INSIGHT
GUIDES

Germany

Directed and designed by Hans Höfer
Photography by Erhard Pansegrau, Siegfried Bucher,
Christoph Zange and others

APA
PUBLICATIONS

As every effort is made to provide accurate information in this publication, we would appreciate it if readers would call our attention to any errors that may occur by communicating with Höfer Media (Pte) Ltd., Orchard Point Post Office Box 219, Singapore 9123.

Information has been obtained from sources believed to be reliable, but its accuracy and completeness, and the opinions based thereon, are not guaranteed.

Germany

Third Edition

Printed in Singapore by Hoefer Press Pte. Ltd

About This Book

When APA Publications planned *Insight Guide: Germany*, several arbitrary decisions had to be made. One was to include in detail only information about the Federal Republic of Germany, best known as West Germany. Since the post-war division of Germany, the communist east German Democratic Republic had evolved into a vastly different political and social entity which only from December 1989 opened up its borders for Western tourists. In subsequent editions of this book, APA Publications will also detail tourist attractions in East Germany now easily accessible. Although the FRG is only the size of the US State of Oregon and is known as the world's third largest industrial country, the great natural attractions have been preserved and the historic sites lovingly restored. We can present only 80 or 90 of the 10,000 surviving castles and fortresses. But here is the glorious Rhine Valley, the marvelous Romantic Road, Heidelberg, Munich and the German Alps. The Travel Tips section describes the rules for visiting the GDR and the easier process for seeing a sample in East Berlin.

For APA founder **Hans Höfer**, *Insight Guide: Germany* was a return home. He set off for Asia and published his first book, *Insight Guide: Bali*. That prize-winning edition set the model for all *Insight Guides* that include fine writing, great photographs and straightforward, clear journalism. From headquarters in Singapore, APA has produced an entire library of new travel literature that makes each tour a complete life's experience.

A team of the best available local writers and photographers was assembled for this book under the guidance of a single project editor, **Heinz Vestner**. Vestner has lived in Munich since 1965 where he studied English, German and Philosophy. He wrote his dissertation on the fiction of Samuel Beckett. Vestner has also traveled widely in Italy, Spain, Yugoslavia, Sweden, England and China. He translated several *Insight Guides* into German and helped produce *Cityguide Berlin*.

Also included in Vestner's team is **Dieter Vogel**, another translator and editor for APA. Vogel studied German literature and studied or lived for long periods of time in the US, Mexico, Peru, Sweden, Iraq, Lebanon and South Africa and almost all of the west-European countries. He has contributed a number of features to this book.

The women in the team includes **Renate Eder** who did her Masters in English Literature and German History at the University of Munich. Eder has worked as a freelance radio journalist and has lived in England and the US. She too has previously done some translating work for APA and for this book, she compiled the Travel Tips section, a mine of practical information.

May Hoff lives in Munich and is a freelance photo-journalist and editor for a travel publisher. Her works have been featured in *Epoca, Traveller's World, Frankfurter Rundshau, the Suddeutsche Zeitung* and various other publications.

Maja Specht also lives near Munich and works as a freelance lecturer and translator for *APA Guides*. She has traveled through most of Europe and visited Mexico, Egypt, Tunisia, Honduras and Guatemala. As Specht comes from Augsburg, she set off "Along the Romantic Road."

Carla Meyer wrote two major articles on Franconia and Munich. She studied German and History in Munich and for six years was an editor with the well-known *Grieben Travel Guide*. For Meyer, writing on Franconia was a nostalgia trip back to the land of her childhood, and she knows Munich, her chosen home, like the back of her hand.

Another writer is **Rainer Vestner**, brother of project editor, Heinz Vestner. Rainer studied History (in Munich of course) and loves to travel. He is also very keen on wine, especially French wines, and even runs a wine shop in Munich.

For **Karl Benz** who lives in Karlsruhe, wine is practically a philosophy, as also is good food. Therefore it follows that Benz should be responsible for the features on "Liquid Bread", "Rivers and Wines" and "German Titbits."

H. Vestner

Vogel

Eder

Meyer

Roger Jopp lives in Munich and studied German and History, a traditional subject combination in the German school system. A teacher by profession, Jopp has only recently been editing school textbooks and his travels have led him to spend eight months in South America and Southeast Asia. He contributed "Origins and Rudiments of Romantic Germany"; "Losing My Heart in Heidelberg..."; "Knights and Castles"; "The Hanseatic League" and "German Science." In addition, he worked with Heinz Vestner to organize and select the historical visual aids.

Another "historian" who worked on this project is **Martin Clemens** who studied History and is interested in philosophy and politics. He works at the Bavarian Archives in Munich and also teaches at Volkshochule (community college). Clemens wrote the article "Rise and Decline of the German Empire".

Dietmar Hertel also lives in Munich where he studied German, History and Political and Social Science. Since 1978, he has been teaching at the University's Institute for Language and Interpretation. He wrote "Land of Poets and Philosophers" and "Romantic Festivals."

A non-academic traveler-writer is **Johannes Schultz-Tesmar**, a resident of Hamburg. He has traveled to more than 150 countries including Antarctic and has published several books including *Suedsee und Antarktis, Australien, Aegypten* and *Neuseeland*. His byline is also familiar to readers of *Die Zeit, Frankfurter Allegmeine Zeitung* and the *Sydney Morning Herald*. For this book he wrote "Living With the Tide", "Along the Baltic Sea Coast" and "The Weser River Valley."

Martin Tzschaschel is also from Hamburg. He works for *P.M. Magazine*, Europe's largest popular science publication and has published features in the *Frankfurter Rundshau* and the *Hamburger Abendblatt*. He wrote the "Volkswagen" story.

Reinhard Böhme, a Frankfurter, wrote "On the Trail of the Brothers Grimm." Böhme is a teacher who has visited Asia 11 times and traveled to 42 countries including the US, Canada, Mexico, Bolivia, Peru and Ecuador.

Joachim von Beust wrote about the Black Forest with the help of his wife Franziska who was born in Freiburg and whose family has lived there for many generations. Although a trained lawyer, Beust worked as a freelance travel-journalist when he discovered his passion for travel while on a one-and-a-half year journey through Asia, Australia, New Zealand and the Pacific. Beust has contributed to several branch papers and magazines. He has also translated a number of *Insight Guides* into German together with Heinz Vestner and Dieter Vogel.

Marcus Brooke has traveled the world pursuing his interest in archaeology and anthropology. He has contributed several articles to newspapers and magazines. Brooke is responsible for the final text-editing to this edition of *Insight Guide: Germany* before it went to press.

Aside from Hans Höfer, three people are largely responsible for the overall photography and artistic format of *Insight Guide: Germany*.

Siegfried Bucher who contributed dozens of pictures, also planned, organized, selected the pictures and arranged visual materials. Bucher teaches Art in Munich and has exhibited his works all over Munich.

Christoph Zange who lives and works in Stuttgart is a freelance photographer and a member of the Professional Union of Artists (Munich). He has exhibited his works, often including photographs of his travels in South America and Southeast Asia.

The major picture contribution comes from **Erhard Pansegrau**, a Berliner who majored in electrical engineering and management. His interest in photography has taken him on extensive travels through Africa and Asia. His pictures have been featured in many calendars and he has produced some lovely volumes of photographs of Berlin and China.

—APA Publications

R. Vestner

Jopp

Schultz-Tesmar

Bucher

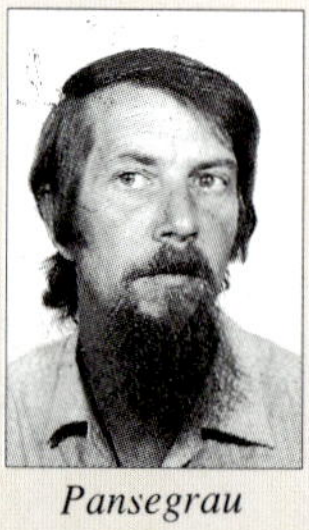

Pansegrau

HISTORY AND PEOPLE

MAPS

Places

PLACES

TRAVEL TIPS

i
Amtshaus
Verkehrsamt

Is Germany a "winter's fairytale," as is claimed by Heinrich Heine, the celebrated German poet? Is Germany the forests, slowly dying and golden red in autumn? Or is Germany the end of the future, packed with hi-tech and industrial plants which threaten to put an end to Father Rhine, the symbol of German Romanticism?

Lying at the heart of Europe, a place of traditions and high culture, and bearing the burden of its recent past, Germany is respected–but seldom loved–by all its neighbors. Germany's economic strength is the envy of all and its thoroughness is often ridiculed. Its beautiful scenery is praised as much as its musicians, poets and philosophers. But what of romantic Germany?

Borders and neighbors: Landing at Frankfurt, the largest airport in Germany, the visitor is already at the center of happenings. A 600-mile (1,000-km) circle around Frankfurt encompasses every European conurbation from southern France to southern Scandinavia, from the English Midlands to eastern Poland. All of Europe's communication routes intersect on German territory, which is surrounded by other states such as Switzerland and Austria in the south; France, the former arch enemy, in the west; and Holland, Luxembourg and Belgium (the Benelux) in the northwest. Then there is the North Sea, of course, the route taken by the Angles and Saxons to England.

Turning to the east, we come to Poland and Czechoslovakia. There is an additional border in the east: the one with the GDR, the other part of Germany, and the Iron Curtain between Germans and Germans, created and built with concrete after the Second World War. To travel the length of Germany start at List, on the island of Sylt in the north and stop at Oberstdorf in the southern Allgäu, a distance of 545 miles (876 km). From Saarbrücken in the west to Furth in the eastern forest it is only 264 miles (425 km) as the crow flies. West Germany covers 95,242 sq miles (246,678 sq km) and is half the size of France or Spain, or about as large as Britain.

Preceding pages: autumnal avenue in Wagner-town Bayreuth; German fairy-tale forest alluring in its dark mystery; timber-frame building basking in the twilight; roundabout on a merry-go-round; wintry forest landscape. Left, agriculture and atomic energy–a symbiosis? Above, punk is fun.

Perfect communications: To develop industry and a national infrastructure, the growth of a transport network is of paramount importance; West Germany is well blessed in this respect. A network of motorways or *Autobahn* covers the whole country. It was begun during the Nazi period, and building increased rapidly especially after the motor

boom of the 1950s. Today, out of a total of 301, 940 miles (487,000 km) of roads, there are 4,910 miles (7,919 km) of motorways and 19,994 miles (32,248 km) of highways of excellent quality. Nearly every village can be reached by cars which carry 75 percent of West Germany's passenger traffic. And, if they were merely carriers to the railheads in the early days, they have now surpassed the railways in terms of passenger traffic.

In 1835, a new era was ushered in when the first German rail track between Nuremberg and Fürth was opened. Today, unprofitable local tracks are replaced by high speed tracks. The rail network, which was nationalized in 1875, was newly-founded in 1918 as the Imperial German Railway, and today bears the name *Deutsche Bundesbahn* (Federal German Railway). Its track covers about 10,850 miles (17,500 km) for passenger traffic and about 15,850 miles (25,500 km) for goods. Because many European commercial and passenger routes pass through Germany, the north-south routes are among the busiest in the world. In spite of this, the passenger division of the railways still run at a loss.

Lufthansa, by far the largest German airline and 75 percent state-owned, is called the *Queen* of the air, and her kingdom is centered around Frankfurt Airport. Domestic air routes are not considered direct competitors of road or rail, especially for the transport of goods. Linking airports to road and rail networks, the relatively short distance between important local destinations, plus high cost and noise pollution all make air travel a problematic form of transport.

Inland shipping in West Germany is a different matter. About 25 percent of goods traffic is carried on German rivers and canals, 70 percent of which is on the Rhine alone. The high cost-effectiveness of freight space, the small number of personnel necessary and the low energy costs make up for the slow movement of transport. Duisburg, in the heart of the Ruhr, is the largest inland port in Europe, and is linked with the northeast by a network of canals, which reach as far as Berlin and which will connect with the Danube in a few years. The Baltic Canal, the Central German Canal and the new Rhine-Main-Danube Canal bring together all of Germany's most important waterways.

Unfortunately, this almost perfect transport infrastructure has inflicted great scars on the landscape. The construction of the Rhine-Main-Danube Canal is very controversial, and further asphalting of woodland and meadow has resulted in ecologists and nature conservationists predicting the irrevocable destruction of the countryside.

From the sea to the Alps: The landscape covered by this close network of transport routes can be divided into three general zones: the North German Lowlands, the Central Uplands and the Alpine foothills, where the Alps form the southern border. The North German Lowlands have been rendered flat by glacial deposits, interspersed with morainic hills, and extend, with the Westphalian Plain, almost as far as the Ruhr. The Lüneburg Heath lies between the Weser and Oder Rivers, and is one of the last great heaths in the country. Journeying south through the Harz and Teutoburg Forest, we come to the largest landscape feature for a long way: the Central Uplands. These are divided many times, and the largest, but not the highest, are the Rhineland Schiefergebirge (slate mountains), with the Hunsrück and Taunus in the south. The legendary German forest is further south, especially in Spessart, Odenwald, Steigerwald, Frankenwald and the Bavarian Forest which is one of Germany's last original landscapes.

Last but not least, in the southwest, bordered by the Upper Rhine Lowlands is the famous Black Forest. On crossing the Danube, which, on the south side of the Swabian Alb and Frankish Alb flows to the Black Sea, the Bavarian Alpine foothills, rounded-off and crowned by the Alps in the south are reached. The German lakes Chiemsee, Starnbergersee and Ammersee, southern tourist centers, are found here. Germany shares the largest lake, Lake Constance in southwest Bavaria, with Switzerland and Austria. The island of Mainau lies in the middle of this lake. It is a small climatic wonder: flowers which would normally find the land too cold, bloom here. And speaking of the weather...

The confounded weather: The weather in Germany is not usually a conversation opener nor the constant topic of conversation, as it is in Britain or in Ireland. Germany belongs to the cool temperate climate zone and rain falls throughout the year. In the northwest, the summers are moderately warm and the winters relatively mild. Towards the east and southeast, the winters get colder and the summers warmer, and the climate is more continental. Average January temperatures are about 34.7 F (1.5 C) in the lowlands and 21.2 F (-6 C) in the mountains. Summer temperatures are between 62.6 F (17 C) and 68 F (20 C) in the Upper Rhine Valley. The statistical average temperature is 48.2 F (19 C), which explains why many Germans visit the sunny Mediterranean beaches. The frost-free period is 222 days on average.

Economy and politics: Germany is one of the leading industrial nations of the world, poor in natural resources and strongly orientated towards exports. Products tagged "Made in Germany" have a good reputation worldwide. Agriculture brings in surpluses, but is engaged in fierce competition in the European Economic Community, resulting in reorganization which affects the livelihood of small farms. Today, 29 percent of the land is farmed, about the area covered by forest.

And politics? The Federal Republic of Germany is a parliamentary democracy for the second time in its history. The parliament, called *Bundestag*, meets in Bonn, the capital, where the seat of government is found. The leading republican is the Chancellor, who is not directly voted into office, but elected by parliament. In the 1980s political life is shaped mainly by four parties: the CDU/CSU, the SPD, the Green Party and the F.D.P. Elections take place every four years. In between there are other elections–to state parliaments, for example, because West Germany is a federal republic and has 11 states: Bavaria, Baden-Württemberg, Rhineland-Palatinate, Hesse, North-Rhine Westphalia, Lower Saxony, Schleswig-Holstein and Saarland, as well as the city-states of Hamburg, Bremen and Berlin, which comes under Allied special powers. These states have not, however, developed out of history, but were founded by the victorious powers as new political units after World War II. The political and administrative backbone is formed by county and parish administration.

Left, at the marketplace in Düsseldorf. Above, motorbike fans talking shop.

THE VOLKSWAGEN

The customs officers at New York's airport were amazed. A German passenger laid down photos and plans showing a bulgy thing on four wheels: advertising material for a new automobile he wanted to sell in America, the man explained. But the officers were not to be fooled: "You can't sell this automobile anywhere in the world." The photos were not declared as advertising material, but as graphic art; the German had to pay $30 tax.

Heinrich Nordhoff's mission (he was head of Volkswagen) had thus begun in the United States. It was Easter, 1949. In Germany, the beetle, initially driven during the war, was selling well. The first model was introduced by its designer Ferdinand Porsche in 1936 and was ordered by the Nazis. It was the prototype of a car that everybody could afford, a *Volkswagen* (people's car), cheap, economical and reliable. Porsche used a streamlined body and an air-cooled rear engine–a technical revolution at the time. For mass production, a huge factory was built in 1938 in Wolfsburg, then a hamlet of 150 inhabitants. The reconstruction of the Volkswagen works after the war–the facilities were destroyed during World War II–became a hallmark of the German economic miracle. And here, in the gigantic American market? Would the people who were already so used to huge limousines accept such a small, bulgy thing? Even the New York sales chief was not convinced, and was fired. He was replaced by two young people in jeans who traveled across the country. "Show the automobile to young dealers wanting to go places," Nordhoff advised them. And that brought success.

The beetle soon became a German export hit, a symbol for "Made in Germany," for German quality, for the economic wonder of post-1945. The unusual but inexpensive and reliable car soon won hearts and five million beetles were shipped to the States in 1971.

A year later the Volkswagen became world champion; 15,007,034 were manufactured, a figure only equalled previously by Henry Ford's legendary tin lizzy.

The VW managers didn't like the name beetle, knowing it meant "dung beetle" in some countries but its success remained unaffected, and the VW made more and more friends the world over. It was exported to 147 countries and even then more than 20 million beetles rolled onto Mother Earth.

Fan clubs were set up. There were beetle socials, beetle races and beetle records; 103 teenagers got in and on to it after first taking out the seats. Connoisseurs collected beetles as marzipan shapes and belt buckles, and the auto even became a film hero.

In Bavaria, a senior citizen still has a beetle with the original engine–from 1939–clocking more than 281,000 miles (449,600 km) on the road. "I treat it with loving care," says the old man, "as if it were my first wife." This has just the same touching effect as the old starting crank and backseat armrests on the first export models. Ah, motoring was still romantic then.

Today, there's no room for romance in auto construction. Instead, modern lightweight technology and catalytic converters are important and these were never planned for the little beetle. However much pleasure it gave, however reliable, this good-natured fellow's days are over.

Today, the "Made in Germany" label is facing tough competition from the "Made in Japan" tag–and not just for cars either.

Her walther vō der Vogelweide. .xlv.

ORIGINS AND RUDIMENTS OF ROMANTIC GERMANY

People must have begun to value the idyllic spots near Heidelberg on the Neckar as early as the Stone Age, since the oldest human bones on German soil, from the age of *homo heidelbergiensis*–about 500,000 years ago!–were found near there. Neanderthal man, already a clever hunter and implement maker, lived about 100,000 years ago near present-day Düsseldorf, before he died about 35,000 years ago, during the last Ice Age. At Lake Constance, the remains of New Stone Age settlements of about 8,000 years ago have come to light.

The Celts: One of the first central European cultures, the *La Téne* culture, which thrived about 800 B.C.–400 B.C., was practised by the Celts, whose origin remains unknown. They settled in northern France and the Balkans and were farmers and tradesmen. In contrast, Germanic people settling to the north of them, built towns which the Romans called *oppida*. The largest settlement south of the Danube was situated near Manching/Ingolstadt, a notable excavation site. About the middle of the first century B.C., Germanic peoples forced their way southwards into Celtic territory. The Romans also tried, with the conquest of Celtic Gaul (58 B.C.) to push their frontiers outwards to the Rhine and the Danube. The entire Celtic settlement area soon belonged to the Roman Empire; the Celts became Romanized and the Germanic tribes became immediate neighbors.

The Teutons: Tacitus, the Roman historiographer, writing in A.D. 60, characterized the Teutons as having "Blue eyes and reddish hair, a large build, very strong in the attack, but not suitable to the same extent for heavy work." He was describing a number of clans living on the northern borders of Imperial Rome and partly on Roman territory.

What made them dangerous to the Romans was their warlike nature and the migration of Germanic tribes between A.D. first and fourth century, the period of human migration which resulted in conflict with the crisis-torn Roman Empire. Between A.D. 100–570, many Germanic tribes such as the Vandals and the Goths, moved from their original settlement areas and traveled far to France, England and North Africa, posing a constant threat to the Roman Empire.

Romans in Germany: About the time of Christ's birth, the roles reversed. Under the powerful Emperor Augustus, the Romans attempted to spread their power in the north, and crossed the Rhine and Danube with their legions to attempt to incorporate Germany into the Roman Empire. But the warriors of the Germanic people, the Cherusci, under their leader Arminius, defeated three of the best Roman legions led by Varus in the Teutoburger Forest in A.D. 9, that the Romans then preferred to accept the Rhine and the Danube as the border. To defend the country against the Germanic people, they built a wall 341 miles (550 km) long, the Limes, parts of which can be seen today. The adoption of Germanic tribes as partners in the Empire, gifts of money, and brisk trading at the border with furs, wine, amber and slaves, helped Rome to keep the situation under control. Towns were built along Roman lines, for example, Regensburg (*castra regina*) Mainz, Trier, and Augsburg. Theaters, baths, paved roads, artistically decorated houses and villas–structures which the Roman soldiers knew from their native country–were reconstructed in distant, inhospitable Germany to make life more bearable.

When at last in A.D. 406, the Vandals crossed the Rhine in large numbers, they ushered in the end of the economically, politically and militarily disintegrating Roman Empire. The history of Germany and Europe henceforth was decided by the Germanic tribes, which took over where the Romans had left off in Western and Central Europe. Many of the Germanic tribes which brought about the fall of Rome have been lost, unfortunately, in the mists of the past.

Clovis, King of the Franks: This fate did not befall the tribe of the Franks. They settled from the middle of A.D. 4th century in present-day Belgium, did not migrate any further, but instead limited themselves to small

Preceding page: modern Germany–the BMW tower in Munich. Left, Minnesinger Walther von der Vogelweide, taken out of an early manuscript (*Manessische Handschrift*).

raids into Roman Gaul. All this changed with the rise of 15-year-old Clovis from the House of the Merowingians, who became monarch of the Franks in A.D. 481, and in A.D. 496, converted to Christianity. In the 30 years of his reign he formed an army of Frankish warriors and enlarged his empire eastwards to the Rhine, westwards to the Atlantic and southwards to Spain.

Wherever the Franks extended their territory were soon to be found bishops, representatives of the Catholic Church which was the state church in Imperial Rome from A.D. 380. During the disintegration of the Roman Empire the bishops performed important administrative functions. Clovis relied on

this administrative structure and the bishops gained security through his power and authority. By his example Clovis won converts for Christianity among the Franks and his expanding empire took Christianity with it.

But the once powerful House of the Merowingians was losing control with the spread of its empire. Real state power lay in the hands of the *Hausmeier*, leaders of the nobility. The *Hausmeier*, especially from the Carolingian family, persistently strengthened their position, held the empire together and even extended it. Who had a right to the crown: the one wearing it as part of tradition, or the one who was *de facto* ruler? This question was answered in A.D. 751 by the Pope who anointed the Carolingian Pippin the new King of the Franks. Pippin divided his empire according to old Frankish custom between his two sons. However, Karl (Charlemagne) and Karlmann soon quarreled over the inheritance and only the premature death of Karlmann saved the empire from fraternal strife.

Charlemagne's Empire: From A.D. 768, Charlemagne was ruler over what was, at that time, the largest empire in Western Europe. Like his predecessor, Charlemagne also did not have a permanent palace. He traveled constantly with his retinue through the country and lived in royal property called *Pfalz*. Here he held court, received messengers and pronounced judgements.

The history of Charlemagne, who has been named "the Great" by later generations, can be read as a succession of wars: that against the Langobards in Italy brought him monarchy over this Germanic tribe; the campaigns against the Arabs in Spain; and the protracted subjugation of the still-heathen Germanic tribes east of the Rhine, especially the Saxons. Charlemagne required more than 30 years to conquer this Germanic people. Charlemagne, the King of the Franks, became the leader of the western Christian world. Only England, southern Spain and southern Italy lay outside his kingdom. He considered himself–albeit in opposition to the East Roman Emperor in Byzantine–the legitimate heir of the Roman Empire. The coronation of the Emperor on Christmas Day in A.D. 800 in Rome was a logical consequence, and the people's acclaim supported the saying: "Charlemagne the Exalted, to the great peace-bringing Emperor of the Romans, crowned by God, long may he live and vanquish."

The Carolingian Renaissance: Charlemagne had two major achievements: administering the Empire and building it up culturally. He unified the legal statues for the various tribes, divided the empire into countries and placed these under the control of administrators who were directly responsible to him. He also systematically brought people well-versed in Latin to his favorite *Pfalz* in Aachen and established schools in abbeys throughout the empire to raise the general level of education. However, the abbeys were more than centers of education in the

Carolingian Empire; they formed model regions where new fruits were planted and new planting methods tried out, for example, the field system still in use centuries later.

Missionaries came from the abbeys and monks' communities, and spread the word. Monks from Ireland (Boniface, Kilian among others) created the first bishoprics and abbeys in the 7th century in mainly heathen Germany (*e.g.* in Würzburg and Fulda). The strict rules of St. Benedict formed the foundation for most monk communities: "Pray and work!" These basic requirements dictated the life of the abbeys and allowed them to prosper as economic and educational centers. Charlemagne, with the help of clerics and lay people educated in the abbeys, was able to introduce Latin as the official language of his empire. The abbey and palace schools taught the art of book illustration, drew up contracts, and produced, with instruction from outstanding learned people like Alkuin of York and Einhard, translations of authors from antiquity, and built libraries to preserve the writings of Caesar, Tacitus, Juvenal and others.

The beginning of German history: Charlemagne, whose empire extended from the Pyrenees to the Elbe, from the North Sea to the Tiber, was neither German nor French, but Frankish. A division into a Germanic eastern Empire and a Roman western Empire was unthinkable during his reign. Yet 30 years after his death, this became a reality. In A.D. 843 his grandchildren divided the empire in the Treaty of Verdun, thus marking the beginning of German history.

The first king of the eastern Empire, Ludwig the German (843-876), ruled over a land which had grown in size and which had also lost some territory, but which was mainly a territorial entity where German, named for the first time as such, represented a unifying influence. In A.D. 911, 40 years after the death of this German king, his last male descendant Ludwig the Child died, ending the Carolingian dynasty in the eastern Empire. Eight years later the right to the monarchy passed to the leader of the Germanic tribe which Charlemagne had so bitterly fought against: to Saxon King Henry.

Otto the Great: It was Otto, Henry's son, whom fate called upon to make one of the most important decisions for Christian Western Europe–to throw back the Hungarians, a warlike nomadic people from the Asiatic steppes. They had forced their way far into German territory, using the disunity of the Germanic tribes and were threatening

Left, Roman watchtower at the Limes. Above, German Imperial orb. Right, bust of Charlemagne.

the very existence of the Empire. In 955, Otto, with an army composed of all the Germanic tribes, met the invaders at Lechfeld in southwest Germany and defeated them decisively. He also removed another danger, the fragmentation of the empire by ambitious princes, by practising clever politics and establishing a strong monarchic system. The church's bishops moved into important political offices; they were educated, experienced in administration, and did not have heirs to make them a danger to the king.

Strengthened in this way, it was possible for Otto, as it had been for Charlemagne, to win the Iron Crown of the Langobard kings, to intervene in the political chaos in Rome

and to incorporate the western Slavs into Catholic Christianity. Otto's coronation as Emperor in A.D. 962 in Rome was thus only the formal recognition, that he was the unchallenged ruler of the Christian world.

Church and Empire: From A.D. 962, without interruption until 1806, the end of the first German Empire, the title of emperor was closely linked to that of the German king: nobody could be crowned emperor without having first been king. Only German kings could be successors of the Roman emperors and defenders of the Catholic church at the same time. The phrase, Holy Roman Empire of Germany, expresses the special position of the German emperor who controlled eternal Rome and acted as both German king and Roman emperor. For centuries this led to the lack of concern for German politics–or its opposite–the lack of concern for imperial politics, especially in Italy. It was difficult to reconcile both tasks. It became even more difficult when the Catholic Church began to question the rights of the German emperor.

Relations between the Carolingians and the church were marked by mutual usefulness: Charlemagne conquered in the name of the church, and the church widened its territory correspondingly. It became indispensable in the administration of the Empire, and thus assured itself of the emperor's benevolence. The church under Otto became a means, finally, to preserve the unity of the Empire against the aristocracy. But however good this partnership, it contained the seed of conflict from the very beginning, and this broke out in the 11th and 12th centuries.

The church had increasingly accepted secular tasks, and its bishops were often princes appointed by the emperor. What was

Left to right: Maria Laach monastery, the climax of Romanesque architecture; knight's armors; historical illustration of the building of a medieval town; knights' duelling.

Knights and Castles

In the poetry of chivalry, a knight's ideals were described and glorified. They were valid throughout Christian Europe as a result of the Crusades, which, from the 11th to the 13th centuries, were joined by all European knights in order to free the holy places of Christianity from the unbelievers, the Arabs. Although the Crusades bringing monstrous sacrifice and brutality, and were, in general, a military failure, Eastern and Western Europe were brought into close and oftentimes fruitful contact, and it is that unified order of trained warrior knights which even today forms our picture of the Middle Ages.

This picture is, however, only partly true. In present-day Germany, it is still possible to visit some of the more than 10,000 castles, now romantic ruins from great days, which were home to the knights. There was, however, nothing romantic in the life of a knight. The training was very tough. Boys born into the nobility went to another castle at the age of seven as *Knappen* (pages) where they had to wait on elders and also learn social poise and good table manners. The appalling standard of etiquette at the dining table is reflected in the etiquette rules, which has to be committed to memory: "Do not burp at the meal table!"; "Do not sneeze into the table cloth!"; "Do not eat with your fingers!" At age 14, the pages became squires and served the knights at tournaments and in battle, and practised swordsmanship, riding and spear throwing. They became knights at about 20 years of age. Reading and writing were not required.

The status of a knight did not necessarily carry a castle with it. Many lived as a group with a rich member of the same order, or even traveled the land as poor knights, without a permanent home. Even with a castle, life was not always pleasant. The hygiene was dreadful; often only the *Kemenate*, the ladies' chambers, were heated. Humans and domesticated animals shared the same quarters, halls lighted by pine torches emitting an acrid smoke that brought tears to the eyes.

The invention and use of firearms made armor useless. The formerly proud and aristocratic order of knights with its ideals and principles became impoverished and eventually disappeared, and was succeeded by another class: the citizens, the tradespeople and craftsmen.

more obvious than to intervene in the election of bishops and only to give those people such ecclesiastical offices who were also acceptable to the secular power? The emperor, of course, accepted this privilege as leader of the Christian world. This secularization of ecclesiastical offices led to a reduction of church authority and also gave theologians the idea that church and politics should be strictly separated, and later, that the Pope should claim dominance over the emperor. The inevitable criticism of the secularization of the church, begun especially in the French abbey Cluny, was taken up by many abbeys in Germany and Italy, and finally argued by the Pope as well. The reform demands of the church thus threatened the power base of the German Empire.

The open conflict between Pope and emperor began in 1076 when Emperor Henry IV appointed, as tradition dictated, the new Archbishop of Milan. Pope Gregory VII, who requested him to alter his decision, was replaced by Henry. The Pope struck back, however, excommunicating Henry and forbidding him to rule over Germany and Italy. The highest Christian authorities were in conflict: which one possessed the real power? The emperor, weakened by the sudden uprising of the opposition of the German nobility, was forced to undertake a journey of penance to Pope Gregory in Canossa in 1077 to avoid excommunication. Henry was thus able to win back his position, but the ecclesiastical authority of the emperor had been severely shaken.

Effects on the monarchy: The leading princes of the Empire no longer recognized the emperor's authority. The nobles, not by birth, was to decide who was to be king. Even the outstanding kings of the Hohenstaufen period, Frederick Barbarossa (1125-90), Henry VI (1165-97), and Frederick II (1212-50) could not win back the old imperial power for ever. The conflict between papacy, nobility and emperor continued; a weakened monarchy remained as a toy of powerful titled interests. The dynasties changed for 150 years and some elections produced two kings who sought a solution in a civil war. In 1356, the choice of the monarch was finally settled with a charter: seven princes (electors) were to choose the king, who was to retain a nominal right, without real authority, to the emperor's title.

Medieval literature: This politically stable period, which went into the 14th century, was fruitful culturally. For the first time a distinctively German literature was in the main: oral poetry of the *Heldenlieder* (Heroes' songs) and sayings and magic chants, such as the *Merseburger Zaubersprüche*, which reached far back into the pre-Christian period. A distinct literary tradition only emerged during the 8th century after Germanic tribes had adopted Christianity, though the heathen Germanic inheritance retained an underlying influence for long after. The old *Heldenlieder* were now written down. In the *Hildebrandslied,* the heroes might call on the Christian God, but the old Germanic virtues of courage in battle, honor and pride take central place.

At the same time, a secular poetry developed, indicating that church dogma alone no longer determined literary content. Material for narratives came from oral tales, sagas, accounts of traveling minstrels, including Oriental tales, which people had come to know through the Crusades.

The year 1170, ushered in the heyday of medieval German literature. One social group especially was described and glorified: the knights, who played a vital role in the Middle Ages. Great poetry and prose was written at the medieval seats of the monarchs, the courts; "courtly" became synonymous with being well brought up, courageous and pure. The knight required strength and intelligence in addition to possessing discipline and ideals of honor, loyalty and understanding. The adventure experienced by the hero in this search for perfection was at the center of chivalrous writings. Material was partly taken from French writings, such as Hartmann von Aue's King Arthur sagas *Erec* and *Iwein*, or was at least influenced by Romance sources, such as Wolfram von Eschenbach's *Parzival.*

Left, medieval peasants at work. Above, in a shoemaker's shop.

Distinctive German traditions were also revived, such as in the *Nibelungenlied*, whose author remains anonymous. Motifs from the period of tribal migration were interwoven, such as the struggle with the Huns and the decline of the Germanic tribes, and heroes such as brave Siegfried or gloomy Hagen embodied Germanic, not Christian, virtues. In addition, there was the *Minne* lyric, devoted to love and worship of a pure, titled woman–referred to as the *Minne*–whose favor was sought. The chivalrous *Minne* singers, who composed material at various courts across the Empire, showed the pleasure–and pain–of love.

The glory and poverty of the courtly period was chronicled by the wandering Minne singers. One of the most famous singers was Walther von der Vogelweide (1170-1230) who described the decline of the Empire, his own lack of a homeland, his helplessness and the beginning of the decline of chivalry in the 13th and 14th centuries. It was a fact that lack of self-control and sloth were increasing among the nobility; instead of heroes' songs, satirical verses were composed which either attacked moral decay or made peasants and citizens the center of attention.

Medieval towns and cities: Tacitus was explicit about the settlement patterns of the Germanic peoples. "It is generally known that Germanic tribes do not live in towns–they live in individual farmsteads far apart from each other." The few towns existing in Germany up to the end of the first millennium A.D., such as Trier, Cologne, Augsburg or Regensburg, were almost all founded on former Roman camps. These towns often became bishoprics, or centers of the spreading Catholic religion, and were thus kept in existence. Later towns developed around points of settlement: abbeys (Munich), castles (Nuremberg), river crossings (Frankfurt), or at the crossing points of the few European trade routes. People collected together where protection in dangerous times was offered, or where there was prospect of good business.

The princes also recognized the advantages of these settlements. They obtained customs duties and taxes, rare goods, excellent craftsmen and safe locations, all of which enabled them to better control their territories. The masses were encouraged to settle in these new towns, which offered special protection, and attracted craftsmen and business people with special concessions. The towns also drew adventurers, disinherited nobles and peasants. Thus, between 1100 and 1250, the number of towns in Germany grew by a factor of 10. Those going to the growing towns to live were

promised freedom after a time. As the settlements grew, so did their prosperity, which increased the self-confidence of the citizens. They built their own fortifications, enclosing a growing number of dwellings, and created their own laws to control communal life.

The towns soon came to recognize their most important functions, and were often able to free themselves from the guardianship of their overlord, whether a bishop or a powerful nobleman. That did not, however, take place without bloodshed. Yet some negotiations were peaceful, since the towns possessed money often needed desperately by the overlord, who sold his rights in the town piece by piece. The citizens developed their own administrative services, with police, courts, authorities and defense.

Business people and craftsmen: Each citizen had a right to certain freedom, but that did not mean that people lived as equals in the narrow, medieval town. The most important class comprised those who gave the town its prosperity, the business people, united in *Gilden* (corporations) which controlled the town. They sat on the town council and dealt with the business of government.

From the 13th century to the 15th century a second economically important class fought for and won its share of control in many towns: the craftsmen. Each craft had a *Zunft* (guild) controlling the price, quality and amount of the manufactured product; excesses were penalized, masters admitted or rejected, and craftsmen no longer able to work were cared for, as were widows. Guilds even organized protests in Augsburg, Braunschweig, Nuremberg and many other towns, and they were even able to place themselves on town councils.

The Gothic minster: The huge Gothic minsters soaring towards the heavens were clear indications of the skill of the craftsmen and the confidence and prosperity of the town's inhabitants. The building of minsters began in the 13th century in Freiburg, Strasbourg, Cologne and Regensburg, and took centuries to complete. This new architectural style, the Gothic, from northern France was the last medieval-style period until it was succeeded in the 16th century by the Renaissance.

The slim, high towers, the pointed window arches reaching upward, were an exact expression of the religious attitude then: the unity of earth and heaven, life on the former being a preparation for life in the latter. Heights and arches reaching skyward symbolized this connection and praised the Almighty; rich decoration on facades, sculptures, adornment, stained glass windows and decorated portals also bore witness to the influence and prosperity of the town.

The lower classes in the towns: But there were others, in addition to the rich business men and artistic craftsmen, who lived in the medieval towns. Between 30 and 60 percent of the town population hovered on the fringes of society, and were inhabitants without civil rights. They included menial persons, beggars and lepers, as well as people with despised professions such as hangmen and gravediggers. These people dependent on the social help of the church or on charities set up by rich citizens. The influential Catholic theologian Thomas Aquinas (1225-74) had earlier stressed that the rich man should use his money with a sense of responsibility. Only those giving to the poor could hope for God's mercy. In many German towns, therefore, hospitals, homes for the aged, or, as in Augsburg, which boasted the *Fuggerei*, a settlement for the town's poor, were established. The Jews lived outside town society. Each medieval town has Jewish communities, usually in settlements separate from the Christians. These Jews, repeatedly the victims of pogroms and persecution, were subject to strict laws laid down by their Christian fellow citizens. The protests against the Jews were usually based on religion, but were often motivated by economic reasons. Jews were excluded in many places from doing the same work as others, so that many were forced to work as money lenders and pawnbrokers, activities officially forbidden to Christians. In times of economic crisis, many citizens were heavily in debt to Jewish creditors who were often driven out or killed.

An important reason for the constantly recurring Christian rage against Jews was the absurd conviction that the Jews caused of the terrible plagues which broke out in the 14th century. These plagues claimed one-quarter to one-half of the European population. The view that the Jews poisoned the fountains overlooked the fact that they lost proportionally more of their population because of the extremely unhygienic conditions which existed in their overpopulated, shut off settlement areas. The plague, or the Black Death, probably brought in by traders returning from Asia, caused severe reverses in medieval communities. Business suffered a depression, the town's power supply connections partly collapsed, and many trade branches stagnated.

The peasants: In the country, where 90 percent of the population lived, the plague claimed a monstrous number of victims since the living conditions of the peasants were, for the most part, still unsatisfactory.

The Germanic peoples originally only knew the free man. In the centuries of seemingly unending upheaval caused by wars and conflicts, newly claimed land was plentiful, and a class of large landowners, mainly nobles, was formed. Many small farmers who constantly had to serve in armies got into difficulties, and made over the land to their lords, thus obtaining release from military service. They then got back their land for cultivation in return for which they supplied the lord with food and services such as road building, help with the harvest, etc. They descended into servitude, to semi-free peasants not allowed to own land. Among those in servitude was another class, the serfs.

They lived on their lord's land, and were not allowed to move away or marry without permission; their children also remained serfs.

Apart from some periods of progress, the economic and legal position of most peasants grew worse during the Middle Ages. Many were not even able to eke out a minimum existence. The lords knew how to jack-up their demands for goods and services. Added to this was the increasing taxation imposed on the land's prices, so that many peasants were unable to shoulder the burden.

Religious devotion and superstition: In these difficult times many found comfort in the Christian religion, which promised compen-

Left, scene in a medieval bagnio. Right, officer cadet in the Thirty Years' War.

sation in the hereafter for earthly suffering. The population–both urban and country–was filled with a devoutness that governed their existence, as seen in the many chapels and pilgrim's churches, in the worship of relics and in the popular religious tracts of the time. However, this Christian zeal also had its dark side, as, for example, the persecution of witches, which engulfed the whole of Europe in the late Middle Ages.

In the 16th century, when this persecution reached its climax, women especially lived in fear of defamation and accusations. Those falling into the hands of the prosecutor of witches, for whatever reason, were as good as dead. Inhuman tortures and trials were used to "prove" witchcraft. If the victim survived the torture, she had to be burned. The last "witch" was executed in 1749.

The crisis in the church: Against the background of religious devoutness, the poor state of the church in Germany was keenly felt. The moral decline of the church and the theological poverty of the clergy were the main objects of criticism. The church used the believers' fear of purgatory and damnation to obtain money for expensive buildings and a luxurious livelihood. For a certain sum of money, anyone could buy himself free of trespasses, and shorten his time in purgatory. This 'sale of indulgences' was profitable for the perpetrators, the princes and the church. In the 15th and 16th centuries, critical theologians constantly attacked the corrupt state of the church. The German Augustinian monk Martin Luther tried to reform the church by provocative theses, which he announced to the public in Wittenberg. The attempt by the church to convict Luther of heresy and his discussions with Church representatives made him popular in Germany. Luther denied the Pope's authority, threw out the special position of clerics between God and the believer, and formulated instead the teaching of the general priesthood of each believer on the basis of the gospel.

The Peasants' Revolt: Luther found support in all social classes, in the lower nobility, as well as among the citizenry and impoverished peasants. Combined with the economic and legal discrimination which peasants had to suffer, Luther's rage against the church's authority in the countryside led to a rebellion against all authority. Luther's view of the "equality of Christian men" was, for the peasants, an argument against serfdom and the unjust social order with its oppressive payments. In 1525, the first abbeys and castles were set on fire in southwest Germany; the uprising, under the leadership of Florian Geyer, spread like wildfire. The counter-offensive of the nobles caused the poorly organized peasants' revolt of 1525 to collapse. Luther, whom the peasants had looked to for support, advised the nobles to punish the rebels, since they had wanted to disrupt God's order, for nothing is more poisonous than a rebellious man. More than 100,000 peasants were killed in the fighting and the ensuing disciplinary action.

The church's unity was destroyed: western European Christianity was in a confessional divide between Catholics and those who came to be known as the Protestants. In the struggle between the princes seeking to maintain their independence against Pope and emperor, the Lutheran teachings were a welcome weapon for many princes, especially in northern and central Germany. The religious question became a matter of territory, and each overlord could decide matters for his subjects. The fragmentation of Germany into sovereign territories was thus strengthened. The formerly uniform empire had become a collection of competing semistates, a situation which has influenced German history from then until now.

Beginnings of modern history: Luther's success would have been impossible without a changed world view and the corresponding changes in science, technology and economics. The medieval belief that life on earth was only a part of an order determined by God, changed in the 15th and 16th centuries. People tried to interpret order in the world using logical methods and saw the success of this interpretation as serving God. In the course of this change of direction, people became more concerned with antiquity.

Beginning in Italy, a rediscovering of Greek and Roman knowledge entered the scene and the Renaissance gradually replaced the Middle Ages. The new consciousness of the place of man was followed by a number of discoveries and inventions. The earth was recognized as a globe; Christopher Columbus discovered America; Martin Behaim completed his world globe (both in 1492); Gutenberg invented printing in 1445, and the possibility of spreading new ideas and inventions thus became a reality.

The way was now prepared for an expansion in knowledge and education. Although universities were founded in the 13th and 14th centuries (Paris, Bologna, Prague), they were usually directed towards theology only. In the 15th century a number of universities were founded in Germany (Leipzig in 1409, Freiburg in 1455) which were given over to secular activities. Reading and writing rooms were set up in the towns as citizens

Left, scene from the Peasants' War. Above, burning of witches.

experienced a growing awareness of the world, and economic reasons encouraged them to give their children a good education.

Reading and writing belonged more and more to daily life. The production of printed books grew. Indeed the Reformation would have been unimaginable as a mass movement without the printed word.

The Thirty Years' War: In spite of the Catholic Church's attempts to check Luther's Protestantism and to reclaim lost ground, Protestantism was the strongest religious and political force until 1600 in Europe. This conflict was intertwined with the rivalry between the emerging sovereign states and the struggle between emperors and princes.

In 1618, the military conflict which began in Bohemia (Defenstration of Prague) spread across central Europe. France and Sweden intervened for the Protestants, Spain and England for the Catholics. "War feeds war!" was the soldiers' cry and that of their leader Wallenstein, to whom the German poet Friedrich Schiller dedicated a drama. The mercenaries were fed and paid from the pillages and fought for the opposing side. People were tortured, raped, their communities besieged, all in the name of Jesus Christ.

Soon nobody knew what the war was about. Central Europe was so desolated and exhausted after 30 years of war that peace negotiations finally led to an agreement. The Treaty of Westphalia in 1648 brought recognition of the confessions and *de facto* division of the German Empire into 1,800 semi-states and territories and a weak unity was provided by the emperor and the common language. The German population was decimated by one-third; epidemics abounded, there was hunger everywhere and the Holy Roman Empire of the German Nation lost its influence in Europe and ceased to exist.

The rise of new nations: Germany recovered slowly from the wounds of the war. Living conditions improved, favored by monarchist Absolutism which princes (e.g. Louis XIV) supported. They saw themselves as the center of the world, placed there by God and committed only to Him.

The two larger states, Hapsburg (Austria) and Brandenburg-Prussia, belonged to the empire and rose in the 17th and 18th centuries to become leading powers. Austria was able to expand south-eastwards at the expense of Turkey, while Prussia absorbed pieces of fragmented territory by the military threat of its well-organized army.

In both states in the 18th century monarchs thought of themselves as "main servants of the state," rather than possessors of the state. King Frederick II the Great (1712-86) of Prussia and Emperor Joseph II (1741-90) of Austria indicated that they were influenced by a new spiritual attitude, the Age of Enlightenment, which was supposed to change the world. "Have the courage to use your own understanding!" was the key revolutionary statement of the German philosopher, Immanuel Kant, instigator of the Age of Enlightenment, which influenced science and every sector of society.

Prussia, under Frederick II, abolished torture, supported religious tolerance and protected the citizen's rights as an individual. However, the Prussian king promoted wars of expansion, the nobility enjoyed every possible privilege and the peasants remained dependent on their landlords. Later German history was soon influenced by the confrontation with revolutionary ideas from France, by the struggle for national unity, and by the rivalry between Germany's two leading powers, Prussia and Austria.

Left, King Frederick II the Great. Right, Martin Luther, the Great Reformer.

"The autumn of the Middle Ages" (Johan Huizinga) brought a series of fundamental social changes with it: the knights lost their position as military bastions and bearers of medieval culture, and disintegrated into petty thieves and highwaymen, also called robber knights. The peasants were disfranchised and increasingly required to perform compulsory services and pay higher dues. In the cities a new class–citizens–rose, who, as merchants and hand-workers, helped the economy towards its breakthrough. Thus it was a new field of activity that opened to the arts, a new clientele. The artists themselves often came from hand-working families. This increased activity in hand-working professions not only brought new inventions with it, but also the development of new techniques in printing and the graphic arts.

Man in the mirror of painting: The Dutchman **Jan van Eyck** (1390-1441) was one of the first painters to use oil instead of tempera. He painted portraits in the modern style. The first nude poses based on human anatomy appeared and the interiors of rooms or church naves were painted with spatial perspective. Late Gothic painting on paneling more or less exhibits these revolutionary transitions to the Renaissance. Striking altar paintings are attributed to **Matthias Grünewald** (about 1460-1528) from Würzburg. His work is rooted in mysticism and even today maintains its expressiveness with its color and light effects and its heightened naturalism which excites the senses.

Many of his works were at first attributed to one of his contemporaries, **Albrecht Dürer** (1471-1528) from Nuremberg. Visits to Holland and Italy made Dürer that great German artist who, without equal, was able to span the late Gothic and Modern periods and achieve classical perfection in the light of humanism and the rebirth from the spirit of antiquity. In the variety of his craft he embodied the ideal of *homo universalis*. He was goldsmith, painter, artist, graphic artist and also a writer as well as an expert in anatomy and the theory and practice of perspective. For centuries he has remained the great German master of portraits. This is shown in his *Self-portrait* of 1500, in his *Portrait of Hieronymus Holzschuher* and in his charcoal sketch, *The Mother of the Artist.* They show human beings filled with great inner strength and their faces as mirrors to their souls, reflecting erudition, sobriety and the objectivity of the intellect.

Dürer's contemporaries include **Hans Holbein the Elder**, who painted *The Altar in the Vineyard*, and **Hans Holbein the Younger**, his son, one of the most important painters of the German Renaissance (1497-1543). Before he died of plague in London he was court painter to Henry VIII, creating celebrated portraits of the English royal family and nobility. These portraits and his self-portrait of 1542 show him to be a master of physiognomy. An impressive work, characteristic of the northern Renaissance, is his woodcut cycle, *The Dance of Death*, which represents the climax of German graphic art.

In the emphasis on shape, which abandons the classical balance of body and intellect, one sees the beginnings of Mannerism, as in the works of Dürer's pupil, **Hans Baldung**

Left, *Traveler Above The Sea Of Fog* by C.D. Friedrich. Right, self-portrait by Albrecht Dürer.

(1485-1545). Typical of this style is the S-shaped distortion of human bodies which are out of proportion (elongated, narrow-limbed trunks, small heads), and the representation of nature from trained experience and invention. **Lucas Cranach the Elder** (1472-1553) painted first in the style of the classical Renaissance. As court painter in Wittenberg, Cranach got to know Luther, and often painted his friend, and his friend's wife and parents, as well as celebrated contemporaries. He was thus known as the painter of the Reformation, although he also undertook work for the Catholic church.

From Mysticism to Reformation: German mysticism is rooted in the Middle Ages. The Dominican monk Johann Eckart, known as **Master Eckart** (1260-1327) preached the concept of *unio mystica*: since the soul stands between God and living creatures and the purpose of life is the realisation of God and our return to Him, mankind can achieve a unity with Christ incarnate by asceticism and through God's mercy. Twenty-eight of his religious principles were repudiated in a heresy trial initiated by the Archbishop of Cologne. In the next 200 years, his teachings had great influence, although often only in the background, on religion and philosophy in Germany, since he wrote and preached in German and not Latin as was usual then.

Johannes Tauler (1300-61) from Strasbourg, another Dominican, continued Eckart's work. At the end of the 14th century, *Theologia Deutsch* appeared anonymously in Frankfurt, and was republished by Luther in 1518. Mysticism was interpreted as German, that is, anti-papal, anti-Roman Catholic theology. These currents encouraged the rapid spread of the Reformation in Germany. Luther's established church meant decentralization and favored the sovereignty of the German princes relative to Pope and emperor; the language of Luther's church and Bible became the common language: German. Luther's demonstrative burning of the papal bulls, his "disappearance" when ex-

communicated by the Roman Emperor Charles V, are themselves symbolic of this German creation of Reformation theology. Since Reformation and Counter Reformation ended in stalemate, the German soul found neither rest nor release here, but became tangled in religious conflict and territorial disintegration.

If mysticism had prepared the way, especially in the broad social classes, for the revolt against the established forces, then humanism acted in educated circles, in the ruling classes and in the orders of knights as a fermentation agent which dissolved in the Reformation movement. Humanists opposed the rigid world view of scholasticism and the intellectual dominance of the church which resulted in the suppression of scientific knowledge from antiquity and the Arabic world. This knowledge, buried for a long time, was the object of new enquiry; the ideal was the well-educated human who was interested in everything and who, due to education and reason, acted honorably.

Most humanists proved to be students of the sources, publishers and translators of material from antiquity. Their scientific languages were Latin and Greek. **Philipp Melanchthon** (1497-1560) attended lectures at the age of 12 at Heidelberg University and became Professor of Greek in Wittenberg at 21, where he forged close ties with Martin Luther. In harness with the hotheaded Luther, the cool, methodical thinker contributed much to the pointed summarizing and propagation of the new teachings. He supported Luther also in the translation of the Bible and in many religious arguments.

Two other celebrated German humanists did not join the Reformation although they both stood completely against the ossification of Papacy and Empire. One was Melanchthon's great uncle **Johann Reuchlin** (1455-1522). As publisher of a Hebrew grammar he made a name for himself and thus facilitated the transmission and textual comparison between source text and Greek translations of the Bible. He demanded the inclusion of the *cabala* in Bible research and stood against the destruction of all Jewish books in a fierce argument among academics prompted by a demand from the Dominicans. The other, **Ulrich von Hutten** (1488-1523), a knight of the Holy Roman Empire, studied languages, law and literature, and was also an author. With his *Dunkelmännerbriefe* (Dark Men's Letters) in 1517, he came out against the Papacy and its moral decline which he had experienced in Rome, and joined Reuchlin's side. His reform programme agreed in many aspects with Luther's ideas. He especially championed a reform of the Holy Roman Empire–the emperor should make himself independent of Rome, and, supported by the orders of knights, rule over the divided princes.

Left, the Isenheim altar, by Matthias Grünewald. Above, a Madonna by Tilman Riemenschneider.

Of German prose and poetry: When **Cola di Rienzo** and **Petrarch** brought humanism to Germany, it was to Prague. They found an admirer especially in **Johann von Neumarkt**, chancellor of Charles IV, who tried to reconstruct in German the intellectual level and artistic rhetoric of Italian and Greek scholarship. For this he radically reformed the language in use in the chancellor's office in Prague, a language which then enjoyed influence and widespread use for the emperor's administrative and legal purposes. Then **Martin Luther** (1483-1546) created the basis of Modern German with his translation of the Bible, his polemic writing, letters, stories, hymns and speeches. Luther's guiding principle, "Look at the way the man in the street speaks," gave the language penetration, liveliness and vividness.

It was the bitter confrontations of the Reformation which awoke the consciousness of a German nation. German humanism went its own way looking for popular values and was conscious of its own language and culture. And there were real beginnings in German literature–in the festival plays and *Meistersang* competitions, in the doggerel verse and comedies of the Nuremberg shoemaker **Hans Sachs** (1494-1576) and in the satire *Das Narrenschiff* (Ship of Jesters) by **Sebastian Brant** (1457-1521). And there was the father of the German novel, **Jörg**

Wickram (died about 1562) and the *Volksbücher* (folk's books).

In these books we read the adventures of fearless knights and merchants; *Fortunatus* (1509) gains prosperity, respect and happiness by the moderate use of magic, while his sons fritter everything away and end up in poverty. There is Countess Genoveva who courageously resists the pursuit and intrigues of wicked obscurantist at the same time as the devil's maidservants, the witches, are being persecuted (*Hexenhammer*, 1487). The pact with the devil was supposed to be the common basis of heresy and magic. In the *Faust* saga and the *Historia von D. Johann Fausten*, this becomes literary material. The motive of restlessness combines with the fear of dissenters and aliens; fear of the evil forces with the feeling of justification in the book *The Eternal Jew* (1602).

Vanitas vanitatum: Happiness finds a place at the edge of the abyss or can only be bought at the expense of eternal damnation; sensuous enjoyment and bravado leads to illness, suffering and death. The feeling of *vanitas*, of the emptiness and transience of the world, dominates at the end of the Middle Ages and in the transition to modern times–reaction to a time of epidemics and starvation, inquisition and war, which threatened an already poverty-stricken existence.

Martin Opitz (1596-1639) produced, in his *Buch der deutschen Poeterey,* rules for refining the language, for gender classification, meter, and a professional ruling that only the nobility may appear in tragedy, while comedy can be left to the lower classes. If German had achieved an entry into science through the great doctor and natural scientist **Paracelsus** (1439-1541) and a recovery in philosophy, now, for the first time, a literature in modern German unfolded. The main forms of lyric poetry were the hymn (**Angelus Silesius**, 1624-77) and the sonnet (**Paul Fleming**, 1609-40; **Andreas Gryphius**, 1616-64). The lyric poet **Friedrich von Spee** (1591-1635), a Jesuit, expressed his opinion in public in a polemical scientific work (*Cautio criminalis*) on the delusionary persecution of witches. While Jesuit drama attempted to win back the stage for Latin, Gryphius produced German comedies and tragedies. He influenced **Daniel Casper von Lohenstein** (1635-83), whose dramas already possessed the flowery language of Mannerism.

Through the novel we meet **Hans Jakob von Grimmelshausen** (1622-76), the authentic recorder of the apocalypse of the Thirty Years' War. He was kidnapped from home at the age of 12 and experienced 14 years of war as baggage boy and musketeer.

In his work *Der abenteurliche Simplicissimus Teutsch*, published in 1669, irony and humor are the final weapons against despair at the senseless poverty of the world. War, famine and epidemics had decimated Germany's population from 17 to eight million. At the end of the war, Germany was a shambles of over 300 mainly tiny principalities, politically powerless, economically disunited, and confessionally at odds.

The court geometry of power: However, a phoenix rose from the ashes: France, Europe's new hegemonic power. Its sun was the absolutist ruler Louis XIV with his "the state is me," and Versailles was the epitome of brilliance and power, art and pomp. In the

collapse of the German Empire, hundreds of sovereign princes made use of the disintegration and all these potentates tried to copy their shining example, the Sun King. Hundreds of princes eagerly sought to imitate the splendor of the French king's court.

In the same manner that the Baroque had conquered the churches north of the Alps from 1600 onwards, it now became the expression of triumphant secular power expressed in the Rococo style of countless palaces, castles and parks. The richly flowing bodies, lines and stuccos forced out the unceremonious severity of the Gothic and Renaissance, and often overloaded space. Greater lightness, grace and playfulness developed. Masterworks of this period include the Residenz (prince's palace) in Würzburg, and the castle Sanssouci in Berlin. Worth seeing also is the castle Nymphenburg in Munich. Here, as in Sanssouci, Herrenhausen in Hanover, and in the Eremitage (hermitage) in Bayreuth, there are geometrically laid-out parks. With their raked paths and studiously trimmed hedges, and in their dominating geometry, they symbolize the sturdiness and graciousness of the quiescent power of the prince. And in this atmosphere of parks, castle courts, mirrored halls and smoking rooms, of the magic of fireworks and fountains, belongs the *Brandenburg Concertos* of J.S. Bach.

Johann Sebastian Bach was born in 1685 at Eisenach (Thuringia). He came from a large family of musicians and was raised by his eldest brother after his parents' premature death. From his brother he received piano and violin lessons, and played in the Duke of Weimar's orchestra. He became the Thomaskantor, or organist and choir director of the Thomas Church, in Leipzig in 1723. Besides numerous concertos, Bach's secular works include *The Art of the Fugue* and *The Tempered Piano*. His ecclesiastical work includes cantatas, chorales, three great oratorios, several masses and the *St. Matthew Passion*. His last work before his sudden death on July 28, 1750, was a fugue with the counter theme B-A-C-H.

Just a month before Bach's birth, **Georg Friedrich Händel**–the other genius of Baroque music–came into the world on February 23, 1685. Händel began his career playing the violin and harpsichord in 1703. While Bach wrote compositions quietly gathering inspiration from his Protestant beliefs and family background, Händel was a restless, resilient fighter. He met other composers and artists, learned the culture of other countries, and traveled often to Italy. With unquenchable creativity he wrote operas, but lack of success twice forced him to abandon this musical form. He took up the struggle again, this time with oratorio. His breakthrough came with *The Messiah*, performed in Dublin and London. The royal court now lay at his feet. He died on April 14, 1759.

Left, entrance portal of the Cologne cathedral. Above, composer J.S. Bach.

The new thinking: However, it was not only courtly splendor which spread from France at this time but also revolutionary thinking. *Cogito ergo sum*–René Descartes' famous thesis–released the natural sciences from religion's tutelage. Physics separated from metaphysics, chemistry from alchemy and magic, and mathematics from proving God's existence, while philosophy not only moved away from religious dogma, but also based itself on findings in natural science.

Gottfried Wilhelm Leibniz (1646-1716) became the founder of this Enlightenment in Germany long before the expression became a slogan for an intellectual emancipation movement. He was also a child genius, studying law, natural sciences and philosophy at the early age of 15, and taking a doctor of philosophy degree at 20. His main interests were research into languages, nature, theology, history, philosophy and technical construction. He was a polymath, a European, and championed Christian unity. When the Academy of Sciences was founded in Berlin in 1700, he became its head. At the same time as Newton, he developed infinitesimal calculus, discovered the dual number system and made a calculating machine. As a philosopher he believed that a pre-ordained harmony ruled between God and Man, soul and body. The *monad* was the unifying substance which made up the universe with all its individual manifestations.

Gotthold Ephraim Lessing (1729-81) supported the new thinking in his dramas and literary criticism. He fought against the rigid dependence on French drama and a schematic, didactic intellectual art as proposed by **J.G. Gottsched** (1700-66) in his *Rules of Literary Art.* Lessing oriented himself on Shakespeare, and was one of the first Germans to recognize the Englishman's importance. He broke through the professional ruling (Opitz), and it was more than just a formal revolution when the high-born *Minna von Barnhelm* appeared in a comedy whereas *Miss Sara Sampson* from the bourgeoisie became a tragic heroine. The conflict between nobility and the hoi polloi became the evident theme of *Emilia Galotti* 15 years before the storming of the Bastille. In *Nathan the Wise* the equality of Judaism, Christianity and Islam was symbolized. Freedom of the individual, fundamental honesty and tolerance belong together in Lessing's view of humanity.

While the colonies in North America were fighting for independence and the first indications of the French Revolution were appearing, Germany developed into a heartland of philosophy. Over 200 philosophical publications with explosive intellectual contents were in circulation. The themes were *The emergence of mankind from its self-inflicted immaturity* and *The courage to use your own understanding*. Where were these sounds coming from? From the darkest corner of the country, from Königsberg, East Prussia. There, on April 22, 1724, **Immanuel Kant** was born. He studied philosophy, theology and natural sciences, and as a teacher taught logic and metaphysics at the University during 1770-97. He died in Königsberg on February 12, 1804.

Influenced by Leibniz, Kant researched into the possibilities and limits of human perception, and to a synthesis of empiricism and rationalism. Critical reason enabled the individual, amid countless individual phenomena, to recognize the essence of a thing (*Critique of Pure Reason*, 1781). In the *Critique of Practical Reason* (1788), Kant determined the degree of human freedom in the inter-relationship between an absolutely valid moral law and the self-interested reason of the individual. As a guideline of the moral will, he formulated the categorical imperative: act such that the maxim of your will at any time can be the principle of a general set of rules! Finally Kant examined the principles of aesthetics in the *Critique of Judgement* (1790). This truly deep and leading thinker, alone in his study, revolutionized philosophy as no one else before him.

Left, philosopher Leibniz during a lecture at court. Above, G.E. Lessing who paved the way for the Enlightenment. Right, Immanuel Kant, progenitor of the German Idealism.

Weimar classicism: Enlightenment and rationalism which began in France and England reached their climax and consummation in Kant. Whereas the ideals of the Age of Enlightenment had political consequences in France, culminating in the French Revolution (1789) they remained without political effect in Germany, where the belief in rationalism fused with a liberal ideal drawing its strength from the return to ancient Greece and Rome. The result was a cultural blossoming unique in Europe and which, as the Weimar Classic period or Goethe period (1780-1830), has been admired the world over ever since. The description of Germany as a land of poets and philosophers stems from this period.

Lessing's belief in tolerance, Wieland's concern with harmony, the classical ideal of beauty of the archaeologist J.J. Winckelmann (1717-68) and the liberal beliefs of the philosopher **J.G. Herder** (1744-1803) together with Kant's revolutionary writings prepared the ground for an intellectual and cultural synthesis probably unequalled in the world and connected forever with the word Weimar. Weimar, one of the innumerable German principalities of the time, became the nerve center of Europe for a generation.

In 1775, Duke Karl August brought together **Johann Wolfgang von Goethe** (1749-1823) and **Friedrich Schiller** (1759-1805), who was Professor of History in neighboring Jena. Schiller, born on November 10, 1759, in Marbach, of a bourgeoisie family, experienced military drill and despotism very early when he was forced to study theology, law and medicine in the duke's school. As a reaction he turned to writing, and sent *Die Räuber* to the theater in Mannheim in 1780. The duke reacted with

a ban on his writing. In 1782 Schiller was able to escape to Mannheim, where he had to work hard to make a living. He was, however, able to continue his writing and his studies in history. When he went to Jena in 1790 only 15 years of close friendship and cooperation with Goethe were left before he died in Weimar on May 9, 1805.

Goethe, on the other hand, was a child of the world from the beginning. Born on August 28, 1746, in Frankfurt, he was encouraged and educated by his mother and house tutors and forced to study law by his father. He had the most varied interests: experiments in alchemy, devotional piety, German architecture, natural sciences, and, as part of his professional duties, mining and military affairs. After studying in Leipzig and Strasbourg, a professional career in Frankfurt and Wetzlar, and the Swiss journey, his Weimar period began in 1775. His first Italian journey (1786-88), in collaboration with Schiller, led to the turning-point in form and material which has since then been known as the Classic in its original sense (*classicus* = member of the highest tax class; therefore something preferred, exemplary, ideal).

The Weimar Classic postulated, in form and content, new ideals rooted both in antiquity and in the Age of Enlightenment. Man was free, could determine his own fate, and had a duty to goodness, truth and beauty. The power of a moral sense and culture was a central theme, as was harmony. Even nature itself appeared as a wonderfully arranged whole without tyranny and cruelty. The *Classic*, culminating in Goethe and Schiller, acknowledged the liberal ideal of Greek antiquity, which **Friedrich Hölderlin**, although unsuccessful, was to call upon later. Many works belong to this period: Schiller's *Maria Stuart, Don Carlos, Maid of Orleans, Wallenstein*, and also theoretical treatises such as *On the Aesthetic Education of Mankind*; and Goethe's *Iphigenie, Egmont, Torquato Tasso* and especially *Faust*, as well as his novels *Wilheim Meisters Lehrjahre* and *Wilhelm Meisters Wanderjahre*, which look far into the future. The moral idealism in these works is closely connected with philosophical idealism which developed at the same time in Germany in critical discussions over Kant's thinking.

The Vienna Classicists: The turn of the 18th century also brought a new climax and hub in music: Vienna. The dominating music of the salons and pavilions was sufficient for punctilious ceremony, for tipping wigs and pigtails, even matching the pleats and coattails, but remained as soulless as the mechanism of a watch. There was no room for feelings and passions. Reform only came into opera with **Christoph Willibald Gluck** (1714-87), who prepared the way for the blossoming of German music composition connected with the names Haydn, Mozart and Beethoven and centered around Vienna.

Joseph Haydn was born on March 31, 1732, of humble parentage. The master of the Vienna boys' choir discovered by chance that Haydn could sing and took him back to Vienna, where he got to know the world of music and the art of composing. In 1761 Prince Esterhazy employed him as choir master in Eisenstadt. Haydn composed many works here, where he also conducted the Prince's festival concerts week after week. When the Prince died in 1790, Haydn returned to Vienna and began the last years of his life with the works *The Creation* (1798) and *The Seasons* (1804). He composed the imperial anthem for Franz I–today the West German national anthem–and was triumphantly received at concerts in Vienna, Paris and London. In Oxford he was offered an honorary doctorate as the best living

composer, but declined and suggested Mozart whose requiem mass was played at Haydn's funeral. He died on May 31, 1809.

Wolfgang Amadeus Mozart, the child wonder from Salzburg (1756-91), gave his first concert at age six. His childhood and youth were spent on music tours throughout Europe, and he played before all the famous people of the time, including the young Goethe. Mozart, whose life burned up like a fierce flame, continues to capture the hearts of music lovers the world over. He had no Esterhazy as patron, but was choir master to the Prince-Bishop of Salzburg, who did not appreciate the true genius of this virtuoso. Often hungry and beset with money problems, Mozart spent his last 10 years in Vienna without a permanent base and died in grinding poverty. Despite problems, this frail, sickly man composed over 600 pieces with tireless dedication, including the operas *Idomeneo*, the *Marriage of Figaro, Don Giovanni*, and *The Magic Flute*. He also wrote symphonies, concertos, sonatas and church music such as his last unfinished work, the *Requiem*, which he worked on till his death on December 5, 1791.

Left to right: Wilhelm von Humboldt, a German polymath; W.A.Mozart, the musical child prodigy; Ludwig van Beethoven, gloomy and tragic.

Ludwig van Beethoven, the first freelance composer in the history of music, was born on December 17, 1770, in Bonn. He was forced to remain there until 1792 because of the invasion of the Rhineland by French Revolution troops. He learnt composition as a pupil of Haydn, was a celebrated pianist and already famous as a composer when the pain of love and the signs of growing deafness threw him into deep despair, as confirmed by his *Heiligenstadt Testament*. Who can fail to hear this despair in the theme at the beginning of his *Fifth Symphony*? From 1816 on, because of his disability, he could only communicate with visitors and guests by conversation books in which questions and answers were written. His *Ninth Symphony*, an arrangement of Schiller's *Ode an die Freude*, emanates strong belief in mankind. Before this he had further developed, extended and revolutionized almost all the traditional music forms as no other before him, using Haydn's and Mozart's composing methods as a starting point. Music was for him a unity of subjective expression and objective idea, an acknowledgement of the worth and freedom of the individual as well as the brotherhood of man. It was an artistic means of moving human beings and leading them to revolutionary exploits.

The only member of the Vienna Classicists who was actually born in Vienna was **Franz Schubert** (1797-1828). Despite money problems and other setbacks, he produced monumental works over a period of 11 years. His chamber and orchestral music, masses, dances and nine symphonies greatly influenced the succeeding generation of musicians. His unique contribution was an opus of over 600 songs and song cycles such as *Die Winterreise*, which paved the way for the Romantic period in German music.

Liberalism and Nationalism: The Holy Roman Empire ceased to exist by 1806; Napoleon had overrun the Diadochi Prussia and Austria. In Vienna, however, music still reigned supreme, and when the ghost of the Napoleonic Wars had gone, a congress was held which led people to say, "there is dancing but no movement forward."

During Prussia's darkest hour, a new intellectual center arose in Berlin. The University founded in 1810 commemorates the linguistic researcher **Wilhem von Humboldt** (1767-1835) and his brother **Alexander** (1769-1859), the great explorer and natural scientist. Both were polymaths in the spirit of the new humanism and civil liberalism. A. von Humboldt founded new branches of knowledge such as climatology, vegetation geography, vulcanicity, and the earth's magnetism. W. von Humboldt founded comparative linguistics and, as Prussia's Minister of Education, set up elementary schools. As political philosopher he defended the freedom of the individual against the total power of the state, and even resigned his ministerial office in 1819 to protest against the reactionary developments of politics in the Europe of the Holy Alliance.

First, a number of the ideas of the French Revolution passed through the gates of Brandenburg with Napoleon's victorious forces. Chancellor Freiherr vom Stein and Prince von Hardenberg reformed Prussia from the ground up during the years (1806-13) it was subject to French rule. This foreign dominance bore a twin brother to German liberalism–German nationalism–which was discharged in a first ecstatic wave in the anti-Napoleonic wars of liberation. The philosopher **J.G. Fichte** made fiery *Addresses to the German Nation;* writers and poets such as **E.M. Arndt** and **F. Jahn** wrote with burning hearts of the basic force and character of the German people. The frenzy to free Germania and to make one German people out of all the German strains, stirred up many who were normally cool. However, when the frenzy evaporated after the event, when Napoleon had been driven out, the former masters again sat firmly in the saddle and reined in the national and liberal spirits because they endangered their territorial power interests.

The rise of German Idealism: The darkest hour of the Prussian state was at the time of the birth of German Idealism, which influenced European thinking into the Modern period as only Plato and Aristotle had done earlier, and which is connected with names Fichte, Hegel and Schelling, all of whom taught in the new nerve center in Berlin.

Johann Gottlieb Fichte (1762-1814) laid the foundations of German Idealism with his *Wissenschaftslehre* (Theory of Knowledge, 1794), completed as an analytical reference to his admired supporter Kant. Fichte rejected the thing-in-itself construction of Kant because he believed philosophy could only take two courses: materialism deriving ideas from the things themselves, and idealism, deriving the things from the ideas. Fichte decided on subjective idealism.

Fichte's successor at Berlin University in 1818 was G.W.F. Hegel (1770-1831). Due to his objective idealism and the discovery of the dialectic in nature and history, Hegel became–unwittingly–a forerunner of Marx. He undertook a monumental challenge: to overcome once and for all the 2000-year division in Western thinking, the dichotomy of spirit and material, belief and reason, self and society, human and God. His focus was the conception of the slowly growing consciousness of the secular spirit out of the

Left, the German princes of poetry–J.W.von Goethe and Friedrich Schiller. Above, *The Poor Poet*, painting by Carl Spitzweg.

dynamic principle of all occurrences. According to Hegel, the secular spirit is in a state of its real self before it relinquishes this to go into its other state, nature, finally returning to itself through the thinking subjects, humans, out of this self-alienation. Truth and freedom of the individual develop at the same time as this growing consciousness of self. History can thus be understood as a step-by-step revelation of God's reason.

Although Hegel logically saw the reconciliation of the real with the reasonable in, of all places, Prussia, King Friedrich Wilhelm III discovered after Hegel's death and before Marx, his philosophy's latent revolutionary content. To remove Hegel's dragon seed from Prussian soil, he brought Hegel's former friend **F.E.J. Schelling** to Berlin. Schelling had turned away from idealism after 1809, to become a mythical, God-feeling Christian. He had, however, already become famous as an advocate of objective idealism. In his ideas on a philosophy of nature and in the work *Von der Weltseele* (secular soul), he developed a pantheistic view of nature recalling Spinoza: reality appears as a beautiful unfolding of secular spirit, and spirit is invisible nature. Recognizing this spirit in the world of the senses is the task of the imagination, that is, of the artist. Yearning for the unity to be re-established with nature grows in the human soul. Schelling thus formulated the central idea of Romanticism.

The nature of Romanticism: German Romanticism had its counterpart in England, France and Italy, yet developed as an intellectual current with its own German character from the beginning of the 18th century until far into the 19th century. In addition, Romanticism grew, like Classical literature and music, during a time of national emergency, weakness and disintegration. Also, it should be understood as the last stage of development of German idealism. Almost all the advocates of the older Romanticism–Friedrich and A.W. Schlegel, Ludwig Tieck, Novalis, W.H. Wackenroder–felt allied to Fichte's and Schelling's philosophy.

They were concerned first with what they considered necessary additions to the picture of life and mankind of the Classic with which they were closely allied. They saw the paradoxical in the Age of Enlightenment and moderation of the Classic was set against emotional subjectivity and irrationality as necessary human constituents. This would not be regained by harking back to antiquity, but would be found in German history with its sagas, fairy-tales and medieval mysticism. To the Romanticists, knowledge and belief, philosophy and religion, human being and nature could not be separated.

They were concerned with universality and "universal poetry," a comprehensive philosophic and poetic style which included all existence in its enigma. Despite this backward-looking adroitness and frequent merging with Catholicism, especially in the "later Romanticism" around Joseph Görres, Clemens Brentano and Joseph von Eichendorff, German Romanticism was the expression of a perceived crisis and the attempt to get out of this crisis into a new cultural synthesis.

If the borders between self and cosmos, between thinking and feeling, between reality and conception were fluid to the Romanticists, then this was also true of the transitions between the individual branches of art. This can be seen in the growing interest then in the opera as speech and sound art form and in the work of **E.T.A. Hoffmann** (1776-1822), who was musician, artist and poet.

Generations later his feeling and its matching art form found their consummation in the works of **Richard Wagner** (1813-86) who marked what was the end of probably the greatest epoch in German intellectual history, an epoch spanning nine decades in which the German soul was expressed completely. Since then classical humanist ideals and romantic sentiments were accepted as typical German character traits and the contribution of Germans to world culture, going beyond the horrors of National Socialism, which cruelly thwarted the ideals of German Idealism, the Classic and Romanticism.

The will to power: The epoch filled with the Weimar Classic, Romanticism and philosophical idealism has been described as the century of the Germans in the history of mankind. Between the end of the 18th and the end of the 19th centuries, philosophers, Arthur Schopenhauer (1788-1860), Friedrich Nietzsche (1844-1900) and Karl Marx (1818-88) made significant contributions.

Their common philosophical starting point was German idealism which they all wished to surmount in completely different ways. Closest to it was **Schopenhauer**, the first Western philosopher who did not proceed from Christian philosophy and its dichotomy. In his main work, published in 1819, *The World as Will and Ideal*, he claimed for the first time that irrationalism was dominant in nature and history. The title illustrates Schopenhauer's main ideas.

G.W.F.Hegel holding a lecture.

In a second-hand bookshop, **Friedrich Nietzsche** found Schopenhauer's main work and read it all at one sitting. From then on, the philosophy of the will characterized Nietzsche's thinking. He described himself in *Thus Spoke Zarathustra* as "the philosopher with a hammer...the destroyer of all existing works," and wanted to be the pitiless arbitrator of all values, knowledge and cultural forms in Europe. With uncanny penetration and prodigious command of the language, he unmasked all existing "eternal truths" of art, philosophy, ethics, religion and metaphysics, and uncovered, long before Freud and Jung, the subconscious inclinations that are "all too human in human beings." His dictum "God is dead" became the fanfare of modern atheism and nihilism.

Like Schopenhauer, the only real and unquestionable quest for him was the will to power, the principle of the living, or quite simply, that of the life-desiring. The prophet of European nihilism thus paved the way for a life and existence of philosophy. Nietzsche died in 1900, mentally deranged, and did not see the start of the 20th century, in which many of his prognoses were confirmed.

A contemporary of Nietzsche pushed the door to the 20th century wide open with his thesis, "The philosophers have only interpreted the world; the main thing is to change it." It was **Karl Marx**, who, together with **Friedrich Engels** (1820-1895), founded dialectical materialism and actually changed the world. Marx was also concerned with surmounting philosophical idealism, but with other intentions and consequences.

Marx developed his politico-economic theory, the *Law of the Development of Human History* (Engels) and attempted in the unfinished *Das Kapital* (1876) to determine from analysis and criticism of capitalistic society, the governing laws which would cause capitalism to bring about its own decline and allow the revolutionary rule of the proletariat to take its place. This would enable the classless society in which each can live according to his abilities and needs.

Whatever one's opinion of Marxist theory, the fact is that it has changed the world. Without Marx, German social democracy would be as unthinkable as the October Revolution in Russia, the Cultural Revolution in China, or the present arms race.

18 Januar

1871.

Germany at the end of the 18th century was neither an empire, state nor a power. The reader may instead imagine a patchwork carpet of 350 principalities and over 1,000 tiny estates, each patch representing a state. Vast numbers of ecclesiastical and secular dwarf states came together in Germany; kings, princes, dukes, counts, knights, abbeys and cities assumed chartered autonomy. It was a medieval hotchpotch of feudal relations, territorial fragmentation and estates. Only two powers had rank and authority in this Augean stable of petty potentates: Prussia and Austria. This loose union of states with the grandiose title 'Holy Roman Empire of Germany' had a perpetual albeit useless parliament at Regensburg, a futile clamp for an empire without centralized power. The emperor had no unified taxes and no army. Only the postal service could receive orders. This was Germany then, stuck in the Middle Ages, out of the mainstream of 200 years, outdated and provincial.

Nobility and peasantry: Four-fifths of the 23 million inhabitants of this curious empire were peasants making a living from the land. In the western part they paid their lords money and provisions, and provided unpaid labor and transportation. The church required 10 percent of the harvest. Only a few peasants owned the land they worked on. Most, as sub-owners, were at the mercy of their lords, the main owners. In the extensive Prussian lowlands east of the Elbe, the peasants and their families still lived as inherited subjects of titled landowners. As serfs they had to perform compulsory work on their knight's or bishop's land for four to six days a week. They could not marry freely without permission. The stick was law, with the landowner as judge. A lawsuit would have been useless. Then there was the burden of royal wars. Peasants were worn down in the army and its retinue while farms and harvests went to waste. The Prussian peasant was also a soldier of the king, and in Prussia's army he could expect inhuman drilling and torment.

A free market is essential: The many small German states hindered the development of business and industry. Each state and town had its own measures, coins and weights. Gulden competed with taler, gold mark with kurant mark. It was no wonder that the small German states' currencies were not accepted abroad and were even laughed at. Guild and customs barriers sabotaged free competition. Each guild master was only allowed a strictly defined amount of raw materials which had to be turned into goods with an exactly laid down number of craftsmen. A wide range of local forms of legislation prevented free movement of people and made it difficult for entrepreneurs to concentrate

workers at one point. But things could not stay that way; Germany's economic unity was becoming a pressing need.

France and Russia had begun a radical clean-up in 1803 in fragmented Germany. A number of small states lost their independence. Napoleon declared Prussia and Bavaria as kingdoms. The 16 southern and western German princes committed open treason and founded a Rhine Confederation under Napoleon's Protectorate. Henceforth, German farmers had to serve in the French army as required by their princes. The Holy Roman Empire of Germany no longer existed. When the Austrian emperor Franz II gave in to Napoleon's ultimatum and dispensed with the crown of Germany in 1806, it marked the inevitable end of the 900-year-old empire.

To gain land in Poland, Prussia had participated for 10 years in the war against France. When France finally threw down the challenge, the twin battles at Jena and Auerstedt in 1806 exposed the extent of Prussia's internal weakness. The army disintegrated without further ado and the king fled. Napoleon marched unchallenged into Berlin. Europe's greatest military state, with its 200,000 soldiers and elderly officers, fell like a house of cards. In the Treaty of Tilsit, Prussia lost half of its territories and inhabitants. It was only due to the Russian Czar that total destruction did not occur. The French occupation weighed heavily on Germany.

Reforms and the War of Liberation: Defeated armies learn quickly, and the Prussians learnt: reformers trod on the plan. The nobleman von Stein, the statesman Hardenberg, and officers such as Scharnhorst, Gneisenau and Clausewitz, recognized that only Prussia, renewed at head and limbs, stood a chance of freeing itself from the burden of the French overlords. Freeing of the peasants was decreed; the guild order was lifted in some trade areas, and civic administration restructured. Above all, the army was reorganized. Mercenaries, running the gauntlet, and the nobles' monopoly of officer posts were abolished. General military conscription was introduced and the flexible French *Tirailleur* tactic adopted.

A national freedom movement grew in Germany. Fichte, the philosopher, made fiery speeches to the German nation in Berlin. Gneisenau demanded mobilization for an uprising against the alien French overlords. After Napoleon's crushing defeat in Russia (1812), the time was ripe. The hesitant German king was presented with a *fait accompli* by the masses and the reforms. In spring 1813, anti-French revolts broke out all over Germany. Supported by Russia, England and Sweden, Prussia finally declared war on France. The entry of Austria into the anti-Napoleon front forced the active, revolutionary-democratic element of the war for German liberation into the background. Now the happenings carried the stamp of Metternich's conservative, dynastic politics. The battle of Leipzig (1813) represented a turning point in world history: Napoleon's army was defeated and France had to retreat across the Rhine. Napoleon's final defeat is connected with the name Waterloo. Germany's fate was to be decided at the victor's Vienna Congress in 1815.

Triumph of the Restoration: Two emperors, six kings, more than one hundred princes, diplomats and numerous titled hangers-on, negotiators, imposters, servants, soldiers of fortune and courtesans danced and wasted away about 20 million gulden in five months. Thousands of peasants had to perform compulsory service for the hunting parties of the elegant nobility when Europe's monarchs came together at the glittering Vienna Congress.

The political mind behind the Donau monarchy, Prince von Metternich, tied together the threads of the new European order. Germany and Italy were again divided into small states, Poland was divided for a fourth time, and Hungary remained repressed. The European reaction was triumphant. The kingdom of God's mercy, feudal control and the church returned to their ancestral positions. The French state of affairs

Preceding pages, the proclamation of the 2nd German Empire in Versailles. Above, the Hambacher Fest in 1832.

had been removed at last, and the moment of the roll back begun. The citizenry was fobbed off with the promise of constitutions and the princes received tempting morsels as booty. Prussia expanded westwards and became the most important power along with Germany. Austria's center of gravity moved eastwards into the extra-German zone. Some 36 principalities and four free imperial cities were combined into a loose German Confederation without a leader.

The only all-German organ was a *Bundestag* in Frankfurt, a cumbersome congress of representatives. This papered-together Confederation only worked when the larger member states of Prussia and Austria joined

forces. When their cooperation ended, the German Confederation disintegrated. The main point of Vienna was that Germany remain divided, powerless, to its neighbors' advantage. The kings of Russia, Prussia and Austria fashioned the final agreement of this great congress of princes. They founded the Holy Alliance of the eastern powers, a confederation of strong absolutism.

Democrats in prison: Students at German universities organized a protest movement against the princes' confederation. Their symbol was a black, red and gold flag. When the pro-Russian author Kotzebue was murdered in 1819 by a student, Metternich reacted with the Carlsbad Decrees. Opposition was suppressed, the students' organization banned, and the universities placed under police control. Many democrats landed in jail, and many more were exiled. "When I think of Germany at night, then I am robbed of sleep" wrote poet Heinrich Heine. A dark period of demagogic persecution, lightened only by news of freedom fighters in other countries, fell over the land. The brave struggle of the Greeks against the Turkish yoke, the Italian and Spanish uprisings, the great independence movement in Latin America, inspired democrats and liberals.

Reaction: In July 1830 the Parisians overthrew their king. This was the signal for an outbreak of dissatisfaction in Europe. There was an uprising in Leipzig; uproar and the burning of a castle in Brunswick; and the police station in Dresden was destroyed. But protests were quickly snuffed out. The Holy Alliance governed with troops, though it was no longer possible to remove the citizens' democratic opposition. In May 1832, some 30,000 people at an impressive meeting at Schloss Hambach demanded a free united Germany. Citizens, peasants, craftsmen and students expressed their bitterness at the wretched conditions and spoke of "eternal damnation to the kings, to the people's betrayers." However, the damned ones still held the reins of power. Metternich's police arrested the speechmakers. Black, red and gold colors were banned.

Two years later, the writer Georg Büchner was to call on the peasants, via the leaflet *Hessischer Landbote,* to rebel against their masters. Academics such as Alexander von Humboldt proposed intellectual German unity. During choir meetings, Schiller celebrations and gymnastics' tournaments of the father of gymnastics, Jahn, the German national movement gained in popularity. The Germans' opposition to the governing nobility was expressed in a liberal movement. The liberals demanded representative constitutions and basic citizens' rights. In the southern German states the monarchs preserved their constitutions, but allowed the citizens a certain right of participation by second chambers. In Prussia, Austria and many other states, however, gloomy absolutism, the single-handed rule of the monarchs, dominated as before. Radical democrats struggled for a democratic republic, for the principle of the people's sovereignty, and for the removal of the monarchies by force. Their most important press organ was the *Rheinische Zeitung* until its ban in 1843; Karl Marx was its chief editor.

Railways and poverty: Literary circles and comfortable conformity (Biedermeier) characterized the period. Those who could afford it, promoted culture and lifestyle. Of course, shares were a part of it all. The Industrial Revolution was knocking louder and louder on Germany's door. In Prussia the number of steam engines trebled, and factories with machines began to force out old manufacturing methods. Locomotive manufacture flourished. In 1835 the first German locomotive traveled the nearly four miles (six km) between Nuremberg and Fürth. The nation was entranced. Rail companies paid high dividends, and it was with railways, canals and new wide roads, with money and steam, that the upward moving citizenry undermined the old feudal society.

Even gloomy Austria, apparently unshakable in its barbarity–the European China–had to look on impotently as modern civilization encroached mile by mile. A German customs union had existed since 1834, and included 18 states with 23 million inhabitants. An important step had been taken towards a unified internal market although Austria remained outside.

The other side of the economic boom showed itself in the growing poverty of the lower classes. Peasants, only able to free themselves from their feudal ties by selling one-third or even one-half of their land, went bankrupt and became paupers. They had to work as day workers or laborers for rich landowners. Unsuccessful hand-workers and mates became workers for wages in the new factories. Inhuman working days of 12 to 16 hours, for a pittance, drove many families to despair and bitterness.

Left, barricade fighting in the year of revolution, 1848. Above, the first German parliament in the Paulskirche in Frankfurt.

In Silesia in 1844, the starving weavers rose and smashed the machines–early capitalism in Germany. The social poverty drove many to emigration. In Switzerland and France, secret revolutionary hand-workers unions demanded utopian communism. Karl Marx and Friedrich Engels worked in Paris, Brussels and London on the theoretical idea of revolutionary socialism. The surrounding air smelled of radical change.

Germany on the barricades: The year 1847 saw a general economic crisis in Europe: failed harvests, inflation, mass starvation, the fall of banks, production deficits, unemployment and a war over potatoes. That winter of 1847-48 was hard. The first tumults and unrest were felt in the cities. Paris began the struggle. Barricades were built in February and shops selling arms were plundered. The citizen's king Louis Philippe and his ministers had to flee, and the Republic was called out in France. The revolutionary waves quickly fanned out to Germany. Peasants burned down castles and did not pay taxes or other dues. Public meetings demanded reforms and a parliament. The monarchs were frightened and in order to prevent matters getting worse, they made concessions. Citizens were made ministers. The *bourgeoisie* was allowed to share in government and provide armed vigilantes.

When an uprising broke out in Vienna, Metternich escaped to England dressed as a woman. The emperor promised a constitution. In Milan, Venice, Hungary and Bohemia, the Austrian troops had to give way to the uprisings. On March 18 it was Berlin's turn to see barricades in the streets. The Prussian king had to order his troops to retreat and then appointed a liberal government. In Posen the Poles demanded their own state. Parliaments were elected in the states of the German Confederation. On May 18, 1848 an elected German National Assembly finally met in St. Paul's church in Frankfurt. Lawyers, professors, government employees and landowners–a total of 586 members–formed the first all-German parliament. All looked anxiously towards Frankfurt, hoping for political reforms.

The failure of revolution: Would the French Revolution be repeated in Germany? Would the National Assembly become permanent, proclaim the nation's sovereignty and abolish the nobility? Nothing of the sort happened. The German citizens talked and talked, but did not touch the old power centers. The National Assembly allowed the individual states to keep their armies. No powerful people's army was created under its command; but nobody could take it seriously without muskets. The liberal majority were afraid to free the peasantry of its feudal obligations without compensation. They betrayed their natural allies–the peasants–in the struggle against the nobility. They failed to support the Polish national movement and opposed the national struggle over Schleswig-Holstein. The German Revolution was stuck in the middle.

The situation was completely in reverse when the citizenry–shocked by the bloody June fighting in Paris–openly went onto the side of the nobility. The absolutist gentlemen knew how to use their power. The Vienna uprising was shot to pieces in October by Field Marshal Windischgrätz. The revolution in Berlin had to contend with General Wrangel. Rebellious Hungary was brought to its knees by the brutal Russian army, acting for the reaction. The Paul's church Assembly, afraid to wield the sword, was broken up by swordsmen.

To the last it had very obediently requested the Prussian king to become German emperor, but the request was angrily rebuffed. The people took up arms again in the early summer of 1849 in order to force a national constitution. A series of regional uprisings failed. Without an organized center it was impossible to defeat the princes' troops. In July, the last redoubt of the revolution, Rastatt, fell to Prussian troops. The revolution had failed: the nobility remained in control.

Otto von Bismarck and the Second German Empire: Calm and order returned to Germany, along with exhaustion and the quiet of the grave. The revolution had been removed, but the problems which caused it have remained. Each new factory, each new railway, each new month of economic activity demanded, without question, the solution to the problem of the multiplicity of Germany's states. The national state has to be created; if not revolutionary and democratic or liberal, then reactionary; if not as a pan-German state (with Austria), then as a single German state (without Austria), under Prussia's leadership. Something had to be done, one way or the other. What actually happened will forever remain connected with the name Otto von Bismarck.

What sort of man was Bismarck? He was born in the year of the Vienna Congress, 1815, the son of a Brandenburger nobleman, a cavalry captain. He had a humanistic education, studied law, and was given to student pranks and free-thinking. When he married, he discovered his Christian faith.

In the 1848 revolution he was on the staff of the pro-Russian and arch-conservative *Kreuzzeitung,* and supported a counter-revolutionary *putsch.* He was able to pass in and out of the Prussian king's court, since the king had noticed Bismarck. However, the loyal vassal had to earn his political spurs. He served eight years as Prussian representative at the *Bundestag* in Frankfurt, and recognized that Prussia could rise only if Austria became weak. From 1859 to 1862 he was ambassador to the Russian Czar at St. Petersburg and had the opportunity to strengthen his pro-Russian attitude, which he kept all his life. After a few months'

Left, the first German railway line between Nuremberg and Fürth. Above, in an iron-and steel works, painting by A.von Menzel.

diplomatic service in Paris, he was ready. It was October, 1862.

First successes: The king summoned Bismarck to lead the Prussian government. He was there to bring the liberals in parliament to their senses, which he did, thoroughly. Without regard for parliament and constitution, he pushed the modernization of the Prussian army. In 1863, the Poles rose anew against the Russian overlord. Bismarck joined in coalition with Alexander II to suppress the Polish freedom endeavors.

Bismarck's first master stroke came a year later. He obtained the support of Austria to win back the tiny provinces Schleswig and Holstein from Denmark in a joint venture. It was not a people's war, not even a war with all the German states fighting together which put Denmark in its place. It was just those conservative dynasties who wore the victor's laurels in the struggle for the sovereignty of the German nation. Then they fell out over the spoils, which was opportune for Bismarck, since the quarrel was about more than the possession of the two Elbe dukedoms. Who gave the orders in Germany: Berlin or Vienna? The Hohenzollerns or the Habsburgers? This question could not be answered by speeches and resolutions, but, according to Bismarck, by "blood and steel."

Königgrätz–A German civil war: Bismarck cleverly kept the other European powers out of the German civil war. Napoleon III was tricked into acting as agent in a Prusso-Italian pact. Austria suddenly found itself again in the pincers of a war on two fronts.

In 1848 Bismarck had raised an outcry against votes for all, speaking of anarchy. Now, as a move against Austria, he introduced the hideous liberal voting rights into the *Bundestag*. He became the Prussian royal revolutionary. He caused, against the will of the small and middle-sized German states, a deliberately calculated war against the Habsburg monarchy. In July 1866, the force of arms decided the issue at Königgrätz.

The Prussian army fought using rifles with needle firing pins and won, and Bismarck became Prussian's hero overnight. His revolution changed the map of Germany: Prussia annexed the kingdom of Hanover, the principality of Hessen-Kassel, the dukedom of Nassau and the free city of Frankfurt. Schleswig-Holstein fell finally to Prussia. Austria and France had to agree to the territorial expansion. The German Confederation disintegrated. Prussia forced Austria out of Germany and in the newly set up North German Confederation, it achieved unchallenged hegemony. Bismarck granted the liberals their national wishes at the expense of their democratic freedom. They thanked him by disunity and an important section went over to the conservatives. As so-called national liberals they were significant supporters of Bismarck's policies.

Franco-German War: After the victory over Austria, Prussia had only one important competitor power in Central Europe: France. Bismarck used the deserted Spanish throne to provoke Napoleon III: a Hohenzollern should reside in Spain. The French emperor could not tolerate a government friendly to Prussia behind France's back. The prince finally had to give up his candidature and Bismarck's provocation should really have failed there and then. However, Napoleon III

went too far. He demanded a humiliating declaration of renouncement from Prussia, which the Prussian king, Wilhelm I, could but would not give. Bismarck added sharpness to the tone of the answer with a little forgery, and thus the desired war resulted.

Led by General von Moltke, the superior German troops triumphed at Sedan on September, 1, 1870. Napoleon III was captured. In France, he was unanimously deposed by the people, who again called out the Republic. German troops marched into Paris and supported the bloody quashing of the Parisian commune. France was forced to accept a bitter peace settlement. Germany annexed Alsace-Lothringen and received five thousand million francs in reparation.

An imperial national state: The Germans achieved their new empire in a strange and notable way. It was not founded in Germany, but in France, in the room of mirrors in the Palace of Versailles. It was not born in a democratic people's movement, but by the diplomatic agreements of German kings and princes; not as a victory of citizens over nobility, but as a victory of royalty and Junkers over the citizenry. An empire, not a republic, was proclaimed on January 18, 1871. This imperial national state was to last for 47 years, until it broke up in the November revolution of 1918.

Germany the industrial state: If four-fifths of the German population at the beginning of the 19th century derived their livelihood from agriculture, this figure had fallen to one-fifth by the end of the century. Germany changed from an agricultural into an industrial state. Places such as Hamburg, Cologne, Munich, Leipzig and Frankfurt grew from suburbs to world cities. In 1848, Berlin had 400,000 inhabitants; in 1914 the figure was four million. Advances in medicine contributed to the rapid population growth.

The five thousand million francs of reparation helped the German economy to achieve an unparalleled boom. In the foundation years (1871–74), joint stock companies sprang up like mushrooms, with speculation and swindles. The Ruhr developed into the greatest industrial zone in Europe with the munitions factory of Krupp in Essen alone employing 50,000 people.

The financial influence of the large money institutes–Deutsche Bank, Dresdner Bank and Commerzbank–penetrated industry and commerce. Takeovers resulted in gigantic monopolies which invested their money abroad. Total German industrial production soared past that of France in the 1870s, drew level with that of England in 1900, and then finally went ahead in the First World War.

The irresistible rise of social democracy: It was not Bismarck's desire to encourage and to lead the Industrial Revolution. The new age passed him and his bonapartist dictatorship. He became superfluous. The Junker

Left, *Rising of the weavers,* etching by Käthe Kollwitz. Above, Otto von Bismarck, the *Iron Chancellor.*

class he represented embodied the land, the stick and the past. Bismarck always remained an opponent of parliamentary government, democracy and especially of the social democratic workers. He tried to break the influence of the social democratic workers' party, advised by K. Marx and F. Engles, by rigid persecution and a ban on political activities. But he could not have helped more. Social democracy increasingly won votes and authority during the period of social legislation (October 1878 to January 1890). In 1912, it formed the largest party in parliament. The social legislation could not prevent the rise of the social democrats. The workers accepted improved sick and retirement benefits but gave no thanks. They demanded the eight-hour day, a Republic, and political power. Bismarck was forced to retire as a failed politician; the new Kaiser, Wilhelm II, no longer had any use for him.

Gunboat politics: German tradesmen and troops gained colonies. In South-West Africa, East Africa, Togo, the Camerons, on some South Sea islands and in China, the black, white and red flag of the German emperor was raised. Krupp, Kirdorf, Hapag, Kaiser Wilhelm and the German Fleet supported German colonial policies. People were looking for a place in the sun.

England, the main competitor, was to be paid back on its own territory–at sea. German imperialism plunged into warship building. The Deutsche Bank dealt business with Turkey and in 1902, the Turkish Sultan granted it the concession for a railway to Baghdad. To tear Morocco (rich in iron ore) away from France, the German government ordered the gunboat *Panther* to Agadir. However, Morocco remained French.

All the European powers were arming for a great war because of the redistribution of colonies and markets. In a secret agreement in 1887, Bismarck had promised Russia help to allow it to penetrate Constantinople, and thus bought Russia's neutrality in case of a Franco-German war. However, his successor did not renew this Reinsurance Pact. In 1907, Russia and England agreed on a mutual definition of their spheres of interest. After two Moroccan crises and Balkan wars, the imperialist powers went into formation for a war which had been in the air for some time: Germany and Austro-Hungary against the Entente of France, Russia and England.

When Serbian nationalists murdered the Austrian Crown Prince Franz Ferdinand in Sarajevo, the Berlin government took the historical chance to rise to a world power by a preventive war. The time seemed ripe; the superiority of the German artillery and infantry supported an attack in the near future. Within two to three years, Russia would have completed the construction of its strategic railways and Baltic Sea fleet, and then have a crushing superiority in numbers of soldiers. However, in the summer of 1914, Russia and France were not ready for war, as the military surmised.

In the period following, the German empire forced its partner in Vienna into a war

against Serbia and threw down the gauntlet to Russia and France. It would be an iron bath for the nation; a short exercise of arms lasting a few months, and the matter would be settled. Von Moltke and the entire general staff thought this way, as did many Germans blinded by patriotic warmongering. All of them were to be mistaken. An avalanche of war, once set in motion, buried the old heap of bones, Europe, for a full four years.

German war aims: "I do not recognize par-

Above, August Bebel, progenitor of the German Social Democracy. Right, Albert Einstein and C.W. Röntgen.

GERMAN SCIENCE

Many people think of Germany as the country of poets and philosophers and names like Goethe, Schiller, Beethoven, Kant and Marx are familiar to almost everybody. Yet this country in the heart of Europe has not only enriched the world culturally but had also fundamentally changed the world through its scientists.

The inventor of the X-ray was W.C. Röntgen, a German who was awarded the first Nobel prize for physics in 1901. Today tetanus and diphtheria are hardly a problem, with the invention of vaccines against these diseases by E.A. von Behring (awarded Nobel prize in 1901). Tuberculosis killed hundreds of thousands, until the causes and the basics of the therapy for this disease were discovered by the German bacteriologist Robert Koch.

Germany has seen inventors and innovators in abundance. Without the inventions of N. Otto, C. Benz and G. Daimler, we might still be walking, not driving, to purchase our cigarettes. Though many people believe that the media like radio and television dominate our daily lives to a disproportionate extent, these communication systems have become an inseparable part of our modern society. And once again it was German scientists such as H. Hertz and F. Braun (awarded Nobel prize in 1909) who originated the foundations of these systems. Knowledge about physical processes has expanded immensely in this country, thanks to German scientists like Max Planck (quantum theory), Albert Einstein (relativity theory), W. Heisenberg (quantum mechanics) and Otto Hahn (nuclear fission). Between 1901, the year the first Nobel prizes were awarded, and 1933, the year the Nazis came to power, Germany was the undisputed "superpower" in the natural sciences. During those years, 31 Nobel prizes were awarded to Germans, as opposed to six to the Americans. The essentials for this high scientific level were established in 1871, at the beginning of the German Reich.

Many of the excellent researchers that Germany generated in such large numbers were Jews. The racism of the Nazis drove away many of them, such as A. Einstein and J. Oppenheimer, mainly to the United States. To this day German science has not yet fully recuperated from this loss.

ties anymore. I only recognize Germans," announced Kaiser Wilhelm at the start of the war. Applause came from all sides, including the Reichstag party and chairman of the social democrats who joined in the end of peace and agreed to war credits. Only Karl Liebknecht, at that time still in the SPD, refused to agree and protested against the capitalist war. Later, together with Rosa Luxembourg, he founded the German Communist Party. Thus August 4, 1914, went into history as the day of shame for the peace-loving, national and reformist SPD.

Chancellor of the Reich, von Bethmann-Hollweg, presented his government's war objectives in a memorandum: conquering the basin of Briey, the gradual weakening of France, subjection of Belgium, Luxembourg and the non-Russian peoples ruled over by Russia; and the setting up of a Central European economic and customs union under German leadership. Others had even more extensive aims but in the end nothing was realized. As the war raged on, the military and economic inferiority of the Austro-German camp became more obvious. France could not be defeated in a *Blitzkrieg*. Over a million soldiers were killed in the battles at Verdun and on the Somme (1916).

Defeat and revolution: Germany was turned into a military dictatorship. A state of siege, censorship and forced labor influenced political affairs. The people were starving, but there was gold for steel. The increasingly detested war was financed continually by loans. Hunger, cabbage stumps and war vegetables did their part. After the peace agreement of Brest-Litowsk in 1917 and the revolutions of February and October, Russia was out of the war–a military success in the east. But the dice tumbled in the west. The French tank attack at Amiens (August 8, 1918) was a black day for the German army. The war could no longer be won militarily. At the end of September 1918, Bulgaria, a pact partner, capitulated. Germany was now cut off from oil supplies from the Balkans. The army command was able to calculate how long it could continue the war with the available oil.

In this situation the General Quartermaster, Ludendorff, made history. A monarchist and conservative from head to toe, he convinced Hindenburg and the Kaiser that an immediate ceasefire was necessary, and that a parliamentary government should be formed. The parliamentary government should take responsibility. The German people thus heard of the entry of SPD into the new government of Prince Max von Baden at the beginning of October 1918, and of the request for a ceasefire. The war was lost and the parliamentary monarchy could not be saved. The revolution continued apace.

Councils or national assembly: In the week of November 3-10, 1918, Germany changed from a military dictatorship to a republic of councils. Princes and military authorities fell. Armed workers and soldiers formed workers and soldiers councils and took over local control. Kaiser Wilhelm II fled into exile in Holland. The hour of social democracy, and that of its chairman, Friedrich Ebert, had come. The "council of the peoples' representatives"–the six-member, social democratic government called itself this–was supposed to plan the formation of a socialist republic of councils required by workers' representatives throughout the country. But Ebert was not thinking of this. He did not want control by conditions. He secretly made sure of the support of the German army; the Kaiser's generals were ready to support social democracy in the fight against Bolshevism.

The first congress of German councils met in Berlin in 1918, with the vast majority of the 489 representatives coming from the SPD. It was decided to hold elections to a national assembly, and the entire political power was entrusted to Ebert's council of people's representatives. The German revolution thus became shunted onto a parliamentary track. "Someone has to be the bloodhound," said the social democrat Gustav Noske and had the rebellious workers shot down by government troops. In the capital Berlin, civil war was raging. Rosa Luxemburg and Karl Liebknecht, leaders of the Communist Party, were killed by a mutinous group of Reich's army soldiers. In this atmosphere of bitter conflict, the representatives of the national assembly were gathering in peaceful Weimar to elect F. Ebert president of the first German democratic republic, the Weimar Republic.

Germany after the November Revolution: Kaiser, kings and princes had fled, and the dynasties in Russia and Austro-Hungary had been removed. Germany was now a republic, with votes for all men and women, the eight-hour day and recognized unions. Social democracy had proved itself as protector of the peace in an emergency. That did not happen without giving credit to the left, where the newly-formed KPD (Communist Party) accused it of treachery. A strongly conservative camp drew incorrigible monarchists, east Elbian Junkers and poisonous anti-Semites, bankers and influential press czars into its growing ranks. They also talked of treachery and knitted a legend of the war being lost from within, by a stab in the back.

And then there was Versailles where, on November 1918, defeated Germany signed a humiliating peace settlement. It lost all its ingredients for a wave of German chauvinism and revengeful feelings. The brown hordes of National Socialism screamed a short while later of "war guilt lies" and "interest rates' bondage." Their leader was Adolf Hitler.

Adolf Hitler: Some Christians believed Hitler to be Satan in human guise, the personification of evil. Others believed him to be a psychopath, a confidence trickster, someone with illusions of grandeur, or a criminal. He was a failed artist without training and profession; one of the Viennese *Bourgeoisie*, who absorbed eastern European anti-semitism and pan-German nationalism; a corporal in World War One and

colonies, Alsace to France, Danzig to the League of Nations, West Prussia, parts of Pommern and Upper Silesia to Poland. The remaining Rhine areas were occupied by victors' troops; the Saar was administered by the League of Nations, and its coal mines went to France. Reparation had to be paid in thousands of millions. The union of Germany and Austria was forbidden, and paragraph 231 burdened Germany with the guilt for World War One. All these provided the

Overwhelming patriotism: masses performing the Hitler salute at a *Reichsparteitag* (party conference).

"grass" in the service of the Reich's army; a speechmaker for a small reactionary postwar party in Munich public houses, in 1923, a failed *Putschist*.

Without Versailles, without the economic crisis with its six million unemployed in Germany, without powerful backers in commerce and Reich's army this unscrupulous demagogue would never have succeeded to the head of the Weimar state. He organized a chauvinist mass movement, with a powerful civil war army allied to the SA and propagated the destruction of Marxism and Jews, and promised to restore Germany to a world power.

And the ruling circles helped him because they needed him. The steel Baron Fritz Thyssen later admitted in a book: "I paid Hitler." Others were to follow Thyssen: the industrialist Borsig, the Cologne banker von Schröder and many more. At the height of the economic crisis, when all political extremes became more extreme and parliamentary government no longer functioned, the leadership of the Reich's army favored a transference of power to the NSDAP (National Socialist Party). After the cabinets of Brüning, Papen and Schleicher had been worn down, President Hindenburg appointed Hitler as Chancellor on January 30, 1933. The NSDAP came legally to power: no *putsch* was necessary.

The Nazis in power: The curtain went up on the barbarity of the Third Reich. The brown terror lasted 12 years in Germany. A fire staged in the Reichstag building heralded the end of parties. The KPD and SPD were banned and persecuted and their leaders thrown into concentration camps. The unions were broken up, and finally all parties abolished. *Führer* democracy was what the fascists called their one-party dictatorship. Factories, offices, schools, universities, radio and press–almost the entire society–were forced into step and regimented.

There were *Sturmabteilungen* (SA) and *Schutzstaffeln* (SS) of the NSDAP, the German Work Front, National Socialist Women's Movement, Union of German Maids, Hitler Youth, Strength Through Joy, and Beauty Through Work. Pompously arranged mass gatherings, torchlight marches and Reich's party conferences were intended to bring about the nation's awakening. The people received stew once a week and learned that general well-being precedes personal advantage.

The fascists made noises about the chosen northern race and began their grisly business of cutting out all unworthy life. The Jews, declared second-class citizens, were attacked and robbed in a horrible *Kristallnacht*, and then led to the final solution with German thoroughness and perfection. Six million European Jews died in extermination camps: Auschwitz, Treblinka, Sobibor, Majdanek, Buchenwald...it was a holocaust like no other.

World War and capitulation: Shortly after coming to power, Hitler, in front of army and navy commanders, reduced Germany's future foreign policy to the concept: "Acquisition by force of new export possibilities," "conquering of new land in the east and its Germanization regardless of opposition." In order to win future wars against the world powers, the USA and the Soviet Union, fragmented Europe must be combined into a large, unified economic body, under German leadership, of course. The Nazis produced a four-year plan of war preparation. Soon tanks were moving on new motorways built for them.

At the beginning, Hitler was able to point to notable successes. In five years he had scraped together what Germany had lost at Versailles. In 1935 the Saar was returned to its German mother; a year later the army moved into the Rhineland; in March 1938, the union of Austria and Germany was greeted; and after the Munich Conference, the Sudeten Germans in Czecholslovakia became Reich's Germans. Then came 1939.

After the dismemberment of the rest of Czechoslovakia, German fascism put war on the agenda. Appeasement from London and Paris had failed as documented by the Munich Agreement of 1938. In a Soviet-German non-aggression pact of August 23, 1939, the two countries divided East Europe between themselves. A week later the Second World War began with the attack on Poland. It was to be the most terrible war in human history, with 50 million dead. For two years German troops marched from victory to victory, spreading shock and terror. In 1941, the fascists ruled Europe and in union with Italy stretched out towards Africa.

When Hitler ordered his troops into the Soviet Union and, after Pearl Harbor, the USA entered the war against Germany, the tide turned. England, the Soviet Union and the USA united to form an anti-Hitler pact. They were economically stronger with mightier battalions. Stalingrad and Normandy saw the end of the second German grasp at world domination. The fall was hard, and the capitulation on May 8, 1945, unconditional. Hitler had wanted to enlarge Germany and to halve it. Now Germany lay in ruins, down and out, bombed to smithereens, occupied and divided.

The *Führer* Adolf Hitler in his classic pose.

When the German army's total surrender was signed on May 8, 1945, the Third Reich lay in ruins. Cities like Cologne, Nuremberg, Hamburg, Würzburg and Dresden had been destroyed by more than half, and entire urban centers had been razed to the ground in a hail of bombs. Millions were afflicted by hunger, homelessness and sickness: Germany was at a low point in its history.

According to Allied agreements reached on September 9, 1944 in London, Germany was divided into four zones: the Soviet in the east, the British in the northwest, the French in the southwest and the American in the south. The former capital, Berlin, received a special status and was divided into four sectors. Administration of the country was carried out by the Allied Control Council made up of the commanders-in-chief of the occupying powers.

The Potsdam Treaty: The conference of the victorious Allied powers was concluded on August 2, 1945, in Potsdam, where Truman, Attlee and Stalin determined the political and economic future of the defeated Reich. War should never again begin on German soil; steps should be taken to remove the roots of fascism. Despite fundamental differences already beginning to appear at Potsdam, German demilitarization and denazification were agreed upon. Germany was to be treated as an economic entity and the democratic reconstruction of the land initiated. Two measures were vital for the remains of the formerly leading industrial nation of Germany: reparation and dismantling of industry. After Potsdam, each occupying power was to realize its claims from its own zone: the Soviet Union was to receive an additional 10 percent from Western zones where the main industrial towns were. If one considers that only 33 percent of the 1936 industrial capacity remained after 1946, it can be seen how difficult the payment of reparation was for ruined Germany.

Denazification and new political beginning: At the same time, Germany's democratization and denazification were initiated as the basis of a new political beginning after 12 years of fascism and fascist thought. The Nuremberg Trials began on September 14, 1945; the International Court of the Allies tried 24 national socialist politicians, military leaders and industrialists, among them Herman Göring, Rudolf Hess and Alfred Krupp, for crimes against humanity and world peace. Some were sentenced to death, others to life imprisonment. A start was made towards denazification of the people

with law 104 and a questionnaire with 133 questions on an individual's life. All the government employees in the American zone, for example, were dismissed if they had been members of the NSDAP (Nazi Party) before May 1, 1937. Punishment ranged from 10 years in prison to removal of the right to vote.

In the Eastern zone, attempts were made with the help of the USSR to use radical change to create real democracy. While in the West the industrialist Flick, who had had Nazi connections, was able to keep his property, in the East, property was taken away and nationalized. Political life got moving again in occupied Germany. In domestic

Left, returning home from captivity. Right, *Trümmerfrauen* (rubble women) building houses after 1945.

politics especially, politicians of all creed were in action again, among them social democrats and communists, who had resisted fascism and were untainted. Political parties began to form–old ones such as SPD and KPD, and new ones such as CSU/CDU and FDP. Names like Kurt Schumacher, Konrad Adenauer, Carlo Schmid and Theodor Heuss contributed towards creating a new democratic Germany. In East Berlin on April 22, 1946, the KPD and the SPD jointly formed the SED with Otto Grotewohl and Wilhelm Pieck as chairmen.

Tension between the now stronger USA and USSR was aggravated in 1947 by the amalgamation of the Anglo-American Bizone with the French zone to form the Trizone. A closer link to the Western sphere of influence was thus achieved. The Cold War, all-important in future political relations in and with Germany, had begun.

The question of survival: The defeat of Germany was not only a historic date for the people: they were living in the middle of the real rubble of the ostensibly 1,000-year Reich, which had disintegrated after 12 years. There was a shortage of clothing, houses, medicine and food. People were living at the subsistence level: the UNO declared 2,650 calories as necessary for survival, but only 1,500 calories, often less than 1,000, were allowed on the ration cards. Only 12 percent of children in Cologne reached normal weight, and in Hamburg there were 100,000 cases of famine. Day-to-day survival was the main concern in life; everything had to be organized, bartered, stored away, stolen. City dwellers drove into the country and bartered pianos and jewelry for eggs, bacon and potatoes. The black market prospered, and corruption was alive in every branch of society. Article for article was the general principle, since money was almost worthless. The *Trümmerfrauen* (rubble women) pulled bricks for new homes out of the ruins of towns and cities. Despite these difficulties, *Otto Normalverbraucher* (average consumer) carefully began to find his bearings to mobilize new forces. Factories had to be repaired and started up; new rail tracks laid; houses repaired and new ones built, especially since there were now 9.5 million refugees from Silesia, East Prussia, Czechoslovakia and other lands.

New cultural life gradually revived on old ground. Writers and artists such as Bertolt Brecht and Heinrich Mann, returned from exile to go to the East zone to participate in Germany's renewal. In the West the literary union *Gruppe 47* was founded, where young writers tried new directions, read their works and expressed their opinions. Theater and satirical cabaret experienced a new growth now that they were free of the stigma of being Nazi standardized art. Young people danced to American music, and smoked American cigarettes; the smell of broth was mixed with a new freedom, often tasting of coca-cola. There was a great need to make up for lost time in music and culture and many accepted everything–uncritically–which came over the Atlantic. Reality in post-war Germany became part of a new situation influencing life as it does today: the confrontation between East and West, between the leading nations of the USA and the USSR.

Siegfried divided: In 1948, the Western Allies, led by the USA, made far-reaching decisions. An economic council was set up in the Trizone and the Western zone was built up as a bastion against the East. About 3.3 thousand million US dollars, made available by the Marshall Plan, flowed into the new area that is almost identical with present-day West Germany. The USA especially wanted to secure Germany's presence in the West, and saw an economically stable Germany as a better market for its own products. American firms invested large amounts of capital in the western part of Germany.

The decisive step towards the country's division was the currency reform in the West zone. On June 20, 1948, each German received 60 marks of the new currency, and savings lost their value. Land property was untouched. After initial resistance, the reform spread the feeling of a new beginning, since the shops hoarded goods in anticipation of this move. The USSR reacted quickly. On June 23, a currency reform was introduced in the East zone. As a result, the first great confrontation occurred over Berlin. The USSR blocked land and sea routes to Berlin and the city had to be supplied daily by an airlift of up to 1,200 flights; potato and raisin bombers droned over the city. The blockade reinforced the American claim of apparent Communist aggression and accelerated the divisions of Berlin and Germany.

In September 1948, the state ministers elected the Parliamentary Council of the West zone. The first chairman was Konrad Adenauer, who announced in 1949 the council's *Grundgesetz* (Basic Law) of the Federal Republic of Germany, which had been worked out by the Parliamentary Council: human integrity was guaranteed, individual freedom protected, and the right of resistance admitted. Property obliged one to engage in social involvement.

Left, the dock at the Nuremberg war crimes trial. Above, the *Rosinenbomber* (bomber) in the Berlin Blockade.

Elections to the first Federal German parliament took place on August 14, 1949. The strongest party was the CDU, founded as a pool of conservative and nationalist German forces. Adenauer was the first Chancellor, at the head of a CDU/FDP government; Theodor Heuss became Federal Republic President, and West Germany was designed as a feudal republic with a Western democracy. The occupying statute remained in force. Again the USSR and the East zone reacted quickly, and a provisional peoples' chamber was formed on October 7, 1949, which announced the constitution of the German Democratic Republic. From now on there were two German states on German soil.

The other Germany: On the other side of the demarcation line between West and East, soon to be known as the Iron Curtain, a sovereign state was formed: the Soviet-occupied zone became the German Democratic Republic. Already, during the period of occupation, an anti-fascist democratic new order had been introduced by the SED as the leading political party. Based on the model of the USSR, reforms in law, administration, agriculture and industry were started. Companies and banks were expropriated and land belonging to rich owners and Junker families was distributed to poor farmers, farm laborers and refugees. Agricultural cooperatives and people's factories called VEB were founded. The intention was to create the first socialist state on German soil. Through this new development, those in the West spoke of brothers and sisters in the East when the topic was German unity, but their relatives were often pitied and laughed at. Everything "over there" appeared smaller, poorer, less free than in the prospering West zones. The result was alienation and envy, the loss of national identity.

The Adenauer period: The Federal Republic of Germany's second *Bundestag* (parliament) was elected in September 9, 1953. It became a personal triumph for one man: Konrad Adenauer. His CDU/CSU received 243 mandates, just one less than the absolute majority. His personality and his party determined politics in West Germany, remaining unchallenged until 1963. The catch-phrases were "security and stability" and "no experiments" and they expressed the self-certainty of these times, which allowed the conservative currents to obtain large majorities.

Important decisions were made during this time in the young republic. The occupation statute was raised in 1955 and the Federal Republic became a sovereign state. Influenced by the Korean War which broke out in 1950, an intense discussion began over Germany's rearmament. Despite great resistance in parts of the country, the Federal Republic joined NATO. The *Bundeswehr* (army) was founded in 1956 and Germany military took to the international stage again. The Federal Republic's integration into the West, one of the government's main aims, had finally been completed.

Another important happening later in the Adenauer era was the signing of the Franco-German Friendship Pact, the nascent reconciliation in 1963 between old enemies, and worked out between Adenauer and De Gaulle. In the same year, J. F. Kennedy visited the Federal Republic, and in his speech in West Berlin he emphasized the close link between West Germany and the USA, ending with the words, *Ich bin ein Berliner* (I am a Berliner). The close political friendship between the United States and West Germany, having grown through economic connections and Western military integration, was at its zenith.

This German-American alliance was to be seen in relation to Adenauer's policy towards the East–there was no effort to follow-up on the verbal demand for reunification. When the GDR or the USSR were active in German politics, for example, Stalin's proposal in 1952 for reunion, the notion was blocked or not taken seriously enough; any action was taken with reluctance.

Left, street fights durings the riots of June 17, 1953. Above, the first chancellor of the West German Federal Republic, Konrad Adenauer.

Adenauer traveled to Moscow in 1955 to obtain the release of all the German prisoners of war. Diplomatic relations were also established with the USSR, but Adenauer emphasized that West Germany's legal position in the question of reunification remained as it was. The USSR, on the other hand, believed in the reality of two states and emphasized East Germany's sovereignty. However, the West German government's claim to be the only legal representative became the Hallstein doctrine of 1955, and a foreign policy criterion. The doctrine meant that diplomatic relations would not be maintained with countries recognizing the GDR–with the exception of the USSR.

Beyond the Wall: The Adenauer era was overshadowed by two events which had found importance for both German states. On June 17, 1953, East Berlin workers struck up a protest against the GDR government's increase in working standards. The SED reacted sternly, claiming the strike was stirred up by supporters of the West, and used Russian tanks against the protesters. The West interpreted these events as an expression of a desire for freedom and the result of a repressed democracy, and in Bonn, the government declared June 17 a national holiday–German Unity Day.

A much stronger straining of the *status quo* in Germany was the building of the Berlin Wall on August 13, 1961. The GDR's Council of State declared the measure as a prevention of the hostile activities of West German and West Berlin "revanchist and militaristic forces," and the wall was built through the city along the sector line, thus closing the border. It was, however, aimed more at stopping the flood of craftsmen, specialist workers and academics who wanted to leave the GDR due to the rising standard of living in West Germany, and the promise of personal freedom under its Western democracy. Despite protests from the Federal German Government and the Allies, the Wall remained and for 28 years until November 1989 was a forlorn symbol of the failure of German reunification politics.

The German economic miracle: In the period 1946-63 there were many crises in the world which had an effect on West Germany: the Korean War (1950-53) and the uprisings in 1956 in Hungary and Poland, which were both bloodily put down by Soviet Russia. During the same year, Britain and France brought about the Suez Crisis, and in 1958 the Cuban revolution, close to the US coast, was successful.

The German economy experienced a great boom during this period–the time of the German economic miracle. West Germany's economic recovery followed the concept of the social market economy. It was supposed to allow free market forces sufficient freedom, but check the socially unfavorable abuses of an unlimited profit economy and industrial monopoly. In fact this ideology of the social market economy concealed the actual restoration of private capitalism in West Germany. The former centers of economic power in the chemical and steel industries, supported and represented by a large number of men who had earned their spurs under Hitler, were re-established very quickly and effectively, favored especially by the USA and the new economic opportunities. The real democratization of Germany moved more and more into the background, while standard of living and progress were the magic words people followed eagerly. Under the Allied (especially US) wing, the West German economy made strides and stormed into the 1950s. In the latter part of the 1950s, it was responsible for half the industrial production of the European Economic Community which had been founded in 1957. The building and automobile industries were the motor of this development, with VW's Beetle becoming *the* symbol of the boom. "Made in Germany" was recognized worldwide as the mark of workmanship of the highest quality. The foreign balance of payments, which had a deficit of three thousand million marks in 1950, achieved a surplus of 1.2 thousand million marks as early as 1955. This trend was strongly influenced by the potential of qualified specialist workers and by the opportunity to introduce the latest technology. A new source of labor was necessary, and on December 20, 1955, an agreement signed by Italy and West Germany enabled Italian workers to be employed in German factories. These foreign workers became the most important figures in the German boom.

New apartments were built everywhere. Automobile manufacturing doubled, making motor vehicle transport for all a possibility, and fostering the rapid increase of tourism, especially to Italy. Pastimes and hobbies experienced their first great revival after years of doing without. Jukeboxes blared the songs of Elvis Presley and Bill Haley, and German 'folk' films celebrated triumphant comebacks. Wages and salaries skyrocketed and an eating orgy which could be satisfied in the first self-service shops, swept the Federal Republic. Television found a place in the living room of German homes, and the Saturday afternoon sports programme became the most popular TV show. In literature and in art, Germany lost giants like Thomas Mann and Bertolt Brecht (both in 1956) while others, such as Heinrich Böll, and Günther Grass became well-known.

The 1950s were also marked by internal political restrictions and the struggle against them. The KPD was banned in 1956, and many of its members lost their jobs or were imprisoned. Social meetings between young people of the East and West were forbidden. Anti-communism became almost an ideology of state. In 1956, however, the longest strike in post-war German history took place: metal workers fought for months for social equality, a reduction of working hours and the five-day week. The SPD followed the spirit of the times, and, with the Godesberg programme in 1959, detached itself from Marxist thought and put itself on the path to becoming the party of the people.

The crisis of the 1960s: In spite of the explosive economic development, the first calls for moderation came from the government in the early 1960s. The rapid growth encountered its first barriers. The CDU/CSU lost its absolute majority in the elections to the fourth *Bundestag*. Adenauer's position weakened and he resigned in 1963. Ludwig Erhard, the father of the economic miracle, became the new chancellor on October 16, 1963. Adenauer's era had come to an end.

The economic miracle began to lose its glitter and the boom lost its momentum. The expansion dynamo of reconstruction became normal, as it adjusted itself to the other industrial nations. In 1967, the first recession was recorded, and felt. Ludwig Erhard was re-elected in September, 1965, but had to resign in 1966. Poor leadership, economic difficulties, and disagreements in foreign affairs as well as the row over tax increases made the way clear for the Great Coalition between the CDU/CSU and the SPD on December 1, 1966. The SPD now came into the government for the first time since 1945. The new chancellor was Kurt Georg Kiesinger, CDU, and the foreign minister was Willy Brandt, SPD. The Great Coalition was able, with the help of the concerted action of industrialists, unions and state discussing economic and political problems together, to overcome the economic difficulties quickly. In 1969 the economy again showed a growth rate of 6.9 percent, and the first serious crisis in the German economy since the war had been successfully surmounted.

The protest movement: During this time the neo-fascist NPD was founded, and national socialist currents came to the surface. In state elections the NDP received up to 10 percent of votes cast. However, at the end of the 1960s, the leftist extra-parliamentary opposition was founded and directed its attention towards two events in particular: the passing of the state of emergency laws in 1968 and the Vietnam War. The state emergency law allowed the state to use the army in a domestic crisis and to limit personal freedom almost completely. Protests of students and young people over the Vietnam War were directed especially at the imperialistic American conduct of the war, at the use of napalm bombs and defoliation chemicals. In this protest movement (called APO) anger and disappointment not only at the self-satisfied politics of Adenauer's era, but also at the Great Coalition were released.

On June 2, 1967, student Benno Ohnesorg was shot down during a demonstration against a visit of the Shah. Bloody riots followed and delivery of the far-right Springer newspapers was blockaded. Radical left-wing groups were formed, and the Red Army Fraction (RAF) traces its roots back to this time. A leader of the student movement, Rudi Dutschke, was seriously wounded in an attempt on his life, and this led to greater dissent in 1968. The state reacted by tightening the laws on internal security.

Against the backdrop of an escalating Vietnam War and the occupation of Czechoslovakia by the USSR and Warsaw Pact countries in 1968, the socio-liberal coalition of the SPD and the FDP under Chancellor Willy Brandt and Vice-Chancellor Walter Scheel was formed in 1969. The government

Left, Italian *Gastarbeiter* (guest workers) on their way back to their native homes. Above, Rudi Dutschke, one of the student movement leaders, at a demonstration.

used the slogan "Dare to try more democracy!" and soaked up the protests of the '68 movement with reform politics in education and social security. The principles of membership in the Western alliance were intact.

The most decisive change brought about by this government was, however, in the field of East-West politics, a change which was encouraged by an increased in trade with the Eastern bloc, which West German industry was also interested in expanding. Leading West German industrialists were interested in trade expansion for more than just charitable reasons. In 1970, agreements with Moscow and Warsaw were concluded, which aimed at reconciliation between nations and a return to normal diplomatic relations. The picture of Willy Brandt kneeling before the monument to the Warsaw Ghetto went round the world, and in 1971 he received the Nobel Peace Prize. In the same year the Berlin covenant and transit agreement with the GDR were signed, both aimed at making contact easier between people in both German states. The government called it "change by coming nearer together." The SPD harvested the fruits of these policies, despite fierce attacks from the CDU/CSU opposition, in November, 1972: for the first time the SPD was the strongest party with 45.8 percent of votes, and it continued the coalition with the FDP. The CDU/CSU remained banished until 1982.

New problems, new leaders: Increasing economic difficulties, reorganization of industry and the increase in the number of unemployed caused the political climate to heat up. Growing environmental pollution together with terrorist attacks, such as those which occurred during the 1972 Olympic games in Munich, did the same. Helplessness and over-reaction after the passing of new laws were the result. In this climate and without solutions at hand, the resignation of Willy Brandt in 1974, revealed the growing differences within the coalition.

Helmut Schmidt, on the right wing of the SPD, became Brandt's successor as chancellor, with H. Dietrich Genscher taking the foreign ministry for the FDP. The economy was faced with the "oil crisis," which led to international economic difficulties which were especially felt in Germany. The contradictions between East and West grew. The period of relief from tension gave way to a climate of rearmament.

Controversy also arose over the issues of atomic energy and environmental pollution. A new protest movement, the ecology and peace movement, began to assemble. Its parliamentary arm, the "Greens," was founded in 1980, and has been represented in the

Bundestag since 1983. This new party developed for a variety of reasons and pledged itself to grass roots democracy, to pacifism and to the sociological and ecological necessities of a society which is supposed to be truly democratic. The belief that the parties in Bonn could find solutions to the problems, shaken as they were by scandals over contributions to political parties such as the *Flick-Skandal*, began to disappear. Rising unemployment figures brought anxiety.

Schmidt's successor as chancellor was Helmut Kohl (CDU), who brought forward new elections to March 6, 1983. His party obtained 48.8 percent of the votes–an impressive victory–and paved the way for a

coalition of the middle with the FDP. The new chancellor announced a spiritual and moral about-turn, as Ronald Reagan had done in Washington. At a time when people were confronted with more and more rockets and armaments, environmental pollution and the problems of livelihood, the new government placed its trust in market forces and in a restrictive domestic and social policy. People's fears took on an invisible but more threatening form, as a radioactive cloud passed over Germany from the Chernobyl nuclear catastrophe. The common fear among Germans of a nuclear war on home soil was understandable as the country bristles with weapons, it being the geopolitical center of the East-West conflict.

Left, a historic event–Willy Brandt going down on his knees in Warsaw, 1970. Above, welcome to West Berlin.

Therefore rearmament, atomic energy, environment and unemployment were the issues prior to the 11th *Bundestag* elections on January 25, 1987. These brought huge losses in votes for the CDU and the SPD, but considerable gains for the FDP and the Greens. The CDU/CSU/FDP coalition led by Chancellor Kohl could thus be continued.

The erosion of the Soviet bloc and the peaceful revolutions in Hungary, Poland, East Germany and Czechoslovakia have reshuffled the political cards in Europe. Germany thus, once again, became a prism that, more than any other country in Europe, reflected this kaleidoscopic development.

The Berlin Wall has tumbled and, after 28 years, millions of East Berliners and GDR citizens are meanwhile allowed to travel hither and thither across the border. At the beginning of December the events in the divided city of Berlin, the perspectives of a cooperation between the two Germanies as well as the summit of the two world leaders, George Bush and Mikhail Gorbachev, off the Malta coast – riveted the world to the TV screens. Let us hope that Gorbachev's statement: "In the final analysis we envision Europe as a commonwealth of sovereign democratic states with a high level of equitable interdependence and easily accessible borders and wide-ranging contacts among people…" will become reality.

Will the present East German government allow joint ventures between East and West? Will a free market economy supersede the centralized economy of the GDR?

Might there even be a reunified Germany? That's a thought that the rest of the world doesn't exactly greet with whoops of delight, least of all Gorbachev who told the French President Mitterand "The day that happens, you will read in the newspaper the name of the marshal who has taken my place." On that night when the Berlin Wall was opened, the Members of the West German Parliament sang the national anthem. But it was the customary third verse they sang: "Einigkeit und Recht und Freiheit", not "Deutschland, Deutschland über alles".

At the beginning of the 19th century Germaine de Stael had already remarked in her famous book *De l'Allemagne* that the "entirety of German nation is similar only in a few main points, for the dissimilarities are so manifold that it is difficult to view such varying religions, forms of government and races from one and the same standpoint."

In other words: *the* German as much existed then, as he does today. Nevertheless, certain clichés about a so-called national character still persist. Mention Bavaria and most people immediately have images of burly Germans in leather shorts, wearing Gamsbart hats. Mention precision and punctuality and the words Teutonic efficiency come to mind. Yet, these are clichés and nothing more. There are Germans who do not dress like the archetypical Bavarian, and German trains have been known to run late.

Club life: Yet, the idea that every cliché is based on fact is still appropriate. Are you acquainted with the saying: "One German makes a philosopher, three Germans make a club?" The former part is, of course, less true, but the latter is very near the truth, because the Germans like their *Verein* (club or society). The choral society or *Liederkranz* (glee-club) is known worldwide and many grow to the same size as the Fischer choirs. And so, fowl-breeders, stamp-collectors, chess-players and sportsmen of all categories and ages also form their own societies. Designations like *Society for the Promotion of Student Living* sound just as peculiar as local curiosities like the *Society for the Restoration of the Monarchy* in Bavaria, the home of the beautiful Ludwig castles. Carnival societies, found usually along the river Rhine, plan their fun and games in an almost military manner and guarantee many days of enjoyment.

Whatever *Verein* it is, members must pay their monthly dues, elect a managing committee, organize an annual festival of the *Verein* and meet other social requirements, not to mention the existing *Vereinsrecht* (law) which regulates this complicated matter. This is German thoroughness at its best.

A completely new form of society is on the rise: the *Bürgerinitiative* (citizen's initiative). This type of society was founded by people of different social and political backgrounds, opposing large projects like atomic plants, new motorways and rocket-bases which destroy both environment and health. Their aim is also to preserve integrated living areas and old town centers. You might discover, during your travels in the Federal Republic, an information stand belonging to one of these groups where people are gathered in discussion.

Suburban life: City living in Germany, as in

other western countries, is fraught with problems of unemployment, living space, high rents and social conditions. Many city dwellers occupy *Trabantenstädte*, densely populated areas without ancient landmarks but with skyscrapers and sterile children's playgrounds, places where supermarkets are poor substitutes for the neighborhood milk and tobacco shop. Many people who live in the estates spend their entire life dreaming about owning their own home.

In so much as they have not been destroyed by the war or by subsequent restoration, more and more old town centers are being reconstructed and are awakening to new life. New pubs and restaurants are springing up alongside green squares. Building facades are being restored and revalued. But all this costs money and leads to higher rents which are unaffordable for many. The tenants move to another part of town and the old quarter changes its character as the new inhabitants bring their own style of living with them. On the other hand, the rents are lower in the areas which are neglected, permitting students and foreigners to live for less but with a disadvantaged lifestyle.

While wandering through the towns and having already admired the promotion or Jugendstil-facades, your journey will take you further through the parks and along rivers flowing through them. This part of municipal nature is usually well cared for and protected, witnessed by the many warning signs: "Keep off the lawn," "Dogs to be kept on the line," "No trespassing," etc. Germans are not fond of these "No-Go" signs and rules, but apparently consider them essential.

Day-to-day culture: The so-called cultural offerings, with which each lord mayor or town council intends to please and to attract visitors and inhabitants are, indeed, necessary. Relatively high contributions derived from taxes are at their disposal. Nowhere else can so many good symphony orchestras –which live on public subsidies–be found, than in Germany. Festival performances, folkloric gatherings, town quarter and street festivals also have a long tradition. Municipal and national stages could not exist without subsidies, while the independent small theaters, which have shot up like mushrooms in recent years, live more on improvisation and enthusiastic audiences than anything else. Did you know that in West Germany, under state regulation, one percent of the money allotted to such buildings as schools and administrative headquarters must be used for art, namely frescoes, murals and sculptures in the courtyards? In fact, Germans seem to be a people devoted to the arts.

Left, a German philosopher? Above, who wouldn't like to get to know her?

According to statistics, a West German has only three books at home which will enable him to be proud of the great classics and the German poets, thinkers, composers, musicians and painters. Are they, however, well-known? Sales of records show that not only pop and soft music, but also the Fischer Choirs and brass band music, are more in demand than either Beethoven or Bach.

Things are not at all easy for the civic spirit –the provision of social welfare–in this still prospering Germany, in spite of the fact that the number of booming private initiatives have been expanding in the Germany of the 1980s. The Germans love their department stores more than their town halls in which every few years they vote for different party representatives in whom they often place little trust. Often it is also made very difficult for enraged citizens to get their way in the face of party machinery and the bureaucracy or to be given a hearing whatsoever. When dealing with the subject that is closest to the hearts of all citizens, the same sentiment is always heard: "Those people up there just do what they like anyway."

The cities: When discussing cities, the usual complaint is that decisions regarding motorways, office blocks, administrative complexes and new airports, are often made without consulting those concerned. Every city has its own peculiarities and characteristic quarter with its festivals and problems–even the cities on the rivers Rhine and Ruhr with about 14,000 inhabitants for every square mile, the industrial centers which also contribute to environmental pollution. Last but not least, is Berlin, in the midst of contradictions, covered in scars, pulsating and lacking in hinterland. Here the punk sits beside his grandmother on a park-bench, holding her ball of wool. Apparently, this city is always at ease.

Rural life: Every third inhabitant of the Federal Republic lives in towns or cities with more than 100,000 inhabitants. There are also about 16 million people living in medium-sized municipalities (*Gemeinden*) of 20,000 to 100,000 persons. That still leaves 40 percent of the populace who live in communities with less than 20,000 and of these almost four million live in villages with less than 2,000 persons. It is worth visiting these small communities–the seat of German daily life–for here tradition and old customs are still likely to be encountered. Clubs thrive in these communities; the choral society intones the song *Am Brunnen vor dem Tore* while the skat society is busy playing; the bowling club is just striking "all nine" and the national costume and rifle club cordially invites you to the *Schuhplattler* (a Bavarian folk dance). These clubs in fact form the cultural backbone of the village and its inhabitants.

Festivals are organized and communal politics discussed–mostly by men–at the *Stammtisch* (table where regular customers meet) in the tavern next to the church. Differences of opinion are often done away with or cannot be excused by one another. However, when the choral society resents its colors or the voluntary fire-brigade celebrates its jubilee or when the village football team plays against the neighboring community, they all come together again.

You will come across the "Kirmes" in the country, which was originally a church festival or a horse or trading market. Every year the inevitable beer tent and sausage stall is set up alongside carousels and ghost trains, offering all sorts of amusement. In the Rhineland the carnivals are in full swing from November till February where pleasure is given a fair chance to outdo sadness. This, unfortunately, doesn't always succeed. Munich is the stronghold of the equivalent event in the south, called Fasching.

Life in the villages and the countryside would not be depicted fully without men-

tioning the role of the church. Nothing much can be achieved in rural areas–where churches are filled–without the approval of the village priest. The chimes of the church bells never fail to accompany the visitor throughout his travels in Germany.

Yet, the archetypical village with its marketplace, linden tree and fountain preserved in aspic, are now difficult to find. Modernization has caught up with the villages during the last 25 years. They have been straightened, flattened, smoothed out and literally covered up. Timbered frames and old walls have often been pulled down in a radical manner and substituted by practical buildings. The villages have lost their own character and many can hardly be distinguished now. What makes matters worse is small farms can no longer survive and articles made by craftsmen cannot compete with those produced by industry. This results in an influx into the cities from the country and the gradual disintegration of traditional structure. Above all, young people seek employment in the cities because to them, the life of a farmer is tough and leaves little time for leisure.

Regional characters: Growing numbers of people who have had enough of the noise and smog of the city, are beginning to form a counter movement in the direction of the country. *The Alternatives,* as they are called in Germany, run farms on a small scale and try to set up new lifestyles. However, they often remain as strangers in the eyes of the villagers, who regard them as outsiders who have little or no interest in village affairs.

This is an attitude which is more likely held by a triumvirate of village mayor, priest and teacher who know how to influence local politics with the help of the representatives of the business world in the area. These same people, however, often wish to preserve the old village structures, a trend which has become apparent especially in recent years. Whereas the cities are densely populated areas and melting pots of many people and interests, the villages, colorfully dotted along the entire countryside, are silent witnesses of German life and history.

Regional peculiarities and differences in dialect, customs and mentality are found in the countryside, but hardly any more in the cities. The typical German is at his most authentic there, namely, the Bavarian, East Fresian, the Rhinelander, Swabian, Saxonian or the Hessian. The Swabian is regarded as thrifty, the Saxonian as reserved and the Bavarian as bad-tempered. The East Fresian is known to be taciturn, the Berliner as cheeky, and the Franconian as cunning and easy-going.

Here we have once again returned to the subject we began with, namely, stereotypes. They are often dreamt up by the very people to whom they are applied and are

Left, at the *Stammtisch* (meeting of regulars). Above, just two out of the millions of German garden gnomes.

passed on by them to succeeding generations. They are just as true as they are false. Drink a few glasses of *Molle und Kare* (spirits) with someone from Schleswig-Holstein and he can become even more talkative than the Berliner who is said to have an especially "big mouth." Also, the charm of a seemingly unapproachable Bavarian, with or without his *Gamsbart* hat and leather shorts, has won the heart of many a female tourist.

Leisure-time in Germany: We can also apply the stereotype to German sportsmen. The German prepares himself for sport in an almost military manner and the winning type must, of course, be blond. The German literally bowls over his opponent at football with

his fighting spirit. Sport plays an important role in Germany–especially, the most popular sports like soccer, handball, and–since Boris Becker and Steffi Graff won Wimbledon–tennis. The fitness wave that flooded in from America like so many other fads, has even reached television.

Cycling is "in" again, not only because it is healthy, but because it involves the environment. Germans are becoming increasingly aware of their spare time and are beginning to take an active part in planning how to use it, adding more importance to it in comparison with everyday work. A typical recreational pastime, for example, is looking after plots (*Schrebergärten*). These are not always on the outskirts of town, but are sometimes in the middle of the city. Vegetables and flowers are cultivated here, a duck's pond dug out, or a little log cabin made for the weekend. Naturally all this is watched over by the German garden dwarf, one of the arch symbols of German sentimentality and narrow-mindedness. These plots are both idyllic small gardens and oases away from the everyday stress and prison-like atmosphere of built-up areas.

The tavern and pub used to be places of communication where one could meet over a glass of beer after work. Visits there have become much less frequent since the goggle box came into existence. In Germany, television has long reached No. 1 on the average leisure-time pop-list. Discussing the television programmes of the evening before often fills each break at work the following day.

The German and his car: Another passion of the German, especially that of the German man, is "The Car." It is a status symbol to be cleaned and polished regularly; it is a holiday "coach" which is often hopelessly overloaded. For a German his car is a hobby and an obsession which he can paint and tune up, dent and repair. To be without a car is, for most people, a nightmare and they would rather be in debt than be without one. Traffic jams during rush hour or at holiday time cannot in any way lessen the German's love of the automobile.

The German travels far on holiday and is to be found in places where he can spend his hard-earned German mark well. The majority spend their holidays in Austria, probably because it is so similar to Germany. Next on the list are Italy, Spain and Yugoslavia. The four most glorious weeks of the year are supposed to relieve the Germans of stress and give them back their peace of mind.

More could be written about the Germans; about their lives, newspapers, politicians, their strikes and prejudices and their hospitality. To quote an old Chinese saying: "To take one look at something is better than to have been told about it a hundred times." Therefore, it is best for you the visitor to have a good, close look at this country than to just read about it.

Left, flower seller in the market. Right, steadily steering an Isar raft.

Krone
erbaut
1480
Einbahnstraße
Holzhäuser Straße
10 - 24 h
0 - 8 h

Deutschland (Germany)
100 km
DANMARK
(DENMARK)
Baltic Sea
North Sea
Westerland
Sylt
Nordfriesische Inseln
Husum
Flensburg
Schleswig
Rödby Havn
Gedser
Puttgarden
Fehmarn
Saßnitz
Rügen
Kiel
Schleswig-Holstein
Helgoland
Warnemünde
Rostock
Itzehoe
Cuxhaven
Lübeck
Elbe
Ostfriesische Inseln
Bremerhaven
Hamburg
DEUTSCHE DEMOKRATISCHE REPUBLIK
(GDR)
Wilhelmshaven
Groningen
Lüneburg
280 km (152 Miles)
Oldenburg
Bremen
Lüneburger Heide
BERLIN
NEDERLAND
(NETHERLANDS)
Niedersachsen
Weser
Celle
(West)
(Ost)
Spree
Hannover
252 km (137 Miles)
Enschede
Osnabrück
Wolfsburg
Hildesheim
Braunschweig
Potsdam
Sanssouci
Arnhem
Bielefeld
Hameln
Magdeburg
Goslar
Münster
Nordrhein-Westfalen
Höxter
Harz
Göttingen
Duisburg
Dortmund
Essen
440 km (238 Miles)
Halle
Leipzig
Elbe
Krefeld
Düsseldorf
Wuppertal
Kassel
BUNDESREPUBLIK DEUTSCHLAND
(FRG)
Dresden
Aachen
Köln
BONN
Erfurt
Marburg
K.-Marx-Stadt
BELGIQUE/BELGIË
(BELGIUM)
Hessen
Fulda
Koblenz
Limburg
Rheinland-Pfalz
Hof
Coburg
Wiesbaden
ČESKOSLOVENSKO
(CZECHOSLOVAKIA)
LUXEMBOURG
Mosel
Rüdesheim
Frankfurt
Bamberg
Bayreuth
Mainz
Trier
Würzburg
Darmstadt
Plzeň
Pfalz
Luxembourg
Worms
500 km
(297,5 Miles)
Saarland
Mannheim
Nürnberg
Metz
Saarbrücken
Heidelberg
Rothenburg
Speyer
Heilbronn
Dinkelsbühl
Regensburg
Karlsruhe
Baden-Baden
Stuttgart
Nördlingen
Donau
Nancy
Passau
Baden
Bayern
Strasbourg
Tübingen
Landshut
Freudenstadt
Ulm
Augsburg
Inn
Württemberg
Dachau
Isar
FRANCE
Donau
München
Lech
Freiburg
Starnberger See
Chiemsee
Mulhouse
Friedrichshafen
Lindau
Salzburg
Füssen
Basel
Konstanz
Bodensee
Oberstdorf
Garmisch-Partenkirchen
Berchtesgaden
Zürich
Zugspitze
2964 m
SCHWEIZ
(SWITZERLAND)
Innsbruck
ÖSTERREICH
(AUSTRIA)

IN SEARCH OF THE ROMANTIC

Romantic Germany: does it still exist? You need not fear. The innumerable fortresses lining the steep slopes along the banks of Old Father Rhine are just as threatening today as in Queen Victoria's time; sonorous bells of Romanesque, Gothic or Baroque churches in the heart of towns and cities still summon the faithful to church services; and German towns are still protected by thick walls and guarded by defiant towers, albeit in a purely symbolic sense. Many of the carefully reconstructed medieval marketplaces with cobblestones, homely half-timbered houses and inviting guest-houses have been turned into pedestrian precincts which makes it easy to drift back into the distant past when such places were the scene of ancient customs and festivals, many of which have been revived. But what about the German forest, once the territory of fierce German tribes dealing the Roman Empire its fatal blow, later the fount and scene of countless fairy-tales and legends, and with its breadth, depth and solitude often deemed a synonym for the German character? It still exists, though the environment is seriously threatened by the destructive power of industrialization.

Romanticism was, and remains, only one characteristic of Germany, whose castles are witnesses of a warlike past characterized by political division and dissolution. Indeed the history of the Germans, this people at the heart of Europe, is more tragic than romantic. For a long time after Charlemagne, it appeared that the first nation-state might arise on German soil as the successor to the Roman Empire and for centuries the Germans were the single stabilizing factor in European politics. However, rivalry between papacy, imperial crown and the regional princes led to the evaporation of this dream, and the Holy Roman Empire of the German Nation became a political and economic patchwork quilt soaked in blood and tears during the Thirty Years' War. A common culture and language remained, but it was not until 1871 that Bismarck's diplomacy and the strength of the Prussian army created a German nation, a centralized Reich. Much of that which is regarded today as "typically German" stems from traditional thought and customs of former centuries and is characterized by their weaknesses. Perhaps this is why Germany has become the home of romanticism, of unrequited national, political and cultural yearnings.

Considering the basic tragic-romantic tenor of German history, one is involuntarily reminded of ancient Greece which, in similar conditions of political disintegration, experienced a golden age of reason and of the arts, comparable to that in the century of the Germans much later. In 1813 Madame de Stael had already called politically-divided Germany the Fatherland of Thought, which later evolved into the phrase, "the Land of Poets and Thinkers". Quite true, for it is questionable if any other European country has produced so many poets, thinkers and musicians of world-renown as has Germany which so often has experienced political misfortune. And when, at the turn of the 19th century, as a result of the Industrial Revolution, the natural sciences and technology changed the face of the world, German, especially German-Jewish intellectuals and engineers were at the forefront.

Unquestionably, the Germans have given the world a lot, but they have also taken and destroyed much. Before the horror of World War I which originated on German soil had faded, the far greater terror of National Socialism cast its shadow over Europe and brought Germany to the lowest point in its history. The fact that Germany today is still a divided country, that there are two states on German soil at the dividing line between East and West may well be the historical price that Germany had to pay.

Preceding pages: crossing the mud–flats by horse carriage; skilfully restored timber frame facades of the 15th century.

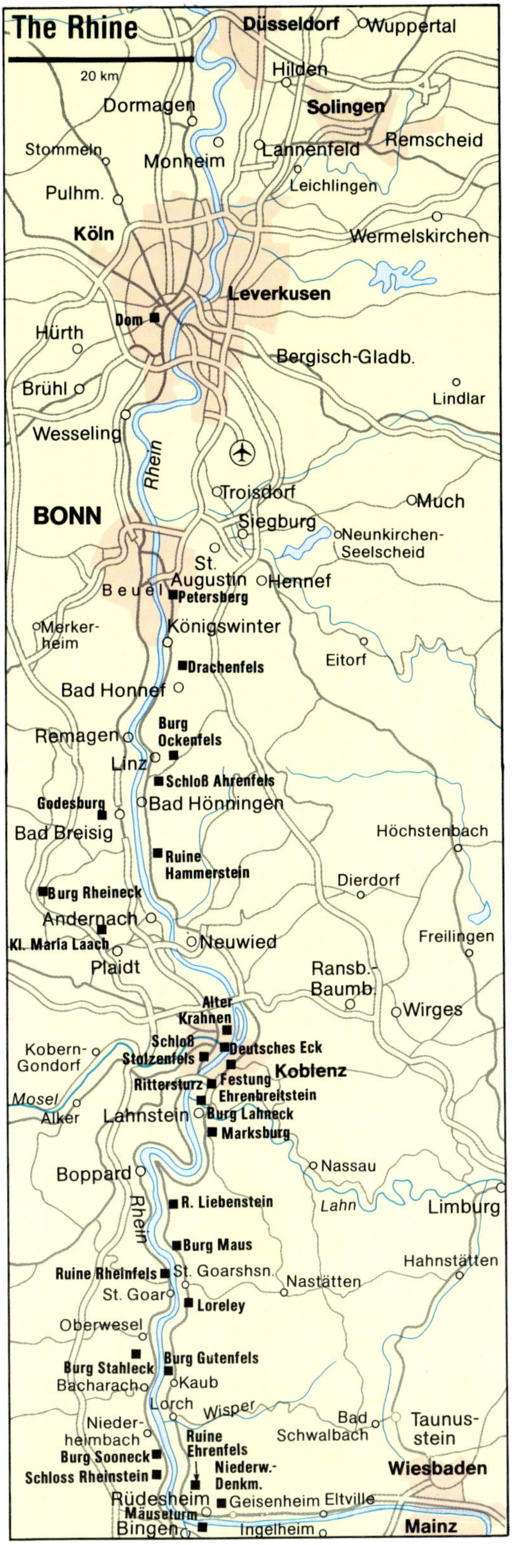

CRUISING FATHER RHINE

The Rhine has always been the most German of the German rivers, the stream-of-fate of the Germans since 55 B.C. when Julius Caesar had the first bridge constructed north of Koblenz. With its vineyards, countless fortresses and idyllic towns to the left and right it has, for centuries, symbolized the ambivalence of the German national character: love-of-life and sentimentality on the one hand, broodiness and inscrutability on the other. The martial and the romantic, industrial and idyllic landscape at one and the same time, Old Father Rhine wears the mask of Janus.

Its 820 miles (1,320 km) makes the Rhine is the second-longest river in Europe, rising in the Swiss Alps to feed into the North Sea, flowing through 542 miles (867 km) of German territory. From Rheinfelden onwards it is navigable for 552 miles (883 km) and is the busiest waterway in Europe. Each month up to 9,000 cargo-vessels sail its waters up and down river, to say nothing of countless pleasure-steamers which ply back and forth, mainly on the romantic stretch between Mainz and Cologne. At least since Queen Victoria and her German Prince Consort Albert traveled this part in torrential rain in 1845, the Rhine has been rated as one of the world's greatest attractions, the epitome of Romantic Germany.

But the Rhine is more than a symbol of Romanticism, more than just a waterway. It is also a river of industry, especially north of Cologne where it flows through Europe's largest industrial area, the Ruhr. It is here, above all, that industrial companies have polluted and contaminated the river to such an extent that the name of the river, derived from the German word *rein* meaning 'pure,' has become a sad joke. Do not be surprised therefore, when boarding one of the white excursion boats in Mainz or further downriver, to find that the Rhine waters are neither blue, bright nor clear.

Johann Gutenberg's workshop: The best place to begin a journey along the

Rhine is at **Mainz** (187,000 inhabitants), which lies not far from Frankfurt, on the left bank of the river and opposite the Mainz estuary. It is a time-honored city which was founded in 38 B.C. by the Romans. After being made the seat of an archbishopric in A.D. 742 by St. Boniface, it soon became the metropolis of German Christianity. In the Middle Ages, Golden Mainz was a powerful city, whose Electors and Archbishops served as the vice-chancellors of the Holy Roman Empire of the German Nation. Today, Mainz is renowned as the capital of the state Rheinland-Pfalz, as the home of *ZDF* (one of the two national TV channels) and, last but not least, as a stronghold of the Rhine carnival. As the center of the wine trade, it is also home to the only vineyard ministry in Germany.

The townscape is dominated by the huge red sandstone complex of the six-towered Romanesque **cathedral** (dating back to A.D. 975), a pillared basilica with three naves and a turbulent architectural and political history. The best view of the entire cathedral complex (sometimes called the cathedral mountains) can be enjoyed from the marketplace. Most prominent of the many museums in Mainz is the **Gutenberg Museum** directly opposite the cathedral. Here the visitor can take a look inside a monastic clerk's office, admire a "Stempelschneider" desk and wonder at old newsprint machines–and, of course, at the reconstruction of Johann Gutenberg's workshop, in which he invented the printing press with movable letters in 1445. The museum's greatest treasure is Gutenberg's 42-page bible, one of the loveliest of the 47 extinct examples printed on parchment which is still in its original binding.

In the evening, the picturesque **Altstadt** entices the visitor to stroll through Mainz's narrow alleys, which boast many votive pictures and fountains. The half-timbered houses and little Weinstuben (wine bars) will almost inevitably lead to a first encounter with the light, sparkling, Rheinhesse white wine which is best enjoyed with

Preceding pages: Rhine valle at Bingen; Rhineland vintner. Below, panoramic view of Mainz with cathedral.

Handkäs mit Musik (cheese with vinegar, oil and finely chopped onions).

From the **Electoral Palace** housing the **Roman-Germanic Museum** on the banks of the Rhine, one can look across to Mainz's sister-town, **Wiesbaden**. It is the capital of the federal state Hesse (population: 280,000), which extends from the right bank of the Rhine to the slopes of the Taunus mountains. From the Baroque castle **Biebrich** (1698-1744) on the banks of the Rhine, the princes of Nassau-Idestein presided over the rise of this spa-town, founded in the Middle Ages, with its 27 hot springs, which became a bathing resort of world-renown in the 19th century.

A glass of wine at Rüdesheim: Mainz is the starting point of Old Father Rhine's most historical and romantic stretch. Between Mainz and Cologne the serpentine river valleys are flanked by needle-sharp church spires, golden weather-cocks, spick-and-span villages, gorges and hills on which terraced vineyards climb in geometrical lines. This is the part which German poets imagined to be paradise on earth and where generations of Anglo-Saxons have cruised up and down. If you do not want to join the Rhine cruise to Cologne or any of the intermediary stops, you can cross the Theodor Heuss bridge and follow the B42 on the right bank of the river, also called the "Rheingauer Riesling-Route," and head for Koblenz as the final destination. It follows the Rhine at the foot of apparently endless terraced vineyards of the Rhinegau area, a spur of the Taunus mountains.

Our first stop will be **Eltville**. Neither highway nor railway has cut it off from the waterfront, for citizens' groups have, after years of struggle, secured the conservation of one of the Rhine's loveliest promenades. The Roman *Alta Villa* was the residence of the Electors of Mainz for 150 years. Eltville's most remarkable building is the **Wohnturm** (living tower) of the elector's castle, which was a refuge during wars and rebellions. Today the village is famous for its sparkling-wine cellars.

At the northern edge of Eltville, a

Below, in lovely Rüdesheim. Right, mighty Germania at Niederwald memorial.

small road branches off the B42 and leads to the wine village of **Kiedrich,** with the ruins of **Scharfenstein** castle and the old monastic complex of **Kloster Eberbach** (monastery) first constructed in A.D. 1116 as a canon's convent of the Augustinian monks on a hill above the Rhine valley. The monastery consists of the original Romanesque church, the cloisters, chapter house, refectory and two hospitals. It is one of those few places filled with such serenity and dignity that can be enjoyed even by those who cannot tell the difference between the Cistercian and Augustinian orders. This is not only because of the well-preserved monastic buildings of the 12th to 14th centuries, but also because of the Cistercians' popularity and industry. At more than 200 locations, the monks were endowed with farms and estates, where they produced their own Rheingau wines which were shipped in their own boats to the monastery's wine cellar in Cologne.

Somehow **Rüdesheim,** with its narrow alley, **Drosselgasse,** lined with ornate *Weinstuben* (wine-bars) has made the big time. It is the favorite destination of millions of Rhine travelers from all over the world. True, the wineries here are famous, and the **Brömserburg** (9th century) which today houses the wine museum, is the oldest Rhine castle, but what else makes Rüdesheim so special? Do not dozens of towns and villages on both sides of the river have half-timbered houses and *Weinstuben* just like the ones in world-famous Drosselgasse? Come what may, Rüdesheim is an established and well-organized tourist attraction which caters to the needs of its visitors. But there is more to Rüdesheim than Drosselgasse. Take a picture of the famous half-timbered houses and then walk on into one of the narrow lanes and you might end up in a small backyard family restaurant and be surprised at how quiet and inexpensive Rüdesheim can be.

Valkyrian Germania: From Rüdesheim the visitor can travel by cable-car up over the gleaming vineyards to the 123 feet (37 m) high **Niederwald Memo-**

Mice tower at Bingen.

rial (unveiled in 1883), whose dimensions and position high above the Rhine are really breathtaking. The sword-swinging lady, dubbed **Germania**, a Valkyrian symbol of Bismarck's unified Germany (1871), gazes defiantly west across the Rhine. Compared with her total weight (6.4 tons) the 23 feet (7 m) long sword in her left hand seems almost a featherweight. This sword stands for a period in German history, when, in the country of poets and philosophers, weapons overshadowed the might of the word as Germany pushed itself into the ranks of the leading European imperialist powers.

Back to Rüdesheim after a trip to Valkyrie, cross the river by ferry to visit the village of **Bingen**, which lies at the confluence of the Nahe and Rhine rivers. From the restaurant in **Klopp** fortress there is a glorious view of the **Mäuseturm** (Mice Tower) of Bingen which is located on a rock in the river. Legend has it that hard-hearted archbishop Hatto withdrew to this spot during a famine in A.D. 996 to escape from the rebellious population, but received his just punishment here when the hungry mice gobbled him up. Of course none of this is true; in reality, the 14th century tower served as a customs-post and later as a signal-tower for the dangerous passage through the **Bingener Loch**, a treacherous rapid near the rock where many ships have foundered.

A pearl-string of castles: The next 16 mile (25 km) stretch along the Rhine past Bingener Loch will help the visitor understand why more poetry, more fables, more songs and modern legends have been inspired by Father Rhine than by any other river. Though almost dead ecologically, and putting aside the rapid development of noisy international tourism, nothing can stop the visitor from absorbing the images of the unique river landscape of the broad, spaciously flowing Rhine, the steep hills and forested rockfaces, the vineyards and the castle ruins. In dense concentration, the castles line both banks of the majestically flowing river. Perched atop vertical crags, they still

he "Pfalz" t Kaub.

seem imperious in spite of their often dilapidated splendor. Nearly all the castles along the Rhine have, at one time or another, been destroyed in successive campaigns by kings, emperors or local rulers who saw them as reminders of medieval days when the lofty eyries were occupied by robber knights and autocratic nobles preying on the domains below them, and impervious to the directives of their overlords. Some cities grouped together to punish the haughty knights who ransacked their caravans, looted their villages and imposed tolls on vessels effected by dropping heavy iron chains across the river.

Shortly before the town of **Assmannshausen**, renowned for its red wine, the ruin of **Ehrenfels** appears on the right bank of the Rhine. In former times the treasures of the Mainz cathedral was stored in this castle which glares sulkily across the river at the fortress of **Rheinstein** on the other bank. Shortly after Assmannshausen, the next fortress, **Drachenstein**, on the left bank, greets the traveler. Then soon after the silhouette of the neighboring fortress of **Sooneck** appears.

You may want to explore the three fortresses on the left bank. If so, you can cross the Rhine by ferry from Assmannshausen and return to the right bank of the Rhine via the well-known wine locality of **Lorch**. However, it is worthwhile to stay on the left bank after crossing the Rhine at Assmannshausen and travel as far as **Bacharach**, an ancient wine center. You can walk the medieval town walls with their well-preserved 14th century defensive towers and look down the narrow alleys of half-timbered houses. The landmarks of this idyllic little town are the **Stahleck** fortress (today a hostel) and, further south, the ruins of **Fürstenberg**. The oldest vintage wine festival is held in early October in the Middle Rhine.

The defeat of Napoleon: After a few minutes' drive by the left bank, one of the Rhine's famous scenic images appears in the middle of the river–the Rhine island Pfalzgrafenstein with the famous **Pfalz**, built in the 14th century

Left to right: Fortresses hail from the steep slopes–Sonneck, Marxburg, and Katz castle.

as a customs post. In those days a chain could be strung across the river to prevent vessels from proceeding until the captain had paid a sum to the customs official. However, it first became famous on account of an event on New Year's Eve 1813-14, when Marshal Blücher, with the help of a pontoon bridge, transported his troops across the Rhine. They were pursuing the Napoleonic forces which had just been defeated at Leipzig. Today it is easier to make the crossing from the right bank to the island and to board the ferry to the small town of Kaub with its imposing fortress of **Gutenfels** (13th century).

Scarcely has the Pfalz at Kaub been passed than the silhouette of the next fortress on the left bank of the Rhine appears: the mighty ruin of **Schönburg** (14th century). Below it lies the small town of **Oberwesel**, which can be reached by ferry from the right bank of the river. Beautifully preserved medieval town walls with 15 watch towers and numerous church towers which include the 243 feet (74 m) high steeple of the **Liebfrauenkirche** and the mighty bell tower of **St. Martin's** (both 14th century) have earned, for Oberwesel, the name "town of towers." The town walls and its towers, together with the picturesque half-timbered houses make Oberwesel a fragment of the Middle Ages with which the visitor might well fall in love.

Loreley and other virgins: Not far beyond Oberwesel, one travels past seven submerged reefs, known as the **Seven Virgins**, who were said to have been turned into stone on account of their prudishness–a legend often told to unwilling girls by impatient lovers. But *she* must have been much lovelier, the blond seductive mermaid Loreley sitting atop a high rock, nine miles (15 km) from Kaub, luring innumerable ships and boatmen who had to pass the rapids of the perilous waters below and who were captivated by her singing and beauty. This early *femme fatale* is an imaginary figure invented in 1801 by the Romantic poet Clemens Brentano and immortalized by Heinrich Heine in

his famous poem of 1823 which was set to music in 1832 by the composer Friedrich Silcher. Since then, Loreley has been regarded as the epitome of Rhine Romance. In real life it is a rugged rock soaring 435 feet (132 m) above the river, whose narrow stretch here was once dangerous to passing ships.

A few minutes after the encounter with the Loreley, another high watermark in a journey along the romantic Rhine awaits: the view of the three fortresses at St. Goarshausen and St. Goar, on the other bank. From vantage points, all three can be seen at once: **Burg Katz** and **Burg Maus** on the right bank above Goarshausen and **Burg Rheinfels** on the other side of the river above St. Goar. The fortress of Rheinfels was built as a powerful medieval fortification for the levy of tolls, and withstood countless sieges before falling without a struggle to the French in 1796, because the garrison had fled. In September, between the idyllic sister towns of St. Goar and St. Goarshausen, visitors will discover "**the Rhine in flames**," a spectacle during which innumerable torches are lit along the Rhine slopes, the castles are illuminated by spotlights, and a colorful display of fireworks is staged.

And the journey continues from castle to castle. High above the old wine-and pilgrimage-center of **Kamp-Borhofen**, on the right bank, are the "hostile brothers," the castles of **Sterrenberg** and **Liebenstein** eyeing one another, but separated by a wall.

Endless vineyards: The white towers of **St. Severus church**, this time on the left bank, herald the town of **Boppard** with its 1.5 mile (two km) long Rhine promenade. This is the central point of the largest wine-growing region of the Middle Rhine; on the **Bopparder Hamm** alone there are about 1.5 million vines. Reside with local families and combine your language studies with easy going life in one of the most romantic resorts of the Rhine valley. Follow the sign to the cable car that from March to October climbs to the **Gedeons-Eck** (990 feet/302 m) offering a magnificent view of the Rhine. A 30-minute walk leads to one of the most fascinating vantage points of the Rhine valley called **Vier-Seen-Blick** (Four-Lakes-View). Here, the meandering Rhine looks like a series of lakes.

Buy a castle: Boppard is the point at which the Rhine begins its loop, the river flowing at first north-west, then suddenly cutting north and west through the breathtaking scenery of the Rhine slate-mountains, before resuming its northerly course shortly before **Braubach**. High above this "town of wines and roses" towers the **Marksburg** (13th century) like a castle of the Holy Grail, thrown into strange contrast by three factory chimneys. Nowhere else can one better appreciate the glories of the knights-of-old whose lives were anything but comfortable. The German Fortress Association is based here and should you wish to buy a fortress, this is the place to enquire.

Diagonally opposite, on the left bank of the Rhine, lies the little town of **Rhens**, which was first mentioned in the 7th century. It was a political center-of-power in the Middle Ages and it was here that the German electors chose the German kings and emperors. The assembly point was the **King's chair**, first documented in 1308, reconstructed in 1843 and moved to its present position in 1923. Downstream, on the right bank, lies **Lahnstein,** at the point where the river Lahn flows into the Rhine. Have lunch here at the famous **Wirtshaus an der Lahn**, where Goethe once took his ease. From the fortress of **Lahneck** (13th century), above the small town, a wonderful view can be enjoyed of the Lahn, the Rhine, and across to the Neo-Gothic castle of **Stolzenfels** on the left bank. The castle was first built in 1836-46 on a 312 feet (95 m) high rock face. The castle on this site was first built in 1250 as a customs station for the Elector of Trier but was destroyed in 1689 by French troops. The structure seen today was commissioned in 1842 by King Frederick IV of Prussia. The castle ruins and parts of the fortification walls dates from the Middle Ages.

Where Rhine and Moselle meet: In a while, when the first Rhine bridge since leaving Mainz comes into view, the traveler knows that he has arrived at **Koblenz** (120,000 inhabitants). Soon the Baroque domes of the **Liebfrauenkirche** and the towers of **St. Kastor** (both 13th century) show up on the left while the silhouette of the **Ehrenbreitstein** fortress appear on the right .

The name Koblenz is rooted in Roman antiquity. The fort **Castrum ad Confluences** was built as early as 9 B.C., and from the 11th century until 1806, it belonged to the territory of the Archbishop, later the Electors of Trier. The city suffered severe destruction in World War II, and most of the facades of its old town buildings have been rebuilt. The best view of the city is from the Fortress of Ehrenbreitstein (access by a road branching off the B42 or by cable-car) more than 300 feet (100 metres) above the Rhine. Here you can take the famous photograph of the **Deutsches Eck** (German corner) the promontory between the Rhine and the Moselle. Of the various museums within the fortress, which also houses the largest youth hostel in the Federal Republic, the **Rhine Museum** is of special interest. From Ehrenbreitstein, return to B42 and cross the Rhine by the Pfaffendorf bridge. Take a stroll down stream from the neo-classical **Schloss** (18th century) near the Rhein promenade, built by the last Elector of Trier to **St. Castor's Church** (founded 836). Proceed to the famous Deutsches Eck named after the former Deutschherrenhaus (House of the Teutonic Order). The monument from which, in 1945, the statue of Emperor Wilhelm II was toppled, is called Monument to German Unity, following a decision by the Bonn government in 1953. From this vantage point one can see the Moselle to the left and the Rhine to the right.

In the middle, above Pfaffendorf bridge, is the famous **wine village**. This was constructed in 1925 as a replica of a winegrowers' village with vineyards and half-timbered houses from the most celebrated German winegrowing regions. Here, whether in the company of a quarter liter of Rhine or of Moselle wine, you will feel on top of the world.

At "Dreiländereck" in Koblenz, the confluence of Rhine and Moselle.

Meandering Moselle River

In the summer of 1986 the Moselle river (German Mosel) between Koblenz and Trier, *the* classical destination of all those in search of romantic Germany, made headlines. Thousands of dead fish were found drifting down the river near Trier and the city brought legal action against French plans to operate a nuclear power plant at Cattenom and empty their sewer into the already polluted waters of the Moselle.

Not only does the river suffer, but the prospects of many people living by it are dim. Between 1979 and 1986, 20 percent of Moselle winegrowers were forced to shut down. Many Moselle vintners working vineyards between 2.5 acres (one hectare) to 45 acres (20 hectares) compete with the rest of the 20 quality winegrowing regions within the European Common Market. Many of the picturesque vineyards which face the river and on whose slaty hills the famous fruity white wine originates, already lie fallow.

Moselle tourism, however, has not been affected by these developments. It is true that the once famous *Moselhecht* (fresh pike) has disappeared from the menus, but trout and carp are still caught in the river. The people here are proud of their *Moselromantik-Service*, a word which has become part of the English vocabulary. The connoisseur of European travel will, on no account, miss his Moselle excursion, and he is sure to find, as did Goethe in 1792 on his boat trip from Trier to Koblenz, "the feeling of relish and well-being which seems to characterize winegrowing areas."

One should not, however, toss aside the Moselle valley as a mere *Weinland*. Few regions north of the Alps have as many historic monuments and fascinating sights as Trier, the Rome of the North and the seat of Roman Emperors. Many of Germany's most beautiful castles and castle ruins represent important chapters of German history that has been written at the Moselle.

Cheer your heart with Moselle wine: Many of the events organized by tourists offices, town and village elders, proprietors of wineries, inns and taverns are centered around the production, the selling and the drinking of wine. Eight different wine educational trails introduce the enthusiast to the growing of the vines. Wine seminars are held for future connoisseurs as well as *Tage der offenen Keller* (open cellar days) where anyone can drop in for a wine tasting session. Wine festivals (*Weinfeste*) are held almost every weekend from April until the end of November. You can even fish the Moselle and spend your holiday at a vintner's house for only DM120 per week (including breakfast and wine tasting).

Following the meandering river: The easiest entry into the Moselle valley from Koblenz is on the B416. **Winningen** is a precursor of a fairyland of steep, slaty hills, castles, old churches, narrow alleys and marketplace lined with half-timbered houses and ancient cellars as well as modern wineries which are unique to the Moselle valley. Have a

Preceding pages, Moselle loop near Bremm. Left, Eltz castle.

look at the backyards or step into one of the cafes which make delicious confectionery. Be sure to visit also the fascinating Moselle castles.

Burg Eltz: One of Germany's most splendid castles four miles (six km) from Moselkern station, it is encircled on three sides by the Eltz river. First documented in A.D. 1150 and since then owned by various branches of the family of the counts of Elce, the castle was spared the ravages of medieval wars and destruction by the French who razed 99 percent of the region's castles about 300 years ago. The towers, high gables and rich ornaments of the oriel windows have fascinated thousands of visitors. The treasures accumulated by the Eltz Counts include a hall of weapons, panel paintings and richly decorated and furnished rooms. A picture of Eltz castle is on all DM 500 bank notes.

Another famous castle, the **Reichsburg Cochem**, first built in 1027, stands about eight miles (13 km) beyond Burg Eltz. The Cochemer Krampen is the first of many idyllic meanders typical of the river course. At Cochem, turn right at the Moselle bridge and see the entrance to Germany's longest railway tunnel (13,790 feet/4,203 m). The marketplace boasts a Baroque town hall from 1739, the Martin's fountain, and half-timbered houses with lovely decorations. The **Moselpromenade** with its cafes, inns and vine taverns, invites a leisurely stroll. Also, the view of the river landscape from the bridge crossing the Moselle to **Kond** (camping site and hostel) is beautiful.

The next stop is **Beilstein**, called the "Mini-Rothenburg" where several popular German films called *Heimatfilme*, were made. Then comes **Zell**, with its famous fountain and wine called *"Zeller Schwarze Katz"* (black cat). About 23 miles (37 km) beyond Cochem is the spa and wine-town of **Traben-Trarbach**, scene of an annual international motorboat racing competition and starting point for a side-trip to **Mont-Royal**, once the largest European fortress under French king Louis XIV, and to the ruins of **Grevenburg**

low, inking ffee at rnkastel. ght, chem stle.

castle (14th century) from where a wonderful view of the Moselle valley with its undulating vineyards climbing up the hills can be enjoyed.

After an 11-mile (22-km) drive you will reach **Bernkastel-Kues** (population: 7,500) which is situated in the heart of the middle Moselle and which is one of the region's best-known winetowns. It boasts one of the most romantic marketplaces in Germany which extends below the ruins of 7th century **Landshut** castle. In the Zentralkellerei, 14 million gallons (65 million liters) of wine, the produce of 5,000 vintners, are stored. Bernkastel is world-famous for its magnificent half-timbered houses, the filigree of its market fountain grating and the elaborate weather vanes on top of the gables, which together form an incomparable ensemble and have embellished calendars for many generations. The traditional *Weinfest der Mosel* in early September, which includes the reception of the wine queen called *Mosella*, attracts more than 200,000 visitors every year.

Cusanusstift is a hospital and hospice in Gothic style, and over 500 years old. It got its name from the famous cardinal and philosopher Nikolaus von Cues (Latin Cusanus: 1401-64) who was a leading figure of German Humanism and who advocated mutual tolerance of all religions. The house he was born in is now a museum dedicated to his life and work, and shows the transition from medieval to modern times.

From Bernkastel-Kues to Trier, the oldest German town, a journey will again take you along the meandering Moselle, past vineyards and through idyllic winegrowing villages like **Piesport** and **Neumagen**, the oldest winegrowing area in Germany since Roman times which are remembered by the *Neumagener Weinschiff* (3rd century).

In Germany's oldest town: Founded by Emperor Augustus in 16 B.C. **Trier** (population: 100,000) ranks as Germany's oldest town and has the most impressive Roman buildings north of the Alps. During its more than 2,000 years' history, it was the resi-

**The ancien
wine ship c
Neumagen**

dence of several Roman emperors including Diocletian and Constantine the Great. Then in the 9th century Charlemagne made it the seat of an archbishophric. From the 12th to the 18th century it was the capital of an Electorate.

Impressive relics of history can be found throughout the towns. Visit the world-famous **Porta Nigra** (2nd century) which was once a fortified Roman gateway and which, at 120 feet (36 m) wide and 100 feet (30 m) high, is the largest and best preserved such structure north of the Alps. In 1040 it was converted into a church, but later, under the rule of Napoleon, was restored to its original state. It was originally constructed without mortar and held together with iron crampons and owes its name to the dark patina which formed on the limestone blocks.

Other remarkable sights dating back to Roman times include the **Aula Palatina**, a basilica built in the 4th century as a coronation hall for Constantine the Great, and the **Kaiserthermen** (imperial baths) which were begun under Constantine the Great, but were never completed. From these baths it is only a short walk to the ruins of the ancient **amphitheater** where 25,000 spectators could watch bloody games or cultural performances. Finally, there is the **Römerbrücke** (Roman Bridge).

Some sights in town will remind you of medieval Christianity. The **Dom** (cathedral) is one of the oldest churches in Germany built in Romanesque style (11th-12th century) and rests on 4th century Roman foundations. Adjoining the cathedral is the 13th century **Liebfrauenkirche**, among Germany's oldest Gothic churches.

From the church it is only a few steps to the **Hauptmarkt**, an impressive and picturesque marketplace in Germany which, with its Gothic, Renaissance and Rococo buildings, is a living textbook of architectural history. Nearby, at Brückenstrasse 10, is the house where Karl Marx, one of the most influential thinkers of modern times, was born in 1818. It is now a museum and attracts pilgrims from all over the world.

**eminder
the past:
parkling
orta Nigra
Trier.**

Rivers And Wines

To discover the German winelands, just follow the Rhine and its tributaries. All the vineyards grow either on the hills which overlook the Rhine valley or along the rivers which merge with it: the Ahr, Moselle, Nahe, Main and Neckar. Germany is renowned for its white wines. Its climate is ideal for the characteristics of this wine which does not have very high alcohol content and which has a somewhat mild taste.

Eighty-seven percent of the wine produced in Germany is white. However, more reds are being produced. A little knowledge about German wines will help you to select, order and appreciate the wine most suitable to your palate.

According to German wine laws, every bottle must state on its label the origin of the wine, the grape used in manufacturing it, and the year of growth. The official control number (AP number) which ensures that the wine has passed the controls and certifies conscientious wine making.

Wines differ in their amount of residual sugar, that is, the quantity of sugar left after fermentation. Generally there are three degrees of sweetness: *trocken* (dry), *haltrocken* (semi-dry) and *lieblich* (sweet). *Lieblich* designates a high content of residual sugar derived either from the grape *Eiswein* or *Spätlese*, or by adding "sweet reserve" (unfermented sweet grape juice) or by stopping the fermenting process. Dry wine does not mean bitterness, however. Dry means that almost all of the dextrose (fruit sugar) has been naturally fermented . These three grades are often indicated by a sticker, the German *Weinsiegel*, with red for the sweeter wines, green the semi-dry wines and yellow the dry wines. It is a matter of taste as to which one you prefer.

German wines are famous for the varieties of grapes which are used in their production. The pride of every vintner is to cultivate that grape which is most suited to his environment. The

Working in a vineyard.

most important grape is *Riesling*, which ripens in late October and produces pungent, fragrant wine, sometimes with a lot of fresh and fruity acid. It is suitable for most meals. Today, the most widely planted grape is *Müller-Thurgau*, which has a milder fragrance and a mellower body. This wine is meant to be consumed early. *Kerner*, a newcomer which produces a fresh, racy bouquet with a spicy body, is the fastest growing variety. *Silvaner*, more than any other grape, reflects the soil in which it is grown, and produces a lighter and sometimes pleasantly neutral wine. *Ruländer* produces an intensive, often heavy wine with a low acid content and lots of character. *Gewürztraminer* is a grape with a low yield but a specific and intense, oftentimes unique character.

Germany is the leading country for discovering new grape varieties which give ample yields and safe harvests in the northern climate. The top red grapes are: *Blauer Spätburgunder* with its intense, full body and its sometimes velvety taste while *Blauer Portugieser*, the second most common red grape gives a milder, lighter wine of pleasant character. *Trollinger*, produced in the Stuttgart region, gives a hearty and fruity wine suitable for daily consumption.

asting
ine.

Note the quality of the wine which is indicated on the label unless the wine is of the poorest quality–*Tafelwein*. Such wines, which are produced from approved grapes in Mosel, Rhein, Main, Neckar and Oberrhein regions, are consumed locally. *Qualitätswein* has more body and is made from approved grape varieties from any of 11 regions. *Qualitätswein mit Prädikat* is the top quality and such wines are also made from approved grape varieties.

Kabinett is the lightest of these and is dry, elegant and delicate. *Spätlese* literally means late harvest and these wines have more body and a pleasant sweetness. *Auslese* are noble wines made from the ripest grapes while nobler and of exceptional quality with a honey-like flavor are *Beerenauslese* wines. *Trokkenbeerenauslese* and *Eiswein* are the crowning achievements of the German wine-maker. The former is made from individual grapes, shrivelled almost to raisins; the latter is from grapes harvested and crushed while still frozen. These wines are rare and expensive.

With the basics, you are now ready to head for the region which offers the wine of your choice. Follow the many wine-roads in the Palatinate or in Franconia; travel along the Moselle and join the winegrowers of Cochem in their wine festival celebrations, complete with benches set up in the marketplace, music from a brass band and the smell of fried sausages. Wine drinkers are sociable characters. This becomes apparent the first time you enter a wine bar. The atmosphere here is quite different from that of the Munich *Hofbräuhaus*–famous for another brand of German conviviality. When in Würzburg, be sure to try the Würzburger PSBocksbeutel, which is found only in Franconia. And if you like to drink Trollinger as much as the local folks, then don't delay. You might probably meet the local wine queen of the Rhine. *Prosit!* Your Health!

HEADING FOR COLOGNE

The side-trip to the Moselle valley concluded, return to Koblenz and head north for Cologne (Köln) on the B42. Soon the flat Neuwied Basin is entered, where the Rhine landscape dramatically changes its character.

In **Bendorf** visit the **Sayner Hütte**, one of the oldest iron foundries in the country. It is a fine example of 19th century industrial architecture with its foundry hall in the shape of a three-naved basilica and its western facade adorned with cast iron filigree work.

Via **Neuwied**, only 1.5 miles (three km) to the north, B42 runs parallel with the railways to Bonn through the Rhine valley. You may stop at **Leutesdorf**, an old wine village on the Rhine bank across the river from Andernach. It is pleasant to stroll among the charming half-timbered houses, the parish church (14th century) and the pilgrimage church and stumble upon one of those small wine restaurants called *Strausswirtschaft*, where you can try the proprietor's own wines and taste typical local snacks.

On the opposite bank of the Rhine lies **Andernach**, the former Roman fort Antunnacum (it can be reached by ferry). Here, another pleasant river walk passes through an old town quarter with its 16th century town hall. A detour to **Maria Laach Abbey**, one of the most celebrated monastic houses in the Rhineland, situated in the geographically interesting upland region called the **Eifel** is a must. The austere beauty of the Eifel, a range of hills averaging 2,000 feet (600 m) in height and of volcanic origin is a major tourist attraction. The Benedictine monastery is centered around the abbey church (1093-1220), one of Germany's most famous Romanesque buildings, whose air of solidity is enhanced by the vast crater lake. The monks are not only well-trained tourist guides: they also run an excellent restaurant, several souvenir shops and a flower shop.

Preceding pages, the Wallraf-Richartz-Museum in front of Cologne Cathedral. Below, in a side arm of the Rhine a Osterspai.

Back on the right bank of the Rhine at Leutesdorf, follow once again the B42. Above the small village of Hammerstein tower is the ruin of the 10th century **Hammersteiner Ley castle**. The early Romantics were bewitched by the view from the castle into the depths of the river. Count Otto von Hammerstein was a very early Romantic. He built the castle to defend his wife Irmgard and himself against the attacks of Emperor Henry II, who had disapproved of his marriage. After a three months' siege the medieval romance ended as Irmgard and Otto were close to starvation.

From the Kaiserberg at **Linz** (do not miss the city gate towers, the late Gothic town hall and the excellent local wine) there is a splendid view of the river and beyond to the Eifel hills and Ahr river valley. In Linz board a ferry again and travel to the bridge at **Remagen**, well known since the end of World War II. The bridge was secured by the Americans who found it miraculously intact, although damaged by German explosives, while all the other 43 bridges over the Rhine had been destroyed by the Nazis. The Americans crossed the bridge just before it collapsed a few days later. The unexpected crossing cut several days off the war and was retold in a Hollywood film. Memorabilia of the dramatic event are shown in the **Friedensmuseum** (Peace Museum) which is located in the only surviving pillar of the former railway bridge.

After crossing the Rhine again at Linz by ferry and traveling along the B42 further north, we come to **Unkel**, with possible detours to **Arenfels castle** and **Ockenfels castle**. The B road leads past the **Siebengebirge mountain range** with its landmark, the **Drachenfels** (Dragon Rock) castle ruins (1,050 feet/ 315 m; 12th century) which are named after Siegfried, hero of the Nibelungen legends, who slew the dragon and bathed in its blood to make himself invulnerable. Another legend is centered around the Siebengebirge (seven mountains), said to have been built by seven giants who dug a channel for the Rhine and left seven lumps of earth.

he "Redoute" t Bad odesberg.

A preliminary capital made permanent: Before 1949 the small, sleepy Rhenish residency of **Bonn** (population: 295,000) attracted visitors as the birthplace of Ludwig van Beethoven, the seat of a renowned university occupying the former Elector's residence, and because of its beautiful marketplace with the Renaissance town hall reminiscent of a small, medieval Bonn.

On November 3, 1949, Bonn was chosen by the Parliamentary Council as the preliminary location for the government of the Federal Republic. Since then, thousands of officials have occupied many of the stately old buildings and the ever-increasing modern highrise blocks housing ministries and administrative bodies. In the evening, government officials and the personnel of more than 120 embassies flock to their homes in the sprawling suburbs of Bonn, consisting of thriving independent villages such as **Poppelsdorf**, **Mehlcm** and **Plittersdorf**. High salaries have made Bonn one of the most expensive German cities.

And yet the old Bonn seems to have survived the massive influx of civil servants and foreign embassies. Walk along the dreamy, tree-lined streets of the **Altstadt** (old town) with its little shops and small pubs; visit the famous **Südstadt** residential district, south of the **Hofgarten park** and **Poppelsdorf Allee** where beautiful patrician houses and facades stand for the self-confidence of Imperial Germany between 1880 and World War I, and maybe then you will understand the feeling of the Greek author Georgos Krommidas, a longtime Bonn resident, "that this sets you back in times long past, where people met in the marketplace..."

Most places of interest are in the old town which can easily be explored on foot. There is the marketplace with the 20th century town hall, where US President Kennedy had his triumphant reception in 1963. (The bridge spanning the Rhine into thc quarter Bonn-Beuel bears his name.) Southwest of it, on **Münsterplatz**, is the venerable Romanesque minster with its 12th century

Beethoven looking down grimly at h[is] home town

cloister. Northeast of the marketplace, at Bonngasse 20 is the **Beethovenhaus**, Ludwig van Beethoven's birthplace (1770-1827). The 16th century building was developed in 1889 into the world's most important Beethoven museum. Imagine standing before the piano–constructed in Vienna for Beethoven and which bears his name–in the very place where the great musical genius was born and lived with his family. The nearby **Beethovenhalle**, a famous cultural center on the Rhine promenade, is the setting for concerts and festivities.

In the old town you will also find the **Koblenzer Tor** (a former town gate) housed in the east wing of the 17th century university building, where **Adenauerallee** starts its way south cutting through the **Hofgarten** and **Stadtgarten** parks, then leading past government buildings like the German Post Ministry and the Foreign Ministry. Further south, located between Adenaueralle and the Rhine promenade, is the heart of political power in the Federal Republic with buildings such as Villa **Hammerschmidt**, official residence of the German president; the **Bundespräsidialamt** (President's office); **Palais Schaumburg**, site of state receptions; and the **Bundeskanzleramt** with its adjoining residence of the German chancellor. The **Bundeshaus** (Parliament building) on the left bank of the Rhine nestles in the shadow of the 30-story **Langer Eugen**, the chamber of representatives.

The district of Bad Godesberg, also called Bonn 2, houses more than 70 diplomatic missions and various Federal ministries. The **Godesberger Redoute**, a Rococo electoral palace built in 1791-92, where once Beethoven gave concerts, is now used for state receptions.

A cathedral city: The most rewarding way to enter the cathedral city of **Cologne** is by train. From the right bank of the Rhine the train slowly moves through the quarter of Deutz and over the impressive **Hohenzollernbrücke** (bridge) while from your window you can enjoy one of the most grandiose city views in the world: the Rhine front with

ust of onrad denauer, ıe Federal epublic's rst hancellor.

its colorful facades and pointed gabled-roofs, above which rise the cathedral towers. Downriver, beyond the **Deutzer bridge,** looms the unique **Severinsbrücke** (bridge), supported by an off-center pillar. Germany's most ambitious building project gets closer and closer, until finally the train stops not far from the left bank of the Rhine about 650 feet (200 m) from the central doorway of the magnificent **Cathedral**.

Photographing Cologne from here is simple and rewarding: The cathedral from below; 509 steps up to the south spire; and Cologne from above with roof spire in the foreground. Then over to the right bank of the Rhine; medieval panorama with river and Cathedral–Cologne's world-famous landmark is always in the picture. Its dimensions: 472 feet (142 m) long, 147 feet (44 m) broad and 143 feet (43 m) high attract everybody within the confines of this city of nearly one million inhabitants, as a magnet attracts iron-fillings.

When, in 1248, Archbishop Konrad von Hochstaden blessed the start of the construction work, Cologne was Germany's largest city and, after Paris and Constantinople, the third largest in Europe and one of the richest in the world. In 1164 the relics of the Magi had been transferred to the old Cathedral. Its importance was enhanced when the idea of a cathedral to house the sepulcher of the Three Magi was born. The design was no longer to be based on the double-chair layout of the old cathedral, but followed modern architecture, that of the French royal cathedrals of Chartres, Rheims and Amiens which had attained a hitherto unknown magnificence of church architecture. The Cologne Cathedral thus became the ideal French cathedral constructed in the Gothic style. By 1320 the choir, including all the interior furnishing and decoration, was finished. In 1560 the medieval construction work was discontinued. It would never have been completed if, at the turn of the 19th century, the spirit of historicism and a wave of enthusiasm for the Middle Ages had not spread across Europe and

Deutz bridg
at Cologne.

nurtured the revival of the Gothic style in the form of the neo-Gothic. In 1842 King Friedrich Wilhelm IV of Prussia laid the foundation stone for the recommencement of work. By 1880 the most ambitious building project of the Middle Ages was completed.

The harmony in the individual parts of the structure is unsurpassed and is the essence of the unity of the Cathedral. The imposing interior is of a clarity which bears the observer up into the heavens, that realm of ethereal elevation which is peculiarly Gothic. Anyone entering the Cathedral is overwhelmed by this impression when looking at the tall windows and the steep vaulting. Above the High Altar is the **Reliquary** of the Magi, 4.5 feet (1.3 m) high, 7 feet (2.1 m) long and 3.5 feet (1 m) wide. It is larger than any comparable gold sarcophagus in the West and contains the sacred remains of the Three Magi. The **Gero Cross** in the Chapel of the Cross is the oldest work of the Crucifixion that has been preserved this side of the Alps (about A.D. 971). The entrance to the **Treasury** is in the north transept. It is one of the richest in the world, with reliquaries, paraments, liturgical articles, codices and ivory works.

Ancient metropolis: The heart of Cologne can be explored on foot. Concentrated within not more than one square mile, there is not only the Cathedral, but also the rich treasures from the time when Cologne was a Roman Imperial City (displayed in the **Roman-Germanic-Museum**), some of the 12 famous Romanesque medieval churches and, fronting the Cathedral, the **Wallraf-Richartz-Museum**, a world famous gallery of European painting. Almost completely rebuilt after the war and only a stone's throw from the Cathedral, the **Hohe Strasse**, Cologne's shopping center and a pedestrian precinct, boasts many department stores, boutiques and some local restaurants.

Cologne was a focal point of Western culture, exhibiting a cosmopolitan flavor of urbane and enlightened liberalism of which Heinrich Böll, 1972 Nobel prize-winner, was so worthy an em-

Striving for the heavens: the interior of Cologne Cathedral.

bodiment. These qualities have their roots in 2,000 years of history since 38 B.C. when the Roman general Agrippa allowed the Roman Germanic tribes to settle on the right bank of the Rhine opposite his military camp. This spot was later named *Colonia Ara Agrippinensis* in honor of the commander. Because of its strategic position on the fringe of the Roman empire, the settlement attracted many merchants and soldiers from the southern lands. At the end of the 5th century, Cologne became a part of the Franconian empire and the sociable Ripuarian Franks molded the character of Colonia, which was made the seat of an archbishopric by Charlemagne. During the Middle Ages Cologne was the most important member of the Hanseatic League. In 1388 a university was established. Since then Cologne has remained the enlightened religious, intellectual and artistic center of the Rhine valley. In 1709 the Italian chemist Giovanni-Maria Farina settled in Cologne and created his celebrated *Eau de Cologne*.

Just by looking through the large windows of the **Roman-Germanic Museum**, south of the cathedral, the visitor realizes that entering the museum will put him on Roman territory. The house was built over the famous **Dionysos mosaic** (2nd century). The 630 sq feet (70 sq m) mosaic consists of more than one million pieces of ceramic or glass and was found during the war when an air-raid shelter was being built. The museum not only has very fine graphic works of Colonia, the town of the Romans, but also tells the history of the settlement from the Paleolithic age until Charlemagne era.

The Romanesque basilica of **Gross Sankt Martin** not far to the southeast of the Cathedral, surrounded by rows of tiny, narrow houses forming the **Old City**, dates back to the end of the 12th century. It was destroyed down to its very foundation walls in World War II. By 1963 it had been restored to its former glory and resumed its role as the distinguishing landmark of the Old City, whose historical character has

Mother and daughter at carnival.

been painstakingly supplemented by the addition of modern architecture.

The spectacular **Cathedral Rhine Project** now houses the famous collections of the **Wallraf-Richartz-Museum**, one of the largest galleries of European painting, as well as the new concert hall **Philharmonie**. Although the architecture of the Philharmonic and the museums may be inspiring as far as the interior is concerned (the paintings provides a visual connection to the Gothic Cathedral itself) the exterior of the gigantic building and the problem of its integration into the cityscape have become matters of controversy.

While wandering through the old part of the city, the visitor should visit one of the famous *Kölsch* beer halls, where the locals drink glasses of beer while discussing the latest news or their grouses. The people of Cologne are friendly and cheerful characters and this is particularly evident during the Cologne carnival when the population overflows with ebullience and love-of-life.

Brühl (nine miles/15 km south of Cologne) is famous for its Baroque castle, **Schloss Augustusburg,** with its beautiful staircase by Balthasar Neumann and large Schlosspark. The well-decorated and furnished palace is used today for state receptions. Near Brühl, **Phantasialand Amusement Park**, at 2,400 acres, is the largest of its kind in Europe, and has model buildings, boat trips, dolphin stunts among other draws.

Aspects of the Ruhr: The largest art dealer's gallery in Germany, if not the world, is at Hamm-Rhynern, on the northeastern edge of the Ruhr. **Gallery Mensing** has everything from model ducks for the pool to full-scale medieval mock-cloisters on its plot of 17.5 acres.

The area north of Cologne between the rivers Ruhr and Lippe, its center between **Duisburg** on the banks of Father Rhine (575,000 inhabitants) and **Dortmund** in the west (620,000 inhabitants) is called the Ruhr (*Ruhrgebiet*). It is known more for its excellent beer rather than as a center of the arts. To most people, it is Europe's largest industrial region with the world's biggest

Kiteflying in the Rhine meadows.

inland port (Duisburg) and the Krupp company, armory of two World Wars.

This area, where nearly six million people live and work, is an impressive testimony to the technical and scientific genius of enterprise which made Germany a leading economic power at the end of the 19th century. Founded on coal mining, it has developed into a vast industrial complex centered on iron, steel, chemicals and engineering. The villages and the towns, the industrial complexes and housing estates have all merged into a unified landscape, such that when a visitor travels on the network of road, rail and waterways, he does not know where one town ends and the next begins. Some years ago a renowned German newspaper wrote: "If you visit the Ruhr, be prepared for a labyrinth of stone, asphalt, steel and concrete, for a maze of roads, waterways and railways, where there is no beginning and no end..."

In recent years there have been many attempts to destroy the stereotyped notion of the Ruhr or *Ruhrpott* as a huge, repulsive industrial complex, where nine percent of the Federal German population live on only two percent of the Republic's surface area. Despite being a center of commercial and economic power and having the faceless character of some of the coal boom towns of the 19th century, the Ruhr has much to offer the traveler.

Moreover, the decline of the coal mining and iron and steel industries has greatly transformed the Ruhr economy and the lives of millions of people. Between 1965 and 1977 the number of jobs in the Ruhr decreased by 300,000. In the southern part, the Ruhrzone, one can even detect a pre-industrial age. People in the valley of the Ruhr river, rimmed by forested hills have, after 100 years of coal mining, rediscovered their castle ruins, half-timbered houses, moated castles and reservoirs and created a host of pleasure resorts and recreational facilities. Billions of marks had to be supplied for the famous structural change at the end of the 1960s which would provide new jobs through

Smoking chimneys in the Ruhr near Duisburg.

the development of service industries and the establishment of government offices in former working-class towns.

Bochum (410,000 inhabitants) in the heart of the Ruhr owed its rise to coal and steel. It no longer operates a mine, but the **Opel car factory** (a sister company of General Motors). In spite of the sentiments of the elder Krupp ("we need workers, not intellectuals") Bochum is also the seat of the new **Ruhr University** with 25,000 students, a Planetarium and the **German Mining Museum**, the best of its kind in the world (demonstration mine, winding house). The **Ruhrstadion** with its 50,000 roofed seats is considered the most modern soccer stadium in Europe.

In **Essen**, the largest city of the Ruhr (665,000 inhabitants) service industries have replaced the 22 mines which were active during the industrial revolution. Today, only one mine is in operation. Thousands flock to the fairs in Essen where the headquarters of 10 influential multi-national companies are based. They include the *Ruhrkohle*, the largest German coal mining corporation, *RWE*, largest European producer of electricity, and the famous *Krupp* factories.

n the heart
f the Ruhr.

Miners and pigeons: Strange as it may seem, the Ruhr can be a delight for the visitor. Theaters and orchestras, museums, cultural events and popular festivals abound in this urban landscape on Rhine and Ruhr. One of the best German museums, the **Folkwang**, is in Essen. The industrial town of **Recklinghausen** has made a name for itself on account of the annual *Ruhrfestpiele* (theater festival) in May-July. The town houses the only **icon museum** in western Europe. The young audience attending the pop concerts at the Dortmund **Westfalenhalle** (seating for 23,000) is, according to cognocsenti, the most musically discriminating in Europe.

How did the miners and steel workers cope with the decline of their industries and the long periods of unemployment? "Factories and plants," says Heinrich Böll, "exude a certain kind of sour sentimentalism." When, after the closure of the mines, the miner's colonies where thousands had been comfortably living, gardening and pigeon breeding were pulled down and replaced by modern apartments, many of the workers formed pressure groups to preserve their old homes, often successfully. The pigeons! More than 10,000 workers still spend 100 to 200 DM a month on their traditional hobby. Their flying race horses can cover 600 miles (960 km) and still return safely to their pigeon house. Nobody can explain the incredible homing instinct of these birds. In Essen the world's first and only **pigeon hospital** has been established and treats 1,500 winged patients per year.

Industrial architecture is another field in which romanticism about the mining era has developed. Twenty years ago factory wings, steel towers and winding houses were deteriorating. Since then hundreds of industrial buildings have been classified as historical monuments. Essen and Dortmund are older cities than Munich and Stuttgart. No town in Germany other than Regensburg and Cologne, has more medieval churches than Dortmund.

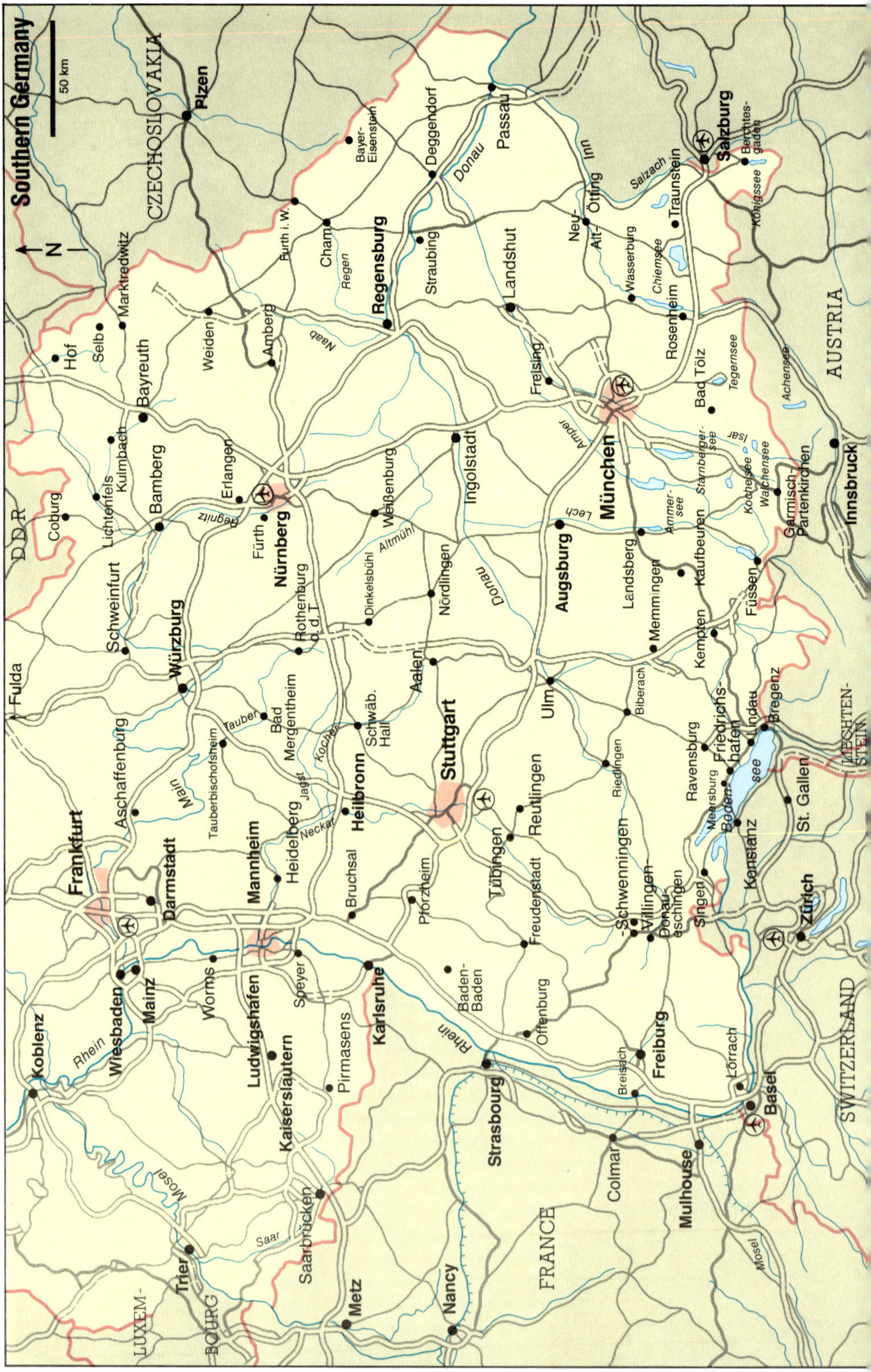
Southern Germany
N
50 km
CZECHOSLOVAKIA
DDR
AUSTRIA
SWITZERLAND
LIECHTENSTEIN
FRANCE
LUXEMBOURG
Plzen
Hof
Selb
Marktredwitz
Bayreuth
Kulmbach
Coburg
Lichtenfels
Bamberg
Erlangen
Weiden
Amberg
Furth i. W.
Cham
Bayer-Eisenstein
Deggendorf
Passau
Regensburg
Straubing
Landshut
Neu-Ötting
Alt-Ötting
Inn
Salzach
Salzburg
Berchtes-gaden
Königssee
Traunstein
Chiemsee
Wasserburg
Rosenheim
Tegernsee
Bad Tölz
Achensee
Innsbruck
Freising
München
Amper
Isar
Starnberger-see
Ammer-see
Kochelsee
Walchensee
Garmisch-Partenkirchen
Lech
Augsburg
Landsberg
Kaufbeuren
Memmingen
Kempten
Füssen
Ingolstadt
Donau
Weißenburg
Altmühl
Nürnberg
Fürth
Regnitz
Naab
Regen
Schweinfurt
Würzburg
Fulda
Aschaffenburg
Main
Frankfurt
Darmstadt
Wiesbaden
Mainz
Koblenz
Rhein
Worms
Mannheim
Ludwigshafen
Kaiserslautern
Pirmasens
Speyer
Heidelberg
Neckar
Jagst
Kocher
Tauber
Tauberbischofsheim
Bad Mergentheim
Rothenburg o. d. T
Dinkelsbühl
Nördlingen
Aalen
Schwäb. Hall
Heilbronn
Bruchsal
Karlsruhe
Pforzheim
Stuttgart
Tübingen
Reutlingen
Ulm
Biberach
Riedlingen
Ravensburg
Friedrichs-hafen
Lindau
Bregenz
Boden-see
Meersburg
Konstanz
St. Gallen
Singen
Zürich
Villingen-Schwenningen
Donau-eschingen
Freudenstadt
Baden-Baden
Offenburg
Freiburg
Breisach
Lörrach
Basel
Mulhouse
Colmar
Strasbourg
Nancy
Metz
Saarbrücken
Saar
Mosel
Trier

SOUTHBOUND

Hopefully the traveler will be more fortunate during the journey along the Rhine than Queen Victoria, who made the trip in pouring rain. If you have included some bottles of Rhine or Moselle wine among your provisions for your remaining travels through Germany, then you had better drink them straightaway. For now the route continues to southern Germany, where not only dry Franconian and Baden wines await you, but also quantities of "liquid bread," that is, Bavarian beer, to say nothing of a cuisine renowned for being particularly solid and hearty. And if you can hardly wait for the chance of seeing women in *Dirndls* and men in *Lederhosen*, then these stereotypes are still very much a reality in Bavaria.

But you may begin like so many before you, by falling in love with idyllic Heidelberg, which is our first destination after Frankfurt. The journey continues into the heart of Franconia, to the Baroque jewel of Würzburg. There, you decide whether to follow the Romantic Road with its string-of-pearls of sights down to the fairy-tale castles of King Ludwig II at the foot of the Alps, or to experience the austere beauty of Upper Franconia and join the Romantic Road via the old imperial town of Nuremberg near Dinkelsbühl.

In Füssen, at the end of the Romantic Road, you have a choice once more of traveling directly to Munich ("the secret capital of Germany") or of driving first along and, because Munich is along the German alpine road, through the bizarre world of the Alps up to the sinister and fantastic Königssee. On the other hand, from here it is well worth taking a trip to the Walhalla and the old Roman settlement of Regensburg. A look at the maps on pages 122, 127, 136-137, 159 and 183 will help you get your bearings to plan your travel route. The suggested routes are marked in color. Repetitions are intended to offer you a variety of possible combinations.

From Füssen you may (instead of heading for Munich) turn west and drive around the largest German inland water, Lake Constance, before traversing the Black Forest via Stuttgart (the city with the Mercedes star) and then returning to Frankfurt. This part of the travel guide offers you two varied routes through the *Musterländle* (model state) Baden-Württemberg; see map on page 214 for information.

Back in hectic Frankfurt you can plan (page 238) the northern part of your journey through Romantic Germany, a place which you are already acquainted with by now.

Preceding pages: nature, religion and modern technology near Raisting; Upper Bavarian women on their way to church.

"LOSING MY HEART IN HEIDELBERG. . ."

Heidelberg, symbol of German Romanticism, with its picturesque lanes and maze of roofs, nestles in a shallow gorge between the River Rhine and the foothills of the Odenwald mountains, where the former emerges from the latter into the Rhine plain.

Again and again the charms of **Heidelberg** have inspired songs and poems by enchanted artists. Friedrich Hölderlin praised the panorama in his *Ode to Heidelberg*. Other poets of German Romanticism such as Scheffel, Brentano, Arnim, Eichendorff and Jean Paul also attempted to capture Heidelberg's uniqueness. They have all made Heidelberg the world-famous town "where one can easily lose one's heart."

Today, about 3.5 million visitors a year attempt to follow up on the fabulous stories they have heard about this beautiful spot on the banks of the Neckar, with the Americans ranking first, followed by the Japanese and the British. Although the city is famous for many historical sites, Heidelberg is no living museum but a town full of vitality. It is the harmonic mixture between the old and the new, between the romantic past and the modern future which acts as a strong stimulus for the visitor.

Let us start with the distant past. About half a million years ago men must have been attracted by the beautiful position it occupies on the Neckar river. The jaw from the *homo heidelbergiensis*, the oldest human bone ever found in Europe, was dug up near Heidelberg. Later, Heidelberg became a Celtic settlement, then a Roman fort. From Roman times onwards, Heidelberg began to prosper and the first documentary evidence of the town can be traced back to 1196. After 1214, Heidelberg was under the control of the dukes of Palatinate, who soon belonged to the *Kurfürsten* (king-elector). For nearly 500 years they chose the German kings and emperors. Monuments from this period can be seen all over Heidelberg. In 1356 Ruprecht I founded the university and commissioned the building of the **Heiliggeistkirche** (Church of the Holy Spirit). During the Thirty Years' War, Heidelberg was besieged and taken by the Catholic General Tilly, who seized rich booty from the famous Palatine Library and sent the books as tribute to the Vatican. Only a few were returned, among them the *Manessische Handschrift*, a brilliantly-illustrated collection of medieval texts which is today on show in the university library.

The castle: The **castle** rests on the northern slopes of **Königsstuhl Mountain**, about 328 feet (100 m) above the town. Even those who are not athletic should approach the castle on foot via the steep Burgweg, starting at Kornmarkt. True, there is a comfortable cable car only a few feet away from this starting point, but its passengers miss that all important first impression of Heidelberg. The **Burgweg** climbs up, passes forbidding vaults and walls and rewards the walker for his efforts with a splendid view of the entire town. A 15-minute walk from the Burgweg leads

ft,
eidelberg
stle from
iloso-
enweg.
ght,
ne in the
nter
town.

directly into the castle's courtyard. Here, you can admire the imposing red walls of sandstone from the Odenwald mountains which command the valley. Started in A.D. 1300, it took 400 years to build the whole complex with its fortifications, domestic quarters and palaces. These structures in varying styles–from Gothic to Renaissance–are eloquent testimony to the rulers' power and their artistic tastes.

To the left of the massive gate tower the oldest palace of the fortified area is to be found. This simple Gothic house was inhabited by the Elector Ruprecht I, who also constructed the Heiliggeistkirche (Church of the Holy Spirit) in the city. On the northern side of the courtyard is the impressive facade of the **Friedrichsbau** which is decorated with the statues of great German kings and the rulers' ancestors. This beautiful palace and its enclosing columns was built in 1607 in Renaissance style.

The most fascinating building within the castle complex is the **Ottheinrichsbau**. Its world-renowned facade is a prime example of German Renaissance. The general impression given by the ornaments and statues is one of perfect harmony and balance. Between the statues of various Christian saints are Roman gods, such as Mars and Jupiter, and the five personified virtues (power, faith, love, hope and justice). The richly-decorated portal resembles a classical triumphal arch and has a relief at the top of the ruler Otto Heinrich of Palatinate, who ordered the construction in 1506. Before taking a closer look at the castle's interior, enjoy another splendid view over the picturesque town and river. Beyond the Friedrichsbau is the castle's terrace, a perfect viewing point, cooled by the gentle breeze coming up the Neckar valley.

A thirsty court fool: Guided tours of the castle are available and take about an hour. Even those who are rushed should not miss the Heidelberg Schloss. It contains the largest wine barrel with a capacity of 55,000 gallons (250,000 liters). It was guarded by Perkeo, the court fool who was known for his legen-

A view of th Neckar rive at Alte Brücke.

dary thirst, and it is said that he died after being persuaded to drink a cup of water instead of the wine to which he was accustomed.

Some of the buildings have been left as ruins, while other parts have been restored for use as banquet and concert venues. The Ottheinrichsbau today also houses the **German Apothecary Museum**, which has an excellent collection of furniture, books, medicines, medical instruments and bottles which were used in earlier times by physicians and chemists. The collections of ancient prescriptions dispensed remedies which are not recommended for visitors such as the *Hortus Palatinatus* (Palatin garden) initiated by the unfortunate ruler Friedrich V, who was German king for only one year. This so-called winter king had a strong passion for splendor and so in 1615 he ordered a magnificent garden to be laid out behind the castle. It is true that he thus weakened the defenses, but it must have been a wonderful garden with its statues, artificial ponds, little caves, gargoyles and colorful flowerbeds. During the Thirty Years' War (1618-48) the garden was partly destroyed and it was not until 1803 that it was restored to its original and also present-day form.

If you are too tired to walk back to the city, take the cable railway. It takes about two minutes to get back to town. From there you can see the castle's mighty facade of red sandstone shimmering like gold in the rays of the late afternoon sun. When floodlit after dark, it seems to float in the darkness. On the first Saturday in June and September, it is illuminated by a display of fireworks.

The historic city: After having arrived back in town, take a rest first in one of the numerous cafes in the pedestrian zone, where cosmopolitan life prevails, before continuing the expedition. The second highlight of Heidelberg is the old part of the town, which sparkles in the mist as you were looking down on it from the castle.

Heidelberg first became important in the Middle Ages and so it is basically a medieval Gothic town with narrow

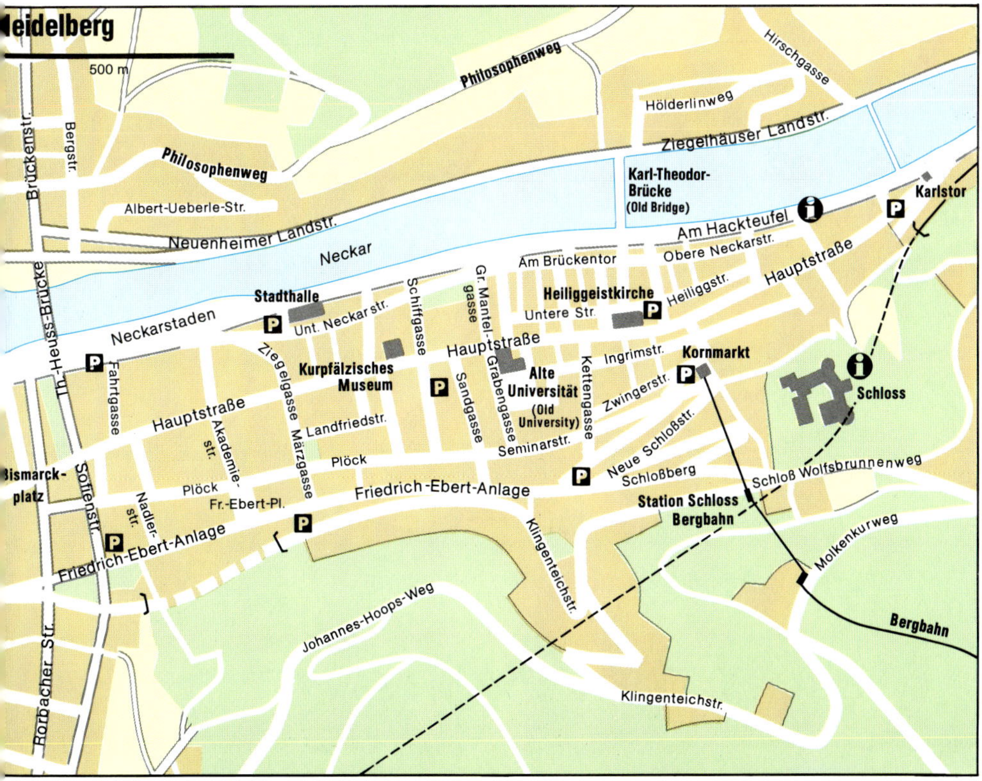

lanes lined by slim houses. Magnificent Renaissance palaces were only added later on. Involvement in the War of the Palatine Succession brought disastrous consequences to Heidelberg. French king Louis XIV claimed the Palatinate throne and so French troops invaded the entire region and, in 1689 and 1693, devastated many towns, including Heidelberg. The second time the town was burned to the ground, the fortification was blown up. For many years the castle remained a ruin, but the citizens decided to revitalize their city. Only a few houses had survived destruction and people built new ones on the medieval foundations, but in the contemporary Baroque style of the 18th century.

Begin by exploring Heidelberg's renowned university at the **Universitätsplatz**. Founded in 1386, this is the oldest university in Germany. During the wars in the 17th century, it lost much of its importance but it was rediscovered in 1805 by Karl-Friedrich of Palatinate. Today there are more than 27,000 students in Heidelberg (one-fifth of the total population of 134,000 inhabitants) and certainly not all of them can be educated in the **Alte Universität** (old university) a building on the southside of the square. At the rear of Universitätsplatz is the **Neue Universität** (new university) erected in 1931 with funds raised in the United States. However, even these two buildings became too small for the students and so another university was built on the other side of the river Neckar.

Although student life has changed dramatically since the times of the famous "Student Prince," there are still traces of those romantic days. One example is the former **Studentenkarzer** (student lock-up) just behind the old university. Until 1914 it served as a prison for students, who were locked up for drunkenness by the university administration. This punishment must have been mild, because the walls of the cells are covered with humorous paintings and graffiti.

Follow **Merianstrasse** and then **Ingrimmstrasse** to the east, to reach the

Members of a student league.

oldest and most traditional quarter of the city. Here is the **Kornmarkt**, the old fish market and the **Marktplatz** (market square). The most famous student inns, **Seppl** and **Roter Ochsen**, are also located in this area on Karlsplatz. But those looking for the *Three Golden Apples* will search in vain. It is only fiction made up by S. Romberg, who composed the world-famous operetta *Student Prince*, which was adapted from the play *Old Heidelberg*. This musical first established the myth of Romantic Heidelberg. Later, a Hollywood film based on this musical, with singer Mario Lanza as one of its cast, enhanced Heidelberg's special reputation still further. Every year in August this musical romance is enacted in the castle courtyard during good weather.

Back in town, there are many buildings around the various markets which are also worth exploring. Do not miss the mighty Gothic **Heiliggeistkirche** (Church of the Holy Spirit) on the Marktplatz, the biggest church of the Palatinate. It houses the monument of Ruprecht I and the rooms of the former Palatinate Library. You may even hear an organ concert here played on one of the most euphonic organs in Germany.

A panoramic bridge: On the opposite side of the street the **Hotel Ritter** stands out on account of its magnificent facade. It survived in 1693 because the French commander chose this house as his residence. Erected in 1592 by the French immigrant Charles Belier, it is one of the most spectacular Renaissance palaces in Germany. A narrow lane called **Steingasse** leads from the Heiliggeistkirche to the River Neckar. The **Alte Brücke** (old bridge) that spans the river here is, together with the castle, Heidelberg's symbol. The great German poet J.W. v. Goethe considered this bridge to be one of the wonders of the world. His opinion was not based primarily on technical criteria, but on the enchanting panorama one enjoys from the bridge. Upstream is the old cloister of the Benedictine **Neuburg**, and downstream the narrow valley softly widens into the Rhine plain.

The world's biggest barrel.

After the bridge, a steep path snakes up the Heiligenberg. The effort of this exercise is well repaid by the marvellous view over Heidelberg and the castle. The so-called **Philosophenweg** (philosopher's path) with its calm and peaceful atmosphere high above the river helps one forget the bustling city. The visitor can walk, meditate, watch the punts on the river and admire the beautiful town stretched out below. Having savored the peace of the Philosophenweg, the visitor might again be eager for the more exciting life of the old town. Continue along the philosopher's path to **Bergstrasse**, which descends to the modern **Theodor-Heuss-Brücke** (bridge). Cross the bridge and enter **Bismarckplatz**, the beginning of the pedestrian precinct.

Students' lifestyle: Those in the mood to become acquainted with another aspect of Heidelberg's romantic past should visit one of the historical students' pubs mentioned earlier. The pubs are still frequented by hard-drinking members of the various student fraternities, some of which perpetuate 19th century drinking rituals and traditional fencing duels to initiate new members. Study the old photographs covering the walls and smile at one or the other of the toasts that are carved into the beams.

But the old quarter has many modern inns, restaurants, pubs and cafes which reflect changing times. These places are popular meeting points for young and old, as comfortable as the historical old pubs. But do not attempt to perpetuate the atmosphere of a long-dead era here. There are many examples of these lively and modern places, such as the **Reichsapfel** or the **Bop**. In Old Heidelberg you can easily discover such places on your own, if you dive into the smaller lanes only a few steps away from Hauptstrasse. Here, where the facades are a little shabbier than those of the main tourist areas, you will find another, but no less romantic and authentic Heidelberg.

Modern Heidelberg: Heidelberg is not a museum: it is a town of vitality and romance. This is guaranteed by the

At Schwetzingen castle

presence of the many students, even those studying such "unromantic" subjects as mathematics, chemistry, medicine or pharmacy. Heidelberg is the seat of the German Cancer Research Center and of the Academy of Science. Heidelberg supplies the world with the most advanced offset-printing equipment. The Heidelberger Druckmaschinen AG is by far the most important exporter of printing presses in the world. Heidelberg also boasts Germany's biggest publishing house of scientific literature, J. Springer, which produces more than 8,000 scientific publications and over 190 specialist journals. In addition, there are many smaller, but successful firms, providing ample evidence that the town's history did not end in the 19th century.

By the way, did you know that one out of seven inhabitants of Heidelberg is an American? Immediately after World War II the U.S. army made Heidelberg its European headquarters. About 20,000 U.S. citizens live here, many of them in their own quarter, called **Patrick Henry Village**, which has its own cinemas, shops, schools and hospitals. The quarter is situated in a southern suburb of Heidelberg, called Little America by its German neighbors.

A day-trip round Heidelberg: Heidelberg is a good starting point for various excursions into this historic region.

The little town of **Schwetzingen** is situated southwest of Heidelberg. Here the former summer palace of the kings' electors which also houses a splendid Rococo theater was erected between 1699 and 1715. The stylish grounds surrounding the castle are among the loveliest Baroque gardens in Germany. They are an attractive mixture between a symmetrically-ordered French garden and one in the markedly less severe English style. This park is a suitable venue for the international music festival held in June every year.

From Schwetzingen, take the road westwards which leads to the Rhine, where the old imperial town of **Speyer** is situated across the river. After entering Speyer (population: 45,000) from the east, you can stop one-quarter of the way on the bridge across the river to admire the perspective of the old town with its mighty cathedral, visible for miles around.

The town was founded by the Romans in the second half of the first century A.D. In the year 343, Speyer was mentioned as a bishopric for the first time. From 1294 to 1797 the city belonged to the seven free imperial towns of the Holy Roman Empire. More than 50 diets were held here, the most important being that of 1529 when the later "Protestant" princes and estates forwarded their protest against the anti-Reformation resolutions of the majority. Speyer survived the Thirty Years' War, but suffered complete destruction in 1689 during the war over the Palatinate succession. As medieval Speyer was virtually annihilated, only a few important monuments of its eventful history still exist.

Romanesque momentum: The most significant is certainly the six-towered Romanesque **cathedral**. This basilica, built between 1030 and 1125, is without doubt unique in its architectural conception and proportions. The basilica's exterior gives the impression of being austere, in spite of the various motifs carved in the capitals on the east side of the apse and the scrolls and palm leaves on the south side. This severity perfectly corresponds with the atmosphere of the interior, where the ornamentation of the architecture conveys a powerful simplicity. Relatively slender, the columns, intersected in the middle with heavy capitals, shore up a gigantic hall. The statues of the eight German emperors who are buried in this church are in this hall. The remains of the imperial tombs (some plundered by the French in 1689) can be visited in the wonderful imperial vault. A visit to the basilica's crypt, the best and largest in Germany, is highly recommended. Romanesque groin vaulting spreads out like a net, accentuated by archstones which are alternately cut in dark red and white limestone. In front of the cathedral is the **Domnapf** (1490) a stone basin which was filled with wine whenever a new bishop was ordained.

The **cathedral gardens** extend behind the cathedral. Here the sculptures of the Salic Emperors, who commenced the construction, still bear witness to the city's rich history. A short distance to the south of the cathedral is the **Palatinate Historical Museum** with its outstanding collection and an interesting **wine museum**. Nearby, at the end of Judenbadgasse, are the remains of the **Jews' Bath**, once part of a synagogue, now lying some 33 feet (10 meters) below ground level. From the cathedral, Speyer's principal street, the Maximilianstrasse, runs west to the **Altportel**, a gate tower of the 13th century. Halfway down, the protestant **Trinity Church**, built between 1701 and 1717, rises above the surrounding houses.

The industrial Baroque town: Leaving northwards, our next stop will be **Mannheim** (population: 310,000) on the right bank of the Rhine. Immediately opposite, on the left bank, lies the industrial city of **Ludwigshafen** (population: 160,000) known worldwide as the headquarters of BASF, the chemical multi-national concern. Situated between two very important highways, this area is of great industrial and commercial importance. Little known is the fact that this region also boasts a remarkable number of architectural places of interest. Above all, Mannheim is marked by the surprising contrast between the bustling industrial port (second largest river port in Europe) and the elegant Baroque architecture.

Thanks to its favorable situation at the confluence of the Rhine and the Neckar, Mannheim soon attracted the interest of the Elector of the Palatinate. In 1606 Elector Friedrich IV ordered a fortress to be built and established a trading settlement. Mannheim was destroyed during the Palatinate Succession War. Thereafter Elector Johann Wilhelm rebuilt the town in 144 rectangular blocks, each of which was designated with a letter and a number. The development in this period accounts for the characteristic criss-cross network in the town center. In 1720 Elector Karl Philipp moved his residence from Heidelberg to Mannheim and soon the town became a center of patronage of the arts. Architects, painters, sculptors and workers in porcelain were attracted by the splendid, new court and created numerous works. In the 19th century the industrial and commercial phase started with the opening up of the Rhine to shipping, and Mannheim, the terminal point of traffic on the Upper Rhine, grew in importance as a river port.

In World War II Mannheim was severely damaged. The post-war rebuilding period has given the town a predominantly modern character, although old buildings remain. The first attraction you will discover after crossing the Rhine river in southern Mannheim and wandering through the Schlossgarten park, is the Baroque **Electoral Palace** (1720-60) the largest Baroque residence in Germany. Beginning at the palace, Mannheim's main street, **Kurpfalzstrasse,** crosses the inner town from one end to the other, intersecting with **Planken**, another main street, at **Paradeplatz**, From here the street leads straight to the marketplace where the

Impressions of two imperial towns. Below, Speyer Cathedral. Right, silhouette of Worms.

old **town hall** and the **Lower Parish Church** (1701-23) are located. They are attached to one another by a tower symbolizing the union of the sacred and the profane. The **Reiss-Museum** can be found in old **Zeughaus** (arsenal) which is a few blocks away. Devoted to the arts and to municipal history, this museum has fine collections of porcelain, a replica of the first pedal-driven bicycle made by Baron Drais in 1817 and one of the world's first cars invented by Carl Benz in 1886.

Continue along Kurpfalzstrasse till the Kurpfalz bridge, which is the point of departure for a round-trip of the harbor. On such a *Hafenrundfahrt,* you can appreciate the other face of Mannheim with its gigantic river harbor which boasts three river jetties and 17 harbors along the two-mile (three km) land peninsula between Rhine and Neckar.

On returning from the trip, it is worthwhile to wander along the Friedrichring as far as the **National Theater** famous because the first performance of Friedrich Schiller's plays, *Die Räuber, Kabale und Liebe* and *Fiesco,* was held in 1782 and 1784 .

An historical setting: The last destination, **Worms** (population: 75,000), is an old imperial town like Speyer and is located on the banks of the Rhine about 16 miles (25 km) northwest of Mannheim. Worms is one of the oldest German towns, dating back to a Celtic settlement which later became a Roman fort. It was the seat of a bishopric since the 4th century. During the great migrations it was named capital of the Burgundian kingdom which was destroyed by the Huns in A.D. 437. These events provided inspiration for the famous *Nibelungen*, one of the earliest epics in German language. Its hero, the blonde Siegfried and villain, the grim Hagen, are still very much alive in Wagner's opera, *Ring of the Nibelungen.* During the Dark Ages, the town played a key role in the rivalries between crown, pope and the dukes. More than 100 diets were held here. One of the most celebrated was the Diet of 1521, when Martin Luther defended his doctrines. The **Luther Monument** on Lutherplatz (1868) still commemorates this event.

The **Municipal Museum** gives a general idea of the town's past, with its splendid collections from the historical and pre-historical periods. The museum is housed in the Romanesque cloister of a former monastery whose church is worth visiting. A short distance away is the oldest and largest **Jewish cemetery** in Europe with 11th century tombstones. Situated in the center of the town is its landmark, the magnificent **cathedral**, a four-tower building with two domes. It ranks with the cathedrals of Mainz and Speyer as one of the most glorious examples of the High Romanesque style (11th–12th century) in Germany. On entering the church through the Gothic south doorway, observe the tympanum which is called the Coronation of the Virgin. On the reverse side is an impressive statue of Christ from the 12th century. Especially worth visiting is the northern aisle with its five excellent Gothic reliefs illustrating events of Christ's life, and the altar created by Balthasar Neumann.

Hotel zum Riesen

INTO THE HEART OF FRANCONIA

Perhaps the best way to forget lovely Heidelberg is by heading east towards **Würzburg**, the world-famous Baroque town. A worthwhile experience is a contemplative journey on one of the white ships of the Neckar Fleet which travel through scenic river valleys and small picturesque towns, past intriguing medieval castles high above the river, and on to a multitude of architectural and artistic treasures. Here is everything the traveler expects to find on a romantic journey through Germany, not only in the typical German low mountain ranges of Odenwald and Spessart but, the region around Würzburg, called **Mainfranken,** will charm you too. On such a voyage the traveler will find splendid wooded districts, vineyards, strange castles built on water and magnificent timber-framed buildings in hospitable but not overcrowded old towns which nestle on the banks of the rivers Neckar and Main.

Along the Neckar valley: Following the B37, we reach the health resort and shipping town of Eberbach on the Neckar via **Neckargemünd** and **Hirschhorn**. The drive from Heidelberg on the romantic road along the Neckar valley gives access to one of the most charming river landscapes in Germany. The **Neckar**, which rises in the Black Forest and flows nearly 248 miles (400 km) before entering the Rhine at Mannheim, is famous for its wooded hill ridges which line its numerous loops and bends and which climb up 1,310 feet (400 m). The town of **Eberbach** harmonizes with the river landscape, the idly-flowing Neckar and the closely-packed line of houses on its banks which are flanked by the defiantly-jutting towers of the old Staufer town. Within 30 minutes the ruins of Castle Eberbach (11th-13th century), once the largest castle of the Hohenstaufen dynasty, can be reached.

Other sights in Eberbach are the timber-framed houses, the **old forge** of 1438 and the public inn, **Wirtshaus Krabbenstein**, which was first mentioned in 1627. The same tavern exhibits frescoes in graffito-style, depicting the ancient professions of the Eberbach population. A 15-minute walk will take you from the town center to the **Gutleut-Häuser** (infirmary) and **Gutleut-Kapelle** (15th century chapel). Those suffering from leprosy were forced to live outside town and were cared for here in the Middle Ages.

Castles around Mosbach: Before driving north from Eberbach through the Odenwald Forest, make an excursion to the south along the Neckar to Mosbach, 15 miles (24 km) on the road called **Burgenstrasse**. First of all, after driving past the ruins of **Stolzeneck Castle,** once inhabited by robber-knights and perched high above the left bank of the Neckar, one arrives in the health resort of **Zwingenberg** with its beautiful castle (13th-15th century). The picturesque little town of **Mosbach**, also known as the **Fachwerkstadt** (half-timbered town) of the Odenwald Forest, originates from a Benedictine monas-

Preceding pages, the sign outside Germany's oldest hotel

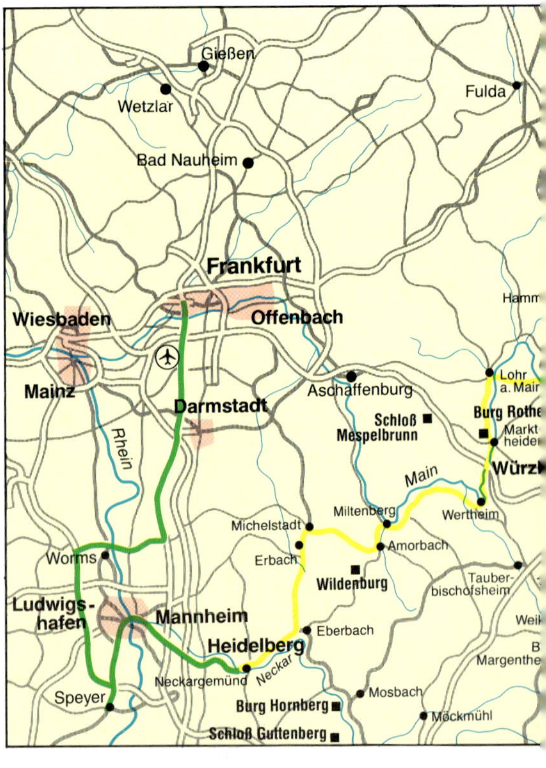

tery founded in the 8th century. Mosbach received the freedom of a city in the 13th century, then became an Imperial City and finally a *Residenzstadt* (seat of the imperial court). The medieval character of the town is most apparent as you walk through the old part of the town, which begins at the **marketplace**. The **town hall** here was built during 1554-58 using parts of the walls from the old Cecilian church of 1300.

Two remarkable fortresses are found not far from Mosbach. **Burg Hornberg**, dating back to 1148, is still one of the most interesting castles in the Neckar valley. For 45 years it was the residence of the knight with the iron hand, Götz von Berlichingen (1480-1562) who is immortalized in Goethe's drama. In his beloved turret-room is a museum commemorating the military exploits of this leading figure in the German Peasants' War. **Burg Guttenberg**, located a few miles to the south near Hassmersheim, is not only one of the oldest, but also one of the best-preserved castles on the Neckar. It is a splendid example of the medieval method of building fortifications and of the development from the type of fortress built for self-defense, to one which served as a residence.

Through the Odenwald: Back in Eberbach, the B45 leads straight through the **Odenwald**, one of the most pleasant mountain landscapes in Germany, to the scenic towns of Erbach and Michelstadt. **Erbach**, a health resort and former residence of the Counts of Erbach, has kept intact the closely-packed buildings and narrow streets of the old town as well as parts of the original city wall. The **town church** of 1748 and the timber-framed **town hall**, of mid-16th century, deserve a visit. The **castle museum** displays interesting collections of old paintings, medieval weapons and armaments and Gothic carving and an imposing line-up of antlers. In the **German Museum of Ivory** which occupies the Erbach banquet hall are examples of ivory carving, pottery and amber-work.

A few miles away the romantic health resort of **Michelstadt** presents one of

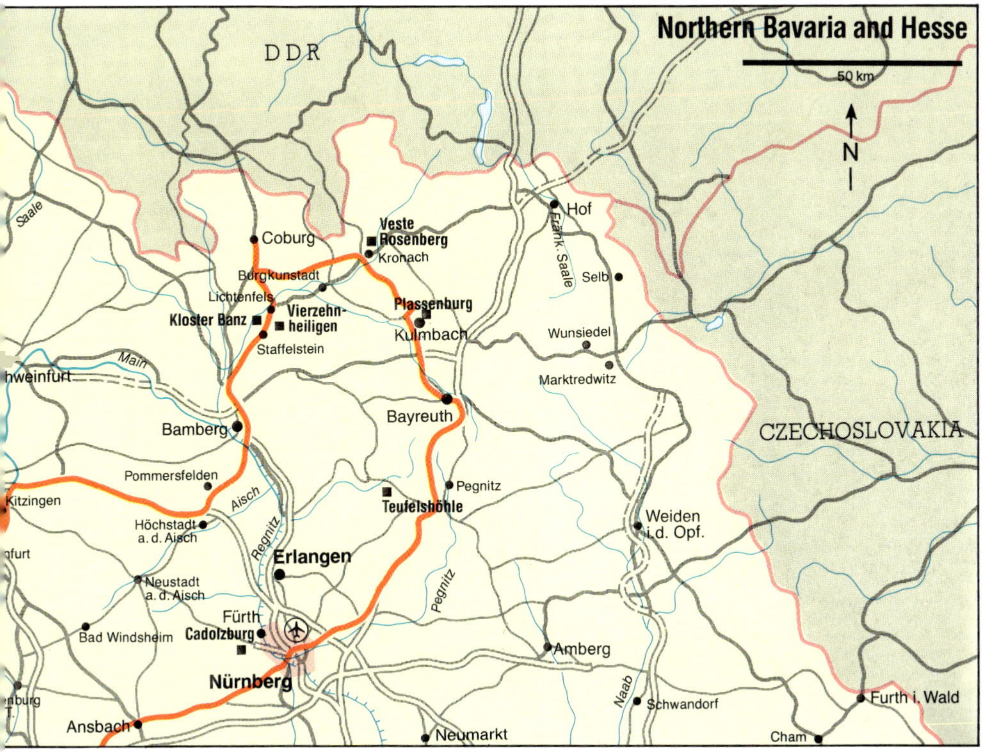

the best-preserved town panoramas in Hessian-Franconia with its romantic corners, beautiful timber-framed houses and its marketplace complete with town hall, a 1484 jewel of medieval civic architecture. The town hall with its big hall, pointed gables and two turrets, is renowned as a site of historical interest. The fountain on the marketplace dates from 1541. The **town church of St. Michael and St. Kilian** is a late Gothic *Hallenkirche* (church with aisles of equal height) which was built in 1461-1507. The Renaissance facade, the **Thieves' Tower**, the remains of the old town fortifications and the **Odenwald Museum** with findings from the Celtic and Roman periods, all merit some attention.

The old Franconian town of **Amorbach** in the Odenwald, 13 miles (21 km) away, boasts an 8th century monastery, and inherits a rich cultural heritage. The **abbey church**, originally Romanesque but reconstructed in Baroque style in 1742-47, are outstanding examples of German Rococo, as evidenced by the exquisite wrought-iron trellis which once separated the monks' church from that of the laymen, and also by the second largest **Baroque organ** in Germany. The latter, with its 3,000 pipes, 63 stops and three manuals has one of the most beautiful tones of any organ in Europe. The late Gothic **town hall** (15th century) together with the marketplace and its *Mariensäule* (Baroque Madonna of 1675) the half-timbered houses and the **Palace of the Princes of Leningen**, built *circa* 1800, with the **Catholic Parish Church** built of red sandstone in 1753 in the background, form an impressive architectural ensemble.

Six miles (10 km) further north is **Miltenberg am Main** which is dominated by **Miltenburg Castle** dating from the 1210. The author Elly Heuss wrote of Miltenberg: "To me, the marketplace and fountain is the perfect embodiment of the German medieval era." The architectural composition consisting of the market-fountain and old timber-framed houses as well as the former official wine-cellars of 1541 and the

Left, romantic memories o Michelstadt marketplace Below, the serene Mespelbrunn wate castle.

taverns **Zur gülden Cron** (1623) and **Weinhaus am alten Markt** (wine tavern) overshadowed by the castle, is world-famous. Several important half-timbered houses also stand in the main street which begins at the marketplace. Observe **No. 136**, Miltenberg's oldest timbered house which was built in 1330; **No. 157**, an imposing late Gothic building from 1470 and, the oldest German tavern, **Zum Reisen**, a typical Renaissance building from 1590 which was mentioned in 1504 as one worthy of a prince. Concerts take place in the courtyard of Miltenburg Castle, accessible through a gate tower called **Schnatterloch** from where there is a superb view over the Main valley right into the Spessart. The cozy taverns and idyllic little *Wirtschaften* (inns) are, as you will discover in the Odenwald, not only of architectural interest. They still cook local culinary specialities such as *Handkäs mit Musik* (a type of cheese made by hand and pickled with a mixture of oil, vinegar and chopped onions) as well as cider and the excellent *Hausmacherwurst* (home-made sausages) served with home-made bread.

Water castles and robbers' inns: From Miltenberg you can easily reach one of the highlights of your journey by following the idyllic road to **Grossheubach** and from there via Eschau and Hobbach to the small town of **Mespelbrunn**. Here, in front of its portals, in the midst of a dense forest, is the picturesque **moated castle** of Mespelbrunn. It was completed in 1564 in Renaissance style and is still owned by the Count of Ingelheim, named *Echter von und zu Mespelbrunn*. Because the castle has retained its original interior, it tells of how noble families lived in bygone times. There is much to view: the **Knights' Hall** with its tiled floor and coffered ceiling, the chapel with its frescoes from 1729, the **Ancestors' Hall**, Chinese Salon, Princes' Room with its Renaissance four-post bed and the circular room, where the family's most famous son, Prince-Bishop Julius Echter von Würzburg, the founder of this city's university, was born in 1545.

ypical ouse front n the way ırough ranconia.

Mespelbrunn castle is situated in the legendary **Spessart**, an upland region of deciduous forest, which is one of the most extensive nature reserves in Europe. The Main river flows around it in a U-shape, thus forming the **Main Quadrangle**. The beauty of the Spessart becomes apparent when you pass through the wide oak-and-backwood forests, idyllic meadows and hill torrents. Be sure to visit the **Wirtshaus im Spessart** (inn) made famous by the fairy-tale of Wilhelm Hauff and since then the scene of robbers' adventures and ghost stories which found their way onto German cinema screens.

From Mespelbrunn you can travel southward on A3 to **Wertheim**, the old Frankenstadt at the confluence of the rivers Tauber and Main. The Main-Franconian character of the town is determined by its narrow lanes and high gabled buildings around the marketplace. Visit **St. Mary's Chapel** (1447), the **town hall** (1540) with its spiral staircase in the tower, and the timber-framed house, the **Vier Gekrönten** opposite the town hall. The cathedral, formerly Romanesque, was converted in 1383 into a Gothic-pillared basilica.

Some 265 feet (850 m) above the Main, towers the ruins of one of the most significant castles of the 12th century. It was demolished in 1619 by dynamite. Above the gateway, the latest addition to the castle, you will discover the archival building of 1745. Several turrets, the restored battlements, the courtyard, the fountain, the castle terrace, the staircase to the palace and the Renaissance gabled tower of 1562 are remains of the original architecture of **Löwenstein Castle**.

Further north, the journey continues along the course of the Main Quadrangle to **Marktheidenfeld** where you face the attractive square with its half-timbered houses. A short distance behind Marktheidenfeld, **Castle Rothenfels** looms 735 feet (224 m) above the Main. The circular wall, the castle keep and the lower story of the castle stem from the 12th and 13th centuries.

City of bishops and wine: Although

Legendary ***Wirtshaus im Spessart***

about half of the 127,000 inhabitants of **Würzburg** are students, the dominant tenor is different from that of a university town. This was a bishopric since the 8th century, and most of what attracts the visitors to Würzburg has its origins in the heyday of the Prince-Bishops.

High above the town, surrounded by vineyards, towers the old fortress of **Marienberg** which was founded in 1201. It forms a rectangle round a courtyard in which are a 13th century keep, a Renaissance fountain temple, and the chapel Marienkirche. The fortress served as a residence for the Prince-Bishops from 1253 to 1719, who used it as a stronghold to curb the growing power of the townsmen. This town showpiece received its Baroque facade under the Prince-Bishop Echter von Mespelbrunn who rebuilt it in Renaissance style and added the **Echter Bastion**. In 1631, after the town was seized by Gustav Adolf of Sweden in the Thirty Years' War, the castle was extended to turn it to a Baroque stronghold with a **Fürstengarten** (park).

Castle above all castles: The town experienced its true heyday in the 18th century under the rule of the House of Schönborn which was very appreciative of the arts. This, in spite of the fact that Prince-Bishop Julius Echter not only founded the **Julius Infirmary** in 1575, but also the old **Würzburg University** in 1582. It was at the university that Wilhelm Conrad Röntgen discovered the X-Ray 300 years later. In 1719 Johann Philipp Franz von Schönborn became Prince-Bishop and moved his residence from Marienberg to the town. A master-builder named Balthasar Neumann was attached to the court. Franz recognized his genius and entrusted him with the planning of the **castle am Rennweg**. Thus, during 1720-44, the castle above all castles came into existence. It was built in southern German Baroque style and ranked as one of the most important castles in Europe.

The left aisle was the first to be constructed in 1720. The rough brickwork shell was not completed before 1744

elow, ürzburg rtress iewed om the old lain bridge. ight, tatues of aints on e old lain bridge.

and the decoration of the interior continued for many years. Neumann created a monument for himself by building the most magnificent **staircase** of the Baroque and Rococo eras. The quadratic walls of the staircase stretch up the two-story building, topped by a single concave vault, 100 feet (30 m) long and 59 feet (18 m) wide. What a challenge the building of this staircase must have been for the engineer, artillery commander and architect Neumann! He was so sure of the solidity of his architectural masterpiece that he offered to have a cannon shot from the staircase-well. The vault has, indeed, survived the bombarding of World War II which caused extensive damage to other parts of the Würzburg Residence.

More famous is the huge **ceiling fresco** painted by the Italian, Giovanni Battista Tiepolo, who was summoned to Würzburg in 1750 to create the largest painting in the world. Tiepolo depicted the Gods of Olympus and allegories of four known continents of that period–Europe, Asia, Africa and America. The painting, completed in 1745, also alludes to the marriage of emperor Friedrich Barbarossa and Beatrix von Burgund in the year 1156.

Tragedy of an artist: Many people visit Würzburg in order to admire the works of the world-famous woodcarver and sculptor Tilman Riemenschneider who came to Würzburg in 1483. In his workshop he carved altars from limestone and gravestone and stone-graphics from sandstone and supplied the whole of Main-Franconia with splendid sculptures. The distinguished citizen became a member of the Upper Council in 1509 and lord-mayor of Würzburg in 1520-1521 (there had been an elected council and lord mayor in Würzburg since 1256). During the Peasants' War, Riemenschmeider, along with other townsmen, supported the oppressed peasants against Prince-Bishop Konrad von Thingen and was consequently imprisoned and tortured for eight weeks after their defeat at the stronghold of Marienberg. Riemenschneider died in 1531, a broken and soon-forgotten man,

Tiepolo fresco in the Residenz.

His name only became of interest to later generations after 1822, when his grave was found during road excavations. The **Main-Franconian Museum** in the Marienberg fortress contains world-famous sculptures by Tilman Riemenschneider including his *Adam und Eva* (1493), as well as an excellent collection of Franconian works of art.

A stroll through the city: Other works of Riemenschneider can be found on a walk through Würzburg starting at the **Hofgarten** (Court Gardens) with its beautiful Baroque group of figures and splendid wrought-iron portals extending behind the Residenz. It is only a few steps to the **Old University,** dating from 1582 with a church in the southern tract which is one of the few notable German Renaissance churches. The nearby early Gothic **Franciscan Church** (1221) houses a Pieta by Riemenschneider. The **Cathedral** can be approached by following Domschulstrasse. It is the fourth largest groin-arched Romanesque basilica in Germany (11th-12th century) and is named after St. Kilian, the Apostle of the Franks and patron of the city, who was murdered in A.D. 68. Riemenschneider designed the tombs of the bishops Rudolf von Scheunburg and Lorenz von Bibra. The **Schönborn Chapel** is built onto the cathedral transept and contains the shrine of the Prince-Bishops of Schönborn, one of the most important works of Balthasar Neumann (1721-36). To the north of the adjoining **Neumünsterkirche** (new cathedral) lies the **Lusam Garden** where the minstrel Walter von der Vogelweide (died A.D. 1230) is buried. In the west crypt is the sarcophagus of St. Kilian.

Rococo statue at Amorbach.

From here the **Domstrasse** leads down to the Main river. A short distance in front of the **Old Main Bridge** stands the Baroque **Vierröhrenburnnen** (fountain) of 1765 and the old **town hall** (13th century) which has been extended several times since then. Nearby its towering **Grafeneckhart,** which was built in 1659 in late Renaissance style, is the **Carmelite Monastery** (1712), a town hall since the 19th century. The originals of the portal figures of Adam and Eve at **Marien Chapel** (1377-1479) are in the Main-Franconian Museum. Balthasar Neumann's burial place is located beside the market gate and the **Haus zum Falken** (Falcon's house). The **Alter Kranen** at the fish market, one of the town's landmarks, is the work of Franz Ignaz Neumann, Balthasar's son (1773).

Cross the Old Main Bridge and walk upstream on the other side of the river towards the Marienberg fortress until **St. Burkhard church** and **Burkharder Tor** (gate) are reached. From here a stepped footpath climbs up to Nikolausberg with the **Käppele**, a picturesque pilgrimage church, designed by Balthasar Neumann, offering beautiful views of Würzburg and the Main.

Metropolis of Franconian wine: St. Kilian, the patron saint of the town and of wine, stands on the Old Main Bridge and his sandstone figure provides a popular motif for photographers. Today Würzburg, which celebrated 1,200 years of wine production in 1979, is the principal center of wine production and marketing in Franconia. The **Juliusspital**, the **Bürgerspital** (infirmaries) and the **State Wine Estate** with its **Court Cellars**, which are considered the most beautiful wine cellars in the world, maintain the largest winegrowing estates in Germany.

For more than 650 years, it is a well-known fact in Würzburg that wine, when consumed in moderation, serves to strengthen and revive the sick and the weak. In 1319, the patrician Johannes von Steren donated the **Bürgerspital zum Heiligen Geist** (Citizens' Infirmary) with its extensive real estate in the form of vineyards, to the people of Würzburg. Elderly citizens, who are cared for here to this day, receive a glass of wine along with their daily meals, as has been the custom for centuries.

Those who have tanked-up with enough culture and information should not miss the wine-tasting in the Bürgerspital Weinstuben, or in the Juliusspital. *Meerfischli*, an old speciality featuring fish as long as your index finger, are eaten complete with head, tail and fins and taste scrumptious when washed down with the Würzburg wines.

The **Stein wine trail** on the northern edge of town (Stein is the oldest brand of wine in the world to carry the name of its origin) is a path nearly three miles (five km) long through one of the best known German vineyard areas.

An outing to the Franconian vineyards around Würzburg is recommended, more so for those feeling tired after a surfeit of sightseeing. Follow the Main south of Würzburg through small villages off the beaten track where the river snakes its way through the hilly Franconian vineyards between meadows and orchards. As you stand on a slope and gaze at the vineyards, the red roofs and the small towers so characteristic in this region, you begin to empathize with this small world. October, the month for grape-picking, is the best time to visit the Franconian wine district. Wine festivals are held each weekend in the villages of as Volkach, Frikkenbausen and Eisenheim.

The Bamberg horsemen: The journey

Franconian market woman.

through Franconian continues on towards the medieval gem of Bamberg, an old imperial and episcopal city first mentioned in A.D. 902.

The **Dom** (Cathedral) is the historical and spiritual focus of the city. The tomb of emperor Heinrich II, who raised Bamberg to an episcopal town in 1007, lies here and is the only Papal tomb north of the Alps. Two tombs, and thus two powers, are not only closely linked to the history of Bamberg, but also to German and European history in the Middle Ages.

A tour of the historic town center will reveal the town's original two-fold division: the ecclesiastical part on seven hills and, at their feet between two arms of the river Regnitz, the island or burgher part. From the **Hauptwache** (main guardhouse) of 1744, the route leads to the Maxplatz with the **Neues Rathaus** (New Town Hall) a Baroque building erected by Balthasar Neumann. The Baroque building style can also be seen at the **Grüner Markt** (Green Market); a few steps away, on the right is the magnificent facade of **St. Martin's Church** (17th century) and on the left is the Baroque house of a burgher, **Raulino House**.

On the border, between the lay and ecclesiastical parts of town, on an island of the river Regnitz, stands the **Altes Rathaus** (Old Town Hall) which is reached via the **Untere Brücke** (bridge). From here there is a splendid view of **Klein-Venedig** (Little Venice) with its fishermen's houses on the right bank of the Regnitz which is the scene of an amusing yearly festival called *Fischerstechen*. The old town hall's unusual location is due to the need, in earlier times, to reconcile the interests of the borough and the episcopal town. Its core is Gothic, with a Rococo doorway, bright balconies on the gate tower, the long side overwhelmed by frescoes, and the **Rottenmeisterhäuschen**, a half-timbered house balanced on one of the bridge's pier-heads.

From here the passage goes through narrow lanes to the **Domplatz**, passing the earlier Dominican church with its

ranconian
witzer-
and at
uchersfeld.

abbey and cloisters from the 14th century, and today home of the celebrated Bamberg Symphony Orchestra. The way via the picturesque stairway of the Katzenberg is also recommended for the **Schlenkerle**, one of the best *Rauchbier* (smoked malt beer) restaurants in Bamberg. The **Domplatz** is a civic jewel dominated by the four-tower Dom (cathedral) the Renaissance gable of the Alte Hofhaltung (Old Residence) and the Baroque facade of the New Residence where the last Bamberg Prince-Bishops lived. The **cathedral**, founded by Heinrich II and consecrated in 1012, burned down twice and was rebuilt in 1237 in the transition period from Romanesque to early Gothic. The **Fürstenportal** (Prince's Door) is very impressive with its deep recesses containing the statues of the apostles standing on the shoulders of the prophets. The statues in the cathedral interior are also masterpieces of medieval sculpture, the most famous being the **Bamberg Horseman**, an idealized portrait of Christian kings and knights in the Middle Ages. The central nave houses the tombs of Heinrich II and his spouse, Kunigunde, sculptured by Tilman Riemenschneider, and the west choir contains the tomb of Pope Clement II, the former Bishop of Bamberg. On the left of the cathedral, in the former chapter house erected by Balthasar Neumann in 1730, is the **Diocesan Museum** with its cathedral treasury of unique exhibits such as Heinrich II's star cloak and the choir cloak of his wife.

The **Alte Hofhaltung** (Old Residence) is separated by only a narrow street from the cathedral. This magnificent Renaissance building (1569) which now houses the Historical Museum, was once an imperial and episcopal palace. Observe the old imperial hall and the gable structure of the Council Chamber. The **Schöne Pforte** (gateway) of 1561 is richly decorated with stone carvings, and the interior courtyard has late Gothic half-timbered buildings from the 15th century. Facing it is the **New Residence**, the largest secular building in the old town, built in about 1700 by L. Dientzenhofer.

The road now leads up to the Michaelsberg, past the **church of St. Jacob**, a Romanesque-columned basilica from the 11th-12th century with a built-on Baroque facade (1771). St. Michael's Church, part of the former Benedictine abbey, and founded in 1015 at the request of Heinrich II, combines Romanesque, Gothic and Baroque in its architecture and decoration. The famous facade above the broad, balustrade exterior stairway (1677) is Dientzenhofer's work. Maternstrasse leads back into town and to the Carmelite abbey and church which was founded in the 12th century. The church's late Romanesque cloisters, the largest in Germany, are from the 13th century. Then comes Bamberg's finest Gothic building, the **Obere Pfarrkirche** (Upper Church) of 1325. Further up the Judengasse is the **Böttinger House,** built in 1713, and considered to be the finest burgher house in the German Baroque.

Fourteen Saints of Intercession: Our journey through the land of the Franks leads us further north, parallel to the Main, where two jewels of Baroque architecture are awaiting between the idyllic little towns of Staffelstein and Lichtenfels. Near **Staffelstein**, and visible from the top of a 1,380 feet (241 m) hill above the Main valley, stand the castle-like buildings of Banz Abbey, occupied by Benedictine monks from 1069 to 1803, and probably one of the greatest achievements of German Baroque. The abbey church of yellow sandstone, with its two-domed towers, is considered L. Dientzenhofer's greatest architectural achievement. The view from the terrace over the Main valley to Vierzehnheiligen Church on the opposite bank should not be missed.

To admire this second Baroque jewel, proceed towards **Lichtenfels**, the center of German basketry. Two miles (three km) south of the town, the road branches left from the B173 to **Vierzehnheiligen Church**, the most famous pilgrimage church in Franconia, named in honor of the 14 Saints of Intercession, who, according to legend, appeared several times to a devout shepherd in the 15th century. The church, high above the Main valley, was built between 1734-51 and became one of the most important consecrated works of Baroque and Rococo. It is a glittering masterpiece of Balthasar. The principal altar, designed by J.J.M. Küchel, is centrally placed. Around it, Neumann made every arch bend 3-dimensional. The columns are set away from the walls, thus creating an uncertainty about the limits of the church and even of its stability.

The "Frankish Crown": Once located in the heart of Germany, **Coburg** is now only a stone's throw from the East German border. Its fortress was the residence of the Dukes of Coburg, and the town is regarded by the well-traveled as a "hidden corner of the German soul."

In the heart of the old town, on the **Marktplatz**, the air is redolent with the aroma of burning pine cones over which the celebrated Coburg sausages are grilled the year round, while, from the town hall (1580) the *Bratwurstmännle* (statue) looks down vigilantly. His staff is said to be the official measure of the Coburg sausages. The Stadthaus from 1600 and a memorial to Prince Albert of Saxe-Coburg (1819-61), Queen Victoria's husband, stand at the Marktplatz.

The **Coburg Veste** has been dubbed the "Frankish Crown," and is one of the largest German castles with a triple ring of fortifications, built about 1200 in the Hohenstaufen style, and, after a fire in 1500, extended over a period of 300 years as a fortress. The Veste was a place of refuge for Martin Luther at the time of the celebrated Augsburg Imperial Diet of 1530. The Prince's Palace with its ducal chamber, chapel and Lukas Cranach room, can be reached from the first interior courtyard. The buildings around the second courtyard contain the valuable art collections of the Coburg Veste, including hunting weapons, Cranach paintings and copper engravings numbering 300,000 works.

Strongest beer in the world: From Coburg, take the B303 to **Kronach**, birthplace of the painter Lukas Cranach (1472-1553). The town offers you a romantic idyll with narrow lanes, impos-

The old town hall on the river Regnitz in Bamberg.

ing houses and a well-preserved medieval town wall with towers and gateways. The 12th century **Veste Rosenberg** fortress, never conquered, towers over the town, and is one of the best preserved fortresses in Germany.

More beer is drunk in Germany per head of the population than anywhere else in the world–and the "beertown" **Kulmbach** (12.5 miles/20 km) south of Coburg, brews the best beers. Crystal-clear spring water from the nearby Frankenwald and Fichtelgebirge uplands is used by four breweries, whose huge chimneys are a local landmark, to brew good, world-famous beers including *Kulminator*, the world's strongest beer. **Plassenburg Castle** overlooks the town. It originated in the 12th century but its present-day appearance is from the 16th century. The castle houses Germany's only museum of 300,000 tin figurines.

Wagner town: Bayreuth, the former residence of the Margraves and a university town since 1975 (population: 70,000) is undoubtedly Richard Wagner's town. Bayreuth is, however, also associated with the poet Jean Paul, who lived here during 1804-25, and with the composer Franz Liszt, who died here in 1886. The cultured Margravine Wilhelmina, Frederick the Great's favorite sister, was also involved with re-structuring the town in the 18th century. She commissioned the architect Saint-Pierre to build the first Bayreuth **opera house**, which is believed to be the best-preserved Baroque theater in Germany. The **Neues Schloss** (New Castle), designed by Saint-Pierre, but in the cooler style of the French Baroque, is also attributed to Wilhelmina's interest in architecture. Richard Wagner's grave and that of his wife Cosima, Liszt's daughter, are in the New Castle park. Liszt is buried nearby.

The **Schloss Eremitage** (Hermitage Castle) is another famous building on the eastern edge of Bayreuth. The **Altes Schloss** (Old Castle) built in 1718, was reconstructed and extended in 1736 according to Wilhelmina's plans. The New Castle, consisting of an 8-corner

Festival theater in Bayreuth.

WAGNER AND WAGNERITES

In 1876, on the Green Hill in Bayreuth, the first performance of the *Ring des Nibelungen* opened the Festival Theater, the only opera house in the world devoted to the works of a single composer: Richard Wagner (1813-83). It was built upon his plans, and financed by public funds and the State of Bavaria's treasury. Romantic, introverted King Ludwig II supported the hopelessly indebted composer, because Ludwig believed he recognized his own sick, dream world in Wagner's plan and works. Since then a community of Wagner-devotees, scattered throughout the world, and often ironically called Wagnerites, make their way to the Green Hill every year to witness–at wickedly expensive prices–one of the world-famous Wagner performances. It has been the dream of many opera singers since 1876 to perform at Bayreuth.

Bust of Richard Wagner.

The story of Wagner's real influence on music began in 1843 with the first performance of *Der fliegende Holländer* (Flying Dutchman) in Dresden. It was a flop compared to the first performance the year before of the opera *Rienzi* composed along traditional lines. This was because *Der fliegende Holländer* showed Wagner's contempt for the traditional Italian and French opera style which, he believed, missed every missionary thought by minimizing the effect of libretto and stage action in favor of the music, which inclined towards mere virtuosity. Stage action in *Der fliegende Holländer* was given decisive weight; the traditional set-number structure of opera was replaced by a rigorous unity and by the musical *Leitmotiv* (leading theme). The basic aim was the *Gesamtkunstwerk* (synthesis of the arts) which is rooted in the Romantic and in which music, poetry, drama, mime and settings are fused and carried a message, Wagner's message. *Tristan and Isolde* continued what began in *Der fliegende Holländer*, the final transition from opera to musical drama, a range of traditional tones never experienced before and climaxing in the *Ring des Nibelungen* (1854-74).

The titles of his musical dramas–*Lohengrin, Tannhäuser, Parsifal, Meistersinger von Nürnberg*–conveyed the spirit of 19th century Germany. Wagner lived in a period of growing German nationalism which had no political fulfilment at first. It nourished the spirit of the Romantic and the medieval Germanic world of sagas, which Wagner revived into a new, politically-orientated artistic form.

During his lifetime, Wagner's work provoked both great admiration and strong rejection. The polarization between his fanatical supporters and equally fanatical opponents led by Nietzsche, reached a sorry climax in the Nazi Wagner-cult. It was Johannes Brahms, his contemporary, who pointed out Wagner's real importance: "Wagner is the best at the moment. Everything else disappears before his importance now which not everyone can appreciate or assess, at the very least the Wagnerites."

sun temple with two round wings, was built in 1753 and has splendid fountains which play four times daily. North of Bayreuth's town center rises the Green Hill where Wagner had the **Festival Theater** built in 1872-76.

Those in a hurry to get to the A9/E8 from Bayreuth to Nuremberg should, nevertheless, detour at the exit **Pegnitz/ Grafenwöhr** and visit **Fränkische Schweiz** (Swiss Franconia) with its delightful and varied scenery. The region was so named by the German Romantics because in the 19th century they imagined Switzerland looked like this. Similarities with the real Switzerland are not necessarily in evidence, though steeply towering, jagged and bizarre dolomite crags are characteristic, such as the twin crags in the romantic crag village, **Tüchersfeld**. However, the climax of a worthwhile detour to this nature park is the mile-long limestone cave, **Teufelshöhle,** near Pottenstein, a fascinating underworld of numerous rocky domes and grottos full of stalagmites and stalactites.

A historic city: Traveling southwards, the next stop is the old Free Imperial City of **Nürnberg** (population: 500,000) which is now Bavaria's second largest city, and an important industrial and commercial center. Despite the world-famous Nuremberg *Lebkuchen* (gingerbread) it is not a city of the pseudo-Gothic–the devastating bombing of World War II made sure of it. After the war, everything had to be rebuilt, giving the old Imperial City its historic significance and charm as Franconia's metropolis.

Although the city was founded relatively late by Emperor Heinrich III in the 11th century as a base for his campaigns in Bohemia, it developed quickly into a powerful trading center. It was raised to a Free Imperial City by Emperor Friedrich II in 1219 and retained this status until its annexation by the Kingdom of Bavaria in 1806. From 1050 until the 16th century, nearly all the German emperors had a residence in the Kaiserburg (castle) whose construction began in the 11th century, and held

In the "devil's cave" at Pottenstein

their imperial diets in the city. During this long period Nuremberg was the unofficial capital of the Holy Roman Empire of Germany, a tradition which Hitler's NSDAP wanted to maintain by staging its party rallies there.

Between the 14th and 16th centuries, the now-wealthy trading center also became a center of art and science. Names like Albrecht Dürer, Adam Krafft, Veit Stoss, Peter Vischer, Hans Sachs, Martin Beheim and Peter Henlein, remind one of this glorious period. However, Nuremberg lost its economic and political importance in the later centuries, and only experienced a new period of glory-filled by the opening of the first German rail track between Nuremberg and Fürth of December 12, 1835–after annexation by the Kingdom of Bavaria in the 19th century. (A construction of German trains and steam locomotives, "dinosaurs of the rail track," can be seen at Nuremberg's **Verkehrsmuseum**.) About 100 years later, however, another less celebrated chapter in German history was written. Between 1933-38, the Nazi rallies with Hitler's demagogic appearances took place: a huge rally arena was especially shaped on the ground by stamping, and the imprints are still there in some places. And Nuremberg was again in the international limelight between 1945-49 when the War Crimes Trials were held here by the victors.

Back in the Middle Ages: Nuremberg's old town is divided geographically into the St. Sebald part and the St. Lorenz part which are both surrounded by a sturdy defensive wall (13th century) with 46 round fortified towers–the landmarks of the city–and four main gates, the Spittlertor, the König- or Frauentor, the Laufertor and the Neutor.

The **Kaiserburg** (emperor castle) built on sandstone crags high above the old town, consists of three architectural parts, each describing a historical period. On the western crags towers the Kaiserburg, erected under the Hohenstaufen Emperor Friedrich Barbarossa in the 12th century; then comes the Hohenzollern **Burggrafenburg**, the

hristkindl arket at uremberg.

original Salic royal castle from the 11th century; finally the **Kaiserstallung** (imperial stables) built by the city of Nuremberg as a corn granary in 1495 and now a hostel. In the 16th century defensive battlements were incorporated into the castle and half-timbered houses for the court employees were built in the outermost courtyard. Once the robber knight Eppelein von Gailingen drove his mount over the ramparts of the Kaiserburg in his legendary attempt to escape from his captors who had condemned him to death. Nowadays, around the castle are a number of cosy taverns where sausages grilled over charcoal (*Rostbratwürste*) can be enjoyed with a hearty "Rauch beer."

Albrecht-Dürer-House is reached through the Tiergartnertor near the castle. The 15th century house where the famous painter lived is now a museum. Then comes **Rathausplatz** (Town Hall Square) with the Evangelical **St. Sebald's Church**, a late Romanesque-columned basilica of 1256. St. Sebald's tomb inside the church is a masterpiece of the German metal founder's art by Vischer from the beginning of the 16th century. The Crucifixion group by Veit Stoss, also from this period, is very moving. Opposite the church is the Fembo Municipal Museum, a splendid late Renaissance building and a typical patrician house from about 1600.

Across Pegnitz river: Cross the river Pegnitz to the **Hauptmarkt** and proceed to the **Townhall**, whose oldest part is a hall with stepped gables (1340). The basement has medieval dungeons with frightening torture chambers. Nearby is the well-known **Gänsemännchen** (1555) the figure of a peasant with two geese whose beaks spout water. At the Hauptmarkt (tourist information center) where the world-famous **Christkindlmarkt** takes place every year before Christmas, observe the **Frauenkirche church** (1349) facing the richly decorated 62 feet (19 m) **Schöner Brunnen** (fountain) of 1396, with a continuous ring of luck. The Frauenkirche has a beautiful facade with the

Winter panorama of the "Burg" at Nuremberg

Michaelschörlein (1508) by Adam Krafft and the celebrated *Männleinlaufen*, a clock which commemorates, at 12 noon daily, the allegiance of the Seven Electors to Charles IV. The interior contains the famous **Tucher-Altar** (about 1400) and two tombstones by Adam Krafft.

Cross the Pegnitz river to reach the **Heilig-Geist-Spital** (hospital) situated on the picturesque Pegnitz and which dates from the 14th century. The German emperor's orb and scepter were kept here until 1796. The interior courtyard has an impressive Crucifixion group by Adam Krafft and the Hansel Fountain from the 14th century. Next stop is the Gothic **St. Lorenz Church** in the Lorenz part of the town. The church was built in the 13th-14th century, and is especially impressive because of its light-filled chancel with monumental star vaulting. Outstanding in its rich and valuable decoration is the **Engelsgruss** (Annunciation), a sculpture suspended from chancel and created by Veit Stoss in 1517. Another work by this artist, the *Crucifix*, can be seen at the high altar together with Adam Krafft's world-famous tabernacle.

Königsstrasse, the shoppers' street, begins at St. Lorenz and passes the **Mauthalle**, which was erected as a corn granary about 1500. The inn with its historic arched cellar roof invites you to stay and enjoy *Veschper* with the famous Nuremberg grilled sausages. Now replenished, you proceed to the **German National Museum** at the Kornmarkt which was founded in 1852 "to save the documents of Germany's Past." A collection of folklore and prehistoric items are exhibited in an art gallery. There is also a copper-engraving room. No other museum offers such a comprehensive insight into the cultural development of the German linguistic area. After passing the early Gothic St. Clara's Church, you arrive at the **Handwerkerhof Old Nuremberg**, a model town illustrating medieval handicrafts, such as coin minting, gold and precious metal forging, a tin foundry and Lebkuchen manufacture.

ı the artisans' ourtyard" ı Nurem-erg.

GERMAN TITBITS

The best places to learn about local eating habits are the *Bäckerei* or *Konditorei* (pastry shop) and the *Metzgerei* or *Fleischerei* (local butcher). These shops are usually owned by one family with the father as master-craftsman ostentatiously having his diploma in a golden frame way behind the counter. Enter these shops and you are in an overwhelming wonderland of food. It is astonishing what German craftsmen can make out of flour and meat. These little shops are bastions of neighborhood shopping and chit-chat.

Germans are proud to have the greatest variety of bread in the world. From *Pumpernickel* to *Weizenbrot*, from rye-bread to sourdough bread there are more than 130 varieties. These include light or dark, fluffy or firm and can be made with different condiments including caraway, coriander, poppy, sesame or sunflower seeds and many more. But the ultimate are the pastries and fancy cakes. Every baker has his specialties. To name them all would be a never-ending endeavor since the names vary from town to town. When you enter a pastry shop, look around, inhale the appetizing aromas and you will soon start to drool. This is one place where it is quite in order to point at the goodies which you wish to try.

From meat to vegetables: The same applies to the butcher, where you can have everything to your heart's desire. German *Wurst* (sausages) are the most varied and most tasteful in the world. Do not miss the *Münchner Weisswurst*, a special boiled veal sausage. Take care, though, to follow tradition and never eat the skin. Also try the *Nürnberger Bratwurst*: special sausages roasted on a grill. Order these by number! The Frankfurter, which some Germans call *Wiener*, is warmed in water. Numerous other varieties are served in different forms, such as *Aufschnitt* (sliced), paté or smoked. Enjoy the selection of *Schinken* (ham).

Usually, out of the big towns, the best places to eat are the restaurants which are owned by the local butchers. But beware: meat in Germany is usually the main dish and sometimes you will be served a very large piece, especially if you order *Wiener Schnitzel*. Methods of preparing the meat vary with the region, be it as *Schweinshaxe* or *Sauerbraten*. There also are many treats to accompany the main dish. Try to sample the *Sauerkraut* in the south, the *Spätzle* around Stuttgart, the fish and stews in the north, and throughout the country, the *Pfannkuchen* or *Dampfnudel* and many kinds of vegetables.

The most common vegetable is the potato. Formerly it appeared at every second meal as *Kartoffelsuppe* (soup), boiled, mashed or fried or in the special German *Kartoffelknödel* (dumpling). Today, the most widespread way of serving potatoes is with applesauce as fried pancakes, called *Kartoffelpuffer*. These pancakes are offered at most eating houses in the large towns together with the famous–or infamous–*Currywurst* (sausage). This prolific

A sumptuou meal.

fast-food of German origin is regarded by some as the incarnation of junk-food and by others as a simple repast. Much depends on the quality of preparation.

It is important to know–or you can be disappointed–that in different parts of the country, different tidbits have the same name. In the south, *Pfannkuchen* is a flat pancake made of flour and eggs which is sometimes served with asparagus or ham. Add the name Berlin and you will be served something else. A *Berliner Pfannkuchen* is a pastry made from fried yeast, coated with sugar and sometimes filled with marmalade. Once, they were a specialty during Lent but today they symbolize the Carnival.

A temple of delicacies: Neither of the two resembles a cake as the word Kuchen would signify. The place to eat the latter fresh and warm is in a cafe. This establishment is indeed the best place to sit and to enjoy an almost infinite variety of tasty morsels. For some Germans it is the only place to be on a Sunday afternoon: to sit, to people-watch, to chat, to drink coffee and to eat the creamiest cakes and the most sumptuous fruit cakes. Here is the true temple to the splendor of food delicacies. Those who have not spent a few hours in a cafe cannot claim to have visited Germany. No other country, other than Austria, can equal the delights of the German coffeeshop about which there are legends, stories and even songs. Nowadays during the day, it is the number one meeting place for everybody, when you can sit, drink tea or coffee and devour heaps of cake. Do not miss the *Schwarzwälder Kirschtorte* (a tongue twister, but sheer bliss to eat), the *Apfelstrudel* (apple pie), the *Linzer Torte*, the *Baumkuchen* (means tree-cake and should look like one) and the *Pflaumenkuchen* (plumcake). In Bavaria, the plumcake is called *Zwetschgendatschi* and you should never attempt to pronounce its name. If you are lucky, you might also find one of the finest specialties of the country: the *Pralinen*. It is worthwhile looking for the few shops which make them the traditional way.

ich
riety at
e baker's.

FOLLOWING THE ROMANTIC ROAD

To travel along the Romantic Road is to experience the panoply of a historical drama extending from Roman times up to the present day. The principals are emperors, kings and countless nobles as well as burghers and peasants, who fought for territorial and human rights. The places they acted in are fascinating towns, magnificent residences, castles, churches and monasteries set in the most varied landscapes between Würzburg on the river Main, and Füssen, at the northern rim of the Alps. Modern times have changed the occasionally-traveled country lane into a busy road, yet innumerable places–a narrow alley at Rothenburg, a palace in Augsburg, the castle of Neuschwanstein–justify the term ‘romantic’ often given to this route. Like the pearls of an exquisite necklace, the jewels of the Romantic Road are bound to one another, examples of the living past.

Charming Tauber valley: Starting from the old residential town of Würzburg, the B27 leads southwest through woods and hilly farmland down the pretty Tauber valley, a tributary of the Main river. Entering **Tauberbischofsheim** over a bridge high above the river, it is hard to imagine the floods which inundated the town in 1985. Wandering through the town you might discover small metal plates about three feet above ground marking the water level during that catastrophe. Higher up so-called *Melusinen* (mermaids) symbolize the town’s close connection with the water. Medieval carpenters depicted these mermaids with cleft fishtail on the half-timbered houses. **Haus Mackert**, the town palace of a wealthy wine merchant and the **Sternapotheke** (pharmacy) opposite, give an impressive entry from the Hauptstrasse into the market square with **Rathaus** (town hall with tourist information) and the Baroque church of **St. Lioba**. The patroness was a relative of the missionary bishop St. Bonifatius and presided here in Tauberbischofsheim around the middle of the 8th century, in one of the first convents in Germany. The fact that the village with its royal court received St. Bonifatius' personal protection gave it the name **Bischofsheim** (home of the bishop). By mid-13th century the bishop and the electoral princes of Mainz gained supremacy over the town and its territory. Today, the wheel in the coat-of-arms and the **Kurmainzische Schloss** (castle) with its **Türmersturm** (watchtower) from the 14th to 16th century are the last remnants of their rule. Converted into a museum, the castle presents a synopsis of the town's cultural achievements. On the other side of the old fortifications you may discover stone toads enjoying a bath in a fountain. Like the mermaids, they symbolize Tauberbischofsheim's affiliation with the river. Toads will again be encountered in the neo-Gothic parish church of **St. Martin** (medieval altarpieces) and the noteworthy **chapel of St. Sebastian**, a former ossuary which has a relief of the Last Judgement.

From Tauberbischofsheim, the journey continues on the B290 along the Romantic Road. En route are the villages of **Distelhausen** and **Gerlachsheim** both of which boast Baroque churches. The former grandeur of the one in Gerlachsheim, which once belonged to a monastery, is reflected in the statue of St. Mary comforting the distressed which stands in front of the impressive complex. Non-religious figures decorate the beautifully-restored half-timbered town hall (1580) of **Grünsfeld** which is a few miles to the left of B290. The famous Tilman Riemenschneider sculpted the tombstone of the countess Dorothea von Rieneck (died 1503) in the parish church of St. Peter and Paul.

Along the country road to **Grünsfeldhausen,** which is worth a visit because of its Romanesque double octagon of St. Achatius, are crucifixes and wayside shrines, which give the area the soberness of *Herrgottsland* (Lord God's country) and *Madonnenländchen* (Madonna's district). Religious sculptures again decorate the old half-

Preceding pages: Neuschwanstein castle in winter; "This march must be possible!" Below, the castle square in Tauberbischofsheim.

timbered and Baroque houses in the center of **Lauda** on the west bank of the Tauber. The vineyards on its steep slopes produce a quality full-bodied white wine whose history is recorded in a 16th-century vintner's house.

Residence of Teutonic Order: The guests at **Bad Mergentheim** (10 miles/16 km from Tauberbischofsheim) drink more water than wine, for the good properties of the spa are supposed to help cure diseases of the liver, gall-bladder, kidneys and other organs. When the source was discovered in 1826 the town saw new life flowing into its charming streets. Celtic tribes might have drunk the vitalizing liquid centuries before, yet a permanent settlement cannot be traced further back than Franconian times (8th century). When the *Deutschritterorden* (Teutonic Order) moved its headquarters to Bad Mergentheim in 1525, the town gained in terms of importance and wealth. Most of the members of the order were nobles, the *Hochmeister* (Grand Master) quite often being a king or duke and they generously invested in the Order's castle which is the most imposing structure in town. The once-secluded buildings, which can be accessible across a drawbridge, are now open to the public. Locals and guests appreciate the walk through the park adjacent to the **Kursanatorium**, as well as the Baroque church (planned by Balthasar Neumann) and the famous spiral staircase. In the castle (municipal offices and a museum) the former assembly room of the chapter has retained its original decoration. Portraits of members of the Teutonic Order and their robes, old furniture, a collection of doll's houses and rustic costumes of local peasants are exhibited in other rooms.

While still an unknown musician, the young Beethoven played in the Schüttplatz opposite the castle, where the Burgstrasse (Automobile Museum now occupies No. 2-4) leads to the **Markplatz**. The statue of Wilhelm Schutzbar, the knight who made Bad Mergentheim the residence of the Teutonic Order, disappears on market days

'he knight's
all in Wei-
ersheim
astle.

amongst the colorful stalls. The 1544 town hall and elegant merchants' houses form an architectural frame around the rectangular market which is guarded by the tower of St. Johannes. Precious works of art, including a 16th-century bronze epitaph, are found in the church of St. Mary which has even older frescoes on the vaulting of the cloister.

Painters, sculptors, and architects: By mere chance the village of **Stuppach** (seven miles/11 km southeast) acquired fame through a painting in its parish church. The priest Balthasar Blumhofer had bought it in Bad Mergentheim, from the estate of the Teutonic Order. Local artists repainted it and made the Virgin Mary with her child resemble a Rubens madonna. Thus it was not until 1908 that specialists identified the canvas as an unknown work by Matthias Grünewald which is remarkable for both its symbolic quality and exquisite technique. Using transparent casein colors, Grünewald depicted Virgin Mary, clad in a fur garment and the child, surrounded by a lush fig tree, roses and lilies. The flowers symbolize immaculateness and virginity.

Past **Markelsheim**, a place to stop for a glass of white wine is **Weikersheim**, the former residence of the counts of Hohenlohe. With an elegant curve the market square merges westwards into the horseshoe-shaped *cour d'honneur* of the castle. The major part of the triangular palace was constructed from the 16th to 18th century. The belfry is a remnant of the 12th century castle keep. The Hohenlohes' wish for a prestigious banquet hall was fulfilled by their architect through an ingeniously constructed coffered ceiling hanging on chains from the roof timbers and spanning a room of 115 feet by 40 feet (35 meters by 12 meters). Life-size plaster sculptures on the walls of the **Rittersaal** (Knights' hall) and the motifs on the ceiling mirror the counts' great passion for hunting. The outstanding luxury for the guest at that time were the toilets, which even Versailles (built later than Weikersheim) lacked. You can even see from outside where they are sited. The weird

Left, section of the Riemenschneider altar in Creglingen. Below, "Will he drain the Meistertrunk in one go?"

lionheads were designed to function, by virtue of their nostrils, as a form of ventilation. The garden with its elegant orangery at the far end, its fountains, obelisks and statues of antique mythology expresses the Baroque love for curves, voluptuousness and allegory. Characters from the court of Count Ludwig (1713-14) were models for the dwarf gallery along the moat.

Röttingen, a few miles to the east, celebrates within its well-conserved town wall the *Bremserfest* in October, (*Bremser* is the local term for young fermenting wine.) From here via Bieberehren, the Romantic Road leads to **Creglingen**, the destination of thousands of pilgrims since the 14th century when–so the legend goes–a farmer found a host of angels ploughing his field. The counts of Hohenlohe thereafter donated a church, and around 1500, Tilman Riemenschneider received the commission for an altar dedicated to the Virgin Mary. His 36 feet (11 m) tall creation surpasses all his other works in its expressiveness. The lack of varnish heightens the intense tension on the faces of the apostles who are moved by the assumption of the Virgin Mary, her life being depicted on the wings of the altar. The coronation scene at the top is even visible when the altar is closed. The **Fingerhutmuseum** (thimble museum) across the road from the church is unique. It has a collection of more than 1,000 thimbles, none more than one inch (2.5 cm) in length, and of the most varied age and origin.

Over the years, next stop **Detwang** by the banks of the river Tauber, has scarcely changed. For over 800 years its main feature has been the Romanesque parish church of St. Peter and Paul which houses one of Tilman Riemenschneider's last works, the **Holy Cross Altar** (about 1515), showing scenes from the Mount of Olives, the crucifixion and the resurrection. Originally sculptured for a chapel in Rothenburg, it came to Detwang in 1563.

Living past: In narrow bends the Romantic Road winds up to the pearl of all medieval towns in Germany:

Stream of tourists at the Plönlein in Rothenburg.

Rothenburg ob der Tauber. The name (as well as the coat of arms) tells the story of its origin and a red castle marks the site, which today is a shady park (Burggarten) on the western edge of the town. The place was well chosen in a period of war when the threat of attack was constant. No wonder that by the middle of the 12th century a settlement surrounded by a wall had grown on the plateau east of the castle. A century later Rothenburg gained the favorable status of a free imperial town, with independent right of legal jurisdiction and defense. The citizens became wealthy merchants dealing in wine, cattle and wool. An outsider, Heinrich Toppler, made the town a powerful element in the German territorial jigsaw puzzle. Toppler's financial and political achievements provided the basis for a rise in population. A new town wall was necessary to guarantee the safety of the settlement. With a few alterations this outer wall is preserved and the **Wehrgang** (battlements) are accessible to the public from **Klingentor** to the **Spitalbastei**. The southernmost bastion is named after the former hospital which in medieval times was located on the outskirts. It offers an enjoyable walk (25 minutes) around the town walls with its numerous embrasures.

Rothenburg's hub is the **Marktplatz** (market square), where all the important streets meet. Here you face one of the most splendid town halls in southern Germany with its Gothic facade (13th century) opposite the **Herrngasse**, its Renaissance facade towards the Marktplatz, and a 16th-century tower, rising up to 180 feet (55 meters). From the tower you enjoy a fantastic view of Rothenburg, Spitalgasse and Schmeidgasse come from the Spitalbastei past Sieberturm and **Plönlein**, an idyllic and probably the most often-photographed square with the view towards **Kobolzeller Tor** (the town gate) in the southwest. Follow St. John's to the **Kriminalmuseum** (Crime museum). The collection of instruments of punishment accompanied by old documents and prints is unique in Europe. The

Dinkelsbühl boys' orchestra.

wooden cage hanging in the front courtyard was, for example, the threat for bakers. If their bread was too light or too small they would be placed in the cage which was then submerged in a pond or river. Remedies for more private problems were so called "neck violins," which quarrelsome women had to wear round their neck, the hand also being locked into the wooden block.

Dancing shepherds: Quite close to this museum of medieval crime and justice is the joyful **Doll and Toy Museum** in Hofronnengasse No. 13. The cobbled road joins the market square at the Renaissance **Herterichbrunnen**. At the end of a war or an epidemic, the shepherds traditionally used to dance around this fountain. The Schäfertänze are performed nowadays in front of the town hall at Easter, around Whitsun, for the summer festivals (June/July) and the *Reichsstadttage* (middle of September). During these times of the year (except Easter), the play *Meistertrunk* (Master Draught) commemorating the siege of Rothenburg by the troops of Tilly during the Thirty Years' War (1631) is performed in the town hall. Witty peasants and country bumpkins are the main characters of the amusing *Hans-Sachs-Spiele* (on stage in the festivals) whilst the puppets in **Trexlers Figurentheater** (at the end of the Herrengasse) entertain every evening.

The most precious work of religious art in Rothenburg is inside the church of **St. Jakob** (north of the town hall). At the beginning of the 16th century the wealthy citizens of Rothenburg commissioned an altar from Tilman Riemenschneider. In the Heilig-Blut-Altar (Holy Blood Altar), in the west choir of St Jakob, he sculpted the most expressive and moving depiction of Christ's passion with the Last Supper as the central episode. Franconian artists also created the miracle-of-colors in the eastern windows and the high altar.

What is said to be the oldest kitchen in Germany is found in the **Reichsstadtmuseum** in the former Dominican convent which was built in the middle of the 13th century. Those wishing to dine or drink in historical surroundings have a wide choice. Try the **"Eisenhut"** or the **"Goldener Hirsch**." However, the most famous is the **Baumeisterhaus** (1596) at the top of Schmiedgasse.

The Baroque castle of **Schillingsfürst** (completed in 1750), which is located in secluded woods on the Frankenhöhe (Franconian Heights), was the residence of the counts of Hohenlohe-Schillingsfürst and the once much-appreciated domicile of Franz Liszt (1811-86) famous musician and composer of the Romantic movement whose statue stands in the park. The castle is situated at the center of the European watershed and it is said its eaves empty via the Tauber and the Rhine into the North Sea and along the Wörnitz and the Danube into the Black Sea. Other than the castle, the **Heimatmuseum** (regional museum) is also worth a visit. Among its exhibits is a model of an old ox-driven pump.

"Little colonel": Back on the Romantic Road, **Feuchtwangen** is the next stop. The history of this town begins with Charlemagne and the foundation of a Benedictine convent (9th century). the wars of the 16th and 17th centuries deprived the town of many stately houses, yet connoisseurs still praise the market square as "Franconia's most beautiful banquet hall." It is dominated by the **Stiftskirche** (collegiate church) with an 1484 altar by Michael Wohlgemut, the teacher of Albrecht Dürer. Further back is the smaller Romanesque **church of St. Johannis** and the **Kasten**, an impressive 16th-century tithe church. The half-timbered house of the **Café am Kreuzgang** gives access to another of Feuchtwangen's treasures, the Romanesque **Kreuzgang** (cloister), which, from June to late August, is the stage for the **Kreuzgangspiele** featuring internationally renowned actors and plays. Artisans demonstrate with enthusiasm the traditional crafts of blueprint, weaving, pewter-making and dyeing in the **Handwerksstuben** above the western wing of the cloister. Their products embellish the most tastefully and lively furnished rooms of the Heimatmuseum, a jewel of its kind in Bavaria.

If you have missed the chance to enjoy a carp in Flasbach or Feuchtwangen, stop at **Dinkelsbühl**, where, by the wall with its 20 towers, the half-timbered homes have been restored or rebuilt according to the traditional Franconian half-timbering method, the town itself surrounded by green meadows and fields, moats, ponds, vegetable gardens and orchards. Its masters excelled themselves in the construction of the **Deutsches Haus** (German house, 15th-16th century) opposite the parish church of **St. Georg**. This towering building symbolizes the wealth of Dinkelsbühl's citizens in the 15th century and marks the crossing of important trade routes. Merchants and farmers delivered their goods at the Schranne. Here stands a coin-operated model of the old town which gives an impression of what Dinkelsbühl looks like when lit up at night. Today the cornbarn of old has a magnificent hall where every July the historical play of the *Kinderzeche* starts with a new council meeting in 1632 when Swedish troops had captured one of the bastions and demanded the surrender of the town. On festival Sundays all Dinkelsbühl joins enthusiastically in a magnificent historical procession finishing with a speech by the "young colonel" next to the **Weinmarkt** (wine market) who once again recalls the town's miraculous change of fortune in 1636. He wears a red and white Rococo army costume which is the traditional costume of the *Knabenkapelle* of Dinkelsbühl, one of the most famous boys' bands in Germany.

While wandering around the town take a look at the idyllic inner courtyard of the **Hezelhaus**, a typical wealthy burgher's house from the golden age of this former free imperial town. The Baroque facade of the house of the German Order with its plethora of coat-of-arms is a stimulating contrast to the neighboring half-timbered houses. Fabulous views over the town can be enjoyed from **Segringer Tor**, the western gate, and from a one-hour walk along the wall south towards **Nördlinger Tor** or north towards **Rothenburger Tor** and the quiet pond, and past the **Spital** (in parts still an old people's home) with an old mangle in the court and an interesting historical museum inside. Dr. Martin-Luther-Strasse leads back to the **church of St. Georg**, one of the most remarkable late Gothic churches in Germany. During the festival week, the night watchman starts his rounds here at 9.30 p.m.

A crater for astronauts: Running southwards, the Romantic Road cuts right through Wallerstein. Both the old castle hill in **Wallerstein** and the 295 feet (90 m) steeple of St. Georg church in the very center of **Nördlingen** are excellent vantage points from which to appreciate the unique structure of the **Ries** landscape, a meteoric crater approximately 16 miles (25 km) in dia-meter. About 15 million years ago a meteorite (diameter 3,937 feet/1,200 m) hit the earth's atmosphere at a speed of 62 miles per hour (100 km per hour). Because the landscape resembles that of the moon the Apollo 14 team received its field-training in the Ries.

In this pan-shaped landscape human traces from 13,000 years have been found. The name *Nordlinga* for a Carolingian court was first recorded in 898. The Free Imperial City of the 13th century, Nördlingen soon became economically powerful by virtue of its *Pfingstmesse*. This Whitsun fair was the hub of all southern German and European trade. Taxes and levies soon financed the perfect round of the tower wall including 11 towers and five gates. The battlements of 2.2 miles (3.5 km) in length are an outstanding attraction in that they are intact, wonderful to walk along and offer a superb sight from the top of the **Daniel**. The church belonging to this steeple, St. Georg, stands right in the middle of Nördlingen, austere in its late-Gothic style (1505) from outside, but decorated with remarkable works of art inside. A few steps north the **Rathaus** (town hall) boasts a Renaissance flight of stairs, below which, in old times, disturbers of the nightly peace and drunkards were detained and earned the scorn and derision of the fool on the wall and the guests of the

An old custom: the sword-dance in Dinkelsbühl.

Reichsadler
Restaurant - Café

Tanzhaus (dancehouse). This is one of the countless half-timbered houses, characterized in the tanners' quarter by long balconies on which the hides were aired. The hospital of old Spital houses a rich historical **Reichsstadtmuseum** (imperial town museum).

The mighty **Harburg**, embodiment of medieval castles, is a mere 10 miles (17 km) east of Nördlingen. It stands atop a limestone hill and overlooks the town of the same name on the Wörnitz river. From the 13th to the 18th century the princes of Öttingen extended and fortified this guardpost of the old trade road from Augsburg to Nuremberg. Today it is one of the largest and best-preserved German fortress complexes. The outstanding art collection in the **Fürstenhaus** is well worth a visit, as is the **Burgschenke** for its traditional atmosphere. Those who visit in June can take part in the historic *Bockfest* festival which dates back to the days of Napoleon Bonaparte.

Where the River Wörnitz flows into the Donau (Danube), it passes around an island called **Werth** in ancient Germany which is the nucleus of modern **Donauwörth**. Its historical monuments, some of them completely rebuilt after the disastrous bombing raids during World War II, are mainly aligned along **Reichsstrasse**. This is a section of the "Imperial Road" which, in the Middle Ages, connected to Bergen in Norway via Nuremberg and Augsburg to Italy. Between the **Fuggerhaus** (1536) with its high gable at the western end of the nowadays lively street and the **Rathaus** (town hall) at the east, there are many splendid houses as well as the parish **Church of Our Lady** with the *Pummerin*, the heaviest bell in Swabia (6.55 tons) which summons the citizens to mass. In the **Tanzhaus**, its facade very much like that of the Fuggerhaus, the burghers used to meet for their Sunday dance in the 15th and 16th centuries. Today, it is a concert hall with a restaurant and an archaeological museum. The imperial eagle, emblem of Donauwörth since 1193, tops the modern **Reichsstadtbrunnen** (Impe-

Aerial view of Nördlingen.

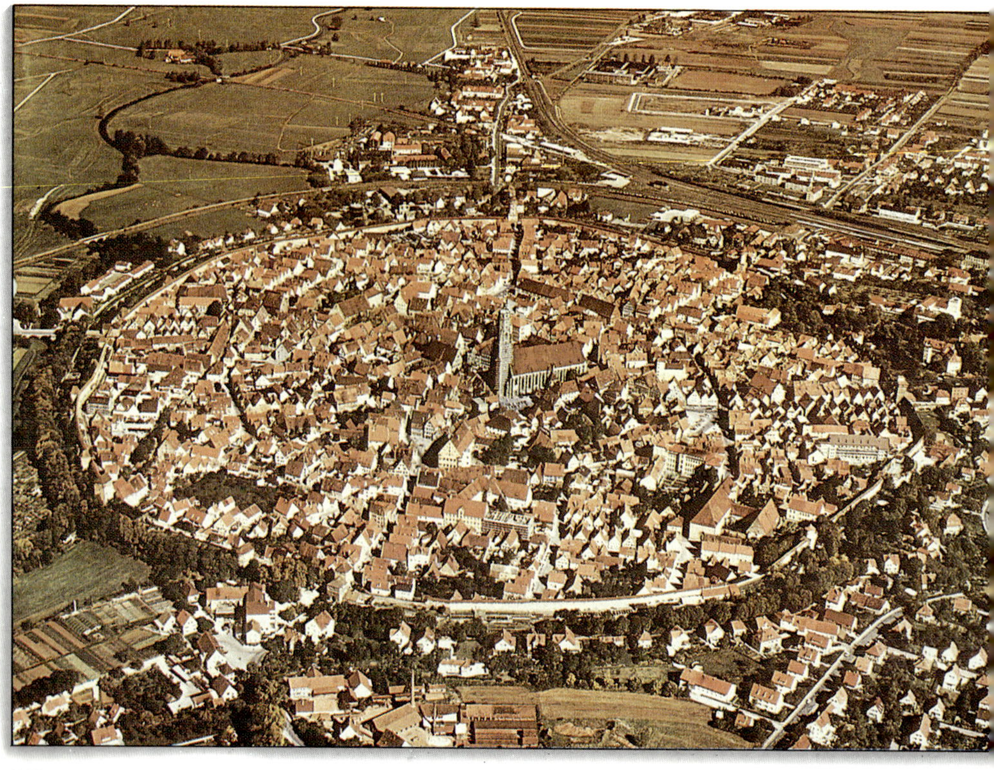

rial City fountain) and gives you a double-headed greeting. Of its medieval bastions, only the **Riedertor** (a gate near the town hall) was not destroyed in World War II. From here a bridge leads to the tiny **Wörnitz island**, the original fishers' quarter. You can walk past the town hall to the picturesque **Färbertör'l** (tanners' gate).

Balloons and flying machines: Reach for the sky, that is the subject of the **Ballonmuseum** in **Gersthofen** on the Romantic Road. This small town on the outskirts of Augsburg has been the Mecca of aerostatics since 1786, when August von Parseval got his first airship off the ground here. The more than 1,000 exhibits in the old five-storied water tower include a genuine balloon basket as well as *objets d'art*, documenting the history of man's non-motorized conquest of the heavens.

The "tailor of Ulm," Albrecht Berblinger, also tried to defy gravity. This man, the first hang-glider pilot in history, attempted to fly over the Danube with a flying-machine he had built in 1811. Presumably on account of the lack of thermal wind over the river he suddenly plunged, much to the amusement of the crowd of spectators, into the cold waters of the river. Today you can still find a plaque on the **Adlerbastei** in **Ulm** (100,000 inhabitants) commemorating this event.

The excursion to Ulm from Augsburg-Gersthofen (43 miles/69 km on the A8) is almost a must, as no other church steeple in the world rises higher than the spire of the town's outstanding Gothic **cathedral** (530 feet/161.6 meters). But during the first phase of building (1377-1533) the self-confident citizens of Ulm, a thriving free imperial town, not only wanted to build the highest tower in the world but also the most spacious church in Christendom. The interior of the minster is capable of holding 29,000 people (twice the population of Ulm at that time) and seems infinitely high to the observer. From the top of the minster you can see the *Ulmer Spatz* sitting on the roof, a sparrow which, as legend has it, showed the citizens how to transport a long beam–lengthwise and not crosswise–through a narrow gate.

Between the cathedral and the River Danube idyllic lanes wind along the town wall and the small canals in the fishers' and tanners' quarters of old. Here you will also find quite old and authentic pubs and taverns serving Swabian specialties. In the **Schwörhaus**, not very far from the town hall (built in 1370) the so-called pledge is read aloud each year by the mayor. It is a 1897 constitutional agreement between the city patricians and the merchant-guilds and the origin of a festival which still takes place every July. The quadrennial traditional fish-catch also has its roots in this document.

Town of the Fugger dynasty: To eat Swabian dishes with your fingers in the medieval manner from a wooden plate, you probably need to make reservations in the **Welser-Küche** (restaurant) in **Augsburg** (250,000 inhabitants). Located in the heart of town it prepares meals from the recipes of Philippine Welser, a famous daughter of this city, where kings, nobles of the realm used to visit the Welser and Fugger merchants in the 16th and 17th centuries.

Augsburg developed from a Roman fort, founded near the confluence of the rivers Lech and Wertach in 15 B.C. By A.D. 100, Tacitus, the famous Roman historian already called Augusta Vindelicům, "the splendid capital of the province Raetia." Alemannic tribes which had expelled the Romans in the 5th century retained Augusta as a capital. And it maintained its key position on one of the most important trading routes from Italy across the Alps–a heritage of the Roman era. The ever-present threat of Hungarian equestrian troops raiding settlements and killing tradesmen was finally removed after the Battle on the Lechfeld in A.D. 955 when the army of Bishop Ulrich of Augsburg defeated the Hungarians and forced them to retreat. Saint Afra, who suffered martyrdom for Christianity in Roman times, and Saint Ulrich have become the town's patrons and the **Ulrichsmünster** (minster) which is dedicated to these saints is a landmark of Augsburg.

Renaissance artists decorated this parish church (late Gothic architecture) which houses the shrine of bishop Ulrich in flamboyant style. Together with the protestant **church of St. Ulrich** it marks the end of **Maximiliansstrasse**. No other street in Germany could match this "avenue" in terms of spaciousness in the 16th century. Augsburg citizens had gained much wealth through linen weaving and trans-Alpine trade and banking. The palace of the mighty Fugger merchant and banker family saw King Charles V of Spain asking for a credit of more than 500,000 florins–in those days an huge sum–to bribe the princes of the realm before the imperial elections. Thereafter he ruled an empire "where the sun did not set," but needed Jakob Fugger to pay his soldiers. Titian stayed in the **Fuggerhaus** to paint Charles V in 1548.

The **Schaezlerpalais** opposite the Hercules fountain may well be the most extravagant town residence of an Augsburg merchant. Lavish white and gold Rococo ornaments embellish the banquet hall which opened with a ball in 1770, at which Marie Antoinette, on her way to Paris, was present. The plainer rooms house the **German Baroque Gallery**.

The **Zeughaus** (arsenal) quite nearby was the first step in Elias Holl's career as municipal architect in Augsburg. With the construction of the **Rathaus** (town hall: 1615-20), however, Holl created a prime example of a Renaissance building and a masterpiece of architectural harmony. The **Goldener Saal** (golden hall) was restored to its original splendor for the 2,000 years' celebrations in 1985. Festivities four centuries ago gave the town council the idea of the **Augustus fountain**, commemorating the founder of Augsburg. The water-goddesses below him symbolize the four main rivers in and around Augsburg. Adjacent is the **Perlachturm** (257 feet/78 meter) tower built 1646-16 by Elias Holl, topped by an onion cupola and once the city tower. Ascend for a panoramic view from April to October.

Sitting in front of the Rathaus an Perlachturn in Augsburg

The Perlachberg road descends to the traditional artisans' quarter, **Jakober Vorstadt**, integrated into the town's fortifications since the 14th century. The house **No. 7** in Auf dem Rain, a narrow alley to the left, is the birthplace of Bertolt Brecht, founder of modern epic theater.

An old folks home: Not only immense wealth, but also social consciousness is associated with the name Jakob Fugger. In 1514 he founded the **Fuggerei**, the first old people's home in the world, where poor elderly Catholic citizens could apply for a small flat at an annual rent of an old Rhenish florin (1.72 DM today), an extremely low rent which is still valid to this day. The rush and bustle of modern times seem to be banned from this peaceful quarter with its neat rows of 53 houses and gardens (museum at Mittlere Gasse No. 18).

Back at the Rathausplatz, the Karolingenstrasse runs north towards the **Dom** (cathedral) and the episcopal palace. What began with the collapsing walls and ceilings in the 10th century was afterwards to become one of the most interesting cathedrals in Germany. By 1065 the Romanesque nave was completed, followed by the towers, the crypt and the huge bronze doors of the southern entrance (11th century), fantastic masterpieces of metalwork and an extraordinary mixture of biblical and profane themes. Within, the south windows open high up in the nave. The oldest series of framed glass windows in the world feature the five prophets of the Old Testament. In the southern court of the cathedral some Roman fragments of columns and funeral monuments are arrayed along a wall near the foundations of what is believed to have been the first Christian church in Augsburg.

A plaque on the wall informs that the first steps were taken here towards the establishment of a new confession of faith. Thirteen years after Luther had proclaimed his 95 propositions, Charles V summoned protestants and his nobles to an Imperial Diet in Augsburg. Melanchthon, Luther's representative, expounded the basic ideas of the Refor-

e 'uggerei," e earliest cial using velopment the world.

mation which became known as the *Confessio Augustana* and, which remained, with slight alterations, the principles of the new religion. But Catholics and reformers reached neither compromise nor agreement until the third Imperial Diet in 1555 resulted in the *Religious Peace Agreement of Augsburg*. Rulers of a territory could now decide on the religion of their state and citizens of the imperial towns were absolutely free in their choice of creed –in theory. Religious wars and the Thirty Years' War ensured that the new liberality did not become a reality until 1650, when, on August 8, protestants in Augsburg celebrated the peace festivals (*Friedensfest*) since then the only official municipal holiday in Germany.

The Romantic Road runs parallel to the river Lech as it heads south from Augsburg to Landsberg. En route it passes through **Klosterlechfeld** where a Renaissance church by Elias Holl commemorates the Battle of Lechfeld in 955 at which the Hungarians were defeated. **Landsberg**, founded by Henry the Lion, derives its name from an old castle of the Bavarian kings and dukes, the Landespurch, which guarded the border between Bavaria and Swabia. There was good reason for the fortification, as the settlement had the only bridge across the river Lech between Augsburg and Schongau. Merchants were shipping salt, the white gold of the Middle Ages, on the Lech or transporting it from Reichenhall to Lake Constance and they were the best clients. The four town walls and gates to repulse the jealous northern neighbors from Augsburg have been well restored and are interesting spots for the visitor, especially **Bayertor** (1425) in the east, and also **Sandauertor** in the north and **Schmalzturm** on the main square. The town offers superb wedding arrangements with the registry office in the outstanding Rococo town hall (also a tourist information office) designed by Dominikus Zimmermann, who had already proven his artistic talents before he became mayor of Landsberg from 1749 to 1754. The bride and groom are

The Gothic sublime of Ulm minster.

later taken by a horse-drawn coach to the **Johanniskirche** (church) which was also designed and decorated by Zimmermann.

A place which is neither romantic nor open to the public is the **Landsberg fortress**. Here Adolf Hitler wrote *Mein Kampf* (My Struggle) in 1923-24 during a period of imprisonment following the failure of his Munich *putsch*.

South of Landsberg the gently rolling hills introduce the traveler to the Allgäu and the Alps, a landscape formed by glaciers, water and gigantic terrestrial movements. Farmers are proud of their dairy cattle, pretty chocolate-colored cows, and their churches, many of them decorated by Baroque and Rococo artists of the famous Wessobrunn School, which gave rise to the name *Pfaffenwinkel* (clerics' corner) for the area south of Landsberg.

The next important stop on the Romantic Road is **Schongau**, 18 miles (30 km) south of Landsberg and once one of the more important trading-posts on the medieval salt route. The **Ballenhaus** (1515) is a reminder of the town's long established mercantile tradition. Do not miss the trip up the **Hohenpeissenberg**, a mountain near Schongau 3,260 feet (988 m) high from where one can see the full extent of the clerics' corner, 11 lakes and the range of mountains of the Bavarian Alps. From Schongau a country road takes you to **Rottenbuch**, where, from 1737 to 1747, Wessobrunn painters, sculptors and masters of stucco decoration devoted their manifold skills to transforming the Gothic basilica into a flamboyant model of Baroque and Rococo Catholicism.

Considering the 10 years of work needed to alter Rottenbuch, the history of the **Wieskirche** (church on the meadow) is all the more astonishing. Dominikus Zimmermann and his brother Johann Baptist needed just nine years to build this Baroque jewel from scratch (1745-54) which is beautifully situated on a solitary meadows. In 1739 a local farmer's wife had detected tears on an effigy of the flagellated Christ, a sculpture she had found among some

elow, ncient tter box. ight, ayertor in ndsberg.

junk and put up in her house. Hundreds of pilgrims came to the tiny chapel she built on the meadow and this finally prompted the abbots of the Steingaden monastery to invest astronomical sums in a magnificent church. Dominikus Zimmermann designed an oval-shaped nave elongated towards the high altar with the miraculous statue. His brother heightened the impression of brightness and space with his remarkable painted illusion of a vaulted ceiling, which in reality is almost flat. By virtue of its harmony with architecture, stucco and painting, to say nothing of the richness of color, variety of form and use of light, the Wieskirche is an unparalleled masterpiece of south German Baroque.

The Wieskirche was commissioned by the abbots of the former Premonstratensian monastery in nearby **Steingaden**, one of the most important buildings along the salt route on the plain north of the Alps, which was consecrated in 1176. The nave and side-aisles of the basilica and parts of the cloisters are remnants of the original Romanesque structure. The master-builder Dominikus Zimmermann is buried in the monastery.

Royal castles: It is only 13 miles (21 km) from Steingaden to **Schwangau**, which, for many visitors, is the climax of the Romantic Road, since it is the region of the famous royal castles Hohenschwangau and Neuschwanstein, with the mountains as a spectacular backdrop.

Hohenschwangau castle was originally a medieval fortress, which was almost destroyed during the Napoleonic wars. In 1833 the Bavarian king Maximilian II had the castle rebuilt in neo-Gothic Tudor style, decorated with frescoes designed by Moritz von Schwind illustrating the tales of Dietrich von Bern. It was here, high above the Alpine lake, that the fairy-tale King Ludwig II spent his childhood, lost in neo-Romantic yearning for the glory of medieval times; dreams to be realized in the castle of Neuschwanstein.

The attempt to turn illusion into reality proved to be the downfall of the

Romanesque simplicity and Baroqu ornament: Left, cloisters in Steingaden monastery. Below, the Wieskirche

Bavarian King Ludwig II. **Neuschwanstein** surpasses every notion of a fairytale creation. A rock plateau high above the **Pöllatschlucht**, which can only be reached by a footpath, was the spot Ludwig chose for what he planned to be the epitome of a knight's castle. A visit to the Wartburg in Thüringen, where the medieval bards had competed in rhyme and music, gave him the idea. So the centre of this pseudo-romantic palace is the **Sängersaal** (bards' hall) where frescoes depict the main plot of Wagner's opera *Tannhäuser*. With its delicately coffered ceiling, candelabra and chandeliers, it occupies practically the whole of the fourth floor. As one approaches the white towers and pinnacles of the castle, perched on a formidable mass of cold grey granite, it looks like a fantastic theatrical set. In fact, it was a theater decorator, not an architect, who drew the first sketches. This may explain the dreamlike atmosphere. After 17 years of construction, Neuschwanstein was still not completed when the king died in 1886, and the magnificent throne hall seems somewhat grotesque considering how little responsibility Ludwig showed for his realm. He himself spent only 102 days at Neuschwanstein castle.

Both Neuschwanstein and Hohenschwangau offer wonderful views of the **Forggensee** which is the largest reservoir in the Allgäu. The river Lech flows into it and both boat trips and water sport facilities are on offer. At its southern end lies the spa town, leisure and winter sport center of **Füssen,** overshadowed by the 16th-century castle **Hohes Schloss**, once the summer residence of the powerful bishops of Augsburg who controlled the trade route along the river Lech. Don't miss the **Knights' Hall** with its beautifully carved coffered ceiling. If you have not done so until now, then Füssen is an excellent place to taste the Allgäu local speciality *Kässpatzen*. What is it? Just try it! Then decide where to move: east towards Munich, or west towards Lake Constance–for Füssen marks the end of the Romantic Road.

üssen at he foot of he Alps.

THE FAIRY-TALE KING

"The king is dead, long live the king," shouted the Bavarians in March 1864 at the large and impressive figure of the 18-year-old crown prince, Ludwig paced behind the coffin of his father Maximilian II, enroute to the family vault at the Frauenkirche in Munich. Until then, he and his brother Otto had spent most of their time sheltered from the public view in the loneliness of the mountains around Hohenschwangau Castle. Here, in the gloominess of a castle built in the shape of a fortress of the Middle Ages, his highly sensitive psyche underwent imprinting accents.

Ludwig's conception of the world stemmed from the Federalism of the Middle Ages and he considered Louis XIV of France the last absolutist representative of that system.

Since his early youth he reserved his greatest passion for the theater, especially the musical theater of Richard Wagner. Upon being proclaimed king, he rescued the heavily indebted Wagner from creditors. Despite difficulties and personal disappointments, Ludwig II financed almost all the escapades of the eccentric composer and, to the displeasure of his ministers, the premieres of Wagner's operas were more important to the king than tedious state affairs.

Other than Richard Wagner, only his cousin Empress Elizabeth of Austria–better known as Sissy–was able to get close to him. Her beauty and her intelligence were symbols of femininity which deserved the utmost reverence. But Ludwig was unable to love and to care for another woman and became increasingly aware of his homophile disposition. In vain he fought against this "sin." Constantly being on the run from the watching eyes of the world, he drifted into solitude. The goal of his often sudden flights was, as in his childhood, the remote Bavarian mountains where he build his fantasy castles.

In 1868, his mania for building that was to last till his death, manifested itself for the first time in the construction of Linderhof Castle. Today, the dreamlike structures of Linderhof, Neuschwanstein and Herrenchiemsee are visited by thousands of tourists, and constitute an important source of revenue for the Bavarian tourist office. But for Ludwig II, the last feudal builder of European history, they proved to be the reason for his downfall. The castles not only required the whole of his own private fortune, but also substantial sums of the state budget. Lavishness, the eccentric lifestyle and the lack of leadership of the monarch constituted the main reasons for the notorious proceedings that placed him under guardianship at the instigation of several ministers and royal relatives. On January 8, 1886, the king, without inquest, was diagnosed as suffering from a progressive mental disorder. After a short political struggle, Ludwig II was taken to Berg to Starnberger Lake, where he drowned or was drowned–something that has not been resolved even to this day. It marked a tragic end to the story of the Fairy-Tale King.

Left, Ludwig II, the fairy-tal king. Right, Hohen-schwangau castle.

Along The Alps

Füssen is not only the terminus of the Romantic Road but it is also a transit point on the German Alpine Road (Deutsche Alpenstrasse) running from Lindau on Lake Constance in the west to lake Königsse in the east. The road passes through the grandiose scenery of the Upper Bavarian alpine foothills. The journey is varied, combining both cultural and scenic enjoyment, but the scenery only too easily deceives with its unscathed picture-book world beneath blue southern skies.

One more royal castle: From Füssen the road crosses the Austrian border and re-crosses into Germany via Reutte until **Linderhof Castle** is reached. In the solitude of the mountains, King Ludwig II of Bavaria built his favorite castle. Following the plans of architect Georg Dallmann, a fantasy Baroque and Rococo structure arose during 1870-79. The 10 relatively small rooms are richly adorned with the almost stifling pomp, having been modeled on the castles of the Sun King Louis XIV.

Two of the most important interior features are the bedroom and the dining room with a table of adjustable height –the Magic Table modeled on German fairy stories. In the large park–only a narrow strip close to the castle was turned into a French garden with the Neptune fountain–are the **grotto** with its lake and a **Moorish pavilion.** It was intended that Richard Wagner's operas would have their premier on a stage in the grotto while Ludwig relaxed aboard his swan-boat on the lake. However, because of poor accoustics this idea was abandoned after one performance. The Moorish pavilion was built for the Paris Exhibition of 1867 and was later purchased by Ludwig. It is said that he smoked his hookah here amidst oriental pomp on hot summer nights.

Oberammergau and its Passion Play: It is only six miles (10 km) through the wide **Graswangtal** to **Oberammergau**, now world-famous for its Passion Plays. In 1633, one in ten of the village's inhabitants died of plague and the survivors pledged as thanks to stage *Christ's Passion* every 10 years (1634 was the first). A commercial enterprise gradually developed and it is now administered by the local council. Strict criteria are used in alloting roles to amateurs: one basic requirement is that the main actor be a native of Oberammergau. The auditorium of the Passion Play theater has 4,800 seats and looks out over the world's largest open-air stage (148 feet/ 45 m) wide, 98 feet/30 m deep). The performance, involving 1,500 Oberammergau people, lasts about six hours. The next performance is due in 1990.

Prominent in Oberammergau's tourist spots are the expensive Upper Bavarian houses with the wide roof overhangs; the facades are decorated with frescoes–the **Lüftelmalerei**. Fine examples are the **Pilatus house** in Ludwig-Thoma-Strasse and the **Rotkläppchenhaus** (Red Riding Hood House) on the outskirts on the road to Ettal. The Baroque church of **St. Peter and Paul** with its superbly painted

'receding ages, he mighty lps, seen rom the ugspitze. eft, nother airy-tale astle: inderhof. elow, a avarian eauty.

dome fresco by M. Günther is worth seeing. The art of the crucifix carvers existed since the Middle Ages and some of the best examples can be seen today in the **Heimatmuseum**.

In the shadow of the steep mountain **Ettaler Mandl** (5,358 feet/1,633 m) lies the Baroque Benedictine abbey **Kloster Ettal**. The dome fresco (1746) depicts 431 figures painted on 13,993 sq feet (1,300 sq m). The Ettal liqueur, found in souvenir shops, is supposed to have medicinal powers.

A twin community: The steep mountain road, from Oberau following the B23, ascends to **Garmisch-Partenkirchen**, located against the backdrop of the Wetterstein Mountains. For the 1936 Olympic Games the two local communities were fused into a twin community with apartment blocks and wide streets. The new hidden picturesque corners of this medium-size town which were then apart thus are found on the fringes.

In Garmisch, a row of splendid houses stands around **Marienplatz**. These include the *Alte Apotheke* (pharmacy) with its black and white graffito facade, and opposite, the house with a richly carved oriel (now a branch of the Raiffeisenbank). The stucco work on the adjoining Baroque church of **St. Martin** was created by the celebrated Wessobrunn artists Michael Schmidt and Leonhard Bader. On the other side of the Loisach river lies the old Gothic church of At. Martin with its 23 feet (7 m) high interior fresco depicting St. Christopher. Nearby, some beautiful Upper Bavarian houses stand in the Frühlingsstrasse. On the way, you pass the old **Husar inn** (closed) with its false window; leaning out are a painted-on dragoon and a hussar. The villa of the celebrated opera composer Richard Strauss stands in the center of a large lawn at the end of Zoppritzstrasse.

Two **Olympic stadiums** are in Partenkirchen–the ice skating and the skiing stadiums. Away from tourist sights, a flight of steps (five minutes from the forest path) on the west slope of the Wank leads to the late Baroque votive chapel of **St. Anton** (18th century). The dome fresco by the Tyrolean painter Johannes Holzer is a masterpiece, the small room receiving depth from the fake architecture depicting scenes from the life of St. Antonius.

Germany's highest mountain, the **Zugspitze** (9,730 feet/2,966 m), can be reached by the rack-railway from Partenkirchen or much faster by the cable railway from nearby lake **Eibsee**. On a clear day the view encompasses Santis and the Grossglockner and the ridge of the Bohemian Forest. Southwest of the **Schneefernerhaus** (Germany's highest hotel with a sunbathing terrace) is the **Zugspitzplatt**, the highest skiing area in Germany.

One of nature's special experiences is the walk from Garmisch-Partenkirchen through the romantic **Partnachklamm**, where tunnels and galleries lead through a steep craggy gorge past waterfalls and a foaming mountain torrent.

An excursion to Mittenwald: Surrounded by arms of the Wetterstein Mountains and the high peaks of Karwendel, Mittenwald some 12 miles (19 km) from Garmisch-Partenkirchen has

"... and what do you think of me?"

preserved much of its village character. Until the end of the 17th century this market town was a major staging post on the old trade route from Italy to Augsburg. It became world-famous for violin construction when Mathias Klotz (his statue stands before the church) returned from Cremona to his hometown. He learned the trade from the great Stradivari and passed his knowledge on to his own countrymen. There are still six violin makers in Mittenwald. The **Violin-Making Museum** in Bellenhausgasse gives an overview of the trade.

The Baroque spire of **St. Peter and Paul**, one of the finest in Upper Bavaria, is the village landmark. The celebrated Wessobrunn master builder Josef Schmuzer created the Baroque room with its stucco decoration. A large number of well-preserved Rococo *Lüftelmalereien* decorate the street houses at the **Obermarkt**.

Mountain lakes: On the way back to **Wallgau**, it is worthwhile detouring through the gentle rolling meadows on the side road to **Klais**, passing by lakes **Lautersee** and **Ferchensee**. An extension of this tour leads to Germany's highest mountain lake, the **Walchensee** (2,630 feet/802 m) which is surrounded by the steep Karwendel and Wetterstein mountains. The sweeping panorama, taking in the Hohen Tauern, the Grossglockner and the Zillertal and Ötztal glacier world may be enjoyed from the **Herzogstand** (5680 feet/1731 m), which can be reached by a chair lift.

The **Kesselbergstrasse** descends in hairpin bends down to lake **Kochelsee**. Just before the village of **Kochel**, a side road branches left to the **Walchensee power station**–the first German high pressure storage power station during 1919–24. In Kochel, the **Franz Marc Museum** is worth a visit; Marc was a celebrated German expressionist and a founder member of the *Blue Rider* artists' group. Visits to the Baroque abbey of **Benediktbeuren** at the foot of the Benediktenwand (5,909 feet/1,801 m) and the **Open-Air Museum Glentleiten** near Grossweil, with its Bavarian farmhouses are worthwhile.

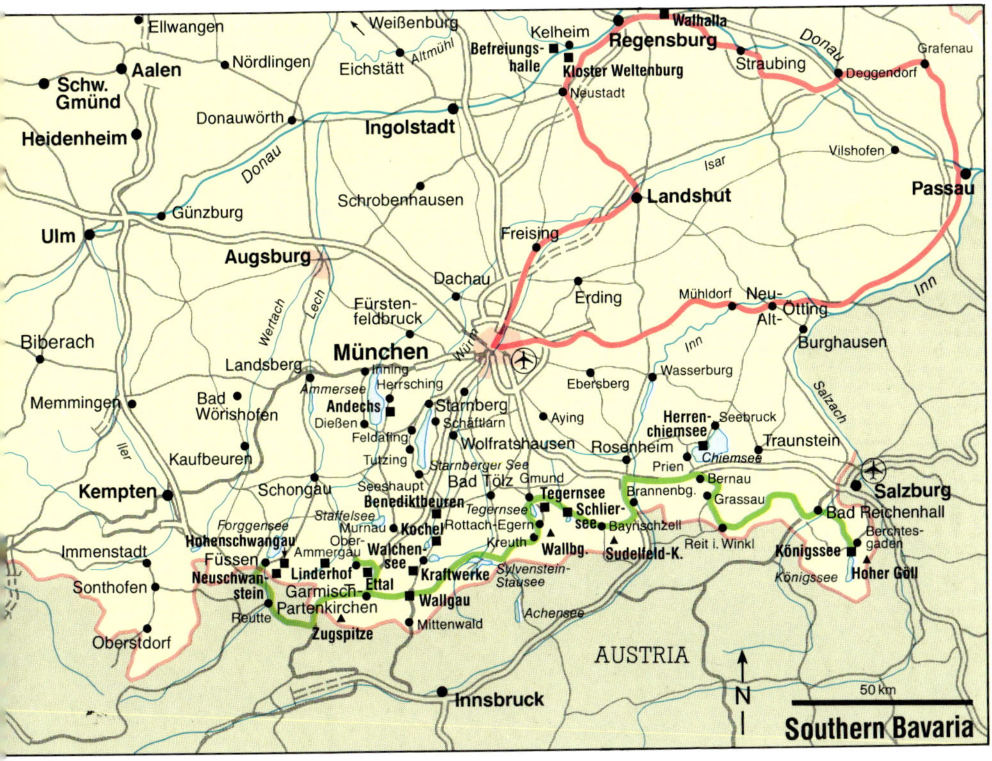

On the alpine road again: Without this excursion to Klais, the route follows the main through-road towards Mittenwald and branches off from this road towards **Wallgau**. The narrow forestry toll road beyond Wallgau follows the natural east-west course of the Isar river with many bends, passing through the thick forest of the **Karwendel Mountains' Nature Reserve**. The elongated **Sylvenstein-Stausee** (dam) in the Isar Valley (Isarwinkel) is two sq miles (six sq km) large and 131 feet (40 m) deep when the water level is normal. After its construction in 1959, the old poachers' village of **Fall** was drowned. A series of sentimental novels by the local writer Ludwig Ganghofer was set here. The new village with the same name was built on a slope above the lake. The best view of the lake is from the wide-arched bridge **Faller-Klammerbrücke**.

From here the tour continues via the Achenpass (3,087 feet/941 m) towards **Kreuth**, a winter resort. Just before Kreuth, a small excursion to **Wildbad Kreuth** is worthwhile. Steep mountain walls overshadow the long, isolated spa hotel. In the elegant foyer, chalybeate spring water splashes into both fountain basins. A plaque records that Czar Nikolaus I and Czarina Alexandra Feodorowna took the waters here in 1838.

A sign beyond Kreuth indicates the cable-car valley station to **Wallberg** (5,650 feet/1,722 m), the starting point for moderately difficult mountain walking in summer. In winter, alpine skiers head for the summit.

Round lake Tegernsee: In the middle of a picture-book landscape with gentle meadow slopes lies lake **Tegernsee**. The monks discovered it first; then came the Bavarian royal family, the Wittelsbachers; and later celebrated artists and singers who settled here. Before, during and after the last war politicians also lived here, followed by Germany's jet-set of the post-war economic boom. The expensive shore land is almost wholly privately owned.

The twin community of **Rottach-Egern** lies at the lake's southern end below the Wallberg. Egern's landmark

Richly decorated farmhouses.

is the Gothic spire of the church of **St. Laurentius**. The altar by Johannes Georg Asam (1690) is worth seeing. The graves of the writer Ludwig Thoma, the poet Ludwig Ganghofer and the celebrated tenor Leo Slezak are found in the churchyard.

Tegernsee town was once the site of influential Benedictine abbey which, after secularization, became a royal castle. All that now remains is the **Church of St. Quirin**. Beyond the Baroque doorway a triple-nave basilica with a ceiling fresco by Johannes Georg Asam opens out. Imposing examples of Upper Bavarian houses can still be found off the busy main road. Another sight is the **Olaf Gulbransson Museum** which contains beautiful, tender portraits by the eponymous Norwegian painter (1873-1958) and famous caricatures which were drawn for the satirical magazine *Simplicissimus*.

Spas and salt: Just before **Gmund**, the road branches off to lake **Schliersee**, with its village of the same name which is a peaceful oasis, especially after busy Tegernsee. The tour proceeds through hilly pastureland with large individual farmsteads at the foot of the Wetterstein range and passes **Bayrischzell**, whose many pseudo-Bavarian buildings appear rather out of place in summer. Then the German Alpine Road climbs steeply in a series of hairpin bends to the skiing paradise **Sudelfeld** (3600-4800 feet/ 1081-1441 m) and threads its way through the steep, rugged walls of the Tatzelwurm (toll). In the dark gorge one is inclined to believe the medieval legend about a dragon barring the way.

Beyond **Brannenburg-Degerndorf** the route crosses the motorway on the German side and winds along side roads via Bernau and Grassau to **Reit im Winkl**. This winter sport resort has good snow especially at the **Winklmoosalm** (3,806 feet/1,160 m), and four clear mountain lakes at other times of the year and it is fantastic for rambles.

The route winds through villages such as **Inzell**, past country inns with beer gardens under old chestnut trees, to **Bad Reichenhall**. The concrete tower

he sign f the guest ouse *Zum chwan*.

blocks may give a poor first impression but a visit to the old town center with its spa will soon counter that. The houses around the spa garden have a distinct air and reveal the splendor of this spa at the turn of the century. In the **Gradierhaus**, liters of the saline water drip daily over the high brushwood grating. The salt content of the air rises due to evaporation, thus giving a healing effect.

The last section of the German Alpine Road is undoubtedly one of the most beautiful Alpine panorama roads. Nearly every bend provides a new and surprising view of the grandiose mountain world of the **Berchtesgadener Land**, whose dominant summit is the **Watzmann** (8,900 feet/2,713 m), Germany's second highest mountain.

Emperor Friedrich I Barbarossa founded the present mountain spa **Berchtesgaden** when he granted the local Augustinian monks the prospecting rights for salt and ore. They discovered the salt, whose deposits have not yet been exhausted. Visiting the **salt mine** is an experience. Dressed like a miner, you travel on the "Hunte" about 1,640 feet (500 m) deep into the mine. In addition to the guide's talk, a film explains the rock salt extraction, the *Sole* (brine) being pumped to Bad Reichenhall. The foundation church **St. Peter and Johannes** (high Gothic) is also one of the sights. The **Schloss**, a former abbey, was home of the popular Bavarian Crown Prince Rupert until 1938. The complex has been added to over seven centuries and has features of the Romanesque, Gothic and Renaissance. Noticeable in the old town center are the Upper Bavarian houses with their pastel-colored facades and delicate stucco. The Lüftelmalerei of the former **Gasthaus zum Hirschen** depicts Bavarian cuisine on the Metzgerstrasse-side.

Hitler's holiday resort: One of the best scenic experiences is the car ride on the **Rossfeld-Höhenstrasse**. The vantage points provide splendid views of peaks such as Watzmann, Hoher Göll, Tennengebirge (range), Steinernes Meer and Dachstein (9,695 feet/2,995 m).

Obersalzberg (3,346 feet/1,020 m) on the north slope of the Hoher Göll was Hitler's favorite spot. In 1835 he had an imposing house built here and received state guests. The house was demolished in 1952 and its ruins are now overgrown. Special buses ascend the **Kehlsteinhaus** (6,345 feet/1,934 m). Hitler's tea house **Adlerhorst** (eagle's nest), is reached by a ski-lift. It is now a restaurant with great views on all sides.

The tour's crowning finale is the boat trip on the lake **Königssee**. The waters of the lake which lies in the middle of the **Berchtesgadener Land Nature Reserve**, are crystal clear . Peak season (the boats do not travel in winter) sees tourists passing through the village of Königssee to the jetties. It is quieter at the **Malerwinkel** (20 minutes on foot) on the east bank, a scene often being portrayed by painters and recorded by photographers. The apses of the **Chapel of St. Bartholomä** along the boat trip are also points of interest. The former hunting lodge of the Prince-Bishop is now a restaurant with a beer garden. A footpath snakes from the lake's southeast end to the small **Obersee**.

Left, St. Bartholomä on lake Königssee. Right, winter mag in Ramsau

Munich: The Secret Capital

The Bavarian capital, with 1.3 million inhabitants, is the third largest German city after Berlin and Hamburg. Its location on the Isar River at the edge of the Alps, surrounded by lakes, with an incomparable range of sporting and cultural activities, acts like a magnet to draw not only Germans, but also foreign visitors. Even the rational *Encyclopedia Britannica* gushes when describing Munich: "a combination of German practicality with Alpine romanticism, or urban thinking with a rural way of life. Although it is thoroughly modernized, it retains something of the genial sociality of the old royal Bavaria."

However, Munich is also a city of art and culture. Its numerous museums and collections are world-famous, as are its music and theater. No other city produces so many films and television programmes. Munich studios are Europe's largest and most modern. The city is not just an international theater and music metropolis: it is also the leading German university center with almost 100,000 students. No wonder that Munich has more publishing houses than any other German city. Apart from this, Munich is now Germany's number one fashion, fair and congress city. The last few decades have seen Munich become one of West Germany's most important economic regions and international companies such as Siemens, BMW, MBB, MTU are based here.

Nevertheless, Munich has, in many ways, preserved a village character and a quiet contemplativeness which is based on the cultivation of Bavarian culture and traditions and its people's profound love of the homeland. This is why Munich is known by the accolades: village of a million; world city with a heart; the unofficial capital city.

A monk's settlement: Officially, Munich dates from A.D. 1158, but a monks' settlement with the name *Munichen* (meaning monks in High German) was already mentioned in a document of A.D. 777. In 1158, Duke Henry the Lion had the bridge over the Isar which belonged to the Bishop of Freising removed, and set it up near Munich. With this one stroke he moved the salt trade route from Reichenhall to Augsburg, thereby pocketing the high taxes levied on this valuable commodity. Emperor Friedrich Barbarossa legalized Henry's action, and soon awarded the new, rapidly-growing parish the right to hold markets and mint coins. The foundation was thus laid for the city's political and economic development, whose name was soon inseparable from that of Wittelsbach. In 1180, the Platinate Count Otto von Wittelsbach was awarded the imperial land of Bavaria by the emperor, and his House then guided the fate of Bavaria for almost 800 years until 1918.

In 1504, Duke Wilhelm IV (1493-1550) selected Munich from all other Bavarian cities to be his residence and the Bavarian capital. The enlargement of the city which began in the 14th century now accelerated, especially under Maximilian I, the Great (1573-

Preceding pages, view of Munich from the English Garden. Below, Mary's Column on Marienplatz

1651) who became Elector in 1623. Munich was also affected by the Thirty Years' War (1618-48). In 1632, the city surrended to the Swedes, who occupied and sacked it for 10 days. After the war the erection of the Mariensäule (Mary Pillar) in front of the Town Hall marked a period of building activity, the high Baroque style experiencing a new blossoming in Munich. Under Prince Max II Emanuel (1679-1726) Munich attained cultural and political rank in Europe.

The following century saw Munich involved in wars and occupation, and, as a result, famine and poverty struck the city. At the start of the 19th century the French occupied Munich for one year and were followed by the Austrians. After the alliance with Napoleon in 1806, as a result of which Bavaria became a kingdom, the city took on a new luster. The influence of Napoleonic political doctrine and secularization, with the dissolution of the monasteries, their property going to the state, and a complete administrative reform, all contributed to Bavaria, and thus Munich, experiencing new political, economic and cultural development. In 1819 the First Bavarian Parliament was opened. With the building of the National Theater and the Prinz-Carl-Palais and the development of the Maxvorstadt, the city's rise to a classical metropolis was assured. Ludwig I (1825-48) is considered to be the second founder of Munich, having had a great influence on the present face of the city.

Capital of the Movement: After the death of Ludwig II, the fairy-tale king, Munich developed into a large modern city under the government of Prince-Regent Luitpold (1886-1912); over 500,000 inhabitants were recorded in about 1900. But hunger, poverty and depression also came to Munich during and after World War I; the revolutionary "pressure from the streets" caused Ludwig III, the last Bavarian king, to abdicate in November, 1918. For the next six months there were bloody street battles which left about 600 dead. It occurred after Kurt Eisner called out the Bavarian Soviet republic in Munich

elow, locken-iel in the unich ty hall. ight, njoying osmopoli-n life on arienplatz.

and shortly thereafter was murdered. The revolution was put down and a new tragic chapter in German history opened, its first lines written in Munich.

It was in Munich that Adolf Hitler rose from being an ordinary member to leader of the NSDAP. On November 8, 1923, he believed himself to be strong enough to call for the fall of the Bavarian and national government. His attempted *putsch* failed; his demonstration on November 9 was forcibly broken up at the Feldherrnhalle, with 16 people meeting their deaths. Since then Munich has been called the capital city of the (National Socialist) movement–an expression which attained an internationally tragic dimension with the 1938 Munich Agreement. World War II led Munich to the edge of catastrophe; about 70 air raids turned the city into a pile of rubble. Today there is nothing in Munich to remind the visitor of this dark period in the city's history. It is now full of life and a kind of total urban artwork awaits the visitor.

Munich's front parlor: One of the busiest squares in Munich, **Karlsplatz**, which is not far from the main station, also known as *Stachus* to the people of Munich, is the starting point of Munich's pedestrian precinct–its front parlor. At the end of the 18th century, Karlsplatz and its imposing **Karlstor** (gate) of 1315 were part of the city walls. A stroll through the pedestrian zone leads past the **Richard Strauss Fountain**, **Deutsches Jagdmuseum** (German Hunting Museum), and **St. Michael's Church**, one of the most famous Renaissance churches in Germany with its Wittelsbach family tomb. On your way, spend a few minutes listening to one of the numerous street musicians–if it is not raining.

Some way up, the Liebfrauenstrasse leads to Munich's landmark, the Late Gothic red brick **Frauenkirche** (Church of our Lady) with its 330 feet (99 m) and 333 feet (100 m) high domed towers. It is just about the most famous and one of the largest Munich churches, being 363 feet (109 m) long and 120 feet (36 m) wide. Consecrated in 1494, it is

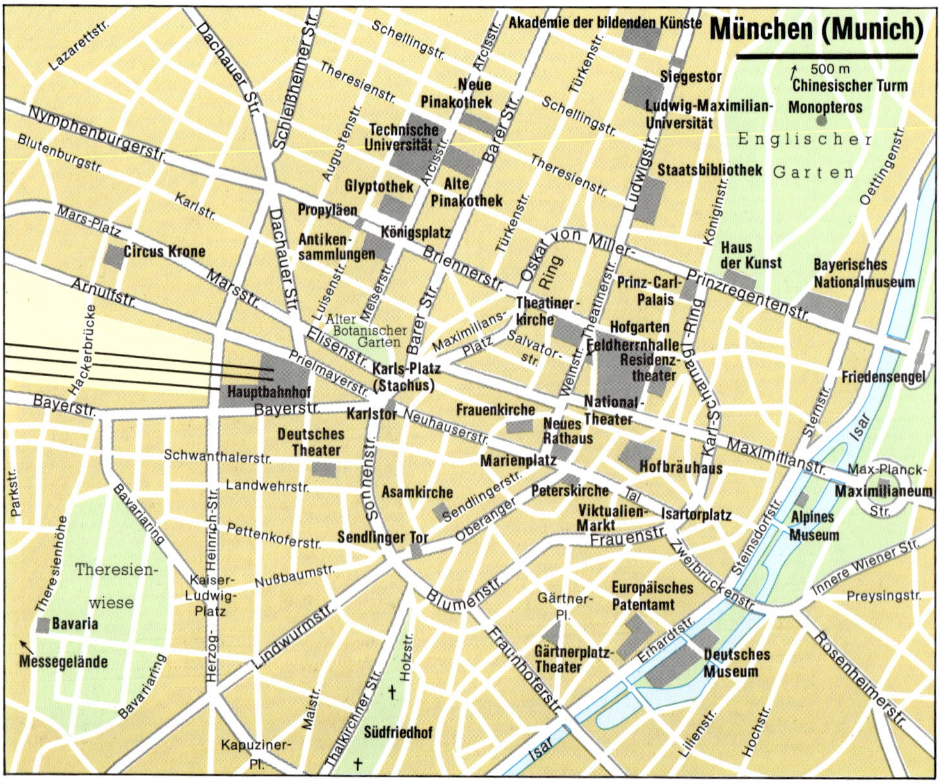

LIQUID BREAD

Medieval monks first mastered the process of making a strong beverage from roasted and fermented barley called beer, and enjoyed this strengthening liquid during their fasting period, Lent. Even today, beer is often referred to as *liquid bread* and is the staple of a German's daily diet. Until now, beer remains the No. 1 beverage in Germany and the Germans are still renowned as the world's greatest beer drinkers.

Yet, this cool and fresh drink with a golden color and a firm foam on top is much more sophisticated than the beverage drunk at the turn of the 15th century. Then it was a dark and sticky liquid to which honey, juniper or myrtle were added. However, after the Dark Ages, the brewers developed a new, successful specialty. By using hops in the brewing process, beer obtained not only its strong and refreshing taste, but also durability. Drive on the *autobahn* from Nuremberg to Munich and you will pass the largest hop-growing area in Germany. In the summer in the typical *Hopfengarten,* these plants grow to 16 feet (5 m) high.

Throughout the year Germans drink vast quantities of beer–about 35 gallons (160 liters) per person. They produce 21 million gallons (94 million hectoliters) annually. Diversity is a strong feature and there are 1,300 different breweries today, although this is 336 fewer than 10 years ago. Of these, 900 are located in Bavaria alone where many are small breweries in the countryside that have not yet been bought out by the large ones such as Löwenbräu, Henninger or Schultheiss.

The characteristics of beer are twofold: light and dark with two different proofs. The lighter proof is *Vollbier* (97 percent of all German beer) with less than 4 percent alcohol. In this group are *Lager, Export*, and *Märzen*. The stronger proof has up to 5.5 percent alcohol and includes *Bock, Doppelbock* and names ending with "...ator," such as *Salvator* or *Optimator*.

'ne erson's ork is nother's leasure!

a testimony to the self-confidence and pride of Munich burghers during the medieval period of prosperity. The Frauenkirche contains the tombs of 46 Wittelsbach princes in its crypt, as well as the tombs of various cardinals of the archbishopric of Munich-Freising. The south tower affords a wonderful view overlooking the city to the Alps, which seem to be at Munich's gates whenever there is the *Föhn*, a Munich specialty. The *Föhn* is a warm, dry mass of air from the Alps which gives the city a few extra sunny days a year, and also produces headaches and irritability.

From Frauenkirche a number of small streets on the right lead to **Marienplatz**. Its layout and atmosphere resembles an Italian square. Here are the **Mariensäule** (Column of the Virgin) the **Rathaus** (Town Hall) and **Altes Rathaus** (Old Town Hall) and, in the background, the towers of St. Peter's. It is the heart of Munich, where the folks of Munich and visitors from overseas mingle daily, or make themselves comfortable on the garden seats of the nearby taverns. Here women in *Dirndl*, (traditional Bavarian rural dress), and men in leathershorts or *Loden* suits, sit next to people dressed in London or Italian fashions from the posh boutiques.

The imposing **Rathaus** (town hall) decorated ornately in the neo-Gothic style with its 283 feet (85 m) high tower, dominates the square. It was built between 1867 and 1908. Punctually at 11 a.m., and between May and October at 5 p.m., you should be in Marienplatz, opposite the Rathaus, to view the **Glockenspiel** (carillon) in the tower. It shows two episodes from Munich history: a tournament held on Marienplatz in 1568, and the *Schäfflertanz* (dance of coopers) commemorating the end of the plague in Munich in 1517.

The **Altes Rathaus** on the eastern edge of Marienplatz was built between 1470-74. Its Gothic hall is one of the most magnificent in Germany, and the only structure apart from the tower of the Altes Rathaus to be reconstructed just like the original after its near total destruction in the last war. It was deco-

View towarc the Theatiner Church

rated in the same manner as the original carvings which had been saved, such as with a frieze of coats of arms from the carved barrel-vaulted ceiling of 1480.

Opposite the Altes Rathaus is the **Heiliggeistkirche** (Church of the Holy Ghost) originally from the 14th century, and renewed in the colorful Rococo style between 1724 and 1730 by, among others, the Asam brothers. The church contains the celebrated **Hammertal Virgin**, a wooden sculpture from the 15th century. Next to the church is the entrance to the **Viktualienmarkt**, a special piece of Munich and Munich life. *Viktualien* is an old word for food, and almost every kind of food can be bought here–from radish to venison, local produce from the country around Munich, and international produce including fish, fruit, vegetable and cheese specialties, Bavarian beer and vintage French wines. It is a land of milk and honey, being both international and Bavarian at the same time. The market women are responsible for this with their ready–sometimes coarse–wit and Munich humor; earthy, quick, but also melancholy and profound.

A passage leads up to *Alter Peter*, as **St. Peter's Church**, the oldest parish church in Munich, is popularly known. The church was destroyed during the last war, but has been reconstructed in its original form. Today, it is again the most richly decorated church in the city. The **Schrank Altar**, named after its contributor, was constructed in 1407, and is one of the oldest and most important altars in Bavaria.

One can pass via the **Rindermarkt** (Cattle Market) diagonally opposite *Alter Peter* into **Sendlingerstrasse** with its **Asamkirche**, a church built by the Asam brothers between 1733 and 1746, and a true jewel of southern German Rococo architecture. The church's interior and exterior are richly decorated; the dominating colors are red-brown and gold, which gives the church an almost mystical air. The **Munich Stadtmuseum** (City Museum) is only a few steps away from the Asam Church. The building, originally the city stables and arsenal from the 15th century, houses permanent and special exhibitions depicting cultural phases in the city's history, such as Munich living styles from 1700 to 1900 or the history of German brewing. (Daily, except Mondays, 9 a.m.– 4.30 p.m.)

Cultural metropolis: Munich is not only Germany's beer capital, but it is also an artistic and cultural metropolis as evidenced by the large number and variety of its museums. The smallest and most original is only a short walk away from Marienplatz in the imposing **Isator**, once part of the city wall opposite the Isar Bridge (1314). In the Curiosities Show of the **Valentin Musäum** (so named, and mispronounced, after the celebrated vernacular singer with his typical, profound Munich humor) you can laugh heartily at a "wonderful, but melted statue of snow."

After this entertaining excursion you cross the Isar, and arrive at what is probably the most famous museum in Germany: the **Deutsches Museum** (German Museum) which is situated on an island in the Isar. This, the largest museum of science and technology in the world, was founded by Oskar von Miller in 1903, and opened in 1925. Over an exhibition length of more than 10 miles (17 km), more than 15,000 exhibits of all sizes demonstrate mankind's scientific and technological history. Almost everything is here: a coal mine in the basement, a planetarium under the roof dome, a trapped alpha particle in the cloud chamber, the first Benz car of 1885-86, the 140-million-year-old fossil of an ichthyosaur, the world's first jet aircraft (an Me262) and even Wernher von Braun's first multi-staged rocket. It would take days, even weeks, to see and to try out–or touch, as the visitor is encouraged–everything in this museum. You can press buttons or levers and feel like a *homo technicus*. For instance, the model of an automatic brick factory spits out tiny bricks as souvenirs.

Emerging exhausted after hours or days in the Deutsches Museum, you can relax with a stroll along the right bank of the Isar as far as the **Maximilianeum**, a building constructed between 1857-74, which towers over the Isar and which today houses the Bavarian *Landtag* (parliament). It is the stately completion of **Maximilianstrasse**, conceived at that time as a grand avenue, which it still is, in spite of the many elegant shops, cafes, boutiques and private galleries. Going down the street towards the town center, one passes the **Völkerkunde-museum** (Museum of Anthropology) with its rich ethnological collections, and then the Munich **Kammerspiele**, one of the best German theaters.

Wittelsbach residence: A few paces further Maximilianstrasse enters the expansively round **Max-Joseph-Platz** which is in the middle of the earlier centers of Wittelsbach influence. (Those who do not visit the Deutsches Museum and Maximilianeum can get here in a few minutes from Marienplatz via Dienerstrasse). The **Alter Hof**, the first palace of the Bavarian dukes in Munich, was built in the 13th century, and extended in the 15th. Its historic character, has, despite modernization, been preserved in the inner courtyard.

The **Residenz** (Palace) on Max-Joseph-Platz is historically and artistically Munich's most important collection of buildings. Construction began at the end of the 16th century with the core being several buildings of the former Residenz which was built in 1385 and extended several times. New buildings, designed by outstanding artists of the Renaissance, Baroque and the Classic periods were added until 1835. The Wittelsbach, who guided Munich's fate for 800 years, resided here until the abdication of the last Bavarian king in 1918. The Residenz has been open to the public as a museum since 1920. Starting at the **Königsbau** on Max-Joseph-Platz (in which the Residenz Museum is housed) the Residenz site includes (clockwise): the **Alte Residenz** (Old Palace) **Festsaalbau** (Ballroom) **Cuvilliés Theater**, **Allerheiligenhof-kirche** (All Soul's Church), **Residenz-theater** (New Palace Theater) and **National Opera** which overlooks Max-Joseph-Platz with its impressive columns. The individual building complexes are linked by no fewer than eight inner courtyards, through which the visitor can walk to the other collections of the Residenz including the **Schatz-kammer** (Treasury) and the **Egypt Collection**. In the **Antiquarium**, state receptions still take place, as do gala concerts in the **Herkulessaal**. (Daily, except Sundays and Mondays, 10 a.m.–4 p.m., Sundays 10 a.m.–1 p.m.)

A visit to Schwabing: After your tour of the Residenz you can pass from Max-Joseph-Platz via Residenzstrasse to **Odeonsplatz** with its **Feldherrnhalle**, completed in 1844 by F. von Gärtner and imitating the Loggia di Lanzi in Florence. In 1923 this was the site of bloody clashes between police and Hitler's party cohorts a day after his appearance in the Bürgerbräukeller. The ochre double towers and imposing 236 feet (71 m) high dome of the adjoining Baroque **Theatiner Church** which was built in the 17th century also suggest Italian influence. The towering church stands to the left of the Feldherrnhalle. Its interior has a magnificent high altar and Wittelsbach tombs.

Modern Bavarian beauty.

Odeonsplatz marks the beginning of **Ludwigstrasse**, planned by Ludwig I as a street of grandeur and built by the architects F. von Gärtner and Leo von Klenze. The street is bordered on both sides by neo-classical facades, including the **Bavarian State Library**, one of the largest libraries in the world, and, shortly before the Siegestor (Victory Gate) the **University**. The **Siegestor** is vaguely similar to the Brandenburg Gate, and stands with its four-in-hand on top exactly one kilometer north of the Feldherrnhalle. It was erected in 1850 as a memorial to the Bavarian soldiers killed in the anti-Napoleonic wars of liberation. Today it carries the inscription: "Dedicated to victory – destroyed by war – an exhortion to peace". Beyond the Siegestor is one of Europe's most famous boulevards: the poplar-lined **Leopoldstrasse**, with its ice-cream parlors, pizzerias, cafes, inns, discos and restaurants on both sides of the street. On warm days one can sit outside and see–and be seen–in the midst of exhaust fumes and dense crowds. Leopoldstrasse was once the artery of the legendary and fabled artists' district of Schwabing, which now is mainly, like Schwabing itself, a place of amusement for Munich's visitors.

Vanity fair: To the east of Leopoldstrasse, just a few steps away, is the **English Garden**. The garden is 900 acres (364 hectares) large and ends up north of Munich. Nobody knows exactly where, because it passes into the Isar water-meadows. It is only clear where it begins: just beyond the **Haus der Kunst** (Museum of Modern Art) a vast building from the Nazi period with a famous collection of 20th-century art, including Picasso, Matisse, Dali, Klee and Warhol. From Odeonsplatz, the fastest way is through the **Hofgarten** (north of the Residenz) beautiful gardens laid out from 1613-17, with arcaded walks in the west and south. The Haus der Kunst is at the beginning of **Prinzregentenstrasse**, a street of fine buildings from the 19th century, and when you are there you should visit the **National Museum of Bavaria**. It is one

iligree like spider's eb–the lympic omplex.

of the most popular museums in Munich, and offers a walk through the history of European art, especially Bavarian culture and art from the early Middle Ages to the present. (Daily, except Mondays, 10 a.m.–4 p.m.).

The visitor who fails to stroll in the English garden cannot really claim to have visited Munich. The English Garden is much more than a landscaped park laid out in the so-called English style between 1781-85 and boasting a Monopteros (Greek temple), Chinese pagoda, three beer gardens and the Kleinhesselohe Lake for rowing. The Garden is Munich life... It is all things to all people with innumerable improvised football pitches and frisbee lawns; it is a test of courage for those plunging into the waters of the Eisbach, or even riding the waves. It is a huge amateur stage for pantomime, acrobats, Zen Buddhists and musicians; a refuge for tramps, a running track for joggers and a racing track for cyclists. Everyone and everything comes together here: solid citizens, tourists, punks, hippies and dogs in their hundreds, as well as the nudists lolling on the grass or strolling uninhibited arm-in-arm on the gravel paths.

District of art: But perhaps you are not really interested in sunbathing, grill parties and the like because you are a passionate art lover. Well, the district where most of Munich's art treasures are concentrated in is the **Maxvorstadt**. First there is **Königsplatz**, one of the most impressive squares in Munich, lined by neo-classical buildings and recently replanned as a green area. You can get there by underground–U1/8. However, from the Odeonsplatz, it is faster to walk. Architecturally important are the Propylaea, the Glyptothek and the Antikensammlung (Collection of Antiques). These neo-classical buildings were erected under Ludwig I and earned Munich the nickname "Isar Athens." The **Antikensammlung** exhibits world-famous Greek vases, and Roman and Etruscan statuettes, glass and terra-cotta work, while the **Glyptothek** is dedicated to Greek and Roman sculpture. Beyond the **Propylaea**,

Sunbathing naked on the banks of the Isar.

a neo-classical archway, the **Lenbach Villa**, is situated in a beautiful garden. The villa was built in 1890 in the Italian style with balconies and patios for the celebrated Munich painter Franz von Lenbach. The municipal art gallery housed here exhibits the works of Munich artists of the 15th-20th century. Worth seeing are the art nouveau works, those of the New Realism and the comprehensive collection of the *Blue Rider* school represented here by Kandinsky, Marc, Macke, Klee and others.

From Königsplatz, we walk to **Karolinenplatz** with its obelisk erected in 1812 as a memorial to the Bavarians killed in Napoleon's Russian campaign. On the left, Barerstrasse leads to the **Alte Pinakothek**, one of the most important European art galleries with works by the European masters of 14th–18th century, such as Dürer, Rubens, van Dyck, Ghirlandaio and Raffael, (Daily, except Mondays, 9 a.m. –4.30 p.m.; Tuesdays and Thursdays 7 p.m.–9 p.m.). Close by is the **Neue Pinakothek**, re-opened in 1981 after its destruction during the last war, in a new complex designed by Alexander von Branca. About 400 paintings and sculptures provide a review of European art from the antique period, the impressionists, symbolism and art nouveau. (Daily, except Mondays, 9 a.m.–4.30 p.m.; Tuesdays 7 p.m.–9 p.m.)

A summer residence: To celebrate the birth of the heir to the throne, Max Emanuel, the art lover Prince Ferdinand Maria of Bavaria presented his wife Henrietta von Savoyen with some land just outside the gates of Munich in the northwest. **Schloss Nymphenburg**, the summer palace of Bavarian princes and kings, was built here by the Italian master-builder Agostino Barelli, and is one of the most important Baroque castle-and-garden sites in Germany. At the beginning of the 18th century, Max Emanuel had the pavilions, galleries and out-buildings (including the orangeries and stables) built, as well as the building which has housed Nymphenburg porcelain manufacture since 1761. The central edifice with its

he fun of raft-trip ownriver.

marble hall–the candlelight concerts of the Nymphenburg summer festival are held here–and the Wittelsbachs' living and reception rooms in the north and south wings should all be visited. The south wing houses the **Gallery of Beauties** which was commissioned by Ludwig I for the Munich Residenz, and also the **Marstallmuseum** (Carriage Museum) with the magnificent carriages, sleighs and ceremonial vehicles of Bavarian kings and princes. One passes from the garden, laid out in the French style, into the park with its **Badenburg** built in 1721 (containing Baroque baths) its **Pagodenburg** built in 1719, the **Magdalenenklause** (1725) and the **Amalienburg** (1739) completed by Franz Cuvilliés the Elder and a masterpiece of the European Rococo.

Assuming you travel to Nymphenburg by car, and enjoy contrasts, you can reach the **Olympic Park** directly via the Wintrich and Georg-Brauchlc ring roads. The underground line U3 also takes you there. This was the scene of the 1972 Games. After the Olympics, and on the same site, Europe's largest sports and recreation center–the Olympic Park–was set up with the wide concrete bowl of the Olympic Stadium, Olympic Hall, many other sports and recreation facilities and the 960 feet (290 m) high TV tower. From the tower's revolving restaurant, the Alps, which are 31 miles (50 km) away is visible during *Föhn* weather. Lightness is the theme for the architecture of the entire site, whose main element is the 18.5 acres (75,000 sq m) tent-like roof. With modern technology and an ideal blend of landscape with architecture, it realizes its futuristic statement. Not far away is the **BMW museum**, similarly futuristic, a strange structure in the shape of a cup at the foot of the BMW administrative tower consisting of four cylindrical shafts linked close together.

Munich's love of life: The visitor can only have a rough idea of Munich, the "total urban artwork," even if he has visited all the places and "done" everything mentioned until now. Munich is a unique paradox of urbanity and local

Village church on the pre-alpine plai

originality, of the rustic and the worldly, of historic luster and seething business activity; i.e., Munich is full of the love of life. There is always something to celebrate–accompanied by beer and good food.

Munich's Fasching is almost as famous as Carnival in the Rhine region, with all the large city halls being involved. One of the highlights is the dance of the market women on the morning of Fasching's Tuesday in the Viktualienmarkt. Before the Munich dweller can recover from the Fasching, he is already rushing off to the Nockherberg to celebrate Munich's "fifth season," the strong beer festival. Spring sunshine sees people passing their afternoons in the beer gardens at the **Nockherberg** enjoying beer with an especially high wort. This marks the start of the beer garden season, a never-ending festival–weather willing–held under ancient chestnut trees for the rich and the poor, the great and the small. Munich has over 100 beer gardens, where the chestnuts provide shade for the *Mass* (tankard) drinkers, who bring packed lunches. There are small, cozy beer gardens with 60 to 70 seats, but also some huge ones, e.g. the **Pagoda** (6,000 seats) and the **Hirschgarten** (7,000 seats). Anyone who has spent a warm summer evening in a beer garden knows that Munich is not just a city but a state of mind. The end of September then sees the start of the world-famous *Oktoberfest* (or *Wies'n* to Munich folks) on the **Theresienwiese** .

A different festival highpoint is the Munich opera season which is held in July-August every year in the National Opera and Cuvilliés Theater. World-famous performers beef up the Bavarian State Opera in works by Strauss, Wagner and Mozart. *Chanson* evenings and ballet are also offered. The festival programme also includes serenades which are performed in the fountain courtyard of the Residenz, the Nymphenburg summer concerts, and the Schleissheim castle concerts.

Upper Bavarian lakes: Each weekend sees vehicles streaming out of the city,

ishing oat on the hiemsee, e "Bavar- n sea."

their passengers intent on swimming, sailing, surfing, rambling, climbing or skiing in the environs of Munich.

Lake Starnberg (22 sq. miles/57.2 sq. km) south of Munich is, geologically speaking, a former glacial basin surrounded by wooded morainic hills. The lake's present name comes from Starnberg, the town on the northern tongue of the lake, easily reached via the A95/952 or the Munich S-Bahn (train). Here, on sunny days, you can view yachts, windsurfers, paddle boats and rowing boats crowding the water because the lake is one of Munich's most popular recreation places.

From Starnberg, you can visit almost any place on the lake, taking one of the white steamers, to **Pöcking** and **Castle Possenhofen**, or to **Feldafing**, a beautiful shore parish with a Pompeii-style villa where the Austrian Empress Sissy secretly met Ludwig II. The health resort **Tutzing** is known for its evangelical academy and the 2,400 feet (728 m) high **Ilka Heights** gives a great view of the lake. A favorite place for visitors is **Berg** on the eastern shore, with Castle Berg and the shore hotel of the same name. Nearby is the votive church with a cross marking the spot where Ludwig II mysteriously drowned in 1886.

From Berg one can travel through the Isar and Loisach valleys to **Wolfratshausen**. Those who manage to obtain one of the rafts which start from here (they are booked up for years ahead) can enjoy, between May and September, a journey with beer, food, brass band and jazz music on the Isar as far as Munich. It makes for a wonderful trip.

Farther away from Munich than Lake Starnberg is **Ammersee** (Lake Ammer). It is about 22 miles (35 km) to the west, and a little smaller and not so crowded as Lake Starnberg. A remnant of prehistoric glacial activity, it is sanding up gradually as rivers wash sediment into it. The shoreline also has a string of attractive recreational and holiday resorts where it is possible to swim, row, sail and fish. The Ammersee is reached via the A96/B12 or by traveling on the S-Bahn to **Herrsching** which is the best-known resort on the lake. A round-trip of the Ammersee can start in Herrsching, and if the weather is fine, the view of the Wetterstein Ridge of the Alps with the Zupspitze, Germany's highest mountain, is wonderful. Return to Herrsching finally because from here all routes lead to **Andechs**, one of the most famous Upper Bavarian pilgrimage sites and abbeys, whose reputation is based on the fine Andechs beer from the abbey brewery.

Ludwig II's Versailles: The proverbial "coffee jaunt" (a Munich saying) to **Salzburg** has in fact, a real basis. The A8, the most heavily-used motorway in Europe during the holiday period, bringing never-ending traffic jams, takes one to this romantic city in neighboring Austria in about 90 minutes. Another reason for making this trip is to visit the **Chiemsee**, yet another one of Bavaria's countless lakes and its island, Herrenchiemsee. The lake, which borders the motorway, is dubbed "Bavarian Sea" because it covers the largest area of any Bavarian inland water (34.5 sq. miles/85 sq. km).

Prien on the western shore of the lake lies in the delightful landscape of the Alpine foothills with the Chiemgau Alps as a backdrop and is a route frequently taken to Herrenchiemsee and Fraueninsel. **Herrenchiemsee** is the largest (810 acres/300 hectares) of the Chiemsee islands and is known because of Ludwig II's castle which was erected here in 1878, in imitation of Versailles. It was intended as the highest expression of princely splendor and regal might of the Bavarian throne. In summer, the stately mirrored hall is the scene of candlelight concerts. The **König Ludwig Museum** gives a summary of the king's life, and his close association with the theater and architecture. **Fraueninsel**, 30 acres (12 hectares) large, has a picturesque fishing settlement, the Benedictine nunnery St. Maria, and is attractive, providing scenic and cultural significance in Bavarian history. The nunnery has been standing since A.D. 766 and, with its combination of Romanesque, Gothic and Baroque, documents central European architectural history.

Right, the magnificen hall-of-mirrors in the castle c Herren-chiemsee.

EASTERN BAVARIA

Nine out of 10 visitors to Munich consider taking day trips to the Alps, with its attractions of King Ludwig's castles and Oberammergau, but few take time to visit such famous Bavarian towns as Regensburg, Landshut and Passau, with their rich past and well-preserved buildings and monuments. However, those who do so, have the opportunity of seeing an highly fertile and diversified hilly country offering such jewels as medieval Regensburg, the first capital of the old German Empire; Landshut, where Europe's most elaborate historical plays are staged; Passau, "one of the seven most beautiful cities in the world;" the largest hops growing area in the world; and Germany's wonderful first National Park in the Bavarian forest.

Need any more superlatives to stimulate your curiosity? Before you are even 25 miles (40 km) north of Munich proper you will see the collections of the largest museum of religious art in the country as well as one of the oldest breweries in the world in the town of Freising. A further 25 miles north and you can take a boat through the deepest and narrowest stretch of the Danube (Donau) which, with a length of 1,764 miles (2,840 km) is Europe's second-longest river after the Volga.

A town without tourist traps: Make up your mind and leave Munich on the motorway A92 (Deggendorf) on B11 or by one of the S-Bahn trains and within 30 minutes you will approach the **Domberg** (Cathedral Mountain) in one of the oldest towns of Upper Bavaria, **Freising**, with its friendly and well-preserved **Altstadt** (old town), famous for its former Benedictine abbey **Weihenstephan**, the beautiful gardens of Staudensichtungsgarten (free entrance) and several bombastic buildings of the Domberg. These include the 12th-century **Dom** (cathedral) with its Baroque interior by the architect Asam and the **Bestiensäule** (column) in the crypt. Then there is the **Diözesanmuseum**, Germany's largest museum of religious art which includes precious paintings, sculptures and doors saved from churches damaged by bombs. Call 0816/13-021 for a visit to **Weihenstephan**, the world's oldest brewery.

Hops capital of the world: The B301, the German Highway of hops passes through Linden avenues and villages, with richly flowered balconies, into the heart of the **Holledau** or **Hallertau** district, the world's largest hop growing region. Between August 23 and mid-September the strong odor of hops wafts throughout **Wolnzach,** the site of the largest hop festival, which had a coronation of the Queen of Hops. Within three weeks, 12 percent of the world's hops production is harvested around the little towns of Hallertau.

Where the past comes to life: Those interested in witnessing Germany's most important historical pageant play *Die Landshuter Hochzeit 1475* (The Landshut Wedding) must tour the old Ducal town of **Landshut** where revivals of late-Gothic festivities are held.

eft,
forest
plete with
yths and
tories, the
avarian
orest.
ight,
cene at the
andshut
rince's
edding.

Landshut is situated 18 miles (30 km) northeast of Freising on the Isar river and rewards even the casual visitor in non-festival years, because of its magnificent and wholly intact medieval townscape, and vivid impressions of activities in the town's main streets seen today as it was in 1475. See the Gothic redbrick **St. Martin's Church** where the Archbishop of Salzburg married Princess Jadwiga of Poland to the Duke's son Georg in 1475. Walk along the town's main cobbled streets with their painted Gothic gabled houses and follow the route of the wedding procession to the **Town Hall**, where Emperor Friedrich III led the bride in the first *Reigen* dance. You can see the door of the bridal room, a special construction for the important event, which was staged for the glory of the Landshut dukedom but was doomed to failure, because Jadwiga did not give birth to the desired heir to the throne. The tourist office arranges film screenings of the 1985 Landshut Wedding in the *Prunksaal* of the Town Hall.

The old Ducal **Stadtresidenz**, built during the 16th-18th centuries, with its magnificent residential apartments, inner courtyard and arcades, is the only real Renaissance palace this side of the Alps. The Residenz houses several museums, a picture gallery and the **Verkehrsverein** (tourist office).

Landshut is dominated by **Burg Trausnitz**, founded as a castle in 1204 and rebuilt as a Renaissance palace in the 16th century to be the seat of the Wittelsbach Dukes of Lower Bavaria. The **Hofgarten** (park) on the eastern slopes offers great views of Landshut.

From the Isar to the Danube: Follow the B299 from Landshut for 28 miles (45 km) to reach Neustadt. From here is it only 11 miles (18 km) parallel to the course of the Danube river to **Kelheim**, situated at the confluence of the Danube and Altmühl and overlooked by the **Befreiungshalle** (Hall of Liberation) a memorial high above the Danube built by Ludwig I to commemorate the Wars of Liberation (1813-15). The town has gained significance since its grand

The Walhalla, a German Parthenon.

Archaeological Museum was opened. Here, you discover how our forefathers hunted the mammoth 80,000 years ago. In 1983 the museum received the European Museum of the Year Award.

From Kelheim take a walk by the right bank of the Danube to the rocky **Donaudurchbruch** (Danubian defile) the narrowest and deepest part of the Danube, and on to famous **Kloster Weltenburg** (one-hour walk). Most visitors, however, take a boat trip from Kelheim for Weltenburg at 30-minute intervals. The trip along this stretch, where the river breaks through the Jurassic limestone, is one of the highlights in the tour of Eastern Bavaria. Weltenburg's monastic church built during 1715-34 is a South German Baroque masterpiece by the Asam brothers.

While in Kelheim, consider a detour to the **Altmühltal**, a scenic river valley, where the **Prunn castle** (11th century) stands guard on a towering rock, 328 feet (100 m) above the river. As a result of the construction of the controversial Main-Danube canal this lovely valley, a popular recreation area, is being transformed and possibly destroyed forever.

Where history is fun: After a nine-mile (15-km) drive on the B16 from Kelheim, the silhouette of the 2,000-year-old city of **Regensburg** (131,000 inhabitants) comes into view. The former Roman legionary camp *castra regina* established by Emperor Marcus Aurelius has been the seat of a bishopric since the days of the Irish missionary St. Bonifatius (739). After becoming a Free Imperial City in 1245, Regensburg developed into a medieval metropolis of Germany and a hub of European commerce, trading mainly with Italy. It became the regular seat of the *Reichstag* (Imperial Diet) from 1663 to 1806.

This gem of an ancient German city is at the northernmost point of the Danube which is navigable from here downstream to the Black Sea. It did not suffer damage during World War II and presents its treasures of Roman and medieval buildings and monuments with the charm of an ever-youthful modern teacher conveying to his class the idea

astern
avarian
armhouse.

that "history is real fun." Stroll through the streets and alleys of Regensburg and discover at each corner significant medallions, staircases, backyards and *Gasthäuser* (inns) built centuries ago.

The best view of town is from the **Steinerne Brücke** (Stone bridge) a masterpiece of medieval engineering (12th century) which spans the Danube with 16 arches over a length of 1,017 feet (310 m). From here a marvelous view of the stately mansions along the Danube with the 345 feet (105 m) spires of the **Dom** (cathedral), the most impressive Gothic structure in Bavaria (1250-1525) can be enjoyed. Its Treasury contains fine reliquaries, crosses, chalices, vestments, etc. The cathedral is also the home of a world-famous boys' choir, the *Domspatzen*.

Near the cathedral, walk into the former **Bischofshof**, the bishop's residence since the 11th century, now a hotel and restaurant. From here it is only a short walk to the arches and tower of the **Porta Praetoria** with its relics from Roman times. Pass the **Bishop's Palace**, turn right at the Niedermünster church with its fascinating excavations and arrive at the picturesque **Alter Kornmarkt** with the Herzogshof, the residence of the Dukes of Bavaria since A.D. 988, which houses a Ducal Hall with a unique *Wappendecke* (ceiling).

Worth seeing is the **Old Town Hall** with its large Gothic hall, once home to the Permanent Imperial Diet. The cellars of the **Reichstagsmuseum** contain one of the last examples of a medieval torture chamber. German law in those days provided that any criminal who did not confess be released once he survived three days of torture, even if he were found guilty by the court. You can sit in the very seat of the doctor who had to decide when to stop the procedure.

Follow Bachgasse to the Benedictine monastery of **St. Emmeran** which was founded in the 7th century, and became a center of monastic culture. Nearby is the residence of the Princes of Thurn and Taxis who, in 1504, introduced the first mail coach service in Europe.

Sometimes even the most energetic history buffs need a break. Many hotels and restaurants in Regensburg not only have pleasant-sounding names and well-restored guest rooms, but also famous local specialties on their menus. Try the Bischofshof restaurant for *Wels*, a Danube fish, or *Tafelspitz* (boiled beef) at moderate prices. Or drop in at the **Historische Wurstküche**, the oldest cooked-sausage house in Germany.

A hall of fame: Some regard it as the quintessential 19th-century monument and the most important artistic production in Bavaria since the Middle Ages. The **Walhalla**, seven miles (11 km) from Regensburg, is modelled after the Greek Parthenon and was built in 1830-42 according to the plans of Leo von Klenze. It is the result of a contest ordered by King Ludwig I of Bavaria for a German *Ruhmeshalle* (Hall of Fame) to honor famous men and women of the German tongue. From the bank of the Danube a grandiose staircase (358 steps) leads to the massive foundation (115 feet/35 m). From the front terrace and, on a clear day, you can enjoy a view of the Danube valley, and that of

Luxuriant flower ornamentation on a Bavarian forester's house.

the Alps as well. The interior of the 219 feet (67 m) long temple fascinates by virtue of its colors. Each side is subdivided into three sections with the busts arranged in groups around a Victory symbol. According to the founder's will, the Bavarian ministerial committee is authorized every two years to name a famous deceased person and enshrine his/her bust in the Walhalla.

About 25 miles (40 km) north of Regensburg is the town of **Weiden**, famous for its fine china, ceramics, lead crystal vases, chandeliers and ashtrays produced by world-famous companies. Some of them cater mainly to foreign customers, offering "factory sales" and even mail order services.

Those who wish to experience the *Oktoberfest* atmosphere but are visiting Germany in August, might want to settle for a day in **Straubing**. It is only 28 miles (45 km) to the southeast of Regensburg and is on the way to Passau for those traveling on the B8. Straubing's Gäuboden Fair is Bavaria's second largest *Volksfest* and its seven beer halls and giant amusement park attract 900,000 visitors each year. Once in Straubing, on the Danube bank at the edge of the Bavarian Forest, do not miss the majestic 223 feet (68 m) high towngate (14th century) and the unique Straubing Roman Treasure (discovered in 1950) in the Gäuboden-Museum.

Attractions of the Bavarian Forest: North of Straubing, cross the Danube and travel through the fertile district of the **Gäuboden–**Bavaria's granary–where wheat, corn, potato and other vegetable fields are separated by poplars and alders. Then enter the natural woodlands of the hilly **Bavarian Forest**, a range which rises up to such peaks as **Lusen** (4,498 feet/1,371 m) **Dreisessel** (4,521 feet/1,378 m) **Rachel** (4,764 feet/1,452 m) and **Grosser Arber** (4,780 feet/ 1,457 m) and its idyllic lake. The forest extends along the border of Bavaria with Czechoslovakia and in the northeast merges into the Bohemian Forest, thus forming the largest continuous forest area in Central Europe. Dubbed "devil's wall" by the locals, the

he nedieval eauty of legensburg vith athedral nd "bridge f stone".

Pfahl, a 87 mile (140 m) long quartz dike 33 to 330 feet (10 to 100 m) wide which has been weathered out of granite-hard gneiss, cuts through the thickly-forested hills and mountains which sometimes darken the horizon with huge fir, spruce and beech trees. It is a landscape with a beauty of its own, depicted in the works of the well-known 19th-century novelist, Adalbert Stifter.

When tired from driving, stop at one of the little pensions for the night, where you can make your own instant coffee in the family's kitchen. People here live mainly from tree-felling and the timber business, or are involved in the widespread glass industry. Tourism also contributes to this region's economy.

Apart from the various museums illustrating typical features of the region–the Glasmuseum at **Frauenau** (the Bavarian forest is known as the leading European centre of glass production) the silver mine at **Bodenmais** and the forest museum at **Zwiesel**–the main attraction of the Bavarian Forest is the **Bavarian Forest National Park** (46 sq miles/120 sq km) near **Grafenau**. Its well-tended network of paths which is nearly 124 miles (200 km) makes this unique refuge of primeval flora and fauna accessible to the holidaymaker. Before visiting the wolves, bears, lynxes, etc. (fenced in, of course) be sure to see the **National Park-Haus** (1982). Its exhibitions, films and the *Erlebnisraum for Children* make it the best museum of its kind in the world.

Via Grafenau, a tourist center of the Bavarian forest, the road from the National Park merges into the B85. About 12 miles (20 km) before Passau, follow the sign *Museumsdorf Tittling* until you arrive at a reconstructed Bavarian village of 50 farmhouses from the 15th–19th century, some 30,000 artifacts and implements of over 30 different crafts, and the first German elementary school.

City of the three rivers: The city of **Passau** (51,000 inhabitants) was ranked among the "seven most beautifully situated towns in the world" by Alexander von Humboldt because of its unique site at the junction of the rivers

In Passau, the biggest organ in the world.

Danube, Inn and Ilz. This gave Passau the name "city of the three rivers." The original town is on a narrow land promontory, formed by the confluence of the Danube and Inn. The **Mariahilf** church stands beyond the Inn. The **Oberhaus** fortress overlooks the **Altstadt** where the town's churches and houses in Italian style are huddled together.

Here, the visitor can stroll for hours through picturesque alleys and lanes which may remind him of Venice, or have a glance at some of the stately *Delikatessengeschäfte* (gourmet shops) or the 600-year-old pharmacy at the Residenzplatz. Be sure to arrive at the nearby **Domplatz** by 11.45 a.m. to buy tickets for the organ recitals in the cathedral (reconstructed in Baroque style since 1668). From May until September at noon, 90 percent of the Passau visitors come here to listen to the heavenly sounds of the world's largest church organ (17,300 pipes and 231 stops).

Nearby are the structures of the **Old Bishop's Palace** and the **New Bishop's Palace**. Before you walk along the Innkai promenade to the Dreiflusseck (confluence of the three rivers) a visit to the **Glasmuseum** in the majestic rooms of **Wilder Mann** next to the old town hall facing the Danube is recommended. Here are some good examples of 19th-century glass manufacturing from Bavaria, Bohemia and Austria.

Do not miss the view at the **Dreiflusseck**, where you can gaze into the ripples of the yellow-green Danube, the muddy-gray Inn and the peat-brown Ilz. From here, start a Danube journey to Linz, Vienna and the Black Sea. The landscape here is beautiful, as depicted in the works of Adalbert Stifter.

Depending on time schedules and interests, choose one of the routes back to Munich. The fastest option is by the A3 to **Deggendorf**, from where the A92 (or B11) takes you via Landshut and Freising to Munich in two hours. The slower but more interesting option is the A3 to the B12 passing **Altötting** and a chance to visit Bavaria's most popular pilgrimage church, before moving on the B12 to Munich.

erial view f Passau nd its ree rivers.

Lake Constance

Having experienced the magic of the Bavarian royal castles near Füssen, the visitor can either turn east along the German alpine road (pages 181-186) towards Munich, or travel through the attractive alpine foothills Allgäu, towards **Lake Constance (Bodensee)**. This hilly country which forms the foothills of the Alps has broad, rolling meadows with rich pasture dotted with brown and white cows. Its rich agricultural land is known for its cheese. It also has several holiday possibilities: in winter, its hill slopes reaching to the Alps, are populated by skiers; in summer, its lakes attract crowds of bathers; and in spring and autumn come the ramblers.

Lake Constance is Germany's largest inland lake, with a surface area of 208 sq miles (538.5 sq km). It is 45 miles (72 km) long, up to nine miles (14 km) wide, and is 827 feet (252 m) at its deepest point. One hundred and four miles (168 km) of its shores belong to Germany, 43 miles (69 km) to Switzerland, and 16 miles (26 km) to Austria. Thus the traveler exploring Lake Constance has to cross several frontiers.

The shape of the lake is often compared to a shoehorn. Where the heel is pushed into this old-fashioned aid, the Bodanrücken Peninsula at the northwestern end projects into the Lake. South of this peninsula lie Gnadensee, Zeller See and Untersee with the monastery island of Reichenau. The northern shore runs down to the Überlinger See (Lake) with the sub-tropical flower island of Mainau. The lake forms part of the course of the river Rhine, which enters near Bregenz in the east, leaves at Stein in the west and heads for Schaffhausen. Because of the unusually sunny and mild climate along its shores, its fertile slopes support fruit-growing and even wine production.

The silent lion: Lindau, where we start circling Lake Constance, is an island town on German soil, and is linked to the mainland by a road and rail bridge. The town's history can be traced as follows: in 15 B.C. the Romans formed a military base on the island. Then fishermen settled here, before a foundation for aristocratic ladies was established in the 9th century , an event which influenced the town's future. It was declared a Free Imperial City at the end of the 13th century and economic boom began with the creation of the Lindau Messengers. This messenger service–a novelty then–undertook work between Italy and northern Europe. The year 1496 climaxes the town's history: the town hall was the venue of a meeting of the Imperial Parliament. In 1803, Lindau lost its Free Imperial City status. In 1806 it passed to Bavaria, to which it still belongs.

The tourist center is the **Seehafen** (harbor) with its broad promenade, hotels and many welcoming cafes. Here, on its homeground, you can drink a glass of Lake Constance wine, considered to be one of the best in Germany, but not normally sold elsewhere. The harbor basin entrance is flanked on one side by the 108 feet (33 m) high lighthouse, on the other by the Bavarian symbol, the lion, which cannot roar because the sculptor forgot its tongue. The **Mangturm** (Tower) is all that remains of the old fortress and stands in the middle of the promenade. From here it is only a few paces to the **Reichsplatz** with its **Lindaviabrunnen** (Fountains) at the back of the **Old Town Hall** (Rathaus) which was built in the Gothic style between 1422–36, and which today bears signs of alterations during the Renaissance. The front and back are decorated with splendid frescoes depicting episodes from the Imperial Diet.

Wealthy citizen and patrician houses with businesses under arcades along the **Maximilianstrasse** bear witness to the former prosperity of the people of Lindau. On a fine day this is a pleasant small town: many of the restaurants and cafes have their tables and chairs on the pavement; vegetable barrows exhibit a morning-fresh selection; and street musicians provide entertainment.

Northwest of Maximilianstrasse stands the **Brigands' Tower** (Diebesturm) on the island's highest point.

eft, trip 'ound the arbor in ndau.

adjacent is the Romanesque **Peterskirche** (church) with frescoes from the Passion story which are attributed to Holbein the Elder. At the **Marktplatz**, with its ancient cobblestones, the town's two most important churches stand opposite one another. Behind the plain facade of the former foundation church, **Maria Himmelfahrt**, lies a splendid Baroque room with rich stucco decor. Across, simple light-green stucco circles are the only decoration on the Protestant church **St. Stephan**. The main feature of its modest interior is the impressive Baroque organ in the gallery. Another splendid sight on the marketplace is the Baroque painting of the facade of the **Haus zum Cavazzan** (No. 6). Today a museum, the municipal art exhibition on show here is one of the largest in the Lake Constance region.

On the Austrian side: From Lindau it is just six miles (10 km) to **Bregenz**, the capital of the Austrian land Vorarlberg. The old buildings of this very provincial-looking town are almost overpowered by the heavy concrete facades of modern purpose-built structures. Bregenz is full of life in July and August when the world's largest marine stage provides the evening setting for famous opera, with equally famous singers–an event not to be missed. A walk along the **Seepromenade** is worthwhile because all Bregenz is here on the weekend. From the end of the Promenade it is possible (when there are no performances) to get a free view of the huge floating backdrops in the lake in front of the steep concrete auditorium. On a clear day–usually in autumn–a trip on the cable car to the 3,491 feet (1,064-m) high **Pfänder** mountain is worthwhile for the scenic view of Lake Constance.

On the Swiss side: From Austrian Bregenz, the Swiss border can be reached in a few minutes. Then comes **Rorschach** with its old corn market and screen weaving. The earlier wealth of Rorschach is indicated by the imposing facades of the patrician houses on the Marienberg and Hauptstrasse. In the Baroque **Kornhaus** a local crafts museum has been set up. Another impres-

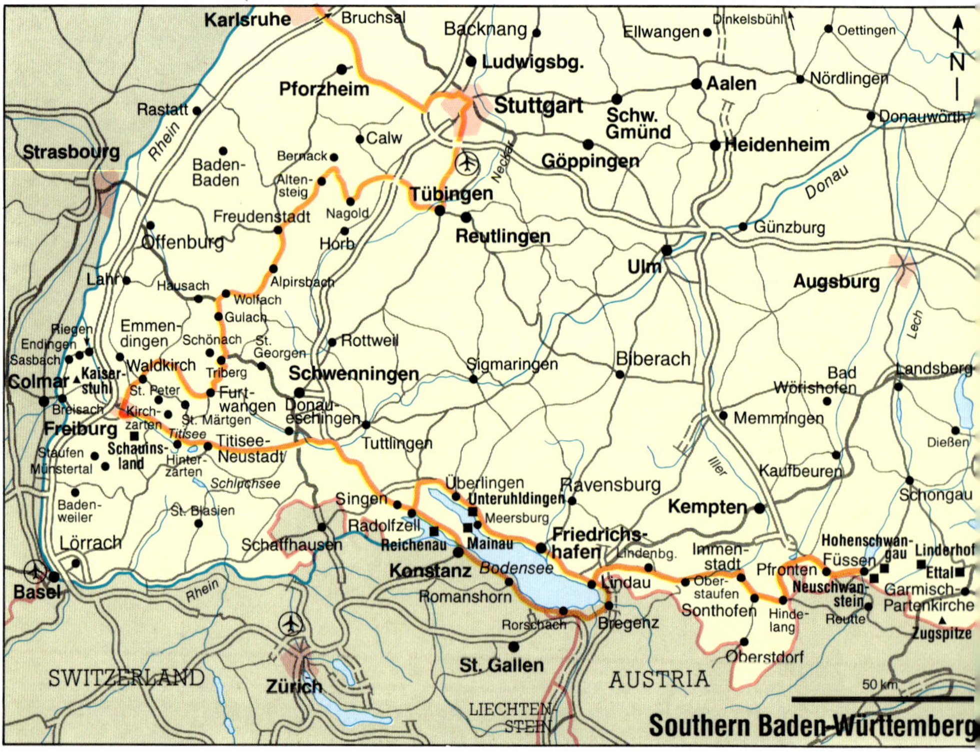

Southern Baden-Württemberg

sive feature from that period is the abbey **Kloster Marienberg**, with the church **St. Columban.**

Romanshorn, about nine miles (15 km) to the west, is a large yacht and ferry port. From here car ferries travel to Friedrichshafen on the German side of the lake. A trip to **St. Gallen** should be made on the way from Rorschach to Romanshorn. St. Gallen's **Benedictine Abbey**, founded in 612, was a cultural center in the early Middle Ages and one of the first education centers in Christian Europe. The foundation church represents a high point in the southern German Baroque, while the Rococo foundation library houses almost 100,000 volumes, dating back to the era of the Carolingians and King Otto.

Kreuzlingen belongs to the growing town of Konstanz (Constance) but is separated by the Swiss border from the rest of the town on the German side. Those interested in art should not miss the Augustine church of the former prebendary foundation. The choir railing, which resembles filigree, catches the eye and is a unique example of artistic wrought-iron work. The story of the Passion is depicted in the wing of the Oelberg chapel. An unknown Tyrolean woodcarver is supposed to have worked for 13 years on this realistic representation of 300 individual portrayals.

Back in Germany: Opposite Kreuzlingen, on a small land bridge between Untersee and Obersee in Germany, lies **Konstanz**. This, the largest town on Lake Constance (population: 80,000), can be traced back to a Celtic fishermen settlement. The Romans built a fort here, named after Emperor Constantinus Chlorus, hence the name. About 540, Konstanz became a bishopric. The most important event in the town's history was the Konstanz Reform Council of 1414–18, when the only selection of a Pope on German territory took place. In the same period the ecclesiastical princes pronounced the death sentence on the Christian reformer Johannes Hus. He was burnt to death on a pile of rubble in front of the town gates in 1415.

Konstanz today is a growing town

ount eppelin uilt the mous rship here Lake onstance.

with many small industries and a university whose campus lies on the outskirts. The historic town center lies in the vicinity of the rail station. Among the main sights is the **Council Building** at Gondelhafen. It was built as a storage room for grain and wine in 1388. The Council met here during 1414–18.

Once the center of German mysticism, it now accommodates the rich in what was the **Dominican abbey**. The early Gothic cloisters (1260–70) now open out onto luxuriously furnished rooms. There is an excellent view from the small island to the **Seestrasse** with its collection of *fin de siècle* houses. The **Rhine tower** at the Rhine landing, close to the busy multi-lane concrete bridge, remains from the old town walls. **Niederburg**, the oldest part of town, lies with its narrow streets between the Rhine gate tower and the Münsterplatz in which is the **Minster**. This cathedral building has a long and complex history. The oldest part of the crypt dates from A.D. 1000, but the Gothic building was only completed in 1856. One famous sight is the early Gothic reproduction of the Holy Sepulcher in the Mauritius rotunda. On a clear day, the climb to the observatory platform below the tower peak is worth its while. The world's historians travel here to examine the delicate early Gothic **Weber Frescoes** (end of the 13th century) in the **House of the Kunkel**. The series of paintings depict the individual stages in the manufacture of silk and linen.

The Wessenbergstrasse (pedestrian precinct) is the main business street. The Menzgasse branches off from it, and gives a view of the splendid facade of the **Zum Deutschen Haus** in which the hotel Graf Zeppelin is located and is said to have been frequented by Count Zeppelin, the airship inventor.

The Rhine Falls: Strongly recommended is the excursion from Konstanz or from Kreuzlingen in Switzerland, along the shore road of the Untersee via Stein, where the Rhine leaves Lake Constance again, to the **Rhine Falls** at Schaffhausen in Switzerland. From the broad shore promenade below the Falls

Roaring falls of the Rhine at Schaffhaus

there is a splendid view of this natural spectacle. Foaming water masses with a width of 490 feet (150 m) drop 310 gallons (1,080 cubic m) per second with a thunderous sound from a height of 69 feet (21 m) to the river basin.

Those who do not wish to view the Rhine Falls can drive from Konstanz along the north shore of the Lower Lake directly to **Radolfzell**. Radolfzell, surrounded by meaningless concrete buildings, has preserved its tiny old town center which is protected by the remains of a mighty town wall. In the former town moat a park with abundant flowers had been created. On the **Mainau Peninsula**, the spa administration is in the **Scheffelschlössle**, originally the home of the writer Josef Victor von Scheffel (1778-1886).

Fruits and flowers: From Radolfzell, the route passes around the much larger **Bodanrücken Peninsula**. A 2.5 mile (four km) long artificially created dam joins the mainland with the **Reichenau Island** which is the most important vegetable-growing area in Germany.

tone-Age abitation: ke-dwelling t Unteruhl- ingen.

Fifteen percent of the three mile (five km) long and one mile (two km) wide island is under huge glasshouses. The **Benedictine abbey** of Reichenau was the spiritual center of West European culture for 300 years (724-1000). Kings such as Charlemagne granted the abbey privileges and Charlemagne's sons were educated by prominent teachers of the time. Three churches remain from the early Middle Age, but today they reflect a faint shimmer of their former magnificence. The monumental frescoes, depicting Christ's eight miracles on the Carolingian-columned basilica **St. Georg** (9th century) in Oberzell are famous. The Romanesque **Minster**–formerly Benedictine abbey–in Mitterzell (11th century) with its annexes, gives only a vague impression of its former splendor. The open roof beams of oak, similar to an overturned ship's hull, are noteworthy. The centerpoint of the Baroque **St. Peter** and **Paul Church** in Niederzell (11th-12th century) is the Romanesque fresco in the apse.

Make an early visit to the famous flower island of **Mainau** on the other side of the Bodanrücken Peninsula on the Überlinger Lake. Only the first arrivals at 8 a.m. enjoy an undisturbed impression of the magic of this sub-tropical flower splendor, which radiates from March to October. The present owner, Count Bernadotte of Sweden, lives in the three-winged castle. A scientist, he started the Lindau Conferences for Nobel Prize winners in science, held every three years.

On the way back to the Stone Ages: On the Lake shore diagonally opposite lies **Überlingen**, once a Free Imperial City and today a lively small town with many old buildings behind the still recognizable former town walls. The steep streets should be explored from the harbor with its long promenade. The best view over the roofs can be enjoyed from the tower of the Gothic Minster **St. Nikolaus**, the largest church in the Lake Constance region. The church's splendidly carved wooden altar dates from the 17th century. In the town hall adjoining the splendid **Council Chamber**, the figures of the imperial representatives by the Überlingen master woodcarver Jacob Tuss (1490) are worth seeing. So is the patrician house of the Reichlin Meldegg, a **puppet museum**. The house displays lifestyles of the era in two forms: one is the original, exhibiting the wealth of the influential trader, and another is the replicas of the originals in miniature from the Renaissance of *fin de siècle*.

High above the shores of Lake Constance stands the pink Baroque pilgrimage church of **Birnau** with its lively Rococo decor. It stands among terraced vineyards three miles (five km) outside Überlingen on the road to Meersburg. Its main attraction is the life-size roguish Baroque putto, *The Honey Licker*.

A few minutes beyond **Überlingen** is Unteruhldingen and a reconstructed Stone-Age village on piles surrounded by water (open-air museum).

Magic of Medieval times: Meersburg, some miles away, have one of the most beautiful townscapes in Germany. The magic of this medieval town, which has never been destroyed, is at its best in the evenings. During the day, hundreds of tourists pass through the steep streets linking the lower and the upper towns, but in the evening it is possible to view in peace the remarkably well-preserved Frankish half-timbered houses. Fountains play, church clock-towers sound, and some inns put out their tables and chairs in the quiet alleys. The historic center is the **Altes Schloss**, the oldest castle in Germany which dates from the Merowingian period. Concerts now take place in the stylish Baroque rooms of the **Neues Schloss**–the former summer residence of the Prince Bishops of Konstanz. The showpiece of the building are the imposing stairways, built according to Balthasar Neumann's plans.

The **Fürstenhäusle** belonged to Annette von Droste-Hülshoff (1797-1848) one of the most celebrated writers of her time, whose book, *Die Judenbuche*, is used in German schools. Her statue stands in front of the bridge to the Old Castle. The upper town gate is marked by the **Rotes Tor** (Town Gate), which Goethe passed through on his journey home from Italy to Weimar.

Nearby is **Friedrichshafen** (52,000 inhabitants) the second largest town on Lake Constance. The main attraction in this anonymous industrial town is the **Municipal Bodensee-Museum** with the Zeppelin Department at Adenauerplatz, in the northern wing of the town hall. Friedrichshafen caught world attention at the end of the 19th century, when shiny silver airships were built. The inventor of these Flying cigars was Count Ferdinand von Zeppelin (1838-1917) from Konstanz. Models of these flying objects hang from the gleaming aluminium ceiling of the museum.

About 140 miles (225 km) to the east, lies **Wasserburg** with the onion tower of the Baroque Pfarrkirche St. Georg. Once owned by the Fugger family, the former castle now houses a luxury hotel. In the Middle Ages, however, Wasserburg achieved notoriety for its trials of witches. In the **Malhaus** on the way to the church, is the site of the torture chamber. The round trip of Lake Constance leads back via **Langenargen** to the starting point of Lindau.

The island of Mainau, an opulent paradise. Right, Hote Graf Zeppel in Konstanz

TIBI
SEMPER GLORIA
Graf
Zeppelin
Gaststätte

Adventuring In The Black Forest

"In my young days I was in charge of the Celts, the Germans and the impenetrable wilderness of the Hercynian Forest. I lived as a hunter amongst wild beasts and found the customs spontaneous and unbridled. I heard the barbarians sing their songs on the other side of the Rhine, their language like the croaking of the raven..."

Emperor Hulian in A.D. 363

A visitor these days venturing into the Black Forest (called Silva Hereyniae by the Romans) with its dark forest-covered hills need no longer look out for wild beasts or barbarians. These days the Black Forest is neither dark nor frightening. There is wilderness, indeed, but a tamed one which has been softened by human effort over the past 2,000 years. As to impenetrability, the Black Forest has long since been made accessible by many roads, railroads and an extended network of walking trails. Today, the valleys of the Black Forest are no longer covered by dense pine woods. Over several decades, the tall, straight and sticky trunks have been ruthlessly cut down in tens of thousands and shipped off down the Rhine to Holland on huge rafts of up to 1,000 feet (300 m) in length. But the people, descendants of the German tribe of Alemans who, in A.D. 260, overran the inhabitants east of the Black Forest and who, by the time of Julian, had forced the Romans to retire to the left bank of the Rhine, are now of a friendly, open and uncomplicated nature.

Their descendants settled exclusively in the Rhine plain and lower valleys, however, and it was only towards the end of the millennium that more remote parts of the Black Forest were colonized. Then, in the 12th and 13th centuries, linear villages developed in suitable places with the fields beginning immediately behind the houses. Irish missionaries founded a number of monasteries which later became powerful abbeys like St. Peter and Hirsau. Secular rulers whose legitimacy derived from the tribal constitutions colonized more land in order to enlarge the territorial base of their political power. By the 16th century, due to intensive clearing of the land through agriculture and logging, the Black Forest, particularly around its navigable river valleys, had seen a significant change. Small-scale industry had developed glass-crafting and watchmaking. These, together with agriculture and tourism, have since then been the backbone of Black Forest economy up to the present.

In the Black Forest tourism has a tradition going back as far as the 18th century. The unique combination of the Rhine plain and mountains rising to a height of 3,950 feet (1,200 m) within only a few miles of one another has always attracted visitors. In the plain, on the one hand, there are hot summer days, warm nights spent outdoors feasting upon opulent food and enjoying delicious wine and the company of an easygoing, cosmopolitan people. The forest-capped mountains, on the other hand, above green picture-postcard valleys, entice the visitor to enjoy extensive walks. Heathcocks and pheasants, buzzards and hawks, deer, foxes, badgers, and hundreds of different butterfly species populate the more remote areas, where the mountain people still cling to their tradition, and, on public holidays, wear their beautifully-adorned costumes. You meet them on your journey through the Black Forest. Commence your visit at the city of **Freiburg** (population 171,000) gateway to the southern section.

A Catholic hedonism: Who does not envy those fortunate enough to study, in this city of forests, Gothic architecture and wine, and where there are countless pubs and open-air restaurants in which to meet and debate into the early hours of the morning? Yet Freiburg is not just a university town with student haunts. Here, town and gown mingle over the superb wine which abounds in the region dominated by the Schauinsland, a mountain well worth a day's excursion.

Freiburg and its university have been thoroughly Catholic since their begin-

idden
ek in
Black
est.

nings. Only 80 years after the city's founding in 1120, its burghers started to build a parish church which grew to be a splendid cathedral in medieval Germany. Its steeple, at 380 feet (116 m) is considered the most beautiful tower of Christianity. The university was a center of liberal humanism renowned in Europe for the first 80 years after its foundation in 1457. Then it became a Jesuit bastion of the Counter-Reformation and remained faithful to this strict Catholic tradition, combined with a dash of liberalism, until the 1920s.

Narrow alleys, paved streets and fast-flowing rivulets called *Bächle*, which in medieval times carried away the waste, characterize the city center around the **Münsterplatz**. This is a pedestrian zone which can be comfortably explored on foot and whose delightful cafes, restaurants and shops make for the perfect tourist haunt. The Münsterplatz is dominated by the most striking Freiburg feature, the **Minster of Our Lady.** It would take an entire book to describe adequately all of its architectural, sculptural and pictorial details. Climbing the airy tower in itself is an adventure, in particular at the hour when the mighty bells seem to make it dance, and the comical and monstrous gargoyles appear to laugh at the panic-stricken visitor.

In front of the Freibu minster.

Around the minster is one of the most picturesque open-air markets in Germany. On a sunny Saturday morning in summer the minster seems to float like a giant steamship in a sea of stalls, vendors, housewives, musicians, tourists, preachers, flowers, meat, bread, vegetables, fruits and grilled sausages.

The soldiers and jesters: The best way to explore the downtown area is to take Münsterplatz as the center of a series of ever-widening circles. The eastern limit is the **Schwabentor**, the old city gate-tower which houses a museum of tiny figures. Nearby, the **Gasthaus Bären** (inn) claims to be the oldest public house in Germany. To the south, the **Gewerbebach canal** was once the artery of the city's medieval economy and to the west, the **Rathausplatz** features Freiburg's early Renaissance town hall. An example of late Gothic architecture is the **Haus zum Walfisch** around the corner of Franziskanerstrasse. In Turmstrasse, behind the town hall, the **Narrenzunfthaus** displays carnival masks and *Häs* (jester's costumes) which today give the *Fasnet* (Alemanic carnival) a touch of wild animistic ritual.

Up, up and away: A visit to the peaceful old Freiburg **cemetery** (Alter Friedhof) with its beautiful tombstones of the 18th and 19th centuries (like the sleeping girl, mysteriously decorated throughout the year with fresh flowers) is one way of escaping the city. Climbing a nearby mountain is another. Just five minutes from Münsterplatz, the **Schlossberg** is an area of lush parkland which is ideal for a pleasant stroll. The **Restaurant Dattler**, which can also be reached by a small funicular, affords one of the best views–and photographic perspectives–of the Münster.

A great escape is a tour up Freiburg's private mountain, the **Schauinsland** (4,210 feet/1,284 m). It is a pleasant ride on tram 2 (to Güntherstal) and bus 21 to

Horben, where the Schauinsland climbs the remaining 2,450 feet (746 m), over a route of over two miles (nearly four km) to the top. A panoramic view, on clear days, of the Black Forest, the Rhine plain and the French Vosges is the reward for making the trip. Public houses, evening spots and cafes, music from classical to rock, and rich Baden cuisine and wine await you. Try delicious *Hechtklösschen* (pike-balls), listen to open-air serenades in the *Kaufhaus* or enjoy a *Viertele* of wine in one of the many *Gasthaus* (inn).

Dallas in Germany: Just a ten-minute drive north on the B3/B294 from Freiburg, one of the most beautiful Black Forest valleys, the **Glottertal**, provides an idyll of pastoral slopes which melt away into lush forests against the sky. Less soothing is the endless array of restaurants, hotels and tourist facilities which line the road.

A more tranquil introduction to the Black Forest is the **Föhrental**, which branches off at the Glottertal entrance. Ascending the Glottertal the traffic, which till now has been a gentle flow, suddenly turns into a traffic-jam, with policemen desperately intent on diverting tour buses and cars from a certain side road. This is the site where the *Black Forest Clinic* is filmed, a German TV version of *Dallas*, featuring a benevolent counterpart of J.R. Ewing, the man everybody loves to hate.

The road climbs on until the huge two-towered abbey of **St. Peter** dominates the panorama. Founded in 1093 by Benedictine monks, the abbey now houses a seminary. On All Saint's Day and Corpus Christi its opulent Baroque church is the destination of colorful processions whose participants still wear traditional costumes.

On to **St. Märgen**, about four miles (seven km) further on with extraordinary views at every turn and with hills and valleys spreading out into the far distance. The Black Forest is made up of dark woods, quiet valleys, unruly creeks and mighty farmhouses whose steep roofs almost touch the ground.

The area around St. Märgen, a charming hill resort centered around an Augustine abbey, offers perfect compromise between remote, natural beauty and the needs of modern-day tourism.

From heaven to hell: When venturing east from Freiburg to the famed lake Titisee, forget your car and take the train. It is a spectacular half-hour trip on a track built in 1887 which, from the **Himmelreich** (realm of heaven) station to the **Höllental** (hell's valley) station climbs about 2,050 feet (625 m) a national record for German railways. The gorge-like valley with its narrow entrance, called **Hirschsprung** (stag jump) because a stag is said to have once jumped from one side to the other, is today characterized by the hellish traffic of a four-lane road cutting through it. A stopover in **Hinterzarten**, a hill resort, should include a meal at the **Parkhotel Adler**, famed for its food and for the fact that French queen Marie-Antoinette once dined here.

At weekends, vehicles of every description deliver thousands of visitors who walk the plane-tree avenue leading down to the picturesque **Lake Titisee**. It

urrounded y vineyards Breisach.

is a tourist's gold-coast with one souvenir shop after the other. Useful items like banners, jugs, T-shirts, walking sticks and cuckoo-clocks which give a deafening concert every hour, are on display. However, the pleasant walk around the lake (1.5 hours) or the challenging hike up the highest Black Forest peak **Feldberg** (4,900 feet/1,493 m) through the scenic **Bärental** valley is nature at its best.

German Tuscany: The maritime winds blowing up the Rhine valley result in a mild climate which is favorable to fruit growing. This, together with the vineyards, beautiful rolling foothills rising to the Black Forest, gives the region south of Freiburg, the **Markgräfler Land**, more than a touch of the Mediterranean. Occasionally, the sky is that special silken, transparent blue and the air that fragrant mellowness which made the Romans crossing the Rhine in 58 B.C. feel at home.

The picturesque little town of **Staufen**, 12 miles (20 km) southwest of Freiburg, became famous in 1539 when the magician Dr. Faustus was beheaded by one of the higher devils at the **Gasthaus Löwen**. The alchemist Faustus who probably blew himself up while making "gold" for the local baron, was later immortalized in J.W. von Goethe's famous drama. Today the "devil" waits in the form of Markgräfler wines and mellow Black Forest fruit-spirits offered in any of the *Gasthaus* lining the streets of Staufen's medieval center.

Possibly a much more profitable relationship than that between the baron and Faustus was between the city of Freiburg with the silver mines in the **Münstertal** valley. One of these mines, the **Schaubergwerk Teufelsgrund**, has been preserved. A Baroque church on the site of a former Irish monastery is at nearby **St. Trudpert**.

The methods of those "liquid gold producers," the bees, can be admired in the fascinating **Bienenkundemuseum** (Bee Museum) in Obermünstertal. The cultural and economic impact of beekeeping on human life since pre-history is recorded in this unique museum.

Up the winding Kaiserstuhl mountain road.

Sulzberg, hidden in a small side valley five miles (eight km) south of Staufen, is remarkable for its variety of religious traditions. **St. Cyriak** is a pure Romanesque basilica which has stood for a thousand years and which, since the Reformation, has served the Lutheran community. One of the oldest (from 1550) and probably the most beautiful **Jewish cemetery** in Germany, which miraculously escaped the depredations of the Nazi regime, can also be visited.

Badenweiler, located on a rounded mountain-slope, has been a spa-town since A.D. 100. The ruins of the **Roman bath** are the best-preserved example of Roman spa-culture north of the Alps. Situated in the **Kurpark**, a lush subtropical park with giant Californian redwoods, the ruins contrast sharply with the modern buildings that have been added to Badenweiler's facilities The town, which prohibits cars, has that hushed clean atmosphere which appeals more to the convalescent than to the transient visitor. Nonetheless, it is well worth a visit with its many walks through beautiful scenery and architecture such as the Hotel Römerbad.

An emperor's seat: The name *Kaiserstuhl* (Emperor's Seat) has nothing to do with the legend that Friedrich Barbarossa, the German emperor, who drowned in 1190 while crusading in Palestine, is resting in a mountain to come forth to re-establish his reign. Rising from the plain west of Freiburg, as though placed there by mistake, the volcanic mountain does, indeed, have something peculiar about it. In summer it heats up to tropical temperatures, with the ground, after a sunny day, easily reaching 70° C. In this climate a great variety of exotic plants and animal life such as wild orchids, unusual butterflies and lizards thrive.

But the Kaiserstuhl also has the perfect climate for growing fruit and wine. Most of it is planted with fruit trees and vines on huge terraces which were bulldozed out of its slopes in the 1970s. From certain angles such as the former volcano rim south of Kiechlingsbergen,

raditional chwarz-vald farm-ouses.

these terraces have a symmetrical fascination all of their own. However, they are also symbols of the conflict between ecology and economy. They have reduced the amount of work devoted to the vineyards by three-fourths, but at the cost of endangering the ecological balance and many species, both animal and plant, have disappeared and large quantities of concrete added to prevent the danger of landslides.

Nonetheless, villages like **Oberbergen** have retained their quiet vintage atmosphere, and the wine does not seem to have suffered as you will notice when tasting hearty *Silvaner* at **Achkarren**, aromatic *Gewürztraminer* at **Bickensohl** or velvet-red *Spätburgunder* at **Oberrotweil**.

The Kaiserstuhl, however, is more than just wine. At the cemetery church of St. Michael in **Niederrotweil**, the altar by the unknown master H.L. is a superb example of late Gothic/Baroque woodcarving. Both picturesque **Endingen**, with its delightful marketplace, to the north and sleepy **Burkheim** to the west, are built on terraces on the banks of the Rhine and have impressive gate-towers. This is an ideal place for a walk in romantic medieval surroundings. You can enjoy other walks up and down the hills of Badberg and Totenkopf or along the Rhine to **Sasbach** (Sponeck ruin and Limburg castle) with a *Gasthaus* always near at hand.

The city of **Breisach**, which is perched on a basaltic rock on the banks of the Rhine southwest of the Kaiserstuhl, is crowned majestically by its minster which was built during the 12th-16th century, and contains a huge wood-carved altar, again by the master, H.L., which is considered to be one of the most magnificent examples of German sculpture. Breisach is a lively town in summer with art festivals, open-air theater and one of the best *Hock* (wine festivals) of the whole region which is held in July. Railway addicts can hop on the Rebenbummler train to **Riegel**, which includes a vintage engine and wooden carriages.

When in Breisach, consider an excur-

Left and right, Black Forest wood carvings of girl and boy.

sion over the border to France. **Colmar**, 16 miles (25 km) west of Breisach, is the place to visit. It has some unsurpassed examples of architecture and art–the **Museum Unterlinden** and the **Eglise des Dominicaines** alone make the trip worth the effort–as well as the best of Alsatian food and wine. Those with time will probably be tempted to prolong their stay and have a closer look at the rest of Alsace.

Time-machines: Since the early 18th century the region between Furtwangen and Triberg/Schonach, on the B500 north of Titisee, has been a center for clock manufacturing with the fabulous cuckoo, which was invented in 1738, becoming its most famous product. In 1985 alone, some 600,000 clocks were sold worldwide.

At the fantastic Uhrenmuseum in **Furtwangen**, clocks of every proportion and design imaginable can be admired. One particularly auspicious piece of engineering marvel is a sewing tailor who, every hour on the hour, has a shoe banged on his head by his wife. A megalomaniac creation, the biggest cuckoo-clock on earth in **Schonach**, is 23 feet (7 m) long, 25 feet (7.5 m) broad and 21 feet (6.5 m) high. Even the cuckoo-bird measures a stately three feet (0.9 m). Those intending to buy should beware of being offered mostly souvenir-kitsch. With luck, however, they may find something special in one of the countless Houses of 1,000 Clocks lining the streets of **Furtwangen**, **Schönwald** and **Triberg**.

A relaxing break from shopping is a visit to **Triberg falls**, where the water cascades down 338 feet (103 m) making these the highest falls in Germany. A train ride from Triberg (even better from St. Georgen, a few miles east of Triberg) to **Hausach** on the *Schwarzwaldbahn* is said to be the most spectacular on German railways.

At the roadside of the B33, nearly two miles (three km) south of Hausach (or 30 minutes' walk from Hausach railway station) is the **Vogtsbauernhof Museum** whose entrance is barricaded by lines of stalls selling "typical" products. The museum displays examples of farmhouses from all over the Black Forest complete with household utensils and ancient farming equipment.

The former Benedictine monastery church in **Alpirsbach**, 12 miles (20 km) northwest of Hausach in the Kinzig river valley, is another must for the Black Forest visitor. It is one of the most beautiful Romanesque basilicas in Germany and had scarcely been altered since it was constructed in 1095-99. A church bench inside is one of the few remaining examples of Romanesque church furniture in Europe.

Black Forest crossroads: Freudenstadt, once dubbed the Swabian Siberia because the snow does not melt before mid-May, is today a hill resort noted for its fresh air and the largest marketplace in Germany. The three major tourist *Strassen* (roads) meet here, bearing the fantasy names of inventive tourist-managers with much less inventive names. On *Freundschaftsstrasse* (Friendship) you can head west to the Rhine plain, on a scenic route: *Schwarzwald-Hochstrasse* (Black Forest High) leads northwest to Baden-Baden and on *Schwarzwaldbäderstrasse* (Black Forest Spas) which is not to be taken literally, you can go northeast towards Pforzheim.

First suggested stop on the latter, 24 miles (38 km) east of Freudenstadt, is **Nagold**, a town beautifully situated in the river valley of the same name. A fresco-painting in the 1,000-year-old **Remigiuskirche** depicts an unusual Holy Mary with the Christ-child holding her hand. The old **Gasthof Post** is an attraction with its beautiful pub-sign and its excellent meals.

"The most beautiful place I know is Calw on the Nagold," the famous writer Hermann Hesse (born 1877) once wrote. And although this reflected his mood when in later years he came back to his hometown, **Calw** still retains, in certain areas, the magical feeling of youth and of summer which the author so successfully recreated in his novels. There is a **Hermann Hesse memorial** at the Heimatmuseum.

The ruins of a monastery and of two churches at nearby **Hirsau** mark the site where once one of the most powerful Benedictine abbeys in Europe stood. This was the Mother abbey of more than 100 monasteries which were members of the Hirsau Congregation. Hirsau headed the first medieval monastic reformation and eventually, having failed in its aims of abolishing the central structure of the church, helped create the papacy in its present form.

Athens on the Neckar: If Germany for a time during its history had the image of being a "nation of poets and philosophers" then **Tübingen** takes credit for having housed a few of its most prolific minds such as Johannes Kepler (1571-1630) who first calculated the elliptic orbit of the planets, and Wilhelm Schickhardt, who, in 1623, invented the world's first mechanical calculator. However, Tübingen attributes its reputation for being an Athens on the Neckar not only to them and philosophers like G.W.F. Hegel and Friedrich Schelling, but also to famous poets like F. Hölderlin, E. Mörike, L. Uhland and W. Hauff. All of them were pupils at the **Stift**, an Evangelical theological seminary which was established in 1536.

Huddled on the slopes of two hills overlooking the Neckar and Ammer rivers, Tübingen has a special charm, its medieval attractions having escaped, unscathed, the destructions of World War II. Worth a closer look are the 15th-century Gothic **Stiftskirche** with the oldest parts of the University behind it (founded 1477) where the reformer Philipp Melanchthon lectured from 1514 to 1518. Below on the Neckar, rising above weeping willows, you can see **Hölderlin Tower** where the insane poet Hölderlin lived from 1807 till his death in 1843. From there, following **Bursagasse** and passing the Stift on the left, you may take a stroll to the half-timbered **Rathaus**, a town hall dating back to 1435. It is located on the old marketplace, where on market days you can meet peasants in regional costumes. Above the marketplace the **Burgsteige** climbs up to the 16th-century **Hohentübingen Castle** (1,220 feet/373 m), offering a scenic view of the roofs of

View over the roofs of Tübingen.

Tübingen and the Neckar, where, on warm summer evenings, you can watch people rowing in lantern-lit boats.

City of the "good star": Stuttgart, capital of the federal state Baden-Württemberg, is, for some, "the biggest village in Germany," and has lived up to the prejudices which other German tribes have nurtured about its Swabian inhabitants. They are regarded as being excessively industrious, as having a highly-developed sense for what is profitable and it is said that "building a house" is their ultimate goal. In fact the city of Stuttgart has been economically successful with its population of 600,000 having the highest income per capita in all of Germany. This is largely because since 1926 "the bright star of the roads," the silver Mercedes star of the automobile company Daimler-Benz, has illuminated the Stuttgart heavens.

The name Stuttgart dates back to a studfarm which was founded about the year 950 by Duke Luitolf, and around which, in the course of time, a settlement grew up as early as 1229 which was known as *Stutkarten*, literally, stud garden. Nowadays the city lies in a basin-shaped valley enclosed by forest-covered hills with orchards and vineyards. Stuttgart is pure hell for bikers because of the steep, cobbled lanes flanked by flights of steps which ascend from the bottom of the valley.

While in Stuttgart, do not miss the 16th-century Renaissance **Altes Schloss** at Schillerplatz. Just opposite, across a broad street called Planie, is the **Neues Schloss** (1746-1807) which houses the Ministeries of Culture and Finance. Behind the Neues Schloss the **Academy gardens** surround the state Parliament building. Opposite the castle park is the **state theater**. Here is the chance to see a performance by the world-famous John Cranko ballet. The **Staatsgalerie**, with one of southern Germany's leading art collections, is located behind the state theater.

A short distance from the center, in the quarter bearing the name Untertürkheim, automobile fans will find the fascinating **Daimler-Benz mu-**

:tuttgart, usy city of ommerce.

seum. On the right bank of the Neckar, in the district Bad Cannstatt, Gottfried Daimler drove the world's first petrol-driven car in the year 1886. This is also where the **Cannstatter Wasen**, the Swabian equivalent of Munich's *Oktoberfest*, is held every autumn.

Gold-town: On their way west to Karlsruhe, those with a predilection for precious things should stop at **Pforzheim**, on the northern fringe of the Black Forest at the confluence of the rivers Enz, Nagold and Würm. Here they can admire the town's renowned gold and jewelry. The jewelers here have a reputation comparable with that of Amsterdam diamond-cutters. About 80 percent of German jewelry is produced in Pforzheim, where 60 percent of the workforce is engaged in manufacture, mainly in small shops. Pforzheim folks, it is claimed, always do their laundry at home, and burn old clothes which others would merely throw away, just in case there are some gold-dust or diamond-splinters hidden in them. When in Pforzheim, do not miss the extraordinary museum of jewelry in the **Reuchlinhaus**, which also houses an art center and a library. Eleven miles (18 km) northeast of Pforzheim, the 12th-century Cistercian abbey of **Maulbronn** is the well-preserved medieval religious complex in Germany.

A rest for Karl: Reliable reports have it that Margrave Karl-Wilhelm of Baden one day was tired of his pious wife and decided to build a new palace where he could dwell in peace–together with his bodyguards consisting of young ladies. At the beginning in 1715 it was just a castle in the middle of nowhere. By 1805 **Karlsruhe** (Karl's rest) had become the capital of the great dukedom of Baden with the city spreading, along geometrical lines, like a fan around the **castle**, with the extensive **Schlossgarten** (park) behind it.

Not surprisingly, most of the attractions are found around the castle, which today houses the interesting **Badisches Landesmuseum**. The **Staatliche Majolika-Manufaktur**, which displays

An old Mercedes-Benz fire-engine.

Fayence pottery; the **Staatliche Kunsthalle**, home of one of the best collections of European painters in south Germany; and the **Botanische Garten** with its Orangerie, are all close by.

So too is the **Bundesverfassungsgericht** (Federal Constitutional Court) which was intended as a custodian of the constitution of the Federal Republic and last arbiter in the major issues of German politics. In practice the Karlsruher judges have become a kind of legal parliament-cum-government, a sort of Solomonic kings in democratic clothing with regulations for each and every problem which is probably what regulation-crazy Germany needs to sort out its affairs. The **Bundesgerichtshof** (Federal High Court) plays a similar role in that its job is to protect the vested rights of the individual; it is the highest Court of Appeal for the German citizen.

European summer capital: The unique combination of German *Gemütlichkeit* and French *savoir-vivre*, enchanting landscape, spa-springs and the most beautiful casino on earth were the foundations on which Baden-Baden built its claim as the European summer capital.

Spa-tradition in Baden-Baden, as might be expected, goes back to Roman times and has been maintained continually since 1507. But the spirit of the imperial times of the 2nd century only returned in 1838 when Jacques Benazet opened his luxurious *salles de jeu* in the **Kurhaus**, the spa-casino, with games of chance adding spice to the dish. Suddenly it became fashionable to visit Baden-Baden. In summer, in addition to European aristocracy, poets and musicians, Baden-Baden always accommodates a few heads of state. Regulars were the Prussian king, Russian princes, even English Queen Victoria, the composer Brahms and, of course, the notorious gambler Dostoievsky.

However, there is more to Baden-Baden than just spa-ing or gambling. At the foot of the Neues Schloss, a romantic Renaissance castle, the narrow lanes of the old town, and the **Lichtentaler Strasse** along the river Oos, are all incentives for long walks.

Playing the tables in Baden-Baden.

ENVIRONMENT AND ECOLOGY

The serious problems caused by the pollution of the Rhine River following a fire at the Swiss Sandoz Chemical Company in Basel, hit the headlines in late 1986. The criminal lack of a sense of civic and ecological responsibility on the part of a few powerful captains-of-industry which could lead to the poisoning of fresh water supplies to millions of people has once again opened the eyes of the public to the ever-present threat of environmental catastrophes.

The dying forests: An even more horrendous vision for an increasing number of Germans is that the very existence of the German forest, which covers 35 percent of the country, is threatened. In their 1986 annual reports on the condition of the forests, the German authorities expressed concern over the more than 50 percent diseased, terminally-damaged or dead woodlands in West Germany. Some fear that in 10–20 years from now there will be no more forests in Germany, as is the case with some parts of Czechoslovakia.

It is, however, virtually impossible to imagine Germany without her forests. Germany is, after all, famous for its vast forest and extensive woodland. It is the birthplace of the Christmas tree, the land of Hansel and Gretel, of Snow White and the Seven Dwarfs, a storehouse of folklore, legend and myth. The woods have played a main role in German art, music and literature and contributed significantly to the moulding of national attitudes. It is still possible for travelers in West Germany to enjoy the varied beauty of the landscape including forests and they might not even be aware of *Waldsterden*–the dying forest syndrome–which has turned out to be one of the most serious environmental disasters of modern times.

Economy versus ecology: "What is killing all the trees?" asked *TIME* magazine in its cover story of September 1985. The causes are apparent: acid rain, ozone smog and other forms of

The dying forest in the Harz.

pollution caused by factories, power plants, domestic chimneys and automobile exhausts. Environmental studies prove that some of the damage could be prevented by imposing speed-limits of 60 miles per hour (100 kmph) on the *Autobahn* and 50 mph (80 kmph) on ordinary roads. Studies have indicated that automobile exhaust emissions increase substantially at higher speeds and that the proposed limits would reduce nitric oxide emission by about 18 percent annually.

The speed-limit was, for a time, one of the country's most controversial issues. Should West Germans temper their racetrack habits and accept speed-limits on the *Autobahn* to save their dying forests? Thirty million cars use the country's roads and most are powered by leaded fuel; only a handful have catalytic converters. The automotive lobby proved too strong. Chancellor Kohl's Christian Democrats coined the slogan against the speed-limit *Freie Fahrt für freie Bürger*, meaning: "Full speed ahead for a free people." A speed-limit, it was intimated, would be tantamount to infringing constitutional rights. Viewed rationally, this argument is difficult to accept, but politically, the economic lobby proved stronger than the ecologic one.

rt
ffected by
ir pollution.

Rise of an ecology movement: At the moment, on the level of national politics, the lobbies of automobile, chemical and power industries and of the building are stronger than millions of environmentalists all over the country. At grassroots level, however, a strong ecological movement has arisen.

During the last decade West Germans have reduced their expenditure on energy by almost 30 percent. Even in small villages large bins are available for the deposit of empty bottles, waste paper, even aluminium. Thousands of sewage works were built in recent years although German rivers have been found to be heavily polluted since 20 years ago. Collection boxes are placed in pubs and supermarkets and agitprop theater in the streets, have saved trees, rivers and meadows from large construction projects such as factories, new *Autobahnen* and nuclear power plants. The ever-increasing anti-nuke resistance by West German rainbow coalitions has succeeded in stopping, or at least delaying, the construction of power plants. At Wackersdorf near Regensburg in East Bavaria, the Bavarian State government intended to erect a nuclear reprocessing plant. Thousands of conservative peasants, housewives and workers protested successfully. Near Stuttgart, a group of pensioners spend their holidays in Bavaria planting young conifers in place of diseased ones in the alpine forests.

In spite of these activities the process of *Waldsterben* seems to be irreversible, partly because there is no consistent policy for environmental protection. The powers-that-be continue to ignore the full extent of the ecological catastrophe, adhering to the dictates of economic interest rather than environmental sense. There is more truth than cynicism in the concerned citizens' comment: "Visit the German forests while they still exist."

Northern Germany
50 km
N
DENMARK
Flensburg
Schleswig
Husum
Kieler Bucht
Baltic Sea
Nordfriesische Inseln
Helgoland
North Sea
Kiel
Cuxhaven
Lübeck
Ostfriesische Inseln
Wilhelmshaven
Bremerhaven
Hamburg
Schwerin
Groningen
Oldenburg
Bremen
Elbe
Weser
Ems
Aller
Celle
NETHER-
LANDS
Hannover
Wolfsburg
Enschede
Osnabrück
Minden
Hildesheim
Braunschweig
Rheine
Hameln
Magdeburg
Bielefeld
Leine
Nijmegen
Bocholt
Münster
Goslar
Rhein
Hamm
Paderborn
Höxter
Göttingen
DDR
Bochum
Dortmund
Essen
Duisburg
Hann. Münden
Halle
Krefeld
Kassel
Düsseldorf
Fritzlar
Fulda
Homberg
Gotha
Erfurt
Weimar
Köln
Schwalm-stadt
Eisenach
Siegen
Marburg
Bad Hersfeld
Aachen
Alsfeld
BONN
Lauterbach
Fulda
BELGIUM
Koblenz
Lahn
Schlüchtern
Coburg
Hanau
Gelnhausen
Wiesbaden
Schweinfurt
Mosel
Frankfurt
Bayreuth
Bad Kreuznach
Mainz
Bamberg
Trier
Darmstadt
Würzburg
LUXEMBOURG
Main
Regnitz
Worms
Ludwigshafen
Mannheim
Saar
Kaiserslautern
Heidelberg
Neckar
Saarbrücken
Speyer
Nürnberg
Pirmasens
Metz
Altmühl
FRANCE
Karlsruhe
Rhein

NORTHBOUND

The travel section of this book is divided into three parts. The first suggests how you can organize your journey through the Rhine-Moselle region and describes everything that awaits you. The second part is *Southbound*, (the largest on account of the wealth of attractions it offers the tourist) where you discover the beauty and the sights of southern Germany.

But it would be a serious mistake to believe that you now know everything about Romantic Germany. For north of the Main line, which the Bavarians jokingly call the "white sausage equator" in order to distance themselves from the north Germans (whom they disparagingly call "Prussians") you will find a great many places of interest, customs and experiences without which your picture of Germany would be incomplete. For Romantic Germany is most definitely more than just Old Father Rhine, Heidelberg, Rothenburg or Munich.

For example a journey to Göttingen, an old and venerable university town, in search of the Brothers Grimm, is just as much a part of Romantic Germany. Along this route and the following stretch through the enchanting valley of the Weser to the proud Hanseatic city of Bremen, one encounters the historical settings of countless fairy-tales and legends: Sleeping Beauty, the Pied Piper of Hameln and Bremen town-musicians.

Away to the west and north of Bremen up to the Danish border extends the coastal landscape of mud-flats, the Frisian Islands and numerous holms shaped by the tides of the North Sea. Here you will meet a very different type of people from that of the Rhine or the Saar. The people of Hamburg for example, inhabitants of the second largest Hanseatic city, are regarded as "the German Britons." From Hamburg it's just a stone's throw to the third pearl of the north, Lübeck, the Hanseatic town made famous by Thomas Mann and the point-of-departure for a suggested route along the coast of the Baltic Sea, with numerous waterways and inland lakes. The maps on pages 238, 251, 263 and 271 are intended to make coordination and planning easier; all routes are shown in color.

At the end of the travel section there is an essay on the former imperial capital, Berlin, the division of which reflected the tragedy of World War II. Since the fall of the Berlin Wall and the process of unification of the two German states which started in November 1989, more interesting destinations for visitors in Brandenburg and Mecklenburg have become accessible. More details on all of the routes can be found in the *Travel Tips*.

Preceding pages: sheep grazing in northern German pastures; going across the sands by horse and carriage.

BfG

ON THE TRAIL OF THE BROTHERS GRIMM

The overseas visitor will most probably land at Frankfurt's Rhein Main Airport. After London's Heathrow Airport it ranks second among the airports in Europe. **Frankfurt** is the hub not only of air travel in Germany, but of road and rail too. Frankfurt is where the major highways meet, and where Europe's largest railway station handles close to 300,000 passengers daily.

The city (population: 650,000) itself, located on the Main river, is a controversial one. Most Germans, with the exception of the Frankfurters themselves, agree that they would avoid living here, and nickname the city "Mainhattan" or "Bankfurt"–because it has played a major role in global commerce since the Middle Ages. Today, more than 350 local and foreign banks are located in the city, together with the Bundesbank (Federal Bank) and the Frankfurt Stock Exchange, the leading exchange in West Germany. That is why the silhouette and townscape of Frankfurt is characterized by towering skyscrapers and glittering complexes.

The city was first mentioned in the 8th century and later became a center of German history. From 855 until 1792, 36 rulers were elected in Frankfurt and from 1502 onwards, Germany's emperors were crowned in its majestic cathedral. Frankfurt's great past can be viewed in a 90-minute walk. The city's landmark and city hall since 1405, **Römer,** along with the Emperors' Hall (*Kaisersaal*) where coronation banquets were celebrated; the square in front with the **Fountain of Justice**; **Haus Wertheim**, a richly decorated 16th-century half-timbered house hosting a cozy inn; the **Historical Museum** the oldest building in the heart of the city; the **Nikolai Church** (A.D. 1290); the **Historic Ostzeile**, a row of houses restored in medieval style; and behind it the **Kaiserdom** cathedral. Nearby is **Paulskirche** (St. Paul's) seat of the first German Parliament in 1848-49. After World War II the damaged Paulskirche was rebuilt for the Parliament of the Federal Republic of Germany, but the choice for the new capital fell upon Bonn. Today, the Goethe Prize–the **Goethehaus**, where the greatest German poet was born and had spent his youth, is just a block away–and the Peace Prize of the German Book Traders' Association, are awarded here.

A good place to start shopping is the **Hauptwache**, once a watch house (1792) and today the heart of the city. Nearby is the **Zeil**, Germany's biggest shopping mall, and the pedestrian zone **Fressgass**, so-called because of the multitude of delicatessens and restaurants. The rebuilt **Old Opera House** stands at the end of the Fressgass. Here, you will also find the so-called Jazzlane with the famous *Jazzkeller*. Frankfurt has a worldwide reputation as a major center for European Jazz.

The Frankfurt museums alone would be reason enough for a visit to this city. No less than eight are placed alongside each other on the bank of the river Main,

eft, old nd new in he business enter of rankfurt. Right, in ront of he "Alter Römer."

including the **Staedel Art Institute and Gallery**, the **German Film Museum**, the **Architecture Museum**, and the **Museum of Arts and Crafts**. Another world-famous museum is the **Senckenberg Museum of Natural History** with its excellent exhibits of giant sauria.

The district of **Sachsenhausen** lies on the south side of the Main. In the pedestrian zone are rows of charming old taverns, some with shady gardens. Here visitors and locals sit and drink *Ebbelwei* (apple wine) and eat *Handkäs mit Musik* (skimmed milk cheese with vinegar, oil and onions).

Other places of interest in Frankfurt are the **Zoo** with its Exotarium, the **Palmengarten** (botanical garden), the **Nizza** (Main River Promenade) and the **Stadtwald**–the largest municipal woods of any German town. Some of Frankfurt's most major fairs are the trade fairs in Spring and in the Fall, the International Book Fair and the bi annual Automobile Exhibition.

Exhibitions from Frankfurt: The Frankfurt urban area and the romantic surroundings offer some rewarding excursions. **Bad Homburg vor der Höhe**, a world-famous spa in the southeast foothills of the **Taunus Mountains** is only about 16 miles (25 km) from downtown Frankfurt. Emperors and czars, kings and dukes, came to seek cures here, where British guests built the first tennis courts on the European continent and also Germany's first golf course. A **Siamese Temple**, a **Russian Chapel** and the world's oldest **gambling casino**, can be found in the spa park.

A bus runs from the Bad Homburg railway station to the nearby **Saalburg**, a reconstructed Roman fort that was built between A.D. 83 and A.D. 260 along the former Roman Empire's border. The **Saalburg Museum** has a unique collection of original exhibits that were found during the excavation.

Another journey of 25 minutes from downtown Frankfurt by S-Bahn (S4) takes you to the delightful town of **Kronberg**, which is dominated by Burg Kronberg, a castle dating from 1230. The old town center has retained its

Aerial view of Frankfurt dubbed "Mainhattan."

medieval character and the nearby **Opel Zoo** provides fun for the children.

The medieval town center of **Oberursel**, the Gateway to the Taunus, can be reached from central Frankfurt by subway (U3) in 25 minutes. The starting point for exploring the Upper Taunus is at the foot of the Feldberg massif. Marked trails and footpaths take you through the **Taunus mountains** from the Hohenmark subway terminus. A bus service runs from here to the **Grosser Feldberg**, at 2,890 feet (880 m) the highest mountain in Taunus, with its observation tower and famous falconry.

The German Fairy-Tale Road: In 1986, the federal state of Hesse celebrated the 200th birthday of two of its most famous sons, Jacob (1785-1863) and Wilhelm (1786-1856) Grimm. As fairy-tale collectors they have made a mark in the lives of many children around the world. (The *Grimm Fairy Tales* have been translated into over 140 different languages.) They were also language researchers who laid down the basic principles of German linguistics and worked on the German encyclopedia. Citizens of eventful times, the Grimm brothers stood up for constitutional law and democracy.

The Hesse and the Weser countryside owe their great wealth of fairy tales and legends to the Grimm brothers who, in the early 19th century at the university of Marburg, rediscovered the almost-forgotten poetry of the ordinary people. The superb achievement of these two men is reason enough to commence a journey along the German Fairy-Tale Road at their birthplace, **Hanau on the Main**. The monument to them in the market square is the actual starting point of this road which is about 370 miles (595 km) long and leads to the Free Hanseatic City of Bremen.

Places to visit in Hanau are the **Deutsche Goldschmiede** (German Goldsmith-house, built 1537-38) on the Alstädter Markt; **Philippsruhe Palace** with its museum; and the health resort of **Wilhelmsbad** with its splendid park. A doll collection at the **Hessische Puppenmuseum** attracts many visitors.

remnant the oman eriod–the aalburg.

Next stop on the Fairy-Tale Road, about 12 miles (20 km) northeast of Hanau area, is **Gelnhausen**. The remains of the imperial palace here are reminders of Emperor Friedrich Barbarossa and his beautiful wife Gela. The **Barbarossa castl**e was built in the 12th century as a residence for Emperor Friedrich I who founded Gelnhausen in 1170 by uniting the three small settlements located in the area, and bestowing upon the community the status of a Free City. In 1180 it was the scene of the first Imperial Diet. During the Middle Ages the settlement was the residence of noblemen and it continued to be a separate community until 1897.

From Gelnhausen, continue through the lovely **Kinzig Valley** and pass through **Wächtersbach,** which has retained its charm as the little residential seat between the nature parks of the Vogelsberg and Spessart mountains. As in many other cities and villages along the route, delightful medieval half-timbered houses border winding lanes. From here it is only a few miles to the spa towns of **Bad Orb** and **Bad Soden**, sources of health in the green valley of the river Kinzig, lined with woods.

Staying on the medieval trade route between Frankfurt and Leipzig, we get to **Steinau an der Strass**, a small, romantic town in the heart of the Bergwinkel area which is one of the most beautiful regions in Germany. Jacob and Wilhelm Grimm spent their childhood in the old **Amtshaus**. Undoubtedly the Bergwinkel scenery and the spirit of this town strongly influenced their creations. Did the prince kiss his Sleeping Beauty awake here in the mighty Renaissance castle with its 115 feet (35 m) tower? Did Hansel and Gretel meet that wicked witch deep in the Spessart forest? In Steinau, the fairy-tale wonderland is well-preserved through the fairy tale puppet theater, *Die Holzköppe*.

In **Schlüchtern**, a historic monastic town in a romantic hilly setting just five miles (eight km) north of Steinau, other memories of the Grimm brothers and also of Ulrich von Hutten (1488-1523),

Still busy in Hanau, the Grimm brothers.

a humanistic knight who fought for a strong and united German Empire, can be found in the **Bergwinkel Museum**.

Reminders of St. Boniface: In Schlüchtern, leave the Fairy-Tale Road for a short side trip to the episcopal town of **Fulda** (population: 60,000) strategically situated in the valley of the Fulda river among the foothills of the Rhön and Vogelsberg massifs. The history of the city of Fulda dates back to 744 when Saint Boniface ordered the Benedictine monk Sturmius to found a monastery on the ruins of an abandoned Frankish Merovingian fortification. It became a center of religion and learning in the Frankish kingdom. After Saint Boniface suffered martyrdom in Friesland on June 5, 754, he was laid to rest in the Church of our Savior in the monastery. The tomb of Saint Boniface, the "Apostle of Germany," became a place of pilgrimage. Under Rabanus Maurus (educator of the German people) the monastery school had already acquired great importance by the 9th century. Here German evolved as a literary language and Fulda became the birthplace of Old High German literature.

The brave ttle tailor" erformed y the heater roup *Iolzköppe*.

Fulda's Baroque quarter is unique in the closed unity of its form. The **Stadtschloss** (City Palace) dates back to 1706–21, when the Prince–Bishops of Fulda had the former Renaissance palace remodelled and extended according to the plans of Johann Dietzenhofer, who also built the **Cathedral** (1704-12). It stands on the foundations of the Ratgar Basilica, one of the largest Carolingian churches north of the Alps and was erected at the beginning of the 9th century to replace the first sepulchral church of Saint Boniface which was no longer able to accommodate the streams of pilgrims. Today, the **tomb of Saint Boniface** lies in the Cathedral crypt. A Baroque alabaster relief edged with black marble depicts his martyrdom. Between the City Palace and the Cathedral is the **Michaeliskirche** (Church of Saint Michael) that Abbot Eigil had built at the beginning of the 9th century, modelled after the Church of the Holy Sepulcher in Jerusalem.

A few minutes drive from the gates of Fulda is Hesse's fine Baroque château, the **Fasanerie**. On top of the **Petersberg** is an outstanding example of ecclesiastical architecture in the Benedictine Abbey whose crypt contains the relics of Saint Lioba. Its frescoes are among the oldest in Germany.

At the Open Air Museum in **Tann,** visitors are introduced in an impressive manner to the life and customs of the Rhön Mountain peasants of bygone days. The **Rhön mountains**, extending between Fulda and Bad Kissingen in the south, are remains of former volcanoes, interspersed by large upland moors and rising to 3,120 feet (950 m) on the **Wasserkuppe,** which is a center for gliding and hang-gliding and also a ski resort. If you are en route to Wasserkuppe, do not miss the **Milseburg mountain** (2,740 feet/835 m) with the remains of a Celtic hill fort.

On the Fairy-Tale Road again: Back in Fulda, travel 15 miles (25 km) to the northeast on the B254 and return to the Fairy-Tale Road in **Lauterbach**, the town where the "little scallywag" lost his sock. Hundreds of thousands of Germany's famous garden gnomes are made here by specialized firms. Many medieval half-timbered houses are around the **Ankerturm**. Other worthwhile visits include the **Riedesel Castle**, the **Eisenbach Castle** and the **Hohaus Palace** with its museum.

Twelve miles (19 km) up the B254 is **Alsfeld**. The focal point of this town is the marketplace with its impressive **town hall** (1512–16), **Winehouse** (1538) and the **Weddinghouse** (1564–71). In addition to religious and secular stone buildings, Alsfeld is known for its 14th-century timber-framed buildings. Many of them have been stripped of additions to the surface in recent years and the original structures have come to light again. Massive beams, carved cornerposts, and inscribed lintels support Alsfeld's claim to being a center of medieval craftsmanship.

About 25 miles (40 km) west, on the B62, lies the university town of **Marburg**, the cradle of German Romanticism. Here the Grimm brothers began their research on the German folktales and stories. Rising above the river Lahn, the old town with its winding lanes and its delightful market square clings to the castle cliff. Marburg's finest building, the **Church of Saint Elizabeth** is a supreme achievement of early Gothic style and a perfect example of a hall church. The **Landgrave Palace** (13th–15th century) with Germany's largest Gothic knight's hall was the scene of the famous "Marburg disputation" between Martin Luther and Zwingli in 1529. Marburg's intellectual image is determined by its university–the world's first Protestant **university**–set up in 1527. The Spanish philosopher Ortega y Gasset said about it: "I owe it half of my hopes and nearly all my intellectual discipline."

Little Red Riding Hood country: The area north of Alsfeld and east of Marburg is called the Schwalm. It is also called Little Red Riding Hood country. The well-known fairy tale originates from here and the costume to which it refers can still be seen. In the towns and vil-

Left, a walk in Fulda. Below, in a side-street of Marburg.

lages, folk costumes are still worn on weekends and during local festivals. The capital of the Little Red Riding Hood country is **Schwalmstadt**, a federation of the two traditional cities of **Ziegenhain** and **Trevsa** and 11 rural townships. The parades at the local fairs at *Salatkirmes* (Ziegenhain) and the *Hutzelkirmes* (Trevsa) are some of Germany's best, featuring traditional and folk costumes, art and customs.

On the Fairy-Tale Road again, you pass through the health resorts of **Neukirchen** and **Oberaula** at the southern approaches of the **Knüll Mountains**. These resorts offer various sports activities and several hiking trails. Twelve miles (19 km) east of Oberaula lies the spa and festival town of **Bad Hersfeld** which celebrated its 1,250-year anniversary in 1986. Every year, on or near October 16, an old German popular festival–the *Lullusfest*–is celebrated in memory of the town founder. Bad Hersfeld is known for its open-air theater festival held in the largest church ruin of Romanesque architecture north of the Alps. Each summer thousands attend the performances in the incomparable atmosphere of the **Stiftsruine**. The spa of Bad Hersfeld offers a stimulating climate and two popular mineral springs called **Lullusbrunnen** and **Vitalisbrunnen**.

Between Bad Hersfeld and Kassel, off the A7, are two remarkable country-towns: Homberg and Fritzlar. **Homberg**, the administrative center for the surrounding countryside, is known for its fabulous half-timbered houses. Especially attractive is the market square with the huge **Marienkirche** (church) and its historical bourgeois houses. The historical **Krone** (1480) is, after the "Riesen" in Miltenberg, the oldest operating guesthouse in Germany.

In **Fritzlar**, some nine miles (15 km) to the north, Saint Boniface cut down a sacred oak tree and founded a Benedictine monastery in 724. By the 9th century, Fritzlar had become an imperial city and later, between the 9th–12th century, played an important role in the German Empire. The visitor will be im-

ime seems
have
tood still
Homberg.

pressed with the unique complexity of the medieval town center, the city walls, towers and the market square surrounded by multi-colored half-timbered houses. The 1,250-year-old history of Fritzlar is rooted in Catholicism and the dominant building is the **Cathedral** (11th–14th century).

City of the Documenta: Fifteen miles (25 km) north of Fritzlar is **Kassel**, the only large city between Frankfurt and Hanover (205,000 inhabitants) and seat of the Federal Labor Court and Federal Social Court.

Due to destruction during World War II, 63 percent of the municipal area consist of green, open spaces. Foremost is the attractive city center with parks, palaces and museums. Dominating the entire scene is the **Hercules Monument** in the **Wilhelmshöhe** hillside park with the **Great Fountain** and its waterfalls and cascades, all designed between 1701–17. **Wilhelmshöhe Palace** was built between 1786 and 1802 in the center of the park. The whole complex was described by the art scholar Dehlio as the most grandiose achievement of Baroque style in its combination of architecture and landscapes.

Since 1955, Kassel has become the forum and venue for artists and art-lovers around the world. The *Documenta*, Kassel's international exhibition of contemporary art, is held every four years and is considered the world's largest art exhibition. Exhibits include those from the **Fridericianum Museum**, Europe's oldest museum, and the Baroque style **Orangery** (early 18th century) in the Karlsaue state park.

The Grimm brothers lived for more than 30 years in Kassel and compiled most of their fairy tales here. The **Brothers Grimm Museum** illustrates their life and works.

Kissing a goose girl: Some 28 miles (45 km) after the A7 from Kassel, you arrive at **Göttingen** (population: 135,000) another historical domain of the Grimm brothers. Göttingen saw its heyday as a commercial center between 1351 and 1572, when it belonged to the Hanseatic League. The town's era of prosperity ended in 1547 with the fall of the Lutheran Schmalkaldic League to which it belonged. The Thirty Years' War also played a part in turning this once-thriving trading center into a sleepy country town. In 1734 the Elector Georg August of Hanover founded the **Georgia Augusta University** and breathed new life into the town. In 1777 the university was Germany's largest with 700 students. Today, it is a leading German university with over 30,000 students. At least 30 Nobel-Prize winners studied or taught in Göttingen. It is not by chance that the headquarters of the famous Max Planck Society was based here in 1945.

The medieval air and former Hanseatic splendor gives Göttingen its attractive atmosphere as evidenced by the picturesque half-timbered mansions, the Gothic churches and the **Old Town Hall** (1369-1443). In front of it stands the "most kissed girl in the world," the attractive **Goose Girl** on the fountain in the market square. By tradition, every post-graduate student who attains his doctorate is required to plant a kiss on the cool beauty's bronze mouth.

Left, "Gänseliesl" fountain in Göttingen. Right, admiring modern art in Kassel.

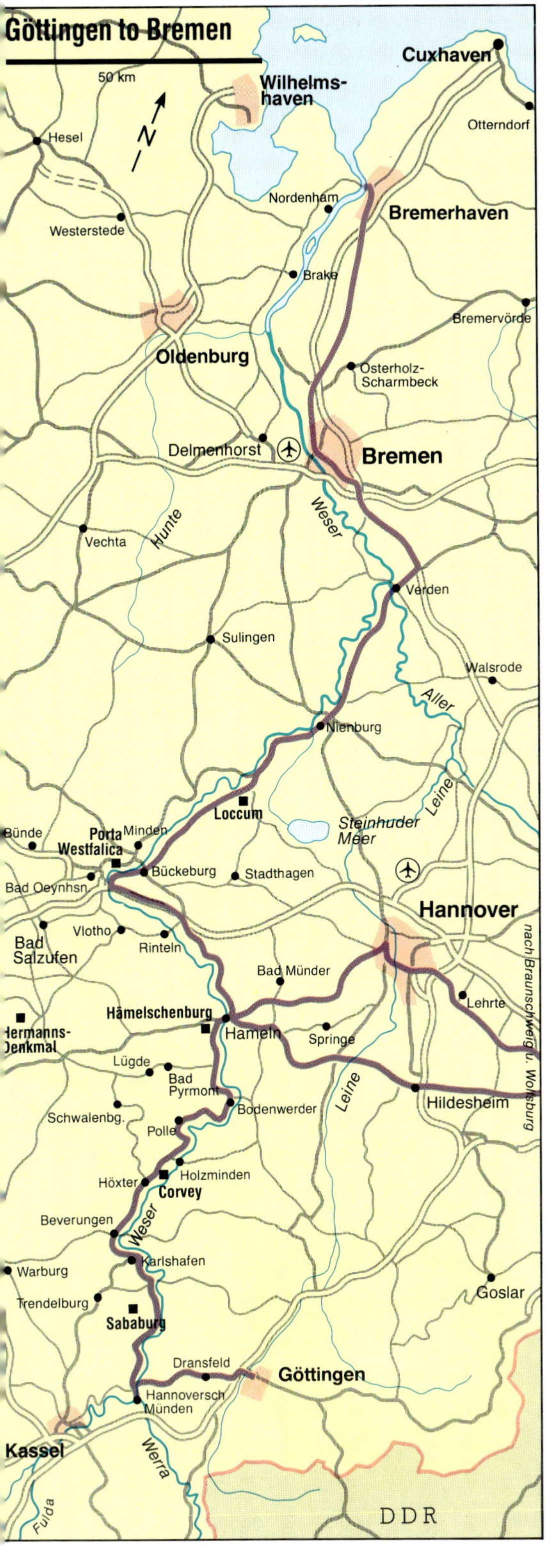

The Weser River Valley

The Weser is one of the loveliest rivers in Germany. It traverses an area renowned for its fairy tales and legends you will encounter at every turn. From Münden, where its tributaries Werra and Fulda merge, the river meanders through a picturesque landscape in Germany before it flows into the North Sea near Bremerhaven, some 270 miles (440 km) northwest of the confluence. The Weser is bordered on both sides by the green hills of the Weserbergland (Weser hill country) which rise to about 1,640 feet (500 m). Barges and boats glide along the river, visible from the "Weser valley road" offering as many scenic sights as the Fairy-Tale Road on the opposite bank.

The present-day traveler exploring this charming and dream-like valley with its many old towns, narrow lanes, crooked half-timbered houses and castles in the distinctive style of the Weser-Renaissance (a style made up of renovated Gothic facades and distinct Renaissance elements) cannot imagine that this region was once the heart of the Holy Roman Empire of the German Nation. Just 500 years ago the Weser valley was the center of a network of major military routes and was visited by many German emperors and kings. At the end of the 16th century the Weser valley was one of the most important grain belts of central Europe and the wealth of both its rulers and citizens is illustrated by the many splendid castles, town halls and patrician houses.

"Where Werra and Fulda kiss each other...": Our journey starts at **Münden**, a picturesque small town founded in 1170 by Henry the Lion, at a place where, according to an old German rhyme "Werra and Fulda kiss each other and lose their own names to become the river Weser." The town escaped destruction during the last war and boasts some 500 well-preserved half-timbered houses built in the 16th and 17th centuries. Worth visiting are the **Rathaus** (town hall), a Renaissance building, the castle **Welfenschloss** (16th-17th century); and the **St. Ägidienkirche** (church) with the grave of the quack healer and British Royal Physician Dr. Eisenbart (1661–1727) who used shock therapy to cure patients. Dr. Eisenbart's play is performed on alternate Sundays in summer. His house still stands in Langenstrasse. There are tours from Münden into the forest of the **Kaufunger Wald**, south of town, and to Molloenfelde, with its unique **Europäisches Brotmuseum** (Bread Museum).

On leaving Münden, follow the river Weser along the B80, called the **Deutsche Märchenstrasse** (German Fairy-Tale Road). It was along this route that the Brothers Grimm compiled many of their famous fairy tales. At the picturesque village of **Veckerhagen**, eight miles (13 km) north of Münden, cross the river by means of a rather old, but ecologically speaking, thoroughly modern ferry to Hameln and then travel on to **Burgfelde** (nine miles/15 km) which has a 12th-century Benedictine monastery with beautiful wall paintings and a bell which was cast in 1470.

Return to the other side of the river and continue on the B80. A few miles beyond Veckerhagen is the village of **Gotstreu**, which in 1722 was the site of a settlement of Waldenser refugees from Italy and France. From here travel three miles (five km) west through the beautiful forest of the **Reinhardswald** to the **Sababurg**, the castle where the Brothers Grimm fairy tale of Sleeping Beauty or Briar Rose (in German: *Dornröschen*) is set. The ballet (*Tchaikovsky*) an opera (*Humperdinck*) and a film (*Walt Disney*) all helped to make the tale world-famous. Close to Sababurg is a zoo which boasts wild boars, wild horses and varieties of oxen.

Back at the river and again on the B80 after some six miles (10 km) we come to the once-busy rafting post of **Gieselwerder**, where the old tavern **Zum Anker** is a reminder of the days of the Weser boatmen who would break for a drink after tying up their skiffs at the river's edge. From here cross to the other side of the Weser again and travel on the B80 through the Waldenser settlement **Gewissensruh** to the white town of **Bad Karlshafen** (9 miles/14 km) founded in 1699 by Count Karl von Hessen-Kassel for Huguenot refugees from France. Discover more about them at the **Deutsches Hugenotten Museum** in Karlshafen. Stay overnight or enjoy a meal in lovely **Trendelburg** (seven miles/12 km) southwest on the B83.

From Karlshafen, journey on down the river to **Beverungen** (six miles/nine km) famous for its trout. Here cross the river again and travel on a secondary road northwards. Six miles (nine km) further on is **Fürstenberg**, which has the second oldest porcelain factory after Meissen (established 1747). Many beautiful porcelain figures can be seen in the excellent **Porzellan-Museum**.

Three miles (five km) from Fürstenberg is the old town of **Höxter** (35,000 inhabitants) which boasts many half-timbered houses, a lovely town hall and its walls. The Romanesque **Kilianskirche** (12th–13th century) is one of the oldest churches on the river. About a mile to the northeast on the right side of

Preceding pages, modern life in the ancient streets of Hannoversc Münden. Below, the impressive doorway of the town ha in Hannoversch Münden.

the Weser stands the former Imperial Abbey of Corvey, site of a number of 12th-century Imperial Diets (*Reichstage*) and a leading cultural center of the Western world then. It was founded in 822 by French Benedictine monks and has a library where the composer of the German anthem, the poet Hoffmann von Fallersleben worked.

Back in Höxter continue along the Weser on the B64 to the historic town of **Holzminden**, five miles (eight km) away on the right river bank. Three miles (five km) northeast lies **Bevern** with its great Weser-Renaissance castle. Four miles (seven km) further on the east is the monastery of **Amelungborn**, built in 1129, one of the oldest in northern Germany.

The lying baron: The next destination is charming **Bodenwerder**, with its well-preserved walls and many half-timbered houses. It was the birthplace of Baron Karl Friedrich Hieronymus von Münchhausen (1720-97) better known as the *Lügenbaron* (the lying baron). His tales from Russia and Turkey, where he served as an officer, were not believed by his countrymen. One of them is about riding on a half-horse which is illustrated by a sculpture in front of the town hall.

Leaving Bodenwerder, travel along the B83 via **Grohnde**, past the huge cooling towers of the atomic power station, before arriving at **Emmern**. A detour at this point to **Hämelschenburg castle** is highly recommended. It is the area's most important castle in the Weser-Renaissance-style built between 1588 and 1610, with lovely gables and step-towers. Make a side trip to nearby **Bad Pyrmont**, which, thanks to its advantageous position, mild climate and mineral springs, rose during the 18th–19th century to become a world-renowned spa-town frequented mainly by aristocrats and artists. The site of this spring is itself impressive and the **Kurpark** with its several palm trees and sub-tropical plants is well worth visiting. After returning to Emmern, travel on for five miles (eight km) to **Hameln** (Hamelin).

iew of
e Weser
alley.

The town of the Pied Piper: Hameln proudly calls itself the town of the Weser-Renaissance, because of its many old buildings in this style. Hameln became world-famous because it is here that the tale of the *Rattenfänger* (pied-piper) took place.

In 1284 a colorfully dressed 30-year-old man called Bundting was asked to combat the mice-and-rat plague which had hit Hameln's grain-barns. After Bundting had successfully piped the vermin away from the village the councillors refused to pay him. When the adults were all in church on a Sunday he took his revenge and whistled 130 boys and girls out of town. They never returned. Historians believe that the pied-piper was a land agent who took the children off as settlers to the East-German territories of Pomerania and Sudetenland. From July till October (Sundays, 12.00 p.m.–12.30 p.m.) the *Rattenfängerspiele* (pied-piper play) is performed at the magnificent **Hochzeitshaus** (wedding house). As you stroll along Bäckerstrasse to the marketplace and turn into Osterstrasse, you will pass old and splendid houses with names like Rattenburg (1568), Löwenapotheke (14th-century pharmacy), Hochzeitshaus with a pied-piper clock and mechanical figures, Dempterhaus (1607) and Leisthaus (1568).

A trip to Hannover: From Hameln it is 20 miles (33 km) on the B217 to **Hannover**, capital of Lower Saxony with 514,000 inhabitants and a major commercial and industrial center. The **Hannover Fair** in April is the largest industrial exhibition in the world. Hannover was founded in 1163 and later became a member of the Hanseatic League. From 1636 till 1866 it was the residence of the dukes and later the kings of Hannover. From 1714 until 1837 the same ruler governed both Great Britain and Hannover until the latter became a Prussian province in 1866.

As a result of the severe damage from World War II, Hannover offers little interest to the visitor. Nonetheless the Ägidienkirche (14th century), the old town hall (15th century) and the

Left, the mendacious Baron Münchhausen on his half-horse. Below, a cathedral of modern times, nuclear plant at Grohnde.

marketplace (14th century) whose tower reaches a height of some 318 feet (97 m) are worth a visit. Not far from the 17th-century castle **Leineschloss** is the grave of the famous philosopher G.W. Leibniz (1646-1716) in the **Neustätter** church. He worked for 40 years as chief librarian of the House of Hannover. The **Kestner-Museum** at Tramplatz 3 is an outstanding art museum in West Germany. The centerpiece of **Maschsee**, a recreational area east of the town hall built in 1936–38, is a lake of about 200 acres (81 hectares). From the western edge take the Herrenhauser Allee to the **Herrenhauser garden**, one of the loveliest man-made Baroque landscaped gardens in Europe.

The motorway A2 takes you from Hannover to **Braunschweig** (Brunswick) the second largest city in Lower Saxony (260,000 inhabitants). It was destroyed during World War II but recovered its economy in the post-war years. It is regarded as the town of Henry the Lion, Duke of Bavaria and Saxony, who took up official residence here in 1166. The fortress of Dankwarderode in the center of the old town with its **bronze lion** is one of his remaining memorials. His tomb, a masterpiece of Romanesque carving, is in the nave of the Romanesque **Dom** (cathedral) built during his reign (1173–95).

Eighteen miles (30 km) north of Braunschweig lies **Wolfsburg**, where Europe's biggest car factory, the **Volkswagenwerk**, was established in 1938. It marked the start of rapid development from a hamlet of 150 inhabitants to a modern city of 130,000. Car enthusiasts can tour the vast facilities of the Volkswagenwerk.

Returning to Hameln, take the B1 to **Hildesheim** (29 miles/46 km) which has been an episcopal city since 815. It was once a treasure house of Romanesque architecture and half-timbered medieval houses until a fire following an air raid in 1945 destroyed most of it. However, there are still some magnificent relics of the past to be found, primarily the Romanesque **cathedral** (11th century) with the **1000-year-old**

Hämelschenburg–country idyll.

rosebush on the outer wall. See the churches St. Michael, St. Martinius (both 11th century) and St. Godehard, a well-preserved Romanesque church. A visit to the **Römer-Pelizaeus-Museum** which houses one of the best Egyptian collections in Europe is a must.

On the way to Bremen: From Hildesheim follow the B1 back to Hameln 30 miles (48 km) and then continue along the right bank of the Weser to the collegiate Romanesque church of **Fischbeck**. Drive through Hessisch-Oldendorf, then turn left into a side-road and on to **Rinteln**, once the seat of a University. A few miles north of Rinteln, visit castle **Schaumburg**, and enjoy a gorgeous view over the Weser valley.

From Rinteln continue through the Weser valley along B514 via **Möllenbeck** and **Varenholz** (another jewel of the Weser-Renaissance) to **Vlotho**. Opposite, on the other river bank, lies **Uffeln**, the mecca of balloon fans. A few miles further west is **Bad Oeynhausen**, a spa which boasts one of the largest thermal springs in the world, the **Jordansprudel**. This 170 feet (52 m) high fountain can be seen in action every Wednesday, Saturday and Sunday. Nine miles (15 km) west of Bad Oeynhausen (take the A64) visit the fascinating Tabak and Zigarren-museum of **Bünde**, to see both the longest pipe and the longest cigar in the world.

Back at Bad Oeynhausen take the B61 to the **Porta Westfalica** (seven miles/11 km) where the Weser, in a breach 2,620 feet (800 m) wide, breaks through the mountains of the Weserbergland into the lowlands of the Norddeutsche Tiefebene–a wide plain which stretches north to Denmark, west to Holland and east to Poland.

On **Wittekindsberg** (886 feet/270 m) you will discover the 285 feet (87 m) high **Kaiser-Wilhelm-Monument** with the last German emperor towering over the landscape.

North of the Porta Westfalica lies the old town of **Minden**, whose13th-century town hall is one of the oldest in Germany. The large cathedral **St. Peter** (10th-13th century) which has a massive Westwerk and a picturesque *Laubengang* (arcade) witnessed the marriage of Duke Henry the Lion and Mechthild of England in 1168. The 1,230 feet (375 m) long **Wasserstrassenkreuz** (waterway crossing) with the **Mittellandkanal** (canal) in a concrete trough at 43 feet (13 m) is unique.

Be sure to make the trip from Minden to **Bückeburg** before trailing the Weser again north to Bremen. Bückeburg was the former residence of the princes of Schaumburg-Lippe. The castle, Little Versailles, has a Baroque gate. Admire the splendid Golden Saloon with the *Götterpforte* (gate of the gods) and the ornate carvings of the chapel in the interior of the lavishly decorated castle. In the park stands a huge mausoleum, one of the greatest in the world.

Back on the banks of the Weser at Minden again, take the B482 with the Weser meandering on the left until reaching the B441 which is followed as far as **Loccum**, a walled monastery with a Romanesque academy (12th century). Today, it is the well-known Protestant institution. A small road from here leads

Still luring children–the Pied Piper of Hameln.

to the **Steinhuder Meer**, the largest German lake between the North Sea and Lake Constance (12 sq miles/32 sq km) which has a maximum depth of nine feet (three meters). Visit by boat the island-fortress of **Wilhelmstein** (18th century) which displays the first workable submarine. Then leave the lake behind and travel on the B6 to **Nienburg**, a regional hub, and back again on the river Weser.

Follow the B215 parallel to the course of the Weser for 37 miles (59 km) until **Verden**, which is known as the "town of horses," at the confluence of the Weser and Aller. The mighty **Dom** (cathedral) in the center of town, built in 786, is the oldest brick-built church in northern Germany. Among other sights to be seen are the **Deutsches Pferdemuseum** (German Horse Museum) and, out of town, the **Sachsenhain**, the place where Charlemagne massacred some 4,500 Saxons.

Old Hanseatic city: After a 25 mile (40 km) drive along the A12 you reach the old Hanseatic city of **Bremen** (population: 550,000) which, together with **Bremerhaven** some 35 miles (57 km) down the Weser, makes up the smallest German federal state.

It is said that the Saxons set out from here in 449 for England on their campaign of conquest. Bremen itself was established in the 8th century and received a bishopric from Charlemagne in 789. It has enjoyed the status of market town since 965 and reached its first golden age in the 11th century. For a long time Bremen was known as the Rome of the North, because it was from here that Scandinavia was Christianized. In 1358 the city joined the Hanseatic League, and in 1646 it became a Free Imperial City. Over this period of 300 years Bremen was in constant competition with Hamburg. This is why the citizens of Bremen today still claim that while Hamburg is Germany's gateway to the world, Bremen is the key (hence the key in Bremen's coat-of-arms)

Today, Bremen is the second largest harbor after Hamburg and is, by tradition, a center for the shipping of grain,

he water unction at linden.

cotton and coffee. Since the end of World War II, it has become a major industrial center where parts of Airbus and Spacelab are produced.

To get to know Bremen, begin your tour from the Tourist Information Office at the Central station. Near here, to the right, is the **Übersee Museum** with an extensive ethnographic collection made up of exhibits from all over the world. From here it is only a short walk over the old town ditch to the old city situated on the Weser. Virtually all the sights can be reached within a few minutes from the marketplace.

The first building worthy of mention is the 15th-century brick-built Gothic structure of the **Altes Rathaus** (old town hall) with its marvelous Renaissance facade. Inside the building is the **Great Hall**, scene of the annual **Schaffermahlzeit**, the world's oldest fraternity meal. The **Ratskeller** (restaurant) is famous both for its Gothic arches and its more than 600 varieties of wine. Under the northwest tower is Bremen's second emblem. The **Street Musicians** of Bremen, dating back to a fairy tale of the Brothers Grimm, is a sculpture which depicts a donkey, a dog, a cat and a cock in the form of a pyramid.

Just opposite the Rathaus is Bremen's third emblem, the 32 feet (10 m) statue of **Roland** (1404) symbol of the city's freedom and independence. He looks down on life around him and faces the **Dom** (cathedral) whose spires rise to 320 feet (98 m) and which embody 1,200 years of history, including the **Bleikeller** (lead cellar) which houses mummies. On the marketplace, the **Schütting** is a 16th-century merchant guild house. Beyond it is the entrance to **Böttcherstrasse**, which was transformed into a street museum with restored medieval buildings. From here it is a few steps to the **Schnoor**, the oldest part of Bremen with its picturesque 15th–18th century burghers' houses and pubs, inns and small shops.

To breathe the fresh air of the North Sea, travel 35 miles (57 km) to the north where the Weser River enters the sea at Bremerhaven.

Left, the "Roland column" sti guards the market plac in Bremen.

THE HANSEATIC LEAGUE

Germany as a political unit did not yet exist when the union of 200 mainly northern German towns, called the *Hanseatic League*, wielded greater economic and political power than any German state prior to 1871. From its inception as a loose association for the protection of German tradesmen, the Hanseatic League developed into a powerful political, economic, and military alliance of cities. At times it had over 200 member cities and, under the leadership of the city of Lübeck, it controlled the North and Baltic Sea trade.

If a city was a member of this alliance, it had to follow the decisions of the *Hansetag* , the congregation of all Hanseatic cities. The most effective, coercive force against independent cities was the so-called *Verhansung*, the boycott of a city by the League. A boycotted city was not permitted to trade nor use the warehouses of the Hanseatic League in major foreign cities like London, Bergen, or Nowgorod. With these measures, the League controlled both the economic and political development of a city. For example, when the workers of Braunschweig managed to become part of the city government, the League, through a trade boycott, forced the city to return to its old government.

Hanseatic *Kogge*.

On the other hand, this kind of manipulation was evened out by the large economic advantages that came with membership in the League: no customs duties, equal units, coins and weights, common trade and common protection against tough competition. The League became so strong that it fought against the Danish King in 1370 to gain free access to the Baltic Sea. The League unified the North and Baltic Sea countries into a single big market. Manufactured goods were exchanged for raw materials of the East much like the "East-West trade" of today. Ships with high walls and sure rudders transported furs, cloth, salt, and grain to every major port in North and Central Europe.

These heavily loaded yet fast cogs, *Koggen* in German, attracted many pirates who at times were supported by some aristocrats. Between 1370 and 1402, even well-protected merchant fleets were captured by pirates, of whom the most famous was Klaus Störtebeker. With the slogan "God's friends, everybody's enemy," the pirates often made daring attacks. Both sides fought mercilessly. The pirates didn't take prisoners but threw captives into the sea. Pirates caught by a merchant ship were executed in the home port of that ship. Their severed heads, on poles, were displayed at the waterfront to discourage further attacks on the League's ships.

With the development of independent national states (Sweden, Russia) in the 16th century, the Hanseatic League, in spite of its successes, began to lose its influence. The last foreign base, London, was given up in 1598. The Thirty Years' War brought about the end of the Hanseatic League. Even today, in many northern cities, buildings still exemplify the rich culture of the past.

ACC 4
ELKE
ACCUMERSIEL
A
W
ACC 2
ACC 2

Living With The Tide

The North Sea is a flat (on average 300 feet deep) peripheral water of the Atlantic, with tides up to 10 feet (three meters) which make the Weser and Elbe navigable for shipping inland as far as Bremen and Hamburg. It is popularly described as the "murderous sea," because it has often gobbled up the land over centuries of sedimentation–the marshes, a fertile coastal strip up to 12.5 miles (20 km) in width–in ferocious floods which have claimed many lives. This is why the flat coast has been protected by dykes behind the mud-flats lying above sea-level at low-tide, when it is possible to walk across them. On the landward side the marshland adjoins the **Geest**, an undulating strip of land with green slopes grazed by flocks of sheep. Flat green marshlands with large farms, sheep and cattle, endless dykes interrupted only by picturesque windmills, church steeples and red-and-white lighthouses await you in this thinly-populated region of the German coastline along the North Sea. It is interspersed by some 160 beach resorts making up the German Riviera, fishing ports and haunting peatbogs on the high Geest behind the marsh to form a striking background. Offshore, the large **Wattenmeer** (mud-flats) is one of the last nature reserves in Europe.

A string of pearls: Coming from the Dutch border, the first German town is Leer, a port called the gateway to East Frisia, and lying between the river Ems and Dollart Bay which forms the border with the Netherlands. From Leer, take the B70 heading for **Emden** on A31, once a pirates' hideout. In the 17th century, Emden (population: 55,000) was the base for the first German merchant fleet which sailed from here to Africa and India. Today, Emden is the largest car-shipping port in Europe. Travel northwards from Emden on the B70, and **Norden** is reached after 21 miles (34 km). A mile to the west on the coast lies **Norddeich**, familiar to sailors for

receding ages, ordsee-allig, urrounded y sea. eft, shing oats in e harbor.

its radio station which sends messages from all over the world.

The "Seven Daughters of the Sea," the East Frisian islands, are arranged like a string of pearls off the coast between the Ems and Weser estuaries. To the north, they are washed by the breakers of the open sea; to the south, they are bordered by the mud-flats. Each of the islands is accessible via different mainland ports. **Borkum**, the most westerly and the largest of the islands (boat ride from Emden, 2.5 hours) is well-known for its 16th-century lighthouse. The eastern end faces the elongated island of **Juist** (off Norddeich) with its high sandhills and the adjacent island bird-reserve of **Memmert**. **Norderney** (boats from Norddeich) is the oldest German beach resort (founded in 1797). **Baltrum** (10 minutes from Nessmersiel), dubbed "Sleeping Beauty of the North Sea," has a sandy beach while **Langeroog** to the east is a bird-lovers' paradise (boat from Besmersiel). The next island on the pearl-chain, **Spiekeroog** (boat from Neuharlingersiel), was once a pirates' lair and the fact that its sandy beach is gradually expanding, demonstrates the continuous eastward drift of these islands. **Wangerooge**, the last and most easterly (boat from Harlesiel), is popular with families.

Pier of tears: If you have had enough of sea and sand, turn south from the coast and head for **Aurich**, once the residence of the princes of East Frisia. From here the B210 leads to **Jever**, a town famous for its Pilsener beer. Less than 13 miles (20 km) to the east is **Wilhelmshaven** (population: 100,000) which is located on the edge of the **Jadebusen** (bay) and, since its construction in 1853 till 1945, Germany's major naval base. Today, thanks to the construction of a 250 mile (400 km) oil pipeline into the Ruhr, Germany's biggest oil port is accessible even to supermarkets.

From Wilhelmshaven travel around the Jadebusen, a bay of the North Sea which, in the Middle Ages, was extended by floods to an area of 80 sq miles (200 sq km) to **Varel** and continue on to **Rodenkirchen**. From here it is

Beach baskets on Sylt.

only 12.5 miles (20 km) along B212 to **Bremerhaven** (150,000) which stands on the right bank of the mile-wide Weser estuary. It can be reached by car-ferry. Today Bremer is Europe's largest fishing and container port, administratively being a part of Bremen. Between 1850 and 1913 and again after the two world wars, Bremerhaven was the gateway to the New World. More than 10 million migrants left Europe from the "pier of tears" (the 4,000 feet/1,200 m long **Columbuskaje**) up to 1913. Since 1945 the port has been the most important supply base for the US Forces in Europe. In the **Deutsches Schiffahrtsmuseum** (German Maritime Museum) the history of seafaring from its beginnings up to the present day is recorded.

The motorways A27 and B6 connect Bremerhaven with **Cuxhaven** (22.5 miles/36 km) which stands at the mouth of the river Elbe where it is one mile wide. Cuxhaven (62,000 inhabitants) is the second largest German fishing port and has been a seaside resort since 1816. From the **Alte Liebe**, an old pier known to sailors, and the nearby **lighthouse** (1803) the view is terrific with ocean liners passing by. The **Kugelbake** is a great beacon which is no longer used, but remains the emblem of Cuxhaven. One pleasant way to see the mud-flats is to take a trip on a horse-drawn cart at low tide to the tiny island of **Neuwerk**, where you can stand beneath the oldest lighthouse in the world (built in 1300).

A fortress of nature: Taking the boat from **Alte Liebe** pier, you can visit the island of **Helgoland** (Heligoland) the mighty red sandstone rock which rises out of the sea like a fortress of nature some 44 miles (70 km) away from the mouth of the Elbe. According to an old myth the devil brought this striking red rock from Norway to its present site.

It was a pirates' lair in the 13th–14th century; then it changed hands among the Danish, English and Germans until, in 1890, it was exchanged for the East African island of Zanzibar and became German. In the following years it was made a naval base and was shelled in World War II. After the war, the island

own houses Husum.

was a practice target for the Royal Air Force before its conversion into a tourist resort in 1952.

The B13 leads from Cuxhaven to **Ottendorf** with the world's largest waterscoop, and then on to **Hemmoor**. Turn left towards Wischhafen and cross the Elbe by car-ferry to Glückstadt. You then arrive at the federal state of Schleswig-Holstein, a long-disputed area in history between Germany and Denmark. It is a harbor town founded by the Danish king Christian IV in 1617.

Through Dithmarschen: Taking the B431 past the controversial nuclear plant at Brokdorf, you arrive at the B5, then turn left towards the town of **Brunsbüttel**, where the **Kielkanal** flows into the Elbe. This 62 mile (99 km) long canal was built in 1895 and connects the North Sea with the Baltic Sea. It is the busiest shipping canal in the world. From here travel along the B5 through **Dithmarschen**, a fertile marshland region which was, until 1559, an independent farmers' republic. At **Meldorf**, 19 miles (30 km) north of Brunsbüttel, the Cathedral of Dithmarschen, a brick church of the 13th century, towers above the low houses on the idyllic marketplace. **Hemmingstedt**, today called Little Texas because of the many oil-wells in the vicinity, was, in 1500, the battlefield between Dithmarschen farmers and the Danish king. Eight miles (12 km) further on lies the town of **Heide**, which boasts the largest marketplace in Germany. The B203 takes you to the seaside resort and shrimp-fishing port of **Büsum**, 13 miles (20 km) southwest. It is also famous for its seal-breeding station. Via **Wesselburen**, birthplace of the German poet Friedrich Hebbel (1813-63) you come to the huge **Eider lock complex**, a dam three miles (five km) long with a built-in lock system to protect the Eider river from the floods since 1974.

Our journey continues parallel to the Eider, north to **Lunden**. In **Friedrichstadt**, four miles (seven km) up north, you might imagine yourself in Holland: there are Dutch-style houses and small *Grachten* (canals) everywhere, because

Lighthouse in the "Marsch".

the town was founded by Dutch refugees in 1621. **Husum** is the place to relax. It was the birthplace and home of the German writer Theodor Storm (1817-88) who portrayed Husum in his stories. Another scenic sight in Husum is the harbor with its shrimp-trawlers, the starting point for boat trips to the Halligen and North Frisian islands.

St. Tropez of the North: Offshore from Husum are the islands of **Nordstrand** (connected by a dam to the mainland) **Pellworm** and the **Halligen**, once a continuous strip of land but later separated by floods in 1362 and 1364. The Halligen are tiny patches of marsh in the middle of the mud-flats whose focal points are farmhouses built on earth mounds called *Warften* to protect them from flooding. At high tide they seem to stand in the middle of the sea. They can be reached either from Husum or from the port of Schüttsiel which is about two miles (three km) north of Husum.

From the Halligen or from the small port of **Dagebüll**, five miles (eight km) north of Schüttsiel, boats depart for the three big North Frisian islands. **Amrum** has nine miles (15-km) of white beach and many old Frisian houses. **Föhr** is the greenest of the three and boasts an excellent **Friesenmuseum** in its capital Wyk. **Sylt**, the northernmost point of Germany, is called the St. Tropez of the North and has fine beaches. In summer many aristocrats, and all who crave to be like them, park their cars on a train at Niebüll on the mainland 25 miles (40 km) from Husum on the B5, and travel over the **Hindenburgdamm** causeway (there is no car-ferry or road link) to this 25 mile (40 km) long and eight mile (12 km) wide playground of the beautiful people. The rail-terminus and capital, **Westerland**, is popular with families and gamblers. **Keitum**, three miles (five km) east, has old but lovely houses and a 12th-century church. At **Wenningstedt**, 2.5 miles (four km) north, you can visit the 5,000-year-old burial site of **Denghoog**. **Kampen**, a similar distance north of Wenningstedt, boasts the towering **Rotes Kliff** (red rocks) and is the place for the jet-set to meet.

Voman in ast Frisian raditional ostume.

WEDEL
5105240
5103930

Hamburg: Gateway to the Seven Seas

Coming to Hamburg, possibly after a 45-mile (74-km) drive from Bremen, you will notice the sign "HH" on the car number plates; it stands for "Free and Hanseatic City of Hamburg." Obviously the city is proud of having been a member of the Hanseatic League.

The town's original nucleus is said to have been the **Hammaburg**, a fort founded by Ludwig the Pious, the son of Charlemagne, in 825 near the site of a Saxon village. That citadel was the beginning of a development into an important commercial town based on a license for free trade issued by emperor Friedrich Barbarossa on May 7, 1189– a day celebrated each year as the birthday of the harbor. The city experienced its first period of economic prosperity between the 13th and 15th century as a member of the Hanseatic League and was designated a Free City by the Augsburg parliament in 1510. Hamburg's claim to be Germany's "Gateway to the Seven Seas" also stems from this Golden Age.

Thanks to poets such as G. Klopstock, G.E. Lessing and M. Claudius, Hamburg was one of Germany's centers of intellectual activity during the 18th century. In 1815 Hamburg became a member of the German Confederation and in 1888 it was incorporated within the customs union of the German Empire created by Bismarck. Amalgamation with the neighboring towns of Altona, Harburg and Wandsbek in 1937 transformed the city into the Greater Hamburg of today. With the establishment of the Federal Republic in 1949, Hamburg remained true to its centuries-old tradition of political independence by becoming the second-largest German city with its 1.6 million population and its land area of some 290 sq. miles (751 sq. km). It is as big as Munich, Düsseldorf and Frankfurt combined. Its favorable location at the head of the long funnel-shaped mouth of the Elbe river has made it one of Germany's leading industrial and commercial centers, and one with the most millionaires in the Federal Republic. So even today, trade is the city's main motivator. The Hamburgians are regarded as the German Britons by the hearty people of southern Germany; on the one hand, because they are reserved, distant, even a little stiff; on the other, because they tend to be objective and worldly-wise.

The Hamburg visitor needs to know two key facts: in 1842 virtually all the old historical buildings were wiped out by a great fire; they were destroyed a second time by World War II bombing raids. Although many of the buildings destroyed have been rebuilt, they are merely replicas. However, this should not prevent the visitor, from getting to know Hamburg's unique atmosphere.

Strolling through the city: A good place to get to know Hamburg is the Central Station. The Tourist Information Office at nearby **Bieberhaus** offers useful information on the city. Sightseeing tours, one of which is in an old-style train, depart from the front of the building at Kirchenallee, close to the beautiful

eft, amburg– ateway) the even Seas. ight, an nviting mile on the Reeper- ahn."

white **Deutsches Schauspielhaus** (theater). Built in 1900 by Viennese architects, it is a prominent architectural work in Hamburg.

Walking instead of riding will give the visitor a more distinct impression, and many of the city's sights are within walking distance. Start at the opposite side of the Central station, passing shops at Mönckebergstrasse. Take a look at **St. Petri Church**, the oldest of the five main Evangelical Churches in the city center. Believed to have been built around 1050, it became a victim of the city's Great Fire in 1842 and was then restored to its original state. Take a few steps back into Steinstrasse to get to **St. Jacobi Church**, first mentioned in 1255. Its Baroque organ behind the altar is one of the most valuable in the world. In 1720 the famous composer J.S. Bach applied for an organist's job, but was not accepted–Hamburg simply could not pay him enough.

Returning to Mönckebergstrasse, do not forget to see the **Rathaus** at the end of it. This magnificent sandstone town hall is the seat of the Senate and the City Council; Hamburg is both a town and a German Land–a state like Lower Saxony or Bavaria. The Rathaus has 647 rooms, six more than Buckingham Palace, and a sumptuous interior. At the back of the pile (Adolphsplatz) you will find Germany's oldest stock exchange–the **Börse**–founded in 1558. The building itself is not so old, because the Great Fire destroyed the original one. The place where the voracious conflagration of 1842 started is the old **Deichstrasse**–an historic area with ancient warehouses and office buildings and some good restaurants with traditional Hamburg atmosphere.

Round the Alster: About half a mile from here the **Jungfernstieg boulevard** leads by the **Alster Lake**, which, in spite of its expansive 450 acres (180 hectares) is not a lake, but a tributary of the river Elbe. The well-known Jungfernstieg cafe, **Alsterpavillon**, was opened by a French emigrant in 1799. It is a favorite meeting point for most people. The same cannot be said of the

In the bottle-ship museum.

neighboring Hotel Vier Jahreszeiten, whose reputation as one of the world's best hotels makes it expensive. Guests to the **Hamburg State Opera** can walk round the corner to Grosse Theaterstrasse 35 where they will find this leading German opera house with a repertoire ranging from the classics to modern works. Here is where Placido Domingo began his illustrious career.

Around the streets and squares, you will be impressed by the chic, glass-roofed shopping centers and arcades. You can also tour the lake; at the Jungfernstieg pier a fleet of white boats offers guided tours of the harbor as well as the principal and lesser channels.

Water and Bridges: These tours are the best ways of visiting **Speicherstadt** (warehouse town). The boat trip gives you a chance to view the biggest warehousing complex in the world, where coffee, tea, tobacco, spices and other goods are stored in Gothic cathedrals–foreign soil in the middle of the city, because the warehouse town belongs to the **Free Port**. This port-within-a-port covers about six sq. miles (10 sq km) and is fenced all round. Its free zone offers customers cargo storage without customs clearance.

Hamburg is surrounded by water and indeed covers 10 percent of the city's surface. Because of this, Hamburg had more bridges than any other city in Europe. On average, the difference between low and high tide is about 10 feet (three m) but over the years the city has had frequent problems with extremely high flood tides and has spent much money on bulwarks.

Gateway to the Seven Seas: The harbor with the old **St. Pauli Elbetunnel** and the **St. Pauli Landungsbrücken** (landing stages) is where the harbor tours begin. Cruise on one of the smaller launches which can go under the low bridges and navigate the narrower side of the channels–the larger crafts are confined to the main parts of the port.

Hamburg's port is the biggest in Germany, being visited by some 15,000 ships each year. In early May, Hamburgians and visitors celebrate the port's

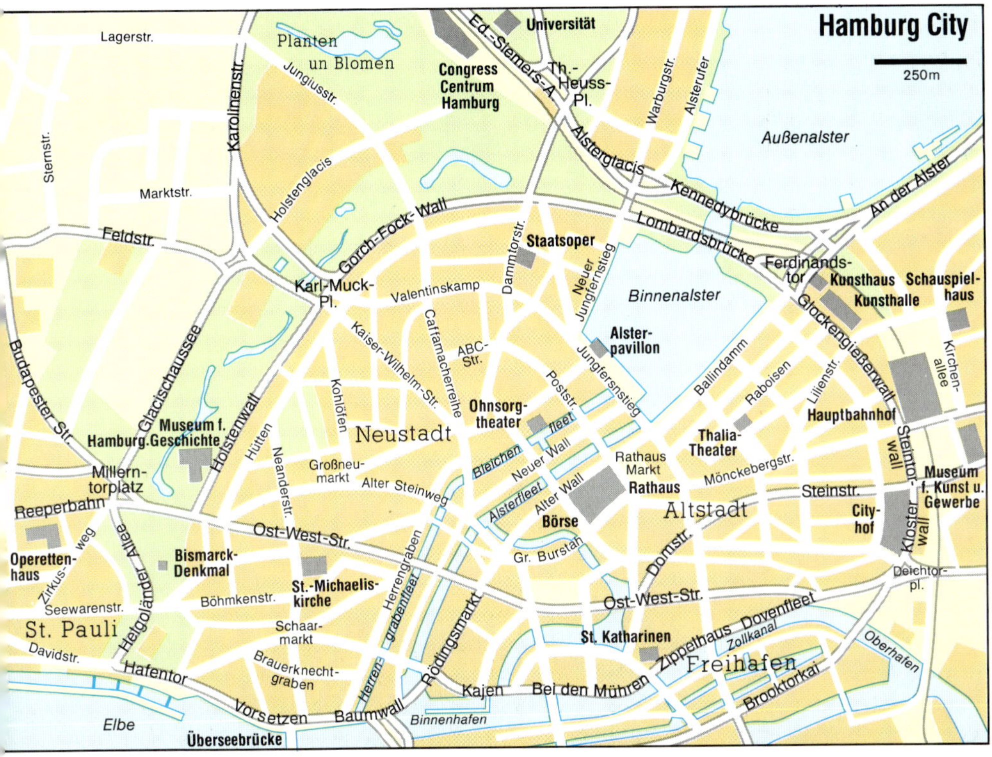

birthday. In 1989, it celebrated its 800th birthday. The old Elbetunnel, leading from Landungsbrücken to the port area of Steinwerder is not so old, but is more appealing than the modernized harbor front. The green rotunda-roofed entrance building, the cages for cars and pedestrians and the tiled tunnel walls make it worth seeing.

The world's most wicked mile: In the port's vicinity, Hamburg's landmark, **St. Michaelis Church**, reaches 430 feet (130 m) high and is well-known to sailors from all parts of the world. This impressive example of Baroque architecture is known as Michel (pronounced meshall) and gives a splendid panorama of the city and the port facilities. Below the church (at Krayenkamp 10) the **Krameramtswohnungen**, built by a mercer's guild as widows' apartments, are fine examples of 17th-century dwellings. Just a short distance from here (at Holstenwall 24) the **Museum für Hamburgische Geschichte** with its collection of ship models lends further insight into Hamburg's history. Inside the building is the **Historic Emigration Office**. If your ancestors left Europe for America between 1850 and 1914 via Hamburg, then this is the place to trace your European roots.

This city district of **St. Pauli** is famous and is a synonym for the nightlife at **Grosse Freiheit**, **Herbertstrasse** and **Reeperbahn**, the world's most wicked mile. Daytime amusement is also offered: the Dom (at Heiligengeistfeld), North Germany's biggest fun-fair is held here thrice a year. (Try the hot apple tarts and the hot Berliner jelly doughnuts!) Early birds should visit the very lively **Fischmarkt** (fish market) at the harborside. On Sundays, from 6 a.m. to 10 a.m., practically every portable item is sold here, Hamburg's most traditional market.

Along the Elbe river: Walking or driving westward along the riverside, the next quarter is **Altona**. Founded around 1520 and becoming part of Denmark 100 years later, the town has belonged to Hamburg since 1937. The **Altona Museum** (Museumstrasse 23) has col-

Shopping mall in Hamburg's Hansaviertel.

lections of ship models, old figureheads and sea maps. Another kind of culture, of a more dynamic kind, is found inside the **Fabrik** (Barnerstrasse 36). The former munitions factory is a busy communication center with jazz, rock, blues, theater and other activities.

Returning to the riverside, the wealthy Elbchaussee leads to the picturesque village of **Blankenese**. This former fishermen's district has developed into a fashionable suburb with romantic spiral staircases and tightly-packed little cottages. The village, situated at the river's edge, offers a beautiful view of the Elbe and passing ships.

About four miles (seven km) from here (driving along the Elbchaussee) and beyond the Hamburg federal state boundary is the **Willkomm-Höft** (Welcome Point), one of Hamburg's greatest attractions for both sailors and landlubbers. Here is where the city begins and ends for every passing ship above 500 GRT. National flags are raised and greetings boom out in different languages. In the basement of the restaurant building is a museum exhibiting miniature ships in bottles.

On the other bank: From the Schulau ferry house the visitor has the opportunity to cross the river by ferry (to Lühe) to visit **Altes Land**, Germany's largest fruit-growing area. (Ask about Harburg and the Altes Land at the Tourist Information office.) Also on this other side of the Elbe river is Hamburg's mountain range, which is for recreation and walking. At the top of the 415 feet (125 m) high **Kiekeberg** (in Ehestorf) is an open-air-museum: a village of farmhouses which has been reconstructed in 16th–18th century styles.

The city also has many recreational areas. The **Planten un Blomen Park** is popular with greenhouses, playgrounds and, in summer, illuminated fountains. It also has the **Wallanlagen** (old ramparts) and the **Old Botanical Garden**. Another open-air-attraction is **Hagenbeck's Tierpark** (on Hagenbeckallee) with its more than 2,100 animals. This privately-owned zoological garden was first opened in 1907 and became a

Below, "Banana Harry," well-known in town, at the Hamburg fishing market. Right, work of the street artist.

model for other cities because of its open-air enclosures.

If it rains (people say that is an essential part of Hamburg) then better go indoors, into Hamburger **Kunsthalle** (Art Museum) with its famous paintings by Bertram, Renoir, Picasso, Kokoschka, Warhol and others. The address is Glockengiesserwall–one minute from the Central station–where the Hamburg tour began. Not far away, at Steintorplatz, is the **Museum für Kunst und Gewerbe** (Arts and Crafts Museum) with its considerable collection of ancient European and Asiatic applied art.

An excursion to the Lüneburg heath: South of Hamburg, Europe's intact heathland region extends over 2,800 sq miles (7,200 sq km) between the Lower Elbe in the north and the Aller in the south. It originated in the Ice Age, when glaciers left behind the base for today's landscape with less fertile soil, covered with heather, broom, juniper and forests of oak and birch–an unforgettable landscape with a touch of melancholy.

Here you will meet shepherds leading their flocks of *Heidschnucken* –sheep with characteristically curved horns and dark shaggy skin–through idyllic landscape. Roasted *Heidschnucken* meat is a specialty of this region, where many people will be delighted to recount old ghost stories. If you are lucky enough to visit this region in August, listen closely to the humming and buzzing of bees in the flowering heather. Their industriously produced honey can be tasted at any time. Numerous *Hünengräber* (megalithic tombs) are a reminder of life and death here in prehistoric times.

Coming from Hamburg by road, take the A7 (route to Hanover) and leave the highway at Garlstorf. One-and-a-half mile (two km) westward, in Nindorf, is **Wildpark Lüneburger Heide**, the first nature park to be established in Germany. The park has since become home to wild boars, otters, and red deer; there is also a playground and pony riding.

The nearby 49,400 acre (20,000 hectare) **Naturschutzpark Lüneburger Heide** extends southwards and is pro-

Sailing boats on the Alster.

tected by the state as an area of great natural beauty. Coming from Garlstorf or Nindorf, take the road to Undeloh or Niederhaverbeck, and in either case drive to the car park: the laws of both nature and man request you to leave your car here. The best ways to experience the peace and solitude of this preserved area is to walk or to ride in a horse-drawn carriage. At its heart is the 554 feet (169 m) high **Wilseder Berg** (mountain). If the weather is good the spires of Hamburg and Lüneburg can be seen from the mountain top. The best time to visit the heath area is at the end of August when the heather is in blossom. On the third Sunday of August, the village of **Amelinghausen** (route B209 to Lüneburg) has a festival to celebrate the election of the heath's queen.

In the heart of the heath: The city of **Lüneburg** about 15 miles (25 km)to the north gave the surrounding heath its name. The town's red-brick or half-timbered houses were once built on the profit from the salt trade. This white gold made the medieval town of Lüneburg wealthy and important for trade. But the town had to pay for its boom: many of the lofty gabled buildings are now at an angle because the ground on which they stand has subsided. Remarkable remnants of the past in the old part of the town worth seeing include **Kloster Lüne** (monastery) **St. Johannis church** and the old street **Am Sande** as well as the second largest town hall in Germany and a 640-year-old crane. Those interested in machines should not miss **Scharnebeck** (just a few minutes northeast) where the big dry dock situated on the Elbe-Seitenkanal is still working. It handles ships of up to 12,000 tons within three minutes.

Heading north, you reach the river Elbe and the town of **Lauenburg**. The old Elbestrasse with its half-timbered houses and the Elbe shipping museum are charming. Lauenburg lies on the border with East Germany and so the only possible direction to travel on the B5 was westwards past Geesthacht with its romantic, thatch-roofed restaurant, **Grüner Jäger**, and back to Hamburg.

lossoming üneburger leide.

CONCORDIA DOMI FORIS PAX

Along The Baltic Sea Coast

While the landscape along the North Sea coast appears to be flat as a pancake, the area north and east of Hamburg towards the Baltic Sea extends into a stretch of land with rolling hills, picturesque towns and villages, meadows with grazing cattle and large forests. Rivers, creeks and lakes extend across the state of Schleswig-Holstein, which is bordered on the east by the Baltic Sea. Typical features are the *Förden*, wide Baltic Sea bays reaching far into the mainland of endless meadows and fields and where it is separated by so-called *Knicks*, rows of dense bushes that cut off the wind.

Lübeck, Queen of Hanseatic League: When exploring this scenic landscape it is best to start at **Lübeck**, the third but once the most important of the three "pearls of the North." It is located only 40 miles (65 km) east of Hamburg to which it is connected by the A1 and the B75. Undoubtedly, this city is one of the prettiest in Germany. Its architecture is mainly in the so-called *Backsteingotik* (brick Gothic) style which developed in the 12th century in northern Germany.

eft, übeck's ndmark, e Holsten ate. elow, e Voss-Eck n Eutin.

The city was founded in 1159 by Duke Henry the Lion on a river-island in the Trave which runs into the Baltic Sea at the present-day Lübeck suburb of Travemünde. After the Danes lost in the battle of Bornhöved in 1227, the city of the seven towers became the main trading center on the Baltic Sea and a Free Imperial City. In the 14th century the Queen of the North, as the city was then called, became the leading member of the Hanseatic League. For 250 years the supremacy of Lübeck was unquestioned. Then the rise of Denmark and Sweden and the Thirty Years' War ended this greatness. In 1937 the city was incorporated into the state of Schleswig-Holstein. Today, Lübeck has 240,000 inhabitants and is the second largest city in Schleswig-Holstein.

Approaching from Hamburg, the seven towers of Lübeck's churches can be seen from far away. **St. Marien** was built during the 13th century and became the model for many brick-Gothic churches in the Baltic Sea area. The organ with its 15,000 pipes and 130 registers is the third largest in Germany. Organ concerts are given from April through October. The **Dom**, the oldest church in Lübeck, has two towers and was built in 1173. In the 13th–14th century it was completed in its present-day shape in Gothic style. Inside this sublime example of the *Backsteingotik* are many art treasures including the huge *Triumphkreuz* of Bernt Notke, a cross with carved figures made in 1466. Other old churches are the small **St. Ägidien** church (14th century) and **St. Jakobi** (13th century); the latter has one of the oldest organs (15th century) in Europe. Worth seeing too are **St. Katharinen** (14th century) and **St. Petri** (gorgeous view from the tower).

All these impressive ecclesiastical edifices are located in the old part of Lübeck. This area is surrounded by water and access to it is via different bridges and dams. The landmark of

Lübeck, the massive and twin-towered Holstentor stands at the western entrance to the old part of town. A former fortified gate within the destroyed city wall, Holstentor was completed in 1477 and is depicted on the 50-mark notes of present-day Germany.

From Holstentor it is a short walk to the magnificent **Rathaus** (town hall) in the town center. It is one of the oldest in Germany and was built between the 13th and 16th century. Unique are the *Windlöcher* (holes in the facade) and the coat of arms of Hanseatic cities on glazed tiles. From the town hall, facing the marketplace, it is only a few steps to the **Buddenbrook House** (18th century) where the brothers Thomas and Heinrich Mann spent their youth. The house is named after one of Thomas Mann's great books which made Lübeck into a shrine of world literature.

If you take the Mengstrasse, you will pass the historic **Schabbelhaus**, one of the city's top restaurants. If you walk down the Breite Strasse you will reach the **Seamen's Guild House**, founded in 1535 for retired sea captains. It is now a restaurant with rough wooden tables, pew benches with high backs, copper lamps and ship models hanging from the ceiling. The **Heilig-Geist-Hospital** (Hospice of the Holy Spirit) another beautiful building some steps away, has a star-shaped vault with wonderful 13th-century frescoes. It was one of the earliest social institutions in Germany and still serves as a home for the elderly.

While strolling you will pass picturesque courtyards and hallways built during the 16th century. Many of these compounds are architectural jewels of small houses and gardens.

Along the Trave River which encircles the old town are several *Salzspeicher* (salt warehouses) where the white gold from Lüneburg was once stored. While in Lübeck, sample its world-famous marzipan served in the cafes around the marketplace.

Resorts and beaches: Northeast of Lübeck you will come to **Travemünde** at the Lübecker Bucht (bay) which, strangely, has been part of Lübeck since

The sailing ship *Passat*, a witness of times gone by.

the 14th century. Travemünde, a fashionable seaside resort of Germany since 1802, has a famous casino, a *Kurhaus*, and a broadwalk over which towers the 520 feet (158 m) tall Hotel Maritim. In the harbor you can visit the four-masted sailing ship *Passat*, formerly used as a *Schulschiff* (school ship) for young sailors and now a youth hostel.

North of Travemünde is a large and popular resort. On summer days you will find the beaches along the coastline crowded with canopied deck chairs and seashell-decorated sandcastles, and the Baltic Sea itself alive with windsurfers and yachts. Along the **Lübecker Bucht**, called "bathub" by the locals, are beach resorts. The most popular are **Timmendorfer Strand, Scharbeutz** and **Haffkrug**. On the way from Travemünde to the Timmendorf beach, you will pass the **Hemmelsdorfer See** (lake) which, at 144 feet (44 m) below sea level, is the lowest spot in Germany. Here you can enjoy smoked fish and visit the local bird park.

To the northwest (take the B76 from Haffkrug) it is only six miles (10 km) to the vast lake district of the **Holsteinische Schweize** (Switzerland of Holstein) a well-loved holiday region in northern Germany. Most of these widely spread lakes–about 200 in this area between Malente, Eutin and Plön–are surrounded by lovely beech and oak forests. The first town you reach is **Eutin**, called Weimar of the North because Eutin was a cultural center in the 18th century when Homer-translator J. H. Voss and the "Goethe painter" Wilhelm Tischbein resided here. Eutin has a pleasant castle with an English-style garden. In summer, thousands of opera enthusiasts gather in the park to listen to the open-air concerts. Favorite pieces are played by famous C.M. von Weber, most acclaimed son of the town. Three miles (five km) to the north is the spa of **Malente-Gremsmühlen** which stands between the lakes **Kellersee** and **Dieksee**. One of the most beautiful lakes of this region is **Ukleisee**, secluded in this forest setting east of town.

At the center of the Holsteinische

t the lakes
f Eutin.

Schweiz is **Plön**, which boasts a Renaissance castle and the **Plöner See** with its 11 sq mile (30 sq km) lake being the largest and most impressive of the lakes. South of the Plön See (by road or by boat from Plön) is the old St. Petri Church of **Bosau** which offers a magnificent view. Six miles (10 km) west lies **Bornhöved**, which, in 789 and 1227, was the scene of two decisive battles against the Danes. From Plön follow the B76 in a northerly direction to **Preetz** with its 13th-century brick-built monastery. Six miles northeast is the **Selenter See**, a beautiful bird paradise. Around the lake stretches the **Grafenecke** with many manor houses and castles such as Keletkamp, Panker and Testorf. Nearby is the **Bungsberg** which, at 541 feet (164 m) is the highest "mountain" in Schleswig-Holstein.

Capital of the North: Ten miles (16 km) north of Preetz on the B76 is **Kiel** (population: 249,000) the capital of Schleswig-Holstein and an important port with a considerable range of industries. The city lies at the inner end of the **Kieler Förde** (fjord) and at the beginning of the most-traveled canal in the world, the 62-mile (100 km) long North-East-Sea canal to Brunsbüttel. Although Kiel was founded in 1233, it only became an important center on the Baltic Sea in 1865. Since the foundation of the Deutsches Reich in 1871, Kiel has been the home of the largest German naval base. Sights include the **Marine Ehrenmal** (16 km east) the **farm-house-museum** at Molfsee (a few miles west of town) and the huge bridge across the Kiel canal in the north. Its bustling **Holstenstrasse**, a pedestrian precinct, is a good example of modern town planning. The promenade **Hindenburgufer** offers an impressive view of the harbor and shipyards. Popular resorts which are linked by delightful boat trips grace the 10 mile (16 km) long Kieler Förde. Since 1882 the July *Kieler Woche* (Kiel Week) has been a world-famous event in which sailing boats from all over the world compete in an idyllic setting.

To continue north from Kiel take ei-

Landscape i Schleswig-Holstein.

ther the B76 for 17 miles (28 km) or the more picturesque B503 for 29 miles (47 km) through the **Dänischer Wohld** (forest) to the fishing port of **Eckernförde** . Here the fishermen land the famous *Kieler Sprotten* (small herrings) smoke and pack them.

From Eckernförde, the B76 continues west to Schleswig. A few miles before Schleswig, stop at the resorts of **Stexwig** and **Heddeby** and visit the remains of **Haithabu** the largest Viking trading place in northern Europe 1,000 years ago. It was linked to the Baltic Sea by the river Schlei and to the North Sea by the rivers Treene and Eider. Today, a new museum houses Viking boats.

Opposite lies **Schleswig**, the oldest town in the state and successor to 11th-century Haithabu. While in Schleswig it is a must to visit the magnificent Renaissance castle **Gottorf** housing the two leading museums in the state: the **Landesmuseum** and the **Museum für Vor-und Frühgeschichte** (Museum of Prehistoric Times) the largest of its kind in Germany. Another attraction is the

sherman
Kiel
rbor.

Nydam Boat, a 4th century Viking boat. Thirty-six men manned the oars. The Romanesque-Gothic St. Petri-Dom contains the famous **Bordesholm Altar** (completed 1521) by Hans Brüggemann with its 392 carved figures crowned by the Holy Virgin.

Northeast of Schleswig is the peninsula **Angeln**, from where the German tribe of the same name sailed to and conquered England in the 5th–6th century. Characteristic of Angeln are the many *Knicks*, long fences which shield the fields and pastures from the wind, and cold megalithic graves.

There are two routes to Flensburg from Schleswig; the shorter way (24 miles/38 km) is via the B76, the historical *Ochsenweg* (ox-road) from Denmark to Hamburg; the longer (52 miles/83 km) but more pleasant route on the B201 passes Angeln via the fishing-port of **Kappeln**. From Kappeln take a six-mile (10 km) detour to the fishing-port of **Maasholm**, famous for its seafood restaurants. Don't miss the smoked eel, a specialty of the area.

Traveling along the B199 from Kappeln, worthwhile detours can be made to the Baltic Sea in the east. At **Ringsby** (25 miles/40 km) from Kappeln) turn right to visit the beautiful white castle of **Glücksburg** (16th-century) which is surrounded by a **Schlossteich** (pond) and which houses a tapestry museum.

Returning to the B199 via Glücksburg, you will reach **Flensburg** (population: 90,000) the Germany's northernmost town and only a few miles from the Danish border. Flensburg was founded 700 years ago and became a trading center. Since the 18th century ships have brought West Indian rum to Flensburg for blending. Today, Flensburg is the gate to Scandinavia, the seat of the German navy school and of the much-feared **Kraftfahrzeugbundesamt**, where all German cars and traffic offenses are registered. At the Nordermarks, the old marketplace, are the **Schragen** (1595) where bakers and butchers once sold their wares. The 16th century brick doorway, **Nordertor**, at the northern end of the old town is the emblem of Flensburg.

Der
Kampf
gegen
Mauer
geht
BLUE
EYES

DAVID'89

MARMORHAUS
MÄNNER
U
U-Bhf. Kurfürstendamm
Anderle
Ku'damm Eck
Danke

SPECIAL BERLIN

Although it is no longer the proud capital of the German Reich, **Berlin** is still a leading metropolis, ranking first in Germany in terms of surface area, population and vitality. The first documentary evidence of its existence dates back to A.D. 1244. In 1307 it amalgamated with the neighboring fishing village of Köln. In 1443 Count Friedrich II von Hohenzollern made the new town his residence and capital of the surrounding region of Mark Brandenburg. After the devastating Thirty Years' War, Berlin was left with some 5,000 inhabitants, but it soon prospered under the rule of the Great Elector Friedrich Wilhelm (1610-88). In 1709 under the Great Elector's son Friedrich I, the first king of Prussia, Berlin became a royal residence. Under Friedrich II the Great (1740-86) the town grew into Prussia's leading manufacturing and business city. A generation later, Prussia's capital became a center of intellectual life in Germany in the wake of the foundation of a university by Wilhelm von Humboldt (1810). During the second half of the 19th century the city developed into the Germany's major industrial and commercial center. It was thus the natural culmination of the city's development that it be made capital of the newly-established German Reich in 1871. After World War I, a new municipal entity called Greater Berlin was established by the amalgamation of Berlin with seven adjoining towns, 59 rural communes and 27 *Gutsbezirke*. During the short period of the Weimar Republic (1918-33) Berlin was the unrivalled center of economic, political and cultural life in Germany and a metropolis comparable to New York, London and Paris. Because it was also the capital of the German Reich under the Nazi regime (1933-45), Berlin suffered the ravages of World War II. In 1945 it was put under a Four-Power administration, a status maintained till today. Political differences between the USSR and the Allies after 1948 led (Soviet blockade) to a division of the city which was formalized by the construction of the Wall in August 1961.

'receding ages, housands of erliners– ast and Vest– elebrate he opening f the Wall. .eft, nusic-box nan in erlin. elow, nemorial o the Allied irlift.

Berlin incorporates a total area of 340 sq miles (883 sq km), more than the total area of Munich, Stuttgart and Frankfurt combined. The three western sectors cover 55 percent of this area. The political island of West Berlin with almost two million inhabitants is fully integrated into the economic, financial and judicial system of the Federal Republic. East Berlin, with its over a million inhabitants, was sealed off by the Wall which had divided the city for 25 years.

Around Kurfütstendamm: The information desk of the Berlin Tourist Office is located at Tegel Airport. The A9 bus departs from the airport for the districts of **Kurfürstendamm** and **Gedächtniskirche** (Memorial Church) in the heart of the city. In the center of pulsating Berlin, these are all that the visitor expects to find in an international metropolis: first-class hotels, palatial cinemas, nightclubs, theaters and a wide choice of cafes and restaurants. The

Kurfürstendamm and its side streets are also Berlin's largest and most elegant shopping district, with department stores, art galleries and flea markets.

The Kurfürstendamm or Ku'damm, was once a sandy riding path leading from the palace at the Spree river to a hunting lodge in the Grunewald forest. After Berlin's rise to the status of an imperial city, a pompous boulevard after the fashion of the Champs Elysées was constructed with imposing apartments in the Belle Epoque style. After World War I, it changed into a chic amusement district and became the playground of a cosmopolitan, frivolous scene. The legendary Romanisches Cafe, a meeting place of the avant-garde in theater, film, painting and literature is still surrounded by many nostalgic memories. The Ku'damm, which is somewhat over two miles (about four km) long, begins–or ends–at the Gedächniskirche (Memorial Church) a ruin left as a landmark to commemorate wartime hubris and destruction. Its old bell-tower, called "hollow tooth" because of its jagged shape, is flanked by a modern octagonal church building and a separate tower. Only a few steps away is the **Europa Center**, a gigantic shopping and business complex, where you will find the *Verkehrsamt* (tourist information). From the roof (282 feet/86 m) one can enjoy a wonderful panorama of the entire city. From the Europa Center, one of the main arteries of Berlin, the shop-lined **Tauentzienstrasse** runs southeast to **KaDeWe** on **Wittenbergplatz**, a Berlin abbreviation for department store of the West, the continent's largest department store with its renowned food and delicacy section.

Berlin's Eiffel Tower: At **the Bahnhof Zoo** station where trains from West Germany arrive, you can take a trip to some of the famous landmarks of Berlin by following **Hardenbergstrasse** past the university quarter to the attractively laid out **Ernst-Reuter-Platz**. From here, along **Bismarckstrasse** you will reach one of Berlin's landmarks, the **Funkturm** (radio tower) which rises 450 feet (138 m) high on the foreground in the district of Charlottenburg. This iron tower looks like a smaller counterpart of the Paris Eiffel Tower. In the same area, opposite the city motorway is one of Berlin's most recent landmarks, the **International Congress Center** (ICC). It was inaugurated in 1979 and looks like a giant spaceship from afar. Also in Charlottenburg, outside Heerstrasse, the **Olympic Stadium** where Jesse Owens triumphed four times in the 1936 Olympic Games.

East of Charlottenburg are the districts of Schöneberg and Steglitz with their many busy shopping streets. After a thorough facelift for the city's 750th year jubilee in 1987, the light sandstone facades of the **Rathaus** Schöneberg (town hall) at **John F. Kennedy Platz** are gleaming again. As the seat of the city government and the political center of West Berlin, it stands out among all the other town halls of West Berlin's 12 districts. This is the reason for the official white-and-red flag with the bear as heraldic animal fluttering on the top of its square tower. When U.S. President

Relaxing at a café on the famous Ku'damm.

John F. Kennedy paid his memorable visit to the city on June 23, 1963, he proclaimed his famous sentence: "*Ich bin ein Berliner*" ("I am a Berliner") from the balcony.

Green Berlin: Both land and air travelers see abundant greenery when they arrive in Berlin. One-third of Berlin consists of woods, fields, parks, lakes and rivers. You may criss-cross parts of the city by boat on the **Spree River** or its canals. Another way of exploring the city's western outskirts is to cruise along the **Havel River** which spreads itself into a chain of scenic lakes, notably the **Tegeler See** and the **Wannsee** which is known as Berlin's bathtub. The place where the Spree joins the Havel is guarded by the 16th century **Zitadelle Spandau** (Spandau Citadel) an imposing water fortress. Another great sight is **Pfaueninsel** (Peacock Island) on the Havel, praised as the most romantic place in the precincts of Berlin, because of the mock-ruin 18th century castle and its natural beauty.

West Berlin's "green lung" is the extensive forest area of **Grunewald** (745 acres/304 hectares) with five small lakes scattered within and the **Teufelsberg** (at 377 feet or 113 m, the highest spot in West Berlin) built on the rubble of demolished buildings in World War II. The largest park in the inner city is the 600 acre (243 hectare) **Tiergarten**, a former hunting ground of the Electoral house. Here, dotted along 20 miles (32 km) of roads and trees, are many of Berlin's historical sights.

Right in the center at the **Grosser Stern** roundabout rises the 220 feet high Siegessäule (Victory Column) built between 1865 and 1873 in honor of the Prussian campaigns against Denmark, Austria and France. The viewing platform is topped by the 26 feet high (eight m) gilded bronze statue of **Victoria**. The Baroque-Classical palace **Schloss Bellevue** (1785) on the banks of the Spree River nearby serves as the official Berlin residence of the West German President. East of Schloss Bellevue, facing the Spree river, stands the fascinating **Kongresshalle** (1975)

'urkish vomen in ront of the 3erlin Reichstag.

dubbed "pregnant oyster" by Berliners until the collapse of its roof in 1981.

Reminders of history: The **Reichstag** further east on the bank of the Spree River, facing **Platz der Republik**, borders closely on the Wall. Erected between 1884-94 in the style of the Italian Renaissance, this monumental building once housed Germany's national parliament. When it was set on fire on February 28, 1933, Germany moved a decisive step further down the path toward Nazi dictatorship. Having suffered severe war-damage, the Reichstag was restored in the hope that it might serve again as the seat of a parliament freely elected by all Germans. In its western wing, an exhibition *Questions Arising Out of German History* attracts over 400,000 visitors annually, mostly German school children.

The wide **Strasse des 17. Juni**, cuts through the district of **Tiergarten**, ending at thc Wall; Junc 17 recalls the East Berlin revolt of 1953. Then, the **Brandenburg Gate**, Berlin's landmark at the end of Strasse des 17. Juni, was still open. For 28 years it lay in the blockaded zone on the East-West border, inaccessible from both sides. Sixty-six feet (20 m) high and crowned with the copper quadriga of the Peace Goddess, it is a replica of the Propyläen Gate of the Acropolis in Athens. It was constructed in 1786-99 and was the first great monument of German classicism.

Pulsating metropolis: Much of Berlin's appeal is based on its role as the center and innovator of German cultural life. West Berlin itself has 13 repertory theaters, among them the **Schiller-theater** near Ernst-Reuter-Platz and the privately-run **Schaubühne** at Lehniner Platz, whose performances are highly regarded both within and beyond the boundaries of the Berlin theater scene. Each night the curtain of the **Deutsche Oper** (rebuilt 1961), 35 Bismarck-strasse, rises for music connoisseurs. It ranks among the world's leading opera houses. In the **Theater des Westens**, 12 Kantstrasse, lovers of musicals and operettas get their money's worth.

Especially interesting to connoiseurs

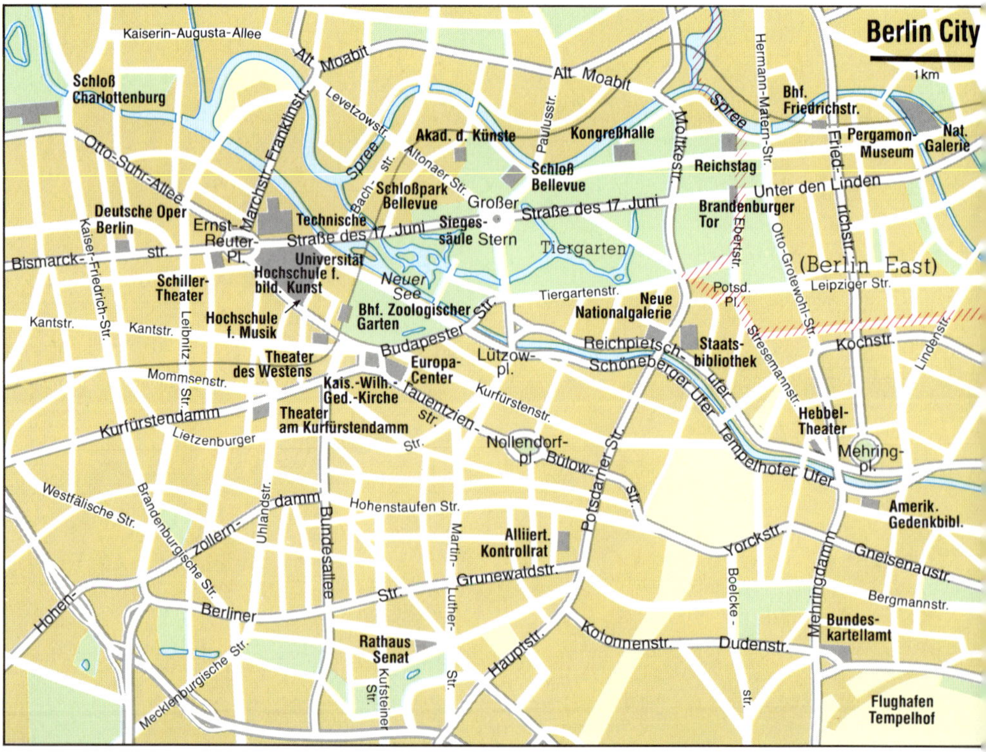

are the so-called fringe talents–less well-known, amateur theater troupes, dancers and musicians perform here, in extended factory lofts and old ballrooms. Berlin has always been a magnet for non-mainstream artists and the avant-garde. They embody the creative potential and give the city its vitality.

At the **Philharmonie** on Potsdamer Platz, the music lover can enjoy concerts given by one of the best orchestras in the world, the Berlin Philharmonic Orchestra, which, until recently, was conducted by maestro Herbert von Karajan. Berlin highlights outstanding cultural events such as the *Berlin Festival Weeks*, which offers a cross-section of international artistic achievements (September). In February/March Berlin is the scene of the world-famous *International Film Festival* in which the Berlin Bear–the city's emblem–is awarded. In November the city is the setting for the *Berlin Jazz Days*.

Encountering Nefertiti: It would take weeks to see all the treasures stored in Berlin's various museums, but even casual visitors can have a good idea of its contents. The Prussian Kings were art collectors, and today their heritage is divided between both parts of the city. West Berlin's largest museum complex can be reached by subway line No. 2 to the residential suburb of Dahlem. Scattered around the **Dahlem Dorf** subway station are the eight museums of the **Stiftung Preussischer Kulturbesitz**. The **Gemäldegalerie** (painting gallery) offers a survey of European paintings during the 13th-18th century with works by Botticelli, Titian, Raphael, Van Dyck, Holbein, Dürer, Cranach, Vermeer, Rubens, and the world's second largest Rembrandt collection. Among other collections, the immense **ethnological department** is especially fascinating. Here pre-Columbian finds, South Sea boats, Oriental artifacts are displayed in theatrical setting. Museums in Dahlem are closed on Mondays.

Berlin's last big castle from the times of the Hohenzollern, **Charlottenburg Schloss**, is now a museum. Construction begun at the end of the 17th century

Berlin Wall at the Brandenburg gate before November 9, 1989.

of what was intended to be a summer residence for Queen Sophie Charlotte. Later kings, however, wanted the castle to compete with Versailles. Thus, in the 18th century the castle was gradually extended with the addition of several wings into a magnificent Baroque palace with a dome-shaped tower, an orangery and a court of justice. Its historic rooms, with collections of paintings and china, as well as the garden, are open daily except Mondays. Another complex houses the **Kunstgewerbemuseum** (Museum of Applied Arts). Its collection surveys the history of design from the Renaissance to the present.

Queen Nefertiti, pharaoh Echnaton's wife, resides opposite the castle. This strange limestone work is the most famous piece in a display of 1,500 objects from the dynasties of ancient Egypt, shown in the Egyptian Museum at 70 Schloss-strasse. Opposite, a similar building, **Stühlerbau**, houses the **Antikenmuseum** (Museum of Antiquities) with Greek and Roman works of art.

Two other art museums and the **Musikinstrumenten-Museum** (Museum of Musical Instruments) lie at the new West Berlin Cultural Forum on the southeastern border of the Tiergarten. The **Kulturforum** at Kemperplatz is home to the celebrated Berlin Philharmonic Orchestra and the Philharmonie. Its futuristic concert hall was built by Hans Scharoun. The **Nationalgalarie** (National Gallery) housed in a glass building designed by Mies van der Rohe, focuses on 19th-20th century art.

After strolling and "culture-vulturing" through the city, you should visit some of the city's 4,000 restaurants, pubs and bars. Because no curfew has been imposed for any of these establishments, Berlin has been dubbed the 24-hour-city, an El Dorado of nightclubs.

The Fall of the Wall: The erosion of the Soviet bloc and the peaceful revolutions in Hungary, Poland, East Germany and Czechoslovakia have reshuffled the political cards in Europe. Germany once again became a prism that, more than any other country in Europe, reflected this kaleidoscopic development.

The Berlin Wall has tumbled and, after 28 years, East Berliners and GDR citizens are meanwhile allowed to travel across the border. In early December the events in the divided city of Berlin, the perspectives of a cooperation between the two Germanies as well as the summit of the two world leaders, George Bush and Mikhail Gorbachev, off the Malta coast, riveted the world to the TV screens. Let's hope that Gorbachev's statement: "In the final analysis we envision Europe as a commonwealth of sovereign democratic states with a high level of equitable interdependence and easily accessible borders and wide-ranging contacts among people..." will become reality.

Beyond the Wall: Foreign visitors can cross safely to East Berlin at **Checkpoint Charlie**, or, when using the subway or the elevated S-Bahn, via **Friedrichstrasse** railway station. Once in East Berlin, tourists head for **Unter den Linden**, Berlin's historic avenue. On the east towards the Spree River, the nondescript modern buildings soon give way to the **Lindenforum**. Here, surrounding **Bebelplatz**, beautiful edifices from the era of the Prussian kings can be seen. The most famous of these kings, Friedrich der Grosse, rides high on his horse on a monument in the middle strip of the boulevard. The **State Opera**, the **Humboldt University**, and the **Museum of German History** all belong to this ensemble of Baroque, Rococo and Classicism. At the **Neue Wache**, a memorial to the victims of fascism and militarism, the East German guard of honor change hourly with a brief ceremony executed in Prussian goose-steps.

Berlin's classic temples of art are on the **Spree Island** at the end of Unter den Linden. Here, the **Pergamon Museum's** archaeological collection boasts unrivalled treasures. The **Pergamon Altar**, the collection's most famous exhibit, was considered one of the seven wonders of the ancient world. The above is just a small selection offered by the Other Berlin, whose modern landmark, the television tower on **Alexanderplatz**, rises 1,198 feet (365 m) above the Wall.

Kaiser Wilhelm memorial church.

For centuries the religious year and the remnants of pre-Christian customs left their imprint on the rural German population. The change of seasons–in spring sowing, in autumn harvesting–resulted in a variety of customs, while in the towns the handworkers' guilds and traders' companies developed their own customs. Still, the rapid industrialization and urbanization of the 19th century have caused many customs to vanish.

It was not until the start of the 20th century that associations were formed in many places to preserve, restore and cultivate traditions. Festivals with traditional costumes and processions were exactly what city tourist departments needed to improve business.

The largest festival in the world: Ever heard of the city where 234,000 gallons (900,000 liters) of beer are drunk within an area of less than one square mile (nearly three sq km) over one weekend? Yes, it's Munich, and it is not just any weekend but the last one in September when the annual *Oktoberfest*, the largest festival on earth, is ceremoniously opened. On Saturday, at 11 a.m. the festival publicans and breweries march in and the leading Bavarian politicians wave from carriages, as once King Ludwig II did to the commoners. Munich's first lord mayor is allowed to broach the first barrel in front of clattering and whirring cameras. *Ozapft is!* is the relieved call, and a cannonade proclaims the news to all Munich.

Those who do not want to miss the parade of actors dressed in exotic costumes of leather and *loden* (green woollen cloth), with plumes of chamois whiskers and eagle-down knicker-bockers, morning stars, and wild beards, must rise early on the first festival Sunday to get a vantage point in the city center. It is led by the *Munich Kindl* (child), astride a horse and followed by costumed groups, riflemen's clubs, folklore groups, musicians and brass bands from Europe and beyond. Over 7,000 participants form a four mile (six km) long procession to the Theresienwiese, scene of the *Oktoberfest*.

Preceding pages, medieval brass band in action. Left, the *Alemannische Fasnacht* in Lindau. Right, the Rhine *Karneval* in Bonn.

It all began in October, 1810, when the Bavarian Crown Prince Ludwig I married the Princess of Saxony, Therese, whose name was then given to the Theresienwiese, where the marriage was celebrated for two days. Although far from the city, the horse races, rifle ranges, and a huge tent captured in the Turkish War, attracted 40,000 visitors, twice the number of Munich's population at that time. The festival then became a permanent institution with more and more visitors but even today the people of Munich refer to

the *Oktoberfest* as *Wies'n* (meadow).

Nowadays, the *Wies'n* lasts until the first Saturday in October–16 days–and almost every year new records are reported. More than seven million visitors came in 1985 for the 175th-year jubilee; they drank 1.3 million gallons (five million liters) of beer and devoured 72 whole oxen, 630,000 fried chickens and 65,000 pigs' trotters. Almost 700 side-shows, merry-go-rounds, stalls, and splendid brass bands in 13 huge beer tents provided entertainment.

The masses start streaming in at 10 a.m. (on Sundays at 9 a.m.) to the *Wies'n,* and the beer flows until 11.30 p.m. when the gates close. In the evenings a seat in the beer tents is difficult to find because many tables and compartments are reserved for the members of Munich firms and large industries, many of which distribute vouchers for two beers and a chicken to their employees.

The fascination of the *Oktoberfest* lies in the variety of impressions, both loud and colorful, and in the beery festive atmosphere. Those fortunate enough to become part of the crowd on that warm, sunny autumn day, preferably at noon or in the afternoon, can allow themselves to be carried along through the alleys of this world of stalls and tents. The aroma of roasted almonds and aniseed, roast ox and chicken, salted fish and sausages and sauerkraut mixes with the beer haze and the smell of horse manure. One is immediately beguiled by the voices from the stalls and merry-go-rounds, by the strains of music from the beer tents. *Hey, Mr. Tambourine Man* comes over from the calypso, disco music blares at the auto-scooter; in the shooting and throwing galleries there are mini-explosions and all are drowned by the rattling, clattering and roaring from the figures-of-eight and roller coasters while in the skies above there is laughter, shrieks and wild cries. It is now time for the first tankard of beer, from one of the open-air beer tents. And in the evening, when thousands upon thousands of lamps and bulbs light up and glitter, it is time to experience the tingling and crawling feeling of the triple loop or the Icarus and to view the wonderful chaos of noise and light from a height of 100 feet (30 m). Your reeling feelings from the ferris wheel combine with the influence of alcohol, and you are soon back in the beer tent. After the second *Mass* (tankard) and while the season's most popular song is playing, you jump onto the bench, clap, sing, link arms and swing along with the rest. When the call comes you will quickly respond: a toast to *Gemütlichkeit*. Sturdy Munich waitresses constantly keep up the supply, the brass band just keeps on blowing, and lights and faces, glitter and sound, beer haze and tobacco smoke start to run together to a single, flowing, blissful feeling of well-being. Yes, indeed, the *Wies'n* is a state of mind!

Folk and church festivals: Those who miss the *Wies'n* need not fear; there are festivals in other places–the *Wasen* in Stuttgart-Bad Cannstatt (16 days starting on the last Saturday in September), the Augsburg *Plärrer* (two weeks, at the end of August or the beginning of September), the Hamburg *Dom* (November), the *Gäubodenfest* in Straubing (August), the *Mainfest* in Frankfurt and Kassel's *Zissel* (both in August).

Folk festivals, fairs or costume festivals take place in almost every town and village at some time of the year. All the stalls and stands with a variety of things, today's bric-a-brac or antiques, are often displayed in the wide square, usually around a church. In earlier centuries the market status was a coveted privilege, awarded personally by a prince or emperor to a place. On market days, traders enjoyed special legal protection. Handworkers and farmers formed a common stream and dancing and all kinds of entertainment were offered. Folk festivals have originated as much from *Kirchweih* (church consecration) as they have from fairs. Churches were consecrated in the name of a saint, and on that day a patron's festival was observed with a special mass in the church. Today, church consecrations usually only provide the date for completely secular festivals. The *Bergkirchweih* in Erlangen, for example, has acquired a wider importance, and has been held at Whitsun since 1755. The huge rock cellars of the Erlangen breweries have been located around the old town shooting house since the 17th century. Erlangen exported the most beer in Bavaria about 1870–ahead of Kulmbach and Nuremberg, and after Munich. And the quality of Frankish beer for connoisseurs is still unmatched. So the beer sampling of the 12 festival days which begins with the Thursday before Whitsun, should not be missed. The stalls, the stands and carousels wind along beneath the old lindens and oaks decorated with Chinese lanterns and lights. Long tables in the open air, the beer cellars and the tents invite one to enjoy Frankish *Bratwürscht* (grilled wuerstels) with beer and brass band music.

Left, *Fischerstechen* on the Danube at Ulm. Above, opera festival in the middle of Lake Constance at Bregenz.

Funny goings-on: The noise of firecrackers has just died away, the light from rockets and garlands bidding farewell to the old year at Silvester, has just been extinguished and almost immediately a series of masked balls begins in the cities. Part and parcel of what southern Germans call *Fasching* or *Fasnacht*, is called *Karneval* by those further north. Irrespective of the name the festival, which lasts several weeks, each provides a superb excuse for colorful jesters to let off steam. The Christian manifestation of the festivals, which is based on former heathen customs, is a turbulent farewell to meat-eating and secular pleasures, and is followed by a period of fasting. The church calendar determines the beginning–in January–and end–on Ash Wednesday, usually in March.

The basis of the custom was probably a fertility and initiation rite, the driving out of winter with its dark forces and demons by opposing them with defending spirits which had their own terrifying masks. The noise of rattles, cymbals and drums produces rhythms which people dance to as they pass along the streets, reminding one of the defense against demons of animistic societies. The artistically carved and frightful devilish spirits, witches' masks and demonic heads of the Alemanni/Swabian *Fasnet* and those in some of the Bavarian Alpine valleys show traces of the old heathen beliefs.

Medieval elements of the *Karneval* appear in jesters' banquets such as those held in Stockach and Grosselfingen, in the occupation of town halls and in the *Weiberfasnacht* (Females' *Fasnacht*) which traditionally is held on the last Thursday of *Fasching*. The symbolic takeover of power by the jesters can be seen in Lindau on Lake Constance.

In the Rhine *Karneval*, centered around Cologne, Aachen, Düsseldorf and Mainz, the *Bütten* speech, with its many references to local and national politics, is read by a jester in a huge wooden barrel called *Bütt*. Satirical criticism is also expressed in the processions on the first Monday before Lent *(Rosenmontag)*, which features masks and floats. If you want to take part in the events, you should learn the local chants–in Cologne, *Kölle Alaaf*, in Mainz, *Helau*. In addition to the traditional jesting in *Fasching* in Bavaria there is also *Skifasching* (Spitzingsee) and the *Schnablerrennen* (with huge pointed sleighs) in Gaissach near Bad Tölz. In Munich, at the Fruit and Vegetable Market, the dance of the market women attracts everybody on *Fasching's* Tuesday.

Horses and riders: Horse lovers will be amply rewarded in Westphalia, Lower Saxony and in Schleswig-Holstein. Large-scale horse markets (Heilbronn, Hamm, Gaildorf) as well as trotting, racing and jumping tournaments are held all over Germany.

In Dithmarschen and Kiel, *Roland's Riding*, which goes back to the training of riders in Roman times, is celebrated. Roland is a wooden figure turning on its own axis; if the rider is not clever enough when thrusting, he is dealt a blow from Roland.

Many mounted processions take place for religious reasons, and the *Kötztinger Pfingstritt* in the Bavarian Forest is a good example. With church bells chiming in the beautiful landscape of the Central Uplands, and costumed horses, flags, fanfare and colorfully-attired riders, the procession of 500 riders starts off on Whit Monday at 8 a.m. and travels through the picturesque Zellertal Valley to hold mass in a field four miles (six

km) away in Steinbühl. The ride is based on a vow taken in 1412: a good Christian was dying in Steinbühl, but the journey through forests and over hills was teeming with robbers and bears. So the Kötzting men formed a mounted escort to accompany the priest to enable him to administer the last rites.

In 1492, the people of Holzkirchen are said to have vowed to save their forests from bark beetle disease. And so, each Whitsuntide, a pilgrimage led by a person carrying a 43 feet (13 m) long candle begins at Holzkirchen and ascends the Bogenberg mountain, east of Donau, near Straubing. The holy blood shed by Christ for mankind is commemorated by mounted processions in

Bad Wurzach and Weingarten; also worth seeing are the old Lake Constance costumes of the women and young girls in the *Blutfest* which is held on the last Sunday in May on the island of Reichenau. Horses and riders also have patron saints such as St. Georg, St. Martin and St. Leonhard; and mounted processions and blessing of the horses occur very often around the saints' days: April 24, November 11, November 6. Worth seeing is the *Goergi-Ritt* in Traunstein (Easter Monday) in connection with the *Schwerttanz* (sword dance) and the *Leonhardifahrten* in Bad Tölz and Kreuth (November 6).

Left, the fearsome dragon of Furth im Wald. Right, medieval jousting revived in Kaltenberg.

Of marksmen, shepherds and fishermen: The season of shooting festivals begins as early as May in the extreme south (*Lenggries*) and in the north (*Fehmarn*) and goes on until the end of August (*Kronach*). For marksmen, the largest of these festivals is in Hanover (first week in July), and has been celebrated for over 450 years. Some 5,000 marksmen and over 130 bands, music corps, marching bands, marksmen's guilds and clubs–some from abroad–take part. A huge folk festival is then held for 10 days with stalls and merry-go-rounds, music and fireworks. Covered wagons, female camp followers and troopers move through the scenes of historic camp life in the *Sehusa marksmen's festival* (beginning of September) held in Seesen in the Harz. Open-air theater, chivalry tournaments, and Renaissance dances form a part, and the *Seesener Hochzeit* (marriage) of 1592 is re-enacted. The *Biberach marksmen's festival* (June/July) has a historical character, having been founded in 1481.

Salt transportation and salt making were formerly important professions. Salt was important and costly, as seen in the modern expression: "He's not worth his salt." At that time salt was brought to Germany from the Tyrol or from the other side of the Alps.

Historical and picturesque festivals are a reminder of this. At Whitsun in Bad Soden-Allendorf, salt manufacture is re-enacted in the fountain festival. *Säumen* was the transport of the salt, and the *Säumer festival* in Grafenau at the golden footpath, the Old Salt Way through the Bavarian Forest to Bohemia, recreates this (first Sunday in August). At Whitsun, Schwäbisch Hall near Stuttgart celebrates a *cake and fountain festival* of salt makers with historical scenes.

The idyllic shepherd's life portrayed in the courtly verses of Baroque and Rococo literature is no longer found in Germany. Clearing of pastures, soil fertilization and motorway construction have driven away shepherds and their flocks. Nevertheless, there is still the tradition of the *Schäferlauf* (shepherd's run) near Stuttgart. Anyone able to run barefoot over stubble for a distance of 150-300 meters wins, and becomes king of the shepherds. Huge processions featuring period costumes and a programme which, according to locality, includes plays, contests, open-air dancing and other entertainment, are played against spectacular medieval backdrops, can be seen throughout the country. One such festival is held during the last weekend in August at the venerable Imperial city of Markgröningen, near Stuttgart, with its beautiful half-timbered town hall. Another such festival is held every two years on one of the first Sundays in July at Wildberg, a meeting point for Black Forest shepherds. Wildberg's medieval attraction is the stone bridge across the Nagold. Heidenheim, with its castle on the river Kocher, holds a similar festival on the last Sunday in May. Another such festival is held on a July Sunday every two years at Bad Urach, a town which boasts both old half-timbered buildings and modern spa facilities and which is picturesquely situated in the Alb.

A shepherd's festival is also held on the edge of the Taunus, in Hungen, north of Frankfurt, on the last Sunday in August because August 24 is the "day" of St. Bartholomew, the patron saint of shepherds. Lüneburg Heath is renowned for sheep-breeding and at Müden, near Oertze, the visitor can witness the famous *Heidschnucken* (sheep) auction. When you have had enough of sheep, go pick a prize lamb at the traditional *Geissbock* auction which is held on Whit Tuesday in Deidesheim.

And how about fish? Anglers' festivals are still frequently found wherever there is a nearby lake or river. Anglers' jousting, whereby contestants stand on boards at the end of their punts and try to push their opponents into the water with poles, are still held. This fun can still be enjoyed in the Nuremberg town center festival held in the second half of September. It can also be seen in the *Sandkerwa*, held in mid-August in Bamberg, Ulm, in Diessen on Ammersee and every five years in mid-August in Starnberg. *Stocherkahnrennen* (punt races) are held in June in Tübingen on the river Neckar.

The Dark Ages Live: Emperors and princesses, knights and knaves, damsels and

maids are still popular material for children and daydreamers. Shining swords, bobbing helmet plumes, rousing fanfares and flags, chargers and couched lances–like to turn back the clock and witness, at least for a day, the life of bygone days? It is amazing how much of the Middle Ages is still present in Germany despite its self-inflicted apocalypse in 1945. In many castles, amidst attractive scenery, in old imperial cities with city walls, gate towers and houses, history is relived in the form of various festivals.

Out of the past they come, on certain days of the year. Emperor Maximilian I, Louis of Bavaria, the unhappy Konrad, the last of the

Stauffenbergs, surrounded by dukes, counts, knights–performed by more than 1500 children dressed in the costumes of different centuries and reenacting the history of their town–Kaufbeuren, in the Allgäu. This *Tänzelfest* lasts 10 days at the end of July, and has processions, historical dances and a knaves' camp reliving scenes from the town's history. Children's festivals have their roots in old school festivals: in May, schoolchildren gather sticks and twigs from the countryside and then carry them in a procession through the town. This tradition is also found in the *Stabenfest* in Nördlingen (second Monday in May) and in the *Rutenfest* which is held in Ravensburg in July.

The *Kinderzeche* in Dinkelsbühl, on the other hand, commemorates the episode in the Thirty Years' War when the town was surrounded by Swedish troops. Capitulation was near, looting and war tributes threatened, and then Lore, the gatekeeper's daughter, gathered all the children and went to the Swedish camp. The commander was so touched that the Swedes withdrew–that is the legend, anyway, which is presented in mid-July every year.

In the Landsberg *Ruthenfest*, a play recalls the time when young maidens jumped from the town's keep into the river Lech on hearing the call: "The Swedes are coming!" In Uberlingen on Lake Constance, this can be witnessed on May 16 and the second Sunday in July, the anniversaries of the Swedish sieges of the town in 1632 and 1634.

Left, standard-bearers at the *Tänzelfest*, Kaufbeuren. Above, Pfingstritt in Kötzting.

The Black Death, the plague, killed many who were spared by the Swedes. The world-famous *Oberammergau Passion Plays* (performed every 10 years, the next one in 1990) are based on a vow of 1634 to save the community from extinction. In July/August, 1991 (triennially), the village of Altdorf near Nuremberg becomes Wallenstein's camp on weekends. The glittering person of the great general from the Thirty Years' War is illuminated in the *Wallenstein-Festspiele* from a different angle: his student days in Altdorf are relived via historic scenes. Other theater performances are part of the festival programme (Schiller's *Wallenstein*) with camp life and a grand procession with over 500 actors parading in period costumes.

Another imperial general was Tilly, who conquered the medieval village of Rothenburg in 1631. Tilly wanted to plunder and sack the village, but the old Bürgermeister Nusch was able to prevent this. He challenged Tilly to a drinking contest with the winner being the first to drink a huge tankard of almost one gallon (3.25 liters) of wine at one go. Nusch won, almost killing himself in the process. The village and the parish councillors were saved. This episode is commemorated in the festival play *Meistertrunk* (master's drink) which is presented together with a 14th century *Schäfertanz* (shepherd's dance) at Easter and/or at Whitsun, and occasionally in summer and autumn. Rothenburg should be visited at Whitsun or during the second weekend of September when the *Reichsstadtfesttage* is celebrated. This portrays life and happenings from 1274, when the village became a Free Imperial City.

Wars and war heroes set the theme in historical festivals such as the *Chilbi* in Waldshut (Sundays/Mondays after August 15), which was besieged in 1468 by the Swiss and, as the supplies were running out, the last sheep was slaughtered and a huge meal feigned on the town walls. The besiegers, believing the town's supplies to be inexhaustible, withdrew. The Hussite wars–after the death of the Bohemian reformer Johannes Hus at the Council of Constance in 1415–provide the material for the *Neunburg Burgfestspiele* (July-August, Fridays and Saturdays) at the edge of the Bavarian Forest. The play *Vom Hussenkrieg* describes the decisive battle of September 21, 1433, for the defense of the Upper Palatinate.

In Furth im Wald, near the Bohemian border, the cruel fate of the people in medieval war is depicted. Each August, for over 500 years, Germany's oldest folk theater has presented the *Drachenstich,* whose theme is that if humans treat each other worse than cattle then the dragon will have its day. However, as in the legend of St. George, a white knight charges onto the scene and slays the 60 feet (18 m) long, electronically controlled, fire-breathing monster with a thrust of his lance into its throat. In neighboring Waldmünchen, the Pandures, who invaded Bavaria in the service of Maria Theresia, are the subject. The town's deliverance is depicted in *Trenck der Pandur*, which is less of a play and more of a folk festival featuring wild riding scenes (July/August).

The peasants' revolt in the Allgäu (1525) is the theme of a play staged in Altusried (near Kempten) on Germany's largest natural stage at the end of both June and August. Over 400 lay actors portray the justified uprising of the oppressed peasants against the tyranny of the princes, and, unlike history, they are victorious. One of the great peasant leaders was Florian Geyer who was followed by his black hordes. In the ruins of his home castle at Giebelstadt (near Würzburg), the *Florian Geyer Festival Plays* are presented annually in his honor. Another legendary figure from this time is the father of the knaves, the knight Georg Frundsberg who was born in 1473 in the castle near Mindelheim (in Bavarian Swabia).

You should also visit the *Ritterspiele* in Kiefersfelden between the end of July and end of August, where plays set in the Middle Ages have been staged since 1618. Knights' tournaments are held in May-June in castle Satzwey/Mechernich near Bonn, in castle Kaltenberg near Munich, and mid-August in the old imperial city of Fritzlar. Here the swords smash against helmets, lances splinter on shields, the Black Knight with closed visor charges in duels and in group combat, and squires hold long-bow archery and axe-throwing contests. The tournament with victory ceremonies, festival and dancing is held in connection with a medieval market.

Of love's pleasure and pain: What would romanticism be without love? The tragic story of the beautiful Agnes Bernauer comes to mind. It was the year 1428 and the young Bavarian duke Albert met the beautiful Agnes in a bathing house in Augsburg after a tournament. As the daughter of the baths' assistant she would not even have been a match for a citizen's son. She could have offered herself–an affair was possible–but this was love. The duke took Agnes back to his court in Straubing and married her there in 1433. The scandal was complete! Family honor was sullied, and the line of accession endangered. Father and sister were opposed, and secular and ecclesiastical court nobility weaved a web of intrigue. The young duke was lured away to a hunt in Landshut. During his absence, they took advantage of the persecution of witches, a rage at that time, with lightning speed. Agnes was drowned in the Donau near Straubing because she was declared a witch on November 12, 1435. The aggrieved duke raged with hate at first. He finally forgave his father, the logic of power triumphing over love. All this is commemorated in the *Agnes Bernauer Festival Plays*, which move 20,000 people in Straubing to tears every four years.

The finale of this festival summary is a spectacular festival of pomp and ceremony known throughout Europe: the *Fürstenhochzeit zu Landshut* (prince's wedding). It is held every four years. In 1204, Landshut was the first place to have a palace of the Wittelsbachs, the Bavarian duke. Duke George married the Polish princess Jadwiga here in 1475, and one of the most joyous festivals of the late Gothic was founded. This wedding has been reenacted since 1903. The present festival lasts three weeks (mid-June–early July) and attracts 500,000 locals and tourists. Small wonder as the old town boasts late-Gothic and Renaissance buildings, castle Trausnitz and the tower of St. Martin. Elaborate costume preparation and the participation of 2,000 Landshut people make it the greatest of Germany's historical festivals. The sheer pleasure with which they take part in the plays, tournaments and the processions is reflected in their faces.

The Rhine in "flames."

TRAVEL TIPS

Getting There

All roads lead to Rome, but if you are flying into the Federal Republic of Germany, all "roads" lead to Frankfurt. The Rhine Main Airport, with 50,000 passengers per day, is the second busiest airport in Europe after London's Heathrow Airport. There are up to 600 international take-offs and landings daily. From here there are also domestic flights to all principal cities: Bremen, Düsseldorf, Hamburg, Hanover, Cologne, Munich, Nuremberg, Saabrücken and Stuttgart. If you are flying to Berlin, you will have to use the American, British or French national carriers.

To book a flight with *Lufthansa* you may go directly to the airline office or to any travel agent. If you book in advance, you may take advantage of the *Flieg & Spar* special rate and save up to 40 percent on internal flights. The *Deutsche Luftverkehrsgesellschaft* is another airline providing domestic flights. They service smaller airports and sometimes connect with major airports. These flights may also be booked with *Lufthansa* or through any travel agent.

Those who prefer to travel by train or by car have several alternatives to reach Frankfurt. There is a 15-minute shuttle service (S15) from Rhine Main Airport to the traffic junction, the Hauptwache. Here, the suburban railway (*S-Bahn*) and the subway (*U-Bahn*) meet. From this point you can travel to anywhere in town on public transport.

Another means of getting from the airport to town is by bus (#61) which takes you to the town center (*Sachsenhausen*). The 15-minute trip costs about three marks. And there are, of course, many taxis waiting to assist you.

Travel Essentials

VISAS & PASSPORTS

A valid passport is the only requirement to enter the Federal Republic. Members of the European Community (EC) only need an identity card. Visitors automatically get a three month permit, but visas are required for longer stays. Within this three-month period you are not allowed to take up any form of employment.

To West Berlin: Traveling to West Berlin, however, is not so simple because you must cross the German Democratic Republic (GDR). If you are traveling by car you need a passport and transit visa. The visa is issued at the border points and costs five marks each way. If you are going by train or scheduled coach you also need a transit visa which is issued free of charge on the train, at the border post. There are four recognized routes from the Federal Republic to West Berlin through the GDR territory:

•From Hamburg: Frontier crossing at Gudow/Zarrentin—motorway to Nauen exit—then trunk road No. 5—checkpoint Staaken/Heerstrasse Berlin.

•From Hannover: Frontier crossing at Helmstedt/Marienborn—motorway-checkpoint Drewitz/Dreilinden Berlin.

•From Frankfurt a. Main: Frontier crossing at Herleshausen/Wartha—motorway-checkpoint Drewitz/Dreilinden Berlin.

•From Munich: Frontier crossing at Rudolphstein/Hirschberg—motorway-checkpoint Drewitz/Dreilinden Berlin.

Into the German Democratic Republic: Visiting the German Democratic Republic is another matter and you need a valid international passport plus a visa. To get the visa, which is issued at the border points, you need a *Berechtigungsschein* (entry license) which can be applied for at the GDR consulate in your own country or at: Reisebüro der DDR, Generaldirektion, Abt. Für besuchsweise Einreisen, Postfach 77, DDR-1026 Berlin.

The cost of a *Berechtigungsschein*, amounts to 30 marks (an additional 15 marks if you are in a hurry).

MONEY MATTERS

The German Mark (D-Mark) is a decimal currency with 100 pfennigs. The coins come in denominations of 1, 2, 5, 10 and 50 pfennigs, and 1, 2, 5 and 10 marks. The notes are in denominations of 5, 10, 20, 50, 100, 500 and 1,000 marks.

Money may be changed at any bank and local money changers (*Wechselstuben*) usually found in train stations, airports and in tourist areas. (For banking hours, see end of section). It is advisable to carry traveler's checks instead of cash. They are safer as they can be replaced if lost or stolen so long as you have the numbers recorded and they can be readily cashed.

Although the Germans are not very fond of credit cards you can pay your bills in hotels, restaurants or big department stores with American Express, Diner's Club, Visa or Master Charge cards. You may have problems, however, in smaller towns or villages. Eurocheques are your best bet since they can be cashed practically everywhere.

CUSTOMS

There are no restrictions on the amount of local or foreign currency you can bring into the Federal Republic. You are also allowed to bring any personal belongings and equipment as well as reasonable quantities of food for your own consumption.

In addition, visitors may bring in limited quantities of tobacco, alcohol, etc., duty free. European citizens (EC) can import 300 cigarettes or 150 cigars or 75 large cigars or 400 g tobacco; 1½ liters of ordinary wine; 750 g of coffee (beans) or 300 g instant coffee; 150 g of tea or 60 g of instant tea; 75 g of perfume; and 3/8 liters of toilet water.

These limits apply to goods bought in ordinary shops. If bought in duty-free shops, there are slightly lower limits. European nationals other than those from the EC have a slightly smaller allowance.

VAT

VAT in Germany (*Mehrwertsteuer*) comes in two rates: 14 percent and 7 percent.

Fourteen percent VAT (MWSt) is added to all goods except food, books and newspapers which are taxed seven percent. For all services such as the hairdressers, also add 14 percent VAT. At restaurants, the menu-price includes 14 percent VAT. VAT can be deducted if you buy expensive articles.

Different regulations apply for EC-Members and other nationalities: EC-Members can deduct VAT if the personal article either cost more than 700 marks or if the customer can prove that tax has to be paid when importing the article. These restrictions do not apply to other nationalities who wish to claim VAT.

To deduct the VAT you must fill in a sales form when buying the article. Present the form and article at customs when you return home. Have it stamped and send it back to the store which will then reimburse you for the VAT.

GETTING ACQUAINTED

TIME ZONES

Germany keeps Central European Time (MEZ) which means it is an hour ahead of Greenwich Mean Time and six hours ahead of New York time. In summer (from the last Sunday in March to the last Sunday in October) it is two hours ahead of Greenwich Mean Time.

CLIMATE

Germany lies within the continental climate zone which means it can be really hot in the summer and bitterly cold in the winter. You will, however, experience a slight change in climate when traveling from the northwest to the southeast. In the north around Hamburg and in Schleswig-Holstein the weather is more oceanic with milder winters and moderately warm summers. Further south the weather becomes more continental with greater variations.

The average temperature in the winter varies from -1° C (30° F) in Berlin to 2.5 ° C (37° F) in Cologne; in the mountains it is between -10° C and -15° C (14° F and 5° F). The hottest spots in the summer can be found in the Upper Rhine Valley around Ludwigshafen/Mannheim. The hottest month is July when it can be as hot as 35° C to 40° C (95° F to 104° F). If you come in summer you will hardly ever be disappointed by the weather since German summers are mostly hot and dry. But of course, it does rain too. July is the wettest month with an average rainfall of 30 ins (750 mm) in the north of Germany and 26 ins (620 mm) in the Rhine Valley. The average rainfall in Bavaria, for example, is 52 ins (1,300 mm) with Oberstdorf in the lead, with rainfall up to 70 ins (1,750 mm).

The Alps are by far the wettest section. This region has another climatic phenomenon — the *Föhn* — a warm dry wind which blows down the Alps into South Bavaria and Swabia. The *Föhn* has two effects: it clears the sky so that one can see the Alps even in Munich, and it also tends to give many people headaches!

The best time to travel to Germany is in the summer from late May to early October. Those who like to ski are best advised to travel from mid-December to March. By the way, warm clothes are not only advisable in the winter since it can be pretty cool in the summer, too. If you choose the summer months for your visit, bring sunglasses and an umbrella.

WHAT TO WEAR

Whatever you do, don't forget a raincoat and your sunglasses because the weather can be very unpredictable indeed. Even if you come in the hottest summer months (July and August) you are advised to bring one warm sweater or cardigan for it can be quite cool in the evenings. And for your trip to the North Sea you should bring a jacket or a raincoat. In case you forget to bring one, you can "go native" and buy a "*Friesennerz*" (a yellow rubber raincoat) and a pair of rubber boots quite cheaply.

Good walking shoes are another must for a visit. It does not matter whether you go walking in the Black Forest or the Lüneburger Heide or hiking in the Laps, a pair of good walking shoes is indispensable. (Especially in the Alps many people die each year because of inadequate equipment.)

Otherwise, casual clothing is acceptable. Jeans and sweat shirts have long been accepted. Most Germans are very fashion conscious, especially in big metropolises like Berlin, Hamburg or Munich. Long evening dresses and tuxedos are still worn when attending the opera, although the trend is beginning to change.

BUSINESS HOURS

Most shops are open from 9.30 a.m. to 6-6.30 p.m. Small shops such as bakeries, fruit and vegetable shops, and butcher shops open as early as 7 a.m., close for 2½ hours at noon, re-open at 3 p.m. and remain open until 6.30 p.m. in the evening. Shops located in the railway stations and airports usually have late shopping hours (some are open till midnight).

Business hours are usually 8 a.m. to 5.30 p.m. Government offices are open to the public in the mornings from 8 a.m. to noon.

The banking hours are: Monday through Friday from 9 a.m. to 12 noon and 1.30 p.m. to 3.30 p.m. In most towns, banks are open until 5.30 p.m. on Thursdays.

PUBLIC HOLIDAYS

The public holidays draw a line right through the Federal Republic. On the one side there are the Catholic states: Baden-Württemberg, Bayern, Hessen, Nordrhein-Westfalen, Rheinland-Pfalz and Saarland, and on the other the Protestant dominated states: Niedersachsen, Schleswig-Holstein, Hamburg, Bremen and Berlin.

The dates in parentheses are national public holidays.

•New Year's Day
(1 January)

•The Magi
6 January in Baden-Württemberg and Bayern

•Good Friday
(changes from year to year; refer to German calendar)

•Easter Monday
(changes from year to year; refer to German calendar)
•May Day
(1 May)
•Christi Himmelfahrt (Ascension Day)
(changes from year to year; refer to German calendar)
•Whitmonday
(changes from year to year; refer to German calendar)
•Fronleichnam (Corpus Christi Day) in Baden-Württemberg, Bayern, Hessen, Nordrheim-Westfalen, Rheinland-Pfalz, Saarland; changes from year to year; refer to German calendar.
•Tag der deutschen Einheit (Day of German unity)
(17 June)
•Mariä Himmelfahrt
Bayern and Saarland; changes from year to year; refer to German calendar.
•All Saints' Day
1 November in Baden-Württemberg, Bayern, Nordrhein-Westfalen, Rheinland-Pfalz, Saarland.
•The Day of Prayer and Repentance
(changes from year to year; refer to German calendar).
•Christmas Day
(25 December)
•Boxing Day
(26 December).

WEIGHTS & MEASURES

Imperial

1 grain	= 0.0648 gram
1 ounce	= 28.35 grams
1 pound	= 0.4536 kilo
1 hundred-weight	= 50.80 kilos
1 long ton	= 1016 kilos
1 pint	= 0.568 liter
1 quart	= 1.1365 liters
1 gallon	= 4.546 liters
1 inch	= 2.540 cm.
1 foot	= 30.48 cm.
1 yard	= 0.9144 meter
1 mile	= 1.6093 kilometers
1 sq. in.	= 6.4516 sq. cm.
1 sq. ft.	= 929.03 sq. cm.
1 sq. yd.	= 0.836 sq. meter
1 acre	= 0.4047 hectare
1 sq. mile	= 259.00 hectares
1 cu. inch	= 16.39 cu. cm.
1 cu. foot	= 0.0283 cu. meter
1 cu. yard	= 0.7646 cu. meter

Metric

1 gram	= 0.03563 oz.
1 kilogram	= 2.2046 lbs.
1 metric ton (1,000 kilos)	= 0.9842 ton
1 liter	= 1.7598 pints
1 centimeter	= 0.3937 inch
1 meter	= 3.281 feet
1 kilometer	= 0.62137 mile
1 sq. cm.	= 0.1550 sq. in.
1 sq. meter	= 10.764 sq. feet
1 hectare (10,000 sq. meters)	= 2.4711 acres
1 cu. cm.	= 0.0610 cu. in.
1 cu. meter	= 35.315 cu. feet

Temperature is measured in the Centigrade (C) scale.

Celsius	Fahrenheit
100	212
90	194
80	176
70	158
60	140
50	122
40	104
30	86
20	68
15	59
10	50
+5	41
0	32
-5	23
-10	14
-15	+5

Electricity

Germany's electrical supply works on the 220-volt system.

COMMUNICATIONS

POSTAL SERVICES

The post offices (*Postamt*) are usually open from 8 a.m. to 6 p.m., with smaller ones closing at noon for lunch. You can have your mail sent to the post office provided it's marked "poste restante." Your mail will be left at the counter that reads, *Postlagernde Sendungen* in the main post office. The postal rates for letters and postcards within Germany are 1.00 mark (letters up to 20 g) and 60 pfennigs (postcards).

The same rates apply for mail to Andorra, Austria, Belgium, Denmark, France, Great Britain, Italy, Liechtenstein, Luxemburg, Monaco, the Netherlands, San Marino, Switzerland and Vatican City. Standard letters (up to 20 g) to all other countries cost 1.30 marks plus 20 pfennigs for air mail; postcards must have a 80-pfennig stamp. The yellow local mail boxes (*Briefkasten*) are emptied at least twice a day (morning and evening); those designated with a red point are emptied more frequently. On Saturdays, however, there is only one service.

For sending telegrams you have to either dial 1131 on a private telephone or go to the post office. The charges are 60 pfennigs per word within Germany and Europe; for overseas telegrams inquire at the post office.

TELEPHONE

In public pay phones (yellow telephone booths) insert 30 pfennigs for local calls. For long-distance calls you may go to a post office where an operator makes the connection. You can use public pay phones with a green label (found at airports and railway stations). You can dial direct but remember to have enough coins with you (10-pfennig-pieces and 1- and 5-mark pieces).

Should you have a language problem, dial 00118 (international directory einquiries).

MEDIA

The Press in the Federal Republic is diverse. The range extends from conservative newspapers like the *Frankfurter Allgemeine Zeitung*, socialist newspapers like the *TAZ* (Tageszeitung) highbrow papers like the *Süddeutsche Zeitung*, to the yellow Press, the most infamous being the *Bildzeitung*. For information on cinema, theater, exhibitions and concerts look in any local paper.

Foreign newspapers and magazines are available in every town. There are also international bookshops especially at railway stations, airports and city centers.

Radio and television broadcasting in Germany is under public law. There are two national TV stations, the **ARD** and **ZDF**, with the ARD having local stations in each state. The ARD also maintains nine radio stations: NDR, RB, SFB, WDR, HR, SWF, SDR, SR, BR. Each state except Rheinland-Pfalz has its own local radio station with three or four channels. On the third channel of all these stations you can hear the current traffic reports (on VHS). The respective wavelengths are indicated on blue signs along the motorways.

For those who know German the main news programmes on TV are *Heute* at 7 p.m. (ZDF), and *Tagesschau* at 8 p.m. (ARD).

EMERGENCIES

Medical Services: The Federal Republic has a national health system whereby doctors' and hospital fees are covered by insurance and only a token fee has to be paid for medication. Treatment and medication is also free of charge for EC Members and certain nationalities (Austrians, Turks and Yugoslavians). All other nationals should ensure that have adequate health insurance before they leave their home country as medical fees are expensive in this country.

People under special medication should either bring a sufficient supply or a prescription from their own doctor. If you have to consult a doctor, contact your consulate for a list of either English-speaking doctors, or doctors who speak your native language.

In the event of an accident, dial 110 for the police who will call an ambulance if necessary, or call the *Rotes Kreuz* (Red Cross).

Useful address for diabetics: Diabetiker-Verband e.V., 6750 Kaiserslautern, Hahnbrunnerstrasse 46, Tel. 0631/7 64 88.

Pharmacies (*Apotheken*) have normal opening hours (8 a.m. to 6.30 p.m.) Every pharmacy carries a list of neighboring pharmacies which are open during the night and on weekends.

GETTING AROUND

ORIENTATION

When driving in Germany observe the following rules: Traffic travels on the right with oncoming traffic on your left. Main road traffic has the right of way. At the junctions of two main roads or two minor roads, traffic coming from the right has priority unless otherwise indicated. Traffic signs follow international standards.

In East Germany driving under the influence of alcohol is banned. It is forbidden to leave the direct route, pick up hitch hikers or to distribute or leave behind any newspapers, magazines or other printed matter. Traffic offenses attract substantial on-the-spot fines, payable in Federal Germany currency. In the event of a breakdown, get help by telephoning a central unit in each area. The telephone numbers can be obtained from petrol stations, motorway telephones, service areas and telephone directory enquiries.

The general speed limit (*Geschwindigkeitsbeschränkung*) in towns and villages is 50km/hour and on open roads it is 100 km/hour. Vehicles towing trailers are limited to 80 km/hour on all roads outside of towns and villages. The recommended speed limit on motorways is 130 km/hour. This is changing, however. Recently the government has been promoting a general speed limit of 100 km/hour on motorways and 80 km/hour on open roads due to the rapid increase in the number of dying trees and forests. Fasten your seat belt if driving, or sitting in the front seat. Violation of this results in a fine of 40 marks. Children under 12 are not allowed to sit in front.

Before setting out make sure you have the following safety equipment in your car: first-aid kit and a warning triangle.

Should you have an accident, switch on your hazard lights and put up the warning triangle at a safe distance from the scene of the accident. Depending on the severity of the damage, you should summon the police. Ask the other party for the name of their insurance company and their insurance policy number, and take note of possible witnesses. And, do not forget to contact your own insurance company immediately.

DOMESTIC TRAVEL

By Car: Germany is renowned for its motorways, the *Autobahnen*. Altogether there are about 8,500 miles (13,600 kilometers) of motorways throughout the Republic, making it one of the densest in the world. The *Autobahnen* are marked with an "A" on blue signs while the regional roads are marked with a "B" on yellow signs.

There are rest stops (*Raststätten*) every 20 to 30 miles (30 to 50 km) along the *Autobahnen*. Here you may drink, eat and use the toilet facilities. Often you will also find hotels at these rest stops; both are open 24 hours. In addition, there are small rest stops every two or three miles (four to five km) offering the opportunity to stretch your legs.

Despite many excellent roads, traffic congestion is the order of the day during the holiday season (from the end of June to the middle of September). It is therefore advisable to check traffic conditions on the local radio stations (Traffic Broadcast/*Verkehrsfunk*). The respective wavelengths (VHR) are indicated on the blue square road signs along the motorways and roads.

Should you get held up, use the diversions

Distance between German Cities

km on the road km by train	Aachen	Augsburg	Berlin	Bonn	Braunschweig	Bremen	Dortmund	Düsseldorf	Essen	Frankfurt/M.	Freiburg	Hamburg	Hannover	Karlsruhe	Kassel	Kiel	Köln	Lübeck	Mannheim	München	Münster	Nürnberg	Regensburg	Saarbrücken	Stuttgart	Trier	Wiesbaden	Würzburg	Wuppertal
Aachen		593	633	91	412	378	150	80	134	259	505	488	353	372	330	581	70	544	317	648	211	475	585	246	446	166	235	369	121
Augsburg	644		586	509	627	755	598	566	583	364	354	784	641	229	484	877	523	840	289	68	660	137	135	373	162	437	371	205	570
Berlin	659	614		598	227	377	488	572	530	555	819	289	282	686	378	370	569	311	631	584	466	437	499	745	624	749	581	537	518
Bonn	100	540	622		383	349	120	77	105	175	421	459	324	288	260	552	27	515	233	564	182	391	501	237	362	150	151	286	84
Braunschweig	430	594	226	394		167	267	351	309	338	602	196	61	469	150	289	346	252	414	625	243	452	562	528	543	590	364	355	297
Bremen	397	700	412	371	183		223	317	275	466	730	119	125	597	278	212	312	175	542	753	171	580	690	656	671	556	469	483	263
Dortmund	161	688	498	151	269	234		63	34	264	509	343	208	397	174	436	83	399	332	653	65	480	590	364	451	269	240	375	35
Düsseldorf	92	614	567	74	338	300	78		29	232	478	427	292	345	276	520	47	483	290	621	135	448	558	332	419	220	208	343	29
Essen	127	653	532	116	303	259	35	40		249	494	385	250	361	207	478	68	441	307	638	108	465	575	349	436	242	225	360	36
Frankfurt/M.	294	362	534	189	381	478	340	264	300		276	495	352	143	193	588	189	551	88	395	326	222	332	202	217	189	32	116	236
Freiburg	529	326	812	425	657	753	581	498	551	278		759	616	135	457	852	435	815	201	412	572	391	481	279	207	343	283	385	482
Hamburg	525	759	291	496	189	119	359	423	382	539	814		154	626	307	93	422	65	571	782	271	609	719	685	700	666	521	512	373
Hannover	376	577	287	342	61	119	208	285	243	357	632	180		483	164	247	287	210	428	639	184	466	576	542	557	531	378	369	238
Karlsruhe	395	272	678	291	523	620	447	365	417	144	134	680	498		324	719	302	682	68	287	439	241	356	144	82	208	150	230	349
Kassel	356	447	433	313	192	290	209	267	244	200	481	353	172	347		400	249	363	269	482	166	309	419	383	398	372	219	209	222
Kiel	633	867	371	605	298	227	467	531	491	647	922	109	288	788	462		515	77	664	875	364	702	812	778	793	759	614	605	466
Köln	71	574	590	34	361	337	97	41	83	222	458	463	309	325	284	571		479	247	578	150	405	515	289	376	177	165	300	55
Lübeck	585	809	290	556	213	179	418	483	442	578	864	66	208	730	375	81	523		627	838	327	665	775	741	756	722	577	568	429
Mannheim	331	309	620	223	467	564	379	301	345	86	195	625	443	61	289	733	260	675		347	384	277	387	132	142	196	92	172	294
München	704	62	675	600	655	761	750	674	715	423	388	820	639	330	508	929	634	870	371		715	167	120	431	220	495	429	281	625
Münster	225	736	472	196	243	173	59	127	87	385	621	291	184	487	220	400	163	351	423	796		542	652	426	513	389	302	436	96
Nürnberg	531	138	477	427	480	586	578	500	540	238	427	646	464	252	329	754	462	696	279	199	623		104	395	187	459	254	108	452
Regensburg	632	141	515	527	581	687	678	601	641	339	442	746	565	392	430	854	563	796	381	139	723	101		505	289	569	364	218	562
Saarbrücken	290	423	738	261	595	639	395	318	360	204	285	743	575	151	413	846	277	792	134	485	440	426	536		226	80	165	290	336
Stuttgart	467	178	681	363	570	669	514	437	482	207	227	727	545	92	406	835	397	778	131	240	560	200	299	245		290	224	164	423
Trier	201	547	781	173	552	527	298	229	273	241	397	656	500	262	362	764	190	716	223	612	353	488	592	89	336		154	354	299
Wiesbaden	254	401	575	152	423	517	302	225	268	42	287	580	398	153	245	688	185	624	83	458	347	280	380	186	225	205		149	212
Würzburg	429	220	515	325	378	484	475	398	438	136	347	543	362	213	227	652	360	594	178	281	520	103	203	329	180	382	177		347
Wuppertal	111	613	546	80	317	291	48	28	46	262	498	415	260	364	243	523	47	479	300	673	117	500	600	317	436	230	224	397	

indicated by blue signs with the letter "U" (*Umleitung*) and a number referring to the diverting road. If your car breaks down on the motorway you can call the breakdown services. Use the orange telephones at the roadside. Black triangles on the posts along the side of the motorway indicate the direction of the next telephone. Listed below are 24-hour breakdown services.

Club	Town	Telephone
ACE	Stuttgart	0711/50671
ADAC	Berlin	030/868686
	Bremen	0421/446262
	Dortmund	0231/171981
	Düsseldorf	0211/19111
	Frankfurt/M	069/74306
	Hamburg	040/23999
	Hannover	0511/8500222
	Munich	089/767676
	Nuremberg	0911/5390222
	Stuttgart	0711/2800111
AvD	Frankfurt	0611/6661666
DTC	Munich	089/8111212

The ADAC (*Allgemeiner Deutscher Automobilclub*) provides road assistance free of charge provided the damage can be repaired within half an hour. Should it take longer, you will have to pay for the repair as well as the cost of all spare parts needed.

Road assistance is free of charge and all recovery costs will be refunded if you have an *Auslandsschutzbrief* (insurance certificate). In fact you should take out the insurance with your national automobile association before you leave home. The other automobile clubs (ACE, AvD, DTC) charge for spare parts, gas and towing.

Cars can be rented (*Autovermietung*) practically everywhere. International companies are Hertz, Inter-Rent, Avis, Europcar, etc. For local car rentals inquire at your hotel's tourist information desk. If you use the services of an international company such as InterRent and you come from an English speaking country, probably all that is needed is your national driver's license and cash, credit card or check deposit. Smaller companies may insist on an international driver's license.

By Train: The German railway system (*Deutsche Bundesbahn*) is a nationalised enterprise. On the whole, it is efficient and will get you to all major places. An hourly service runs from each major city in the Republic by the intercity trains (IC).

You can travel from Munich to Hamburg in less than eight hours. If you board an IC-train at 8.37 a.m. in Munich you will arrive in Hamburg at 4.15 p.m. There are lunch-cars, first- and second-class cars and even a telephone service on the trains for an additional fare of 5 marks (*IC-Zuschlag*) one way. IC-trains do not run at night. If you wish to travel at night board a *D-Zug*, which travels slightly slower because it makes more stops on the way. Another type of train, the *E-Zug*, stops even more often, but has the advantage of getting you to smaller towns.

The *Bundesbahn* is not only very efficient, it also has some attractive fare structures. One person pays 20 pfennigs (0.20 marks) for one km and each accompanying person (up to a maximum of five) only pays 10 pfennigs. These are the basic fares. If you are traveling more than 450 km (280 miles) the first person pays 180 marks and each accompanying person pays only 90 marks (*Sparpreis*). The only restriction is that the return trip falls on the following Saturday or Sunday. However, if you should begin your journey on a Saturday or Sunday, you can return on any day.

Those not in a hurry can save even more money. If within 10 days you are covering more than 300 km (187 miles) the first person pays 120 marks and each accompanying person only pays 60 marks. Since fare structures change from year to year it is advisable to check it at any railway station.

By Bus: Buses are a primary means of transportation in cities and they connect the smaller villages in the countryside. But there is no national coach network like the *Greyhound* in the United States.

The overland buses are a substitute for the railway system and wherever the *Deutsche Bundesbahn* does not go to, there will be a bus to take you you to the most remote corners of Germany.

Information on the regional bus service is available at either the railway stations or the tourist information centers.

PUBLIC TRANSPORT

A widespread network of public transport systems is available in every large city.

Those cities having a population of

Intercity Train Network

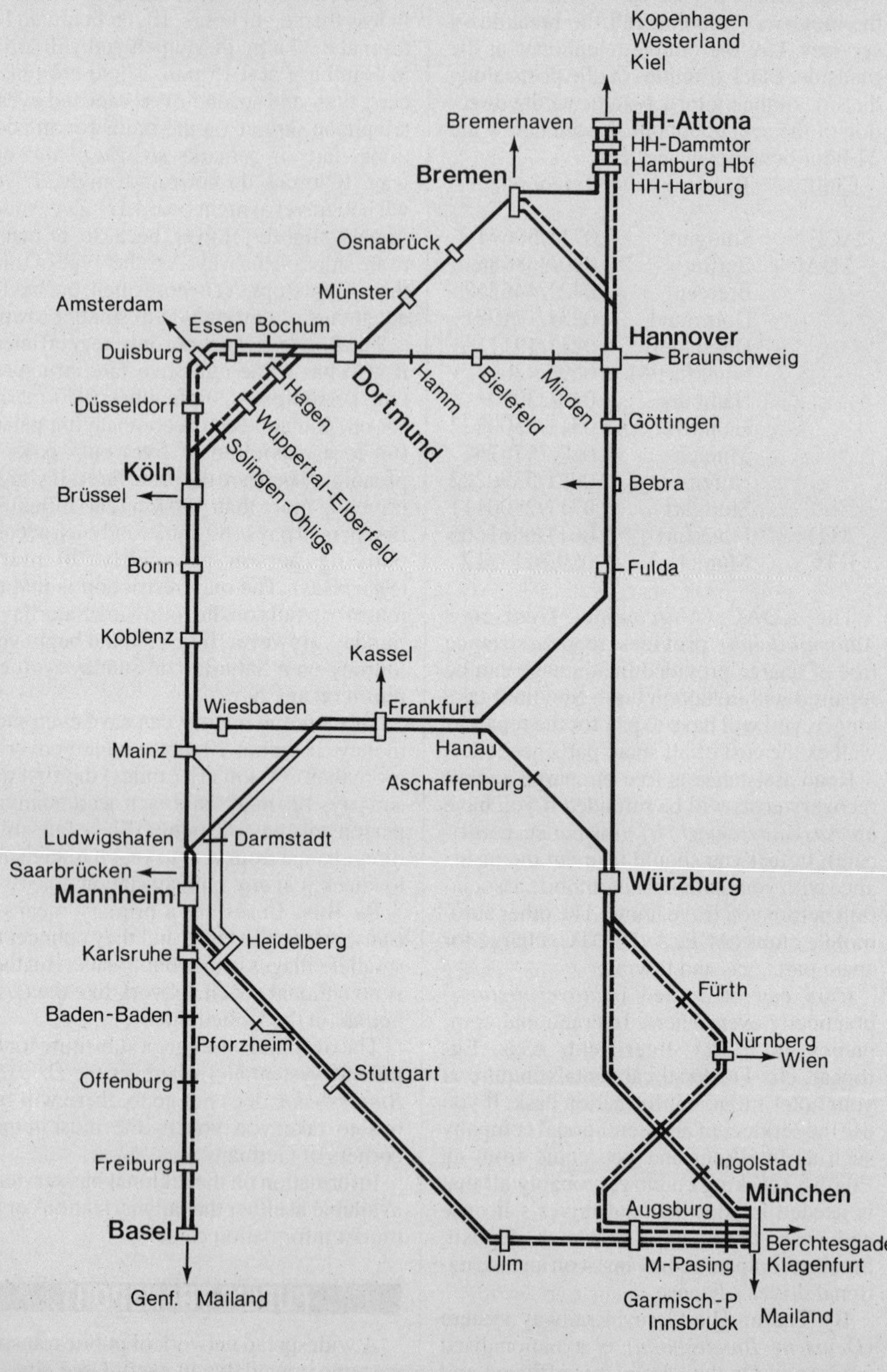

100,000 and more, offer an efficient bus system that runs frequently and usually very punctually. You can buy the bus tickets from the driver or at automats available in the bus or at the bus stop.

In large cities like Berlin, Hamburg, Cologne, Munich, Frankfurt, Stuttgart, the bus lines are integrated with the underground (*U-Bahn*) the tram, and the *S-Bahn* into one large public transport system. The same ticket may be used for all four means of transport.

The trams (*Strassenbahnen*) runs on rails throughout the city. The speed at which they travel allows for sightseeing, although there is the danger of getting into a traffic jam. Still, they are substantially faster than the trams in San Francisco. Look out for yellow signs with a green "H" at bus and tram stops; they list the time schedules.

Underground (*U-Bahn*) stations are usually identified by a sign showing a white "U" on a blue background. Every station has detailed route maps displayed on the wall.

The S-Bahn will transport you at about the same speed as the *U-Bahn*. The *S-Bahns* are short trains that travel to the suburbs of the larger cities, and within the city they travel mostly underground. For people living in the outskirts and suburbs it is a fast way of getting into the city. *S-Bahn* stations are identified by a white "S" on a green background. The price of tickets varies from town to town. For more detailed information contact the respective information office in each town or city.

Taxis: Taxis are more comfortable than public transport although they are the most expensive form of transport available. You can recognize them by their beige color and the taxi sign on the roof (illuminated if the cab is not occupied). In every large town there are special taxi stands, but you can also call for them. (Usually the telephone numbers are listed on the first page of the telephone directory). You should memorize the yellow taxi i.d. number in case you leave something behind in the cab or wish to complain about the driver. In some towns there are also minicars and call cars which are cheaper and which also have ample space for luggage.

Shopping

WHAT TO BUY

Germany, being a popular tourist haunt, offers lots of souvenirs to take home. The shop to look out for is the *Andenkenladen* which has anything from valuable souvenirs to all sorts of knick-knacks. Beer mugs (*Bierkrüge*) are typical gifts. You find them made out of glass, ceramics and tin, colorfully painted or plain. Especially fancy, and therefore more expensive, are the mugs with the tin-lid. For those who do not like beer, there are typical wine glasses. White wine, for example is served in *Römer*, which are bulbous glasses.

Traditional articles of clothing in the north of Germany are the *Schiffermütze, Seemannspullover* and the *Friesennerz*. The *Schiffermütze* is a blue sailor's cap similar to what ex-Chancellor Helmut Schmidt wore. The *Seemannspullover* is a big blue sweater sailors wear at sea. It is very comfortable for rough winds over the North Sea coast. Another indispensable garment in this part is the *Friesennerz*, a raincoat made out of yellow rubber.

In practically every town you will find a *Fussgängerzone* pedestrian zone with all kinds of shops, big department stores, and small specialised shops. Here is everything your heart desires. Cigarettes may be bought in vending machines (*Zigarettenautomat*) either in the streets, restaurants or other public places if you have a number of one or two mark coins. Cigarettes, cigars and tobacco may be bought in newspaper shops which also stock postcards, writing supplies, magazines and newspapers.

FOOD DIGEST

German cooking is not only varied, but differs from region to region. For example, the Northern Germany *Labskaus* will not be found in Southern Germany. Listed below are restaurants, including the most typical meals, we discovered while traveling from the south to the north of the Republic.

WHERE TO EAT

•Bavaria

Krautwickerl: Minced meat rolled into white cabbage, usually eaten with potatoes.

Weisswürste: Spiced veal and pork sausages which are mainly eaten with sweet mustard (*Weisswurstsenf*). They usually accompany a late morning beer during a Frühschoppen (morning beer).

Leberkäs: Meat paste, taken hot or cold.

Semmelknödel: Bread dumplings often served with *Schweinebraten* (roast pork).

Reiberdatschi: Thinly grated raw potatoes baked in deep fat. Served with apple sauce. In other regions of Germany they are called *Kartoffelpuffer*.

Hollerküchl: Elderberry blossoms dipped in pan cake dough and fried.

Gugelhopf: Cake made out of yeast with raisins, nuts, almonds etc.

Dampfnudel: Huge yeast dumplings, with plums and served hot with vanilla sauce.

•Württemberg/Baden

Flädelsuppe: Clear soup with pancake.

Spätzle: A kind of pasta made of flour, egg, salt and water, grated and boiled, *Spätzle* are served as a side dish with meat and vegetables.

Maultaschen: Another form of pasta filled with minced meat and spinach. *Maultaschen* are either served as soup or as a separate dish with salad.

•Hesse

Metzelsuppe: Soup with liver and blutwurst (blood sausage).

Handkäs mit Musik: Curd cheese served with onions.

Kasseler Rippchen: Smoked pickled loin of pork, named after a Berlin butcher named Kassel.

Zwiebelkuchen: Yeast cake (almost similar to pizza) filled with onions and bacon and usually served with a glass of young wine (*Federweisser*).

Äppelwoi: Hard cider, another very popular drink.

•Rhineland

Sauerbraten: Braised pickled beef lard with bacon, usually served with potatoes and vegetables.

Hunsrücker Festessen: Sauerkraut and pea's *Hunsrücker* pudding with potatoes, horse radish and ham.

Halver Hahn: Rye bread or roll with cheese and mustard.

Kölsch: Light-colored, surface-fermented beer. (Note that apart from beer, wine is also a popular beverage; there is a variety of excellent wines to suit the connoisseur.)

Spekulatius, Muzenmandeln: Almond cookies.

•Westphalia

Westfälischer Schinken: Delicious ham, best when eaten with Pumpernickel bread.

Mettwurst mit Linsen: Pork or beef sausage with lentils.

Westfälischer Reibekuchen: Made of grated raw potatoes and buckwheat flour.

•Lower Saxony

Braunkohl mit Brägenwurst: Kale with brain sausage.

Heidschnuckenbraten: Roast lamb served with potatoes.

Braunschweiger Mumme: Very strong dark beer with a high malt content, usually mixed with ordinary beer.

•North Germany—Hamburg—Bremen

Kohl mit Pinkel: Cabbage with coarse sausage and potatoes.

Labskaus: Salted meat, herring and mashed potatoes served with fried egg and beet root.

Lübecker Schwalbennester: Veal olive filled with mashed hard boiled eggs.

Lübecker Marzipan: Favorite sweet, containing lots of almonds ground into a paste.

Rote Grütze: Pudding made from red berries—mainly raspberries—and served with fresh cream. In other regions this dish is called *Götterspeise*. It may be green when it contains a woodruff extract.

•Berlin

Berliner Schlachtplatte: Fresh blood and liver sausage, pig's kidney and fresh-boiled pork.

Berliner Weisse mit Schuss: Wheaten beer with a shot of raspberry juice or woodruff extract.

SPORTS

Germans enjoy both participative and spectator sports. There is a sportsclub in every town and many athletic clubs in the cities specialising in one discipline, such as wrestling, weight lifting, or boxing.

The most popular sport is soccer. During the national soccer league season, millions of German men follow the results of the games that are usually played on Saturday afternoons and shown in excerpts at 6 p.m. over TV. Going to a soccer game has the same significance as the American's attendance at a baseball or basketball game. Here is the list of all the clubs in the national soccer league for your information:

1. Bayern München
2. Hamburger SV
3. Borussia Dortmund
4. Werder Bremen
5. Mönchengladbach
6. Bayer Leverkusen
7. I. FC Köln
8. I. FC Kaiserslautern
9. VfB Stuttgart
10. I. FC Nürnberg
11. Bayer Uerdingen
12. VfL Bochum
13. Fortuna Düsseldorf
14. SVW Mannheim
15. Eintracht Frankfurt
16. Karlsrucher SC
17. FC Homburg
18. St. Pauli-Hamburg

You may enquire at the hotel reception or the local tourist office on sports activities. Since Steffi Graf and Boris Becker became successful, tennis has become very popular.

Other popular sports are handball, volleyball, squash, basketball, athletics, cycling, motor sports and swimming. There are parks for the dedicated jogger.

Language

A few common phrases

Good morning.	*Guten Morgen.*
Good Afternoon.	*Guten Tag.*
Good evening.	*Guten Abend.*
Good night.	*Guten Nacht.*
Goodbye.	*Auf Wiedersehen.*
I don't understand.	*Ich verstehe Sie nicht.*
Do you speak English?	*Sprechen Sie Englisch?*
Could you please speak a little slower?	*Könnten Sie bitte etwas langsamer sprechen?*
What's that in English?	*Was heisst das auf Englisch?*
Yes.	*Ja.*
No.	*Nein.*
Please.	*Bitte.*
Thank you.	*Danke.*
Never mind.	*Bitte; keine Ursache.*
Turn to the right! (left)	*Biegen Sie nach rechts ab!* (*links*)
Go straight on!	*Gehen Sie geradeaus weiter!*
above/below	*oben/unten*

Taking a room

Where is the next hotel?	*Wo ist das nächste Hotel?*
Do you have a single room?	*Haben Sie ein Einzelzimmer?*
Do you have a double room?	*Haben Sie ein Doppelzimmer?*
Do you have a room with a private bath?	*Haben Sie ein Zimmer mit Bad?*
How much is it?	*Wieviel kostet das?*
How much is a room with full board?	*Wieviel kostet ein Zimmer mit Vollpension?*
Please show me another room!	*Bitte zeigen Sie mir ein anderes Zimmer!*
We'll (I'll) be staying for one night.	*Wir bleiben* (*Ich bleibe*) *eine Nacht!*
When is breakfast?	*Wann gibt es Frühstück?*
Where is the toilet?	*Wo ist die Tiolette?*
Where is the bathroom?	*Wo ist das Badezimmer?*

In a foreign town/on foreign roads

Is there a bus to the center?	*Gibt es einen Bus ins Stadtzentrum?*
Is there a guided sightseeing tour?	*Werden kommentierte Besichtigungstouren durchgeführt?*
church	*Kirche*
memorial	*Denkmal*
castle	*Schloss*
old part of town	*Altstadviertel*
Where can I buy souvenirs?	*Wo kann ich Souvenirs kaufen?*
Do you know a nightclub/disco?	*Kennen Sie einen Nachtklub/eine Disko?*
Where is the nearest cinema?	*Wo ist das nächste Kino?*
What film does it show?	*Was für ein Film läuft dort?*
Where is the post office?	*Wo ist das Postamt?*
Where is the nearest bank?	*Wo ist die nächste Bank?*
Where can I change money?	*Wo kann ich Geld wechseln?*
Where is the pharmacy?	*Wo ist die Apotheke?*
What time do they close?	*Wann schliessen Sie?*
open	*geöffnet*
closed	*geschlossen*
close	*nah*
far	*weit*
cheap	*billig*
expensive	*teuer*
free (of charge)	*kostenlos*
price	*Preis*
change	*Wechselgeld*
Have you got any change?	*Können Sie wechseln?*
telephone booth	*Telefonzelle*
Is this the way to the station?	*Ist das der Weg zum Bahnhof?*
Where is the platform?	*Wo ist Gleis eins?*

Where is the airport?	*Wo ist der Flughafen?*
Can you call me a taxi?	*Können Sie mir ein Taxi rufen?*
Can you take me to the airport?	*Können Sie mich zum Flughafen fahren?*
Where do I get a ticket?	*Wo kann ich eine Fahrkarte kaufen?*
departure	*Abfahrt*
arrival	*Ankunft*
When is the next flight/train to...?	*Wann geht der nächste Flug/Zug nach...?*
to change (flights/trains)	*umsteigen*
exit	*Ausgang/Ausfahrt*
entrance	*Eingang/Einfahrt*
travel agency	*Reisebüro*
picnic area	*Rastplatz*
gas (petrol) station	*Tankstelle*
bridge	*Brücke*
crossroads	*Kreuzung*
no parking	*Parken verboten*
no stopping	*Halten verboten*
one-way street	*Einbahnstrasse*
hospital	*Krankenhaus*
ferry	*Fähre*
fee	*Gebühr*
height	*Höhe*
width	*Breite*
length	*Länge*
Have you anything to declare?	*Haben Sie etwas zu verzollen?*
customs	*Zoll*

In a restaurant

Do you know a good restaurant?	*Kennen Sie ein gutes Restaurant?*
Can you recommend anything?	*Können Sie etwas empfehlen?*
Could we order a meal, please?	*Können wir bitte bestellen?*
menu	*Speisekarte*
lunch	*Mittagessen*
evening meal	*Abendessen*
knife	*Messer*
fork	*Gabel*
spoon	*Löffel*
napkin	*Serviette*
beer	*Bier*
wine	*Wein*
bread	*Brot*
cheese	*Käse*
meat	*Fleisch*
sausage	*Würstchen*
honey	*Honig*
noodles	*Nudeln*
potatoes	*Kartoffeln*
rice	*Reis*
jam	*Marmelade*
egg	*Ei*
milk	*Milch*
coffee	*Kaffee*
tea	*Tee*
sugar	*Zucker*
butter	*Butter*
Can we have the bill, please?	*Können wir bitte bezahlen?*
to pay	*bezahlen*
tip	*Trinkgeld*
to complain	*sich beschweren*

Days of the Week

Monday	*Montag*
Tuesday	*Dienstag*
Wednesday	*Mittwoch*
Thursday	*Donnerstag*
Friday	*Freitag*
Saturday	*Samstag, Sonnabend*
Sunday	*Sonntag*

Months

January	*Januar*
February	*Februar*
March	*März*
April	*April*
May	*Mai*
June	*Juni*
July	*Juli*
August	*August*
September	*September*
October	*Oktober*
November	*November*
December	*Dezember*

Numbers

0	*Null*
1	*eins*
2	*twei*
3	*drei*
4	*vier*
5	*fünf*
6	*sechs*
7	*sieben*

8	*acht*
9	*neun*
10	*zehn*
11	*elf*
12	*zwölf*
13	*dreizehn*
14	*vierzehn*
15	*fünfzehn*
16	*sechzehn*
17	*siebzehn*
18	*achtzehn*
19	*neunzehn*
20	*zwanzig*
30	*dreissig*
40	*vierzig*
50	*fünfzig*
60	*sechzig*
70	*siebzig*
80	*achtzig*
90	*neunzig*
100	*hundert*
200	*zweihundert*
1000	*tausend*
2000	*zweitausend*
1 000 000	*eine Million*

Ordinals

1st	*erste*
2nd	*zweite*
3rd	*dritte*
4th	*vierte*
5th	*fünfte*
6th	*sechste*
7th	*siebte*
8th	*achte*
9th	*neunte*
10th	*zehnte*
11th	*elfte*
12th	*zwölfte*
13th	*dreizehnte*
20th	*zwanzigste*
21st	*einundzwanzigste*
100th	*hundertste*
1000th	*tausendste*

Fractions

½	*Hälfte*
⅓	*Drittel*
¼	*Viertel*
¾	*drei Viertel*

Further Reading

HISTORY & SOCIETY

Bailey, George. *Germans.* (1972)

Bradley, John. *The Illustrated History of the Third Reich.* (1978)

Calleo, David. *The German Problem Reconsidered: 1860-1978.* (1980)

Craig, Gordon. *The Germans.* (1982)

Dawson, William H. *German Life in Town and Country.* (1977)

Holborn, Hajo. *A History of Modern Germany: 1840-1945.* (1969)

Jones, Brangwyn G. *Germany: An Introduction to the German Nation.* (1970)

Kirsch, Henry. *German Democratic Republic: A Profile.* (1985)

Lowie, Robert H. *Toward Understanding Germany.* (1979)

MacDonald, Ian. *Get to Know Germany.* (1975)

Moore, James. *Let's Visit Germany.* (1983)

To get to know and understand the German mentality, read any of the classical works by Goethe and Schiller, Heinrich Heine and Friedrich Hölderlin, to name a few. Below is a selection of German and English/American authors:

Grass, Günter. *Headbirths*; *The Germans Are Dying Out*; and *The Flounder.*

Mann, Thomas. *The Buddenbrooks.*

Mansfield, Catherine. *In A German Pension.*

Stael, Madame de. *Germany.*

Twain, Mark. *A Tramp Abroad.*

GERMAN LANGUAGE

Kershul, Kristine. *German in 10 Minutes a Day.* (1981)

CULTURE PLUS

TOURIST ATTRACTIONS

There is much to see in Germany—castles, palaces, country houses, museums, nature parks, etc. The selection listed below is restricted to castles, nature parks and adventure/amusement parks according to the tours described in the book.

CRUISING FATHER RHINE

• Castles

Schloss Biebrich, 5 km (3 miles) SE of *Wiesbaden*, built in the 18th century.

Schloss Gutenfels, in *Kaub* (12th century).

Burg Pfalzgrafenstein, also in *Kaub* (14th century).

Burg Katz, close to *St. Goarshausen.*

Burg Thunberg (known as "Maus"), near *St. Goarshausen.*

Burg Rheinfels, the ruins from the 13th century throne above *St. Goar.*

Burg Lahneck, 8 km (5 miles) SE of *Koblenz.*

Feste Ehrenbreitstein, above *Koblenz.*

Schloss Stolzenfels, 12 km (7.5 miles) S of *Koblenz.*

Burg Stahleck, ruined castle from the 12th century in *Bacharach.*
Burg Sooneck, near *Niederheimbach.*

Burg Reichenstein, near *Trechtlinghausen.*

• Nature parks

Nassau, via the motorway *Cologne-Frankfurt* exits: *Höhr-Grenzhausen, Montabaur, Diez, Limburg.*

Rhein-Taunus, via the motorway *Cologne-Frankfurt* or via the B260 *Wiesbaden-Bad Ems*, B54 *Limburg-Wiesbaden.*

MEANDERING MOSELLE RIVER

• Castles

Burg Eltz, overlooking *Moselkern* was originally built in 1157.

Reichsburg Cochem, 13 km (8 miles) from *Burg Eltz.*

Burg Landshut, ruins found in *Bernkastel-Kues.*

HEADING FOR COLOGNE

• Castles

Ruine Hammerstein, ruins date back to the 10th century.

Burg Drachenfels, ruins lie on a hill overlooking *Königswinter.*

Schloss Augustusburg, castle and hunting lodge dates back to 1689 and can be found in *Brühl.*

• Nature parks

Rhein-Westerwald, Siebengebirge, Kottenforst-Ville: These three nature reserves can be reached via the motorway *Cologne-Frankfurt* (any exit from *Bonn Siegburg* to *Montabaur*) as well as on the motorway *Cologne-Koblenz* (any exit from *Bonn-Lengsdorf* to *Koblenz*).

• Amusement Park

Phantasialand Brühl, just outside *Brühl* is a huge amusement centre.

"LOSING MY HEART IN HEIDELBERG..."

• **Castles**

Heidelberger Schloss, beautiful Renaissance castle overlooking the river Neckar in *Heidelberg*.

Schloss Schwetzingen, former water castle is within the beautiful garden in *Schwetzingen* near *Heidelberg*.

Kurfürstliches Schloss, the Electoral Palace in *Mannheim* is the grandest Baroque residence in Germany.

• **Nature park**

Bergstrasse-Odenwald, in the northeast of *Heidelberg* and can be reached via the *Mannheim-Frankfurt* and *Heidelberg-Darmstadt* motorways.

• **Adventure Park**

Holiday-Park, nature reserve is in the middle of a forest on the B39 4 km (2.5 miles) W of *Speyer*.

INTO THE HEART OF FRANCONIA

• **Castles**

Burg Eberbach, ruins are a few miles outside the town of *Eberbach*.

Burg Stoltzeneck, ruins date back to 13th century and lie just before Zwingenberg.

Burg Guttenberg, a few miles south of *Hassmersheim*.

Schloss Erbach, baroque castle in the town of *Erbach*.

Mildenburg, built in the 15th century and situated in the middle of *Miltenberg*.

Wasserschloss Mespelbrunn, castle was built in the 15th century and can be found at the gates of *Mespelbrunn*.

Burg Löwenstein, ruins overlook the town of *Wertheim*.

Burg Rothfels, castle ruins overlooking the Main Valley at *Marktheidenfeld*.

Festung Marienberg, the old fortress is the landmark of *Würzburg*.

Residenz, beautiful baroque castle in the middle of *Würzburg* (Residenzplatz).

• **Nature parks**

Bergstrasse Odenwald, via the *Mannheim-Frankfurt* and *Heidelberg-Darmstadt* motorways.

Naturpark Bayerischer Spessart: Take any of the exits between *Aschaffenburg* and *Marktheidenfeld* on the motorway *Frankfurt-Nuremberg*.

FROM BAMBERG TO NUREMBERG

• **Castles**

Schloss Weissenstein, baroque castle in *Kulmbach*.

Altes Schloss, landmark of *Bayreuth*, dating back to the 18th century.

Neues Schloss, rococo castle built during the 18th century in *Ludwigstrasse*, *Bayreuth*.

Schloss Eremitage Burg , castle in the northeast of *Bayreuth* overlooking the old *town of Nuremberg*.

• **Nature parks**

Naturpark Frankenhöhe, can be reached by the *Nuremberg-Ansbach*, exits: *Aich-Ansbach, Ansbach-West* motorways.

Naturpark Hassberge, northwest of *Bamberg*.

• **Adventure park**

Erlebnispark Schloss Thurn, adventure park and zoo, near *Forchheim*.

FOLLOWING THE ROMANTIC ROAD

• **Castles**

Kurmainzisches Schloss, castle dates back to the 11th century and houses a museum in *Tauberbischofsheim.*

Schloss Bad Mergentheim, dominates the town of Bad Mergentheim

Castle of Weikersheim, one of the most important castles of *Baden-Württemberg*. It is known for its beautiful interior.

Schloss Harburg, 12th century castle overlooking the town of *Harburg*.

Schloss Leitheim, rococo castle near *Donauwörth.*

Schloss Hohenschwangau, rebuilt in the 19th century, this castle stands opposite *Neuschwanstein.*

Schloss Neuschwanstein, "Fairy-tale Castle" built by King Ludwig II of Bavaria. This castle and Schloss Hohenschwangau are a few miles east of *Füssen.*

• **Nature parks**

Naturpark Frankenhöhe, via the motorway *Nuremberg-Ansbach* (exits *Aich, Ansbach, Ansbach-West*).

Augsburg-Westliche Wälfer, on the motorway *Ulm-Munich*; leave the Autobahn at *Augsburg, Adelsried, Zusmarshaussen* or *Burgau.*

ALONG THE ALPS

• **Castles**

Schloss Linderhof, rococo castle also built by Ludwig II and lies a few miles east of *Oberammergau.*

• **Nature park**

Alpenpark und Nationalpark, the national park extends around lake *Königssee.*

• **Amusement park**

Märchenpark Ruhpolding, fantasyland close to *Ruhpolding*.

MUNICH – THE SECRET CAPITAL

• **Castles**

Schloss Herrenchiemsee: King Ludwig II built this castle on the *Herreninsel*, one of the three islands in the Lake Chiemsee.

Schloss Nymphenburg: The castle and various hunting lodges are in the northwest *Munich.*

Residenz, lies in the heart of *Munich.*

Schloss Oberschleissheim, dating back to the 18th century lies some 15 km (9 miles) north of *Munich.*

• **Amusement park**

Märchenwald im Isartal, fairyland near *Wolfratshausen* (28 km/17.5 miles southeast of *Munich.*

EASTERN BAVARIA

• **Castles**

Burg Trausnitz, a castle overlooking *Landshut.*

Stadtresidenz, Renaissance palace which lies in the heart of *Landshut.*

• **Nature parks**

Nationalpark Bayerischer Wald, via the Passau-Regensburg motorway.

Bayerischer Wald: The Bayerischer Wald (Woods) practically merges with the National park.

CIRCLING AROUND LAKE CONSTANCE

• **Castles**

Schloss Mainau, castle located on the peninsula of *Mainau.*

Altes Schloss, Neues Schloss: The old and the new castles are both found in the town of *Meersburg.*

ADVENTURING THE BLACK FOREST

• Castles

Schloss Hohentübingen, 16th century castle overlooking *Tübingen.*

Neues Schloss, new castle dominates the centre of *Stuttgart*, the Schlossplatz.

Altes Schloss, old castle lies opposite the **Planie** (*Stuttgart*).

Grossherzogliches Schloss, focal point of *Karlsruhe.*

Neues Schloss, Renaissance castle overlooking *Baden-Baden.*

• Nature parks

Naturpark Schönbuch, via the *Stuttgart-Degerloch* motorway (exit: *Stuttgart-Degerloch*) and from the *Stuttgart-Singen* motorway (exits: *Böblingen, Herrenberg, Tübingen*).

• Adventure parks

Altweibermühle Tripsdrill, This huge adventure park lies 23 km (14 miles) east of *Heilbronn.*

ON THE TRAIL OF THE BROTHERS GRIMM

• Castles

Saalburg, Roman castle which lies 7 km northwest of *Bad Homburg.*

Schloss Philippsruhe, 18th century castle is located in *Kesselstadt*, a surburb of *Hanau.*

Kaiserpfalz, ruins of Barbarossa's castle are in *Gelnhausen.*

Burg Brandenstein, castle lies just outside of *Schlüchtern.*

Stadtschloss, castle was completed in 1730 and lies in the centre of *Fulda.*

Schloss Eisenbach, 13th century castle lies 4 km (2.5 miles) south of *Lauterbach.*

Schloss Hohhaus, castle goes back to the 18th century and houses the museum of *Lauterbach.*

Landgrafenschloss, medieval castle (13th-16th century) rises above *Marburg.*

Schloss Wilhelmshöhe, 956-foot (287 metre) long castle which lies on the boundaries of Kassel.

• Nature parks

Hessischer Spessart, via the *Frankfurt-Nuremberg* motorway, any exit between *Aschaffenburg* and *Marktheidenfeld.*

Hessische Röhn, park stretches E of *Fulda* and can be reached via the *Frankfurt-Kassel* motorway (exits: *Bad Kissingen, Bad Brückenau, Fulda-Süd/Nord, Hühnfeld*).

Hoher Vogelsberg, park begins 20 km (12.5 miles) SE of *Lauterbach* and can be reached via the *Giessen-Kassel* and *Würzburg-Kassel* motorways.

FOLLOWING THE WESER VALLEY TO BREMEN

• Castles

Welfenschloss, castle on the shore of the Werra in *Münden* (*Hannoversch-Münden*).

Sababurg, castle about 20 km (12.5 miles) north of *Münden.*

Trendelburg, castle close to the *Sababurg*, on B83.

Hämelschenburg, Renaissance castle close to *Emmern.*

Leineschloss, castle on the edge of the old town of *Hannover.*

Schaumburg, castle north of *Rinteln.*

Schloss Bückeburg, surrounded by moat, castle dates back to the 12th century in *Bückeburg*.

• **Nature parks**

Naturpark Münden, nature park stretches east of *Münden*. Take exit *Münden-Lutterberg*.

Naturpark Solling/Vogler, park can be reached via the *Göttingen-Nord, Norten-Hardenberg* and *Northeim-West motorway exits*.

Weserbergland Schaumburg-Hameln: on the northern edge of the park is the *Bielefeld-Hannover* motorway. Take exits *Eilsen, Rehren, Bad Nenndorf, Lauenau*.

• **Adventure parks**

Rasti-Land, amusement park which lies 32 km (20 miles) east of *Hameln*.

Potts Park Minden, 10 km (6 miles) west of *Minden*.

LIVING WITH THE TIDE

• **Castle**

Schloss Oldenburg, 17th-18th century castle in the centre of *Oldenburg*.

• **Adventure park**

Babyzoo Wingst, zoo with baby-animals only. 20 km (12.5 miles) southeast of *Otterndorf*.

HAMBURG – GATEWAY TO THE SEVEN SEAS

• **Castle**

Schloss Ahrensburg, the white castle of *Ahrensburg* lies 32 km (20 miles) northeast of the centre of *Hamburg*.

• **Nature parks**

Naturpark Harburger Berge: Take the *Hamburg-Bremen* motorway and use exits *Emsen, Nenndorf, Hittfeld*.

Naturschutzpark Lüneburger Heide, west of *Lüneburg* ; can be reached via the *Hannover-Hamburg* motorway (exits: *Behringen/Evendorf, Egestorf, Garlstorf*).

ALONG THE COASTLINE OF THE BALTIC SEA

• **Castles**

Schloss Eutin, 17th-18th century castle lies on the shores of the *Gross Eutiner See*.

Schloss Gottorf, Renaissance castle on an island in the *Schlei-Bay, Schleswig*.

Schloss Glücksburg, white water-castle dating back to the 16th century.

• **Nature parks**

Naturpark Aukrug, on the *Hamburg-Kiel* motorway exit *Neumünster*.

Naturpark Westensee, on the same motorway further north, exit: *Blumenthal-Bad Bramstedt*. If you go on the *Hamburg-Flensburg* motorway, use exit *Warder*.

Hüttener Berge, this northernmost park can be reached on the *Hamburg-Flensburg* motorway, exits *Rendsburg-Büdelsdorf, Owschlag*, or *Schleswig-Gottorf*.

• **Adventure park**

Hansaland, on the shore of the Baltic Sea, 10 km/6 miles from *Timmendorfer Strand*.

ART GALLERIES & MUSEUMS

Museums and art galleries are usually open daily except Mondays.

ART GALLERIES

Neue Galerie/Sammlung Ludwig
Komphausbadstrasse 19
5100 Aachen
Tel. 0241/472561

Suermondt-Ludwig Museum
Wilhelmstrasse 18
5100 Aachen
Tel. 0241/472580

Staatsgalerie am Schaezler-Palais
Maximilianstrasse 46
8900 Augsburg
Tel. 0821/510350

Staatliche Kunsthalle
Lichtenthaler Allee 8a
7570 Baden-Baden
Tel. 07221/23250 or 25390
(Changing exhibitions)

Brücke-Museum
Bussardsteig 9
1000 Berlin 33
Tel. 030/8312029

Gemäldegalerie
Arnimallee 23/27
1000 Berlin 33
Tel. 030/8301217

Nationalgalerie
Potsdamer Strasse 50
1000 Berlin 30
Tel. 030/2662662

Kunstalle
Arthur-Ladebeck-Strasse 5
4800 Bielefeld
Tel. 0521/51247980

Städtisches Kunstmuseum
Rathausgasse 7
5300 Bonn 1
Tel. 0228/773686. 772440

Kunsthalle
Am Wall 207, 280 Bremen
Tel. 0421/324785

Herzog-Anton-Ulrich-Museum
Museumstrasse 1
3300 Braunschweig
Tel. 0531/1551

Wilhelm-Lehmbruck-Museum
Düsseldorfer Strasse 51
4100 Duisburg 1
Tel. 0203/28132630

Kunstmuseum Kunsthalle
Pempelforter Strasse 50
400 Düsseldorf
Tel. 0211/8992460

Städtische Kunsthalle
Grabbeplatz 4
4000 Düsseldorf 1
Tel. 0211/131469

Museum Folkwang
Goethestrasse 41, 4300 Essen
Tel. 0201/774783

Städelsches Kunstinstitut
und Städtische Galerie
Schaumainkai 63
6000 Frankfurt am Main 70
Tel. 069/617092

Karl-Ernst-Osthaus-Museum
Hochstrasse 73, 5800 Hagen
Tel. 023331/207556

Hamburger Kunsthalle
Glockengiesserwall
2000 Hmburg 1
Tel. 040/24825-2612

Kunstmuseum Hannover
mit Sammlung Sprengel
Kurt-Schwitters-Platz
3000 Hannover 1
Tel. 0511/1684400

Landesgalerie im Niedersächsischen
Landesmuseum Hannover
Am Maschpark 5
3000 Hannover 1
Tel. 0511/883051

Staatliche Kunsthalle
Hans-Thoma-Strasse 2
7500 Karlsruhe 1
Tel. 0721/1351

Neue Galerie Staatliche
u. Städtische Kunstsammlungen
Schöne Aussicht 1, 3500 Kassel
Tel. 0561/156266

Staatliche Kunstsammlungen
Schloss Wilhelmshöhe
3500 Kassel
Tel. 0561/36011

Kunsthalle zu Kiel
Düsternbrooker Weg 1
2300 Kiel 1
Tel. 0431/5972781

Wallraf-Richartz-Museum
Museum Ludwig
An der Rechtsschule, 5000 Köln
Tel. 0221/2212379

Kunsthalle Köln
Josef-Haubrich-Hof 1, 5000 Köln
Tel. 0221/2212335
(Changing exhibitions)

Wilhelm-Hack-Museum
Städtische Kunstgalerie
Berliner Strasse 23
6700 Ludwigshafen
Tel. 0621/5043411

Städtische Kunsthalle
Moltkestrasse 9
6800 Mannheim
Tel. 0621/5043411

Städtisches Museum
Abteistrasse 9
4050 Mönchengladbach
Tel. 02166/270394

Alte Pinakothek
Barerstrasse 27
8000 München 2
Tel. 089/23805216

Neue Pinakothek
Barerstrasse 29
8000 München 22
Tel. 089/23805195

Schackgalerie
Prinzregentenstrasse 9
8000 München 22
Tel. 089/224407

Staatsgalerie moderner Kunst, Haus der Kunst
Prinzregentenstrasse 1
8000 München 22
Tel. 089/292710

Städtische Galerie im Lenbachhaus
Luisenstrasse 33
8000 München 22
Tel. 089/521041-3

Westfälisches Landesmuseum für Kunst und Kulturgeschichte
Domplatz 10
4400 Münster
Tel. 0251/591251

Kunsthalle
Lorenzer Strasse 32
8500 Nürnberg 1
Tel. 0911/162853

Saarland-Museum Moderne Galerie
Bismarckstrasse 13
6600 Saarbrücken
Tel. 0681/66361

Staatsgalerie Stuttgart
Konrad-Adenauer-Strasse 32
7000 Stuttgart 1
Tel. 0711/2125108

Von-der-Heydt-Museum
Turmhof 8
5600 Wuppertal 1
Tel. 0202/5636231

MUSEUMS OF NON-EUROPEAN CULTURE

Ägyptisches Museum
Schlosstrasse 70
1000 Berlin 19
Tel. 030/3201261, 3201267

Museum für Indische Kunst
Takusstrasse 40
1000 Berlin 33
Tel. 030/8301361

Museum für Islamische Kunst
Takusstrasse 40
1000 Berline 33
Tel. 030/8301391

Museum für Ostasiatische Kunst
Takusstrasse 40
1000 Berlin 33
Tel. 030/8301381

Kestner-Museum
Trammplatz 3
3000 Hannover 1
Tel. 0511/1682120

Agyptologische Sammlung der Universität
Marstallhof
6900 Heidelberg

Roemer-Pelizaeus-Museum
Am Steine 1
3200 Hildesheim
Tel. 05121/1979

Museum für Ostasiatische Kunst
Universitätsstrasse 100
5000 Köln
Tel. 0221/405038

Staatliche Sammlung Ägyptische Kunst
Residenzstrasse 1
8000 München 2
Tel. 089/298546

MUSEUMS OF SCULPTURE

Georg-Kolbe-Museum
Sensburger Allee 25
1000 Berlin 19
Tel. 030/3042144

Skulpturengalerie
Arnimallee 23
1000 Berlin 33
Tel. 030/8301252

Kunstsammlungen der Ruhr-Universität
Universtätsstrasse 150
4630 Bochum
Tel. 0234/7004738

Akademisches Kunstmuseum der Universität
Am Hofgarten 21
5300 Bonn 1
Tel. 0228/737282

Liebighaus/Museum alter Plastik
Schaumainkai 71
6000 Frankfurt am Main 70
Tel. 069/638907

Staatliche Kunstsammlungen
Schloss Wilhelmshöhe
3500 Kassel
Tel. 0561/36011

Skulpturenmuseum der Stadt Marl
Rathaus
4370 Marl 1
Tel. 02356/105614

Glyptothek
Königsplatz 3
8000 München 2
Tel. 089/286100

Europäischer Skulpturenpark
Schloss,
3533 Willebadessen

MUSEUMS OF ETHNOLOGY

Museum für Völkerunde
Arnimallee 23
1000 Berlin 33
Tel. 030/8301-1

Übersee-Museum
Bahnhofsplatz 12
2800 Bremen 1
Tel. 0421/3978357

Museum für Völkerkunde
Schaumainkai 29
6000 Frankfurt am Main 70
Tel. 069/212-5391

Städtisches Museum Museum für Völkerkunde
Gerberau 32
7800 Freiburg i. Breisgau
Tel. 0761/216-3324

Oberhessisches Museum
Abtlg. Vor-und Frühgeschichte
u. Völkerkunde
Asterweg 9, 6300 Giessen
Tel. 064/306-2477

Hamburgisches Museum für Völkerkunde
Binderstrasse 14
2000 Hamburg 13
Tel. 040/44195-1

Niedersächsisches Landesmuseum
Völkerkundeabteilung
Am Maschpark 5
3000 Hannover
Tel. 0511/883051

Museum für Völkerkunde der Universität Kiel
Hegewischstrasse 3
2300 Kiel
Tel. 0431/5973620

Rautenstrauch-Joest-Museum für Völkerkunde
Ubierring 45
5000 Köln 1
Tel. 0221/311065, 311066

Staatliches Museum für Völkerkunde
Maximilianstrasse 42
8000 München 22
Tel. 089/224844, 224846

Linden-Museum Stuttgart
Staatliches Museum für Völkerkunde
Hegelplatz 1
7000 Stuttgart 1
Tel. 0711/2050-3221

Museum für Völkerkunde
Steinstrasse 19
3430 Witzenhausen
Tel. 0554/3203

FESTIVALS

Germany is a country where festivals are given pride of place. In the Calendar of Events below you will find the most important local festivals throughout the year. (See also Romantic Festivals pages 295-302.) For more detailed information ask at the local tourist information (*Fremdenverkehrsamt*, or *Verkehrsverein*, or *Verkehrsamt*, or *Verkehrsbüro* or *Fremdenverkehrsverein*).

JANUARY

Munich
Schäfflertanz Shrovetime. (Usually February/March).
Faschingszug (parade).

Cologne
Karnevalszug. (parade).

Mainz
Rosenmontagszug. (Rose Monday parade).

MARCH

Verden
Lätare-Spende. On the first Monday after Laetare Sunday, the people of Verden are given bread and herring following an old tradition.

Rothenburg ob der Tauber
Schäfertanz. Shepherds' Dance on the marketplace at the end of March, and several dates in the summer.

MAY

Rothenburg ob der Tauber
Meistertrunk. The Master Draught is a historical play commemorating the rescue of the town in the 17th century. Performed at Whitsun and on certain Sundays in summer.

Höxter
Conveyer Musikwochen. Classical concerts which take place in May and June.

Überlingen
Schwedenprozession. The procession takes place on a Sunday in May and another Sunday in July.

Nördlingen
Stabenfest. Historical festival usually on the second Monday in May.

Island of Reichenan (Lake Constance)
Blutfest. Festival in traditional costume on the last Sunday.

WHITSUN

Rothenburg ob der Trauber
Reichsstadfesttage. Traditional festival held at Whitsun and on the second weekend in September.

Kötzting
Pfingstritt. Cavalcade on Whitmonday.

Schwäbisch Hall
Kuchen-und Brunnenfest. This cake and fountain festival of salt makers is held at the market square of this town near Stuttgart.

Erlangen
Bergkirchweih. Church consecration and secular faith.

MAY – SEPTEMBER

Brühl
Schlosskonzerte. In the castle of Brühl the works of the classical masters are performed from May to September.

Hameln

Rattenfänger-Spiele. Pied Piper Play is an open air performance from May to September, Sundays from 12.00 p.m.—12.30 p.m.

Oberammergau

Passionsspiele. The Passion Play takes place every 10 years. (Next performance in 1990).

MAY – OCTOBER

Regensburg

Orgelwochen. The organ concerts are held in the church of the friary (Minorettenkirche) of the Municipal Museum every Sunday from May to October.

Donauwörth

Kammerkonzerte. Candlelight concerts are held in the Castle of Leitheim from May to October.

JUNE

Lüneburg

Bach-Woche. Mainly the works of Johann Sebastian Bach are performed in daily concerts in the second week of June (8 p.m.)

Göttingen

Händel-Festspiele. Händel's concerts and operas are staged daily for a week.

JUNE – JULY

Oldenburg

Kultursommer. A festival of concerts, folk dances and theatre performances.

Landshut

Landshuter Fürstenhochzeit. The Landshut Wedding is a historical play which takes place every four years. (Next in 1992).

JUNE – AUGUST

Bad Segeberg

Karl-May-Spiele. Wild West in Germany. Open air performances June—August.

Bad Hersfeld

Festspiele in der Stiftsruine. *Romeo and Juliet* is one of the plays performed in the ruins of the Stiftskirche each summer.

Passau

Die Europäischen Wochen. During the European Weeks operas, concerts and dramatic performances are held at the Nibelungen Halle, mainly in the evenings.

JUNE – SEPTEMBER

Meersburg

Internationale Schlosskonzerte. Classical concerts in the castle every Saturday.

JULY

Cuxhaven

Wochenende an der Jade. Festival in the harbor with windsurfing and music.

Ansbach

Rokokospiele im Schloss. Plays, concerts and dances from the 18th century. Several performances daily.

Dinkelsbühl

Kinderzeche-Woche. Traditional festival where children perform historical plays and parades commemorating the rescue of children in the Thirty Years' War.

Kaufbeuren

Tänzelfest. Children's festival with crossbow shooting, puppet theatre and parades.

Mindelheim

Frunsberg Festspiele. Festival pageants all over town.

Straubing

Agnes-Bernauer-Festspiele. Tragic plays of Agnes Bernauer every four years. (Next performance in 1992).

Ravensburg

Rutenfest. Children's festival with sticks.

Überlingen

Schwerttanz. Sword dance at town hall.

JULY – AUGUST

Neunburg

Burgfestspiele. Pageant plays at the edge of the Bavarian forest.

Waldmünchen
Trenck der Pandur. Folk festival with wild riding scenes.

Kiefersfelden
Ritterspiele. Pageant of medieval times.

Altdorf (near Nuremberg)
Wallenstein-Festspiele. Theatre performances and processions.

Heidelberg
Schlosspiele. Classical concerts in the castle of Heidelberg.

Constance
Internationale Musiktage. An international musical festival.

Bayreuth
Wagner-Festspiele. At this festival, the famous works of Wagner are performed daily for one month.

AUGUST

Frankfurt
Mainfest. This festival in August takes place on the Römer and by the banks of the river Main.

Kassel
Zissel. Folk festival.

Straubing
Gäubodenfest. Folk festival.

Grafenau
Säumerfest. Festival in commemoration of the salt transports.

AUGUST – SEPTEMBER

Augsburg
Plärrer. Folk festival.

SEPTEMBER

Stuttgart
Cannstatter Wasen. Folk festival in the suburb of Cannstatt.

Koblenz
Rhein in Flammen. Fireworks along the Rhine.

Nuremberg
Nürnberger Kulturzirkus. Festival with music and theatre performances.

SEPTEMBER – OCTOBER

Munich
Oktoberfest. Also known as *Wies'n* among the local people. Traditional beer-drinking festival with a ceremonial participation of innkeepers, the mayor and other VIP's of the town. Usually begins in the last week of September and continues through the first week of October.

OCTOBER

Bremen
Bremer Freimarkt. This folk festival is held in the second half of October.

Fürth
Michaelis-Kerwa. Festival at the beginning of October.

NOVEMBER

Hamburg
Hamburger Dom. Big fair on the Heiligengeistfeld.

NOVEMBER – DECEMBER

Nuremberg
Christkindlmarkt. The most famous Christmas market in Germany. It begins in the last week of November and lasts until Christmas Eve, December 24.

WHERE TO STAY

Germany is a country which welcomes tourists from around the world. You will have no trouble finding suitable accommodation anywhere in the Federal Republic. It may not be as luxurious or as inexpensive as you would wish, but even in the smallest village there is always some room available.

In the peak season (June-August) it is advisable to book in advance if you are visiting a popular place. You may do so through: Allgemeine Deutsche Zimmerreservierung, Beethovenstrasse 69, 6000 Frankfurt/Main, Tel. 069/75721.

To make advance bookings, contact one of these **hotel chains** which have properties in almost all the cities and sometimes in smaller towns:

Crest Hotels,
Isenburger Schneise 40,
6000 Frankfurt/M 71,
Tel. 069/6781234

Hilton International,
Kaiserstrasse 47,
6000 Frankfurt/M1,
Tel. 069/250102

Holiday Inn International,
Mailänder Strasse 1,
6000 Frankfurt/M 70,
Tel. 069/01305678

Penta Hotels GmbH,
Auguste-Viktoria-Strasse 15,
6200 Wiesbaden,
Tel. 06121/377041

Romantik Hotels KG,
Freigerichsstrasse 5,
8757 Karlstein a.M.,
Tel. 06188/5020 u. 6891

Sheraton Hotels & Inns,
An der Hauptwache 11,
6000 Frankfurt/M 1,
Tel. 069/01303535

SRS (Steigenberger Reservation Service)
Postfach 164 40,
6000 Frankfurt/M 16,
Tel. 069/215718

For tourists on a budget, enquire at the central office of the **German Youth Hostel Association** at: Deutsche Jugendherbergswerk, Bülowstrasse 26, Postfach 220, 4930 Detmold.

Those wishing to explore Germany by automobile can obtain camping information from: **Deutscher Camping-Club**, Mandlstrasse 28, 8000 München 40.

Various categories of accommodation are available: *Hotels*, *Pensionen* (pensions), *Gasthäuser* (inns), *Privatzimmer* (private lodgings). Hotels and pensions almost always guarantee average or above standard accommodation, whereas inns are likely to be simpler.

In the list below you will find the type of accommodation arranged according to prices; LL stands for deluxe, L stands for luxury, where the starting price is 150 marks (for a double room) M stands for moderate and costs between 90 and 150 marks, E stands for economy with a price range of 50 to 90 marks per double room. Single rooms are usually just over half the standard price. Breakfast is included.

CRUISING FATHER RHINE

•Mainz

Hilton, Rheinstrasse 68, Tel. 06131/2450 (L)

Europahotel, Kaiserstrasse 7, Tel. 06131/671091 (L)

Central-Hotel Eden, Bahnhofsplatz 8, Tel. 06131/674001 (M-L)

Moguntia, Nackstrasse 48, Tel. 06131/671041 (M)

Hammer, Bahnhofsplatz 6, Tel. 06131/611061 (M)

Grünewald, Frauenlobstrasse 14, Tel. 06131/674084 (M)

Am Römerwall, Römerwall 53, Tel. 06131/232135 (E-M)

•**Wiesbaden**

Nassauer Hof, Kaiser-Friedrich-Platz 3, Tel. 06121/1330 (L)

Aukamm-Hotel, Aukamm-Allee 31, Tel. 06121/5760 (L)

Penta Hotel, Auguste-Viktoria-Strasse 15, Tel. 06121/377041 (L)

Rhein-Taunus Hotel, Mainzer Strasse 166, Tel. 06121/7050 (M)

Luisenhof, Bahnhofsstrasse 7, Tel. 06121/39431 (M)

Am Kochbrunnen, Taunusstrasse 15, Tel. 06121/520061 (M)

Hotel de France, Taunusstrasse 49, Tel. 06121/520061 (M)

Oranien, Platter Strasse 2, Tel. 06121/525025 (M)

•**Eltville am Rhein**

Sonnenberg, Friedrichstrasse 65, Tel. 06123/3081 (M)

Rosenhof, Martinstrasse 9, Tel. 06123/3360 (E-M)

•**Rüdesheim**

Central-Hotel, Kirchstrasse 6, Tel. 06722/2391 (M)

Rheinstein, Rheinstrasse 20, Tel. 06722/2004 (E-M)

•**Lorch**

Arnesteiner Hof, Schwalbacher Strasse 8, Tel. 06726/9371 (E)

•**Kaub**

Zum Turm, Zollstrasse 50, Tel. 06774/306 (E)

•**Lahnstein**

Kaiserhof, Hochstrasse 9, Tel. 02621/2413 (E)

•**Rhens**

Königstuhl, Am Rhein 1, Tel. 02628/2244 (M)

•**Boppard**

Bellevue-Rheinhotel, Rheinallee 41, Tel. 06742/1020 (M-L)

Rheinlust, Rheinallee 27, Tel. 06742/3001 (E-M)

Rheinkrone, Mainzer Strasse 4, Tel. 06742/5088 (E)

•**Oberwesel**

Römerkrug, Marktplatz 1, Tel. 06744/8176 (E-M)

•**Bingen**

Köppel, Kapuzinerstrasse 12, Tel. 06721/14770 (E-M)

Rheinhotel Starkenburger Hof, Rheinkai 1, Tel. 06721/14341 (E-M)

Rheingau, Rheinkai 8, Tel. 06721/17496 (E)

Am Rochusberg, Rochusstrasse 17, Tel. 06721/12532 (E)

MEANDERING MOSELLE RIVER

•**Winningen**

Moselblick, Tel. 02606/2275 (M)

•**Beilstein**

Langhans, Auensteinerstrasse 1, Tel. 07062/5436 (E)

•**Zell**

Grüner Dranz, Balduinstrasse 13, Tel. 06542/4276 (E-M)

•**Traben-Trarbach**

Moselschlösschen, Neue Rathausstrasse 12, Tel. 06541/710 (M-L)

Krone, An der Mosel 93, Tel. 06541/6363 (M)

Bernkastel Kaiser, Markt 29, Tel. 06531/3038 (M)

•**Neumagen-Dhron**

Zur Post, Römerstrasse 79, Tel. 06507/2114 (E)

•**Trier**

Europa Parkhotel Mövenpick, Kaiserstrasse 29, Tel. 0651/71950 (L)

Holiday Inn, Zurmaiener Strasse 164, Tel. 0651/23091 (L)

Petrisberg, Sickingenstrasse 11, Tel. 0651/41181 (M)

Deutscher Hof. Südallee 25, Tel. 0651/46021 (E-M)

Feilen-Wolff, Kölner Strasse 22, Tel. 0651/86763 (E)

HEADING FOR COLOGNE

•Koblenz

Brenner, Rizzastrasse 20, Tel. 0261/32060 (L)

Hohenstaufen, Emil-Schüller-Strasse 41, Tel. 0261/37081 (M-L)

Kleiner Risen, Kaiserin-Augusta-Anlage 18, Tel. 0261/32077 (M)

Continental-Pfälzer Hof. Bahnhofsplatz 1, Tel. 0261/33073 (M)

Trierer Hof, Clemensstrasse 1, Tel. 0261/34060 (E-M)

Minerva, Cantadorstrasse 13a, Tel. 0211/350961 (M)

•Duisburg

Duisburger Hof. König-Heinrich-Platz, Tel. 0203/331021 (LL)

Novotel, Landfermannstrasse 20, Tel. 0203/300030 (L)

Plaza, Dellplatz 1, Tel: 0203/22375 (M)

Stadt Duisburg Goldene Treppe, Düsseldorfstrassc 124, Tel. 0203/22375 (M)

Rheingarten, Königstrasse 78, Tel: 0203/5001 (M)

•Essen

Sheraton, Huyssenalle 55, Tel. 0201/20951 (LL)

Essener Hof, Teichstrasse 2, Tel. 0201/20901 (L)

Europa, Hindenburgstrasse 35, Tel. 0201/232041 (M)

Arcade, Hollestrasse 50, Tel. 0201/24280 (M)

Arosa, Rüttenscheider Strasse 149, Tel. 201/72280 (LL)

Behr's Parkhotel, Alfredstrasse 118, Tel. 0201/779095 (M)

Ruhr-Hotel, Krawehlstrasse 42, Tel. 0201/775172 (M)

Parkhaus Hügel, Freiherr-vom-Stein-Strasse 209, Tel. 0201/471091 (M)

Romantik-Hotel Residence, Auf der Forst 1, Tel: 02054/8911 (L)

Recklinghausen Die Engelsburg, Augustinessenstrasse 10, Tel. 02361/25066 (M)

Barbarossa, Löhrhof 8, Tel: 02361/25071 (M)

Landhaus Quellberg, Holunderweg 9, Tel: 02361/41014 (M)

Wüller, Hammer Strasse 1, Tel. 02361/41051 (E)

"LOSING MY HEART IN HEIDELBERG..."

•Speyer

Löwengarten, Schwerdstrasse 14, Tel. 06232/71051 (M)

Goldener Engel, Mühlturmstrasse 1a, Tel. 06232/76732 (E-M)

Am Wartturm, Landwehrstrasse 28, Tel. 06232/36066 (E)

•Worms

Domhotel, Obermarkt 10, Tel. 06241/6913 (M)

Pfeddersheimer Hof, Zellertalstrasse 35, Tel. 06247/811

•Mannheim

Steigenberger Hotel Mannheimer Hof, Augusta-Anlage 4, Tel. 0621/45021 (L)

Holiday Inn, N 6, 4, Tel. 0621/10710 (L)

Intercity-Hotel, Im Hauptbahnhof-Ostfügel, Tel. 0621/22925 (M)

Holländer Hof, U 1, 11-12, Tel. 0621/16095 (M)

Seitz, Seckenheimer Strasse 132, Tel. 0621/444858 (E)

Wegener, Tattersallstrasse 16, Tel. 0621/444988 (E)

•Heidelberg

Prinzhotel, Neuenheimer Landstrasse 5, Tel. 06221/40320 (L)

Alt-Heidelberg, Rohrbacher Strasse 29, Tel. 0622/15091 (L)

Schönberger Hof, Untere Neckarstrasse 54, Tel. 06221/22615 (M)

Reichspost, Gaisbergstrasse 38, Tel. 06221/222252 (M)

Haus Sedlmayer, Gerhart-Hauptmann-Strasse 5, Tel. 06221/20203 (M-L)

Romantik Hotel Zum Ritter St. Georg, Hauptstr. 178, Tel. 06221/20203 (M-L)

INTO THE HEART OF FRANCONIA

•Neckargemünd

Zum Ritter, Neckarstrasse 40, Tel. 06223/7035 (M)

•Eberbach

Kettenboot, Friedrichstrasse 1, Tel. 067271/2470 (E)

Krone-Post, Hauptstrasse 1, Tel. 0627/2310 (E-M)

•Erbach

Odenwälder Bauern-und Wappenstuben, Schlossgraben 30, Tel. 06062/2236(E)

•Michelstadt

Drei Hasen, Braunstrasse 5, Tel. 06061/615 (E)

•Amorbach

Badischer Hof, Am Stadttor 4, Tel. 09373/1208 (E)

•Miltenberg

Jagdhotel Rose, Hauptstrasse 280, Tel. 09371/2001 (M)

Hopfengarten, Amberggasse 16, Tel. 09371/2031 (E)

•Grossheubach

Haus Carmen, Eichenstrasse 14, Tel. 0937/1353 (E)

•Wertheim

Schwan, Mainplatz 8, Tel 09342/1278

Marktheidenfeld Zum Löwen, Marktplatz 3, Tel. 09391/1571 (E)

•Würzburg

Maritim, Pleichertorstrasse 5, Tel. 0931/50831 (L)

Walfisch, Am Pleidenturm 5, Tel. 0931/47081 (M-L)

Grüner Baum, Zeller Strasse 35, Tel. 0931/47081 (M-L)

Würzburger Hof, Babarossaplatz 2, Tel. 0931/50360 (E-M)

Franziskaner, Franziskanerplatz 2, Tel. 0931/50360 (E-M)

•Bamberg

Bamberger Hof Bellevue, Schönleinsplatz 4, Tel. 0951/22216 (M-L)

National, Luitpoldstrasse 37, Tel. 0951/24112 (M)

St. Nepomuk, Obere Mühlbrücke 9, Tel. 0951/25183 (M)

Barock-Hotel am Don, Vorder Bach 4, Tel. 0951/54031 (E-M)

Graupner, Lange Strasse 5 Tel. 0951/25132 (E)

•Coburg

Blankenburg, Rosenauer Strasse 30, Tel. 09561/75005 (M)

Goldene Traube, Am Viktoriabrunnen 2, Tel. 09561/9833 (E-M)

Coburger Tor, Ketschendorfer Strasse 22, Tel. 09561/25074 (E-M)

Gasthof Goldenes Kreuz, Herrengasse 1, Tel. 09561/90473 (E)

Staffelstein Rödiger, Zur Herrgottsmühle 2, Tel. 09573/895 (E)

•Lichtenfels

Preussischer Hof, Bambergerstrasse 30, Tel. 09571/5015 (M)

Gasthof Müller, Kloster-Banz-Strasse 4, Tel. 09571/6021 (E)

Kronach Sonne, Bahnhofstrasse 2, Tel. 09261/3434 (E)

•Kulmbach

Hansa-Hotel Hönsch, Weltrichstrasse 2a, Tel. 09221/7995 (E-M)

Christl, Bayreuther Strasse 7, Tel. 09221/7955 (E)

Dobrachtal, Tel. 09221/2085 (E)

•Bayreuth

Bayerischer Hof, Bahnhofstrasse 14, Tel. 0921/22081 (M-L)

Königshof, Bahnhofstrasse 23, Tel. 0921/24094 (E-L)

Am Hofgarten, Lisztstrasse 6, Tel. 0921/69006 (E-M)

Goldener Anker, Opernstrasse 6, Tel. 0921/65500 (E-M)

Gasthof Goldener Löwe, Kulmbacher Strasse 30, Tel. 0921/41046 (E)

•Nürnberg

Carlton-Hotel, Eilgutstrasse 13, Tel. 0911/203535 (L)

Grand Hotel (Penta), Bahnhofstrasse 1, Tel. 0911/203621 (L)

Deutscher Hof, Frauentorgraben 29, Tel. 0911/203821 (M-L)

Prinzregent, Prinzregentenufer 11, Tel. 0911/533107 (M)

Viktoria, Königstrasse 80, Tel. 0911/20381 (M)

Am Heiderloffplatz, Am Heiderloffplatz 9, Tel. 0911/44951)E-M)

Am Ring, Am Plärrer 2, Tel. 0911/265771 (E-M)

Burghotel, Schildgasse 16, Tel. 0911/203040 (E)

•Tauberbischofsheim
Henschker Bahnhofstrasse 18, Tel. 09341/2336 (E)
Am Brenner, Goethestrasse 10, Tel. 0934/3091 (E)

•Bad Mergentheim
Park Hotel, Lothar-Daiker-Strasse 6, Tel. 07931/56100 (L)
Victoria, Poststrasse 2, Tel. 07931/5930 (M-L)
Bundschuh, Cronbergstrasse 15, Tel. 07931/3043 (M)
Deutschmeister, Ochsengasse 7, Tel. 07931/7285 (E)

•Weikersheim
Laurentius, Marktplatz 5, Tel. 07934/7007 (E)

•Röttingen
Rebstöckle, Rothenburger Strasse 2, Tel. 09338/531 (E)

•Creglingen
Gasthof Krone, Hauptstrasse 12, Tel. 07933/390 (E)

•Rothenburg ob der Tauber
Eisenhut Hermgasse 3, Tel. 09861/2041 (L)
Mittermeier, Vorm Würzburger Tor 9, Tel. 09861/2259 (M-L)
Merian, Ansbacher Strasse 42, Tel. 09861/3096 (M)
Gasthof Glocke, Am Plönlein 1, Tel. 09861/3025 (E-M)
Romantik Hotel Markusturm, Rödergasse 1, Tel. 09861/2370 (L)

•Ansbach
Am Drechselgarten, Am Drechselgarten 1, Tel. 0981/89020 (M-L)
Christl, Richard-Wagner-Strasse 41, Tel. 0981/8121 (E-M)
Platengarten, Promenade 30, Tel. 0981/3217 (E-M)

•Feuchtwangen
Gasthof Wilder Mann, Ansbacher Berg 2, Tel. 09852/719 (E)
Gasthof Lamm, Marktplatz 5, Tel. 09852/500 (E)
Romantik Hotel Greifen-Post, Marktplatz 8, Tel. 09852/2002 (M-L)

•Dinkelsbühl
Eisenkrug, Dr.-Martin-Luther-Strasse 1, Tel. 09851/3429 (M)
Blauer Hecht, Schweinemarkt 1, Tel. 09851/811 (E-M)
Goldene Rose, Marktplatz 4, Tel. 09851/831 (E-M)
Gasthof zur Goldenen Krone, Nördlinger Strasse 24, Tel. 09851/2293 (E)

•Nördlingen
Am Ring, Bürgermeister-Reiger-Strasse 14, Tel. 09081/4028 (E-M)
Sonne, Marktplatz 3, Tel. 09081/5067 (E-M)
Altreuter, Marktplatz 11, Tel. 0908/4319 (E)
Mondschein, Bauhofgasse 5, Tel. 09081/86074 (E)

•Donauwörth
Traube, Kapellstrasse 14, Tel. 0906/6096 (E)
Zu den Drei Kronen, Bahnhofstrasse 25, Tel. 0906/21077 (E)
Donauwörther Hof, Teutonenweg 16, Tel. 0906/5950 (E)
Park-Café, Sternschanzenstrasse 1, Tel. 0906/6037 (E-M)

•Augsburg
Steigenberger Drei-Mohren-Hotel, Maximilianstrasse 40, Tel. 0821/510031 (L)
Turmhotel Holiday Inn, Imhofstrasse 12, Tel. 0821/577087 (L)
Alpenhof, Donauwörther Strasse 233, Tel. 0821/413051 (M)
Langer, Gögginger Strasse 39, Tel. 0821/578077 (E-M)
Dom-Hotel, Frauentorstrasse 8, Tel. 0821/153031 (E-M)

•Landsberg
Goggl, Herkomer Strasse 19, Tel. 08191/2081 (E-M)

•Bad Wörishofen
Kurhotel Residenz, Bahnhofstrasse 8, Tel. 08247/3520 (L)
Kurhotel Fontenay, Eichwaldstrasse 10, Tel. 08247/1011 (M)

Gasthof Adler, Hauptstrasse 40, Tel. 08247/2091 (E)

•**Schongau**
Holl, Altenstädter Strasse 39, Tel. 08861/7292 (M)
Alte Post, Marienplatz 19, Tel. 08861/8058 (E-M)

•**Schwangau**
König Ludwig, Kreuzweg 11, Tel. 08362/81081 (M)
Weimbauer, Füssener Strasse 3, Tel. 08362/81015 (E-M)

•**Füssen**
Sailers Kurhotel, Bildhauerstrasse 3, Tel. 08361/7089 (E-M)
Kurhotel Filser, Säulingstrasse 3, Tel. 08363/2068 (E-M)
Fürstenhof, Komotener Strasse 23, Tel. 08362/7006 (E-M)

ALONG THE ALPS

•**Oberammergau**
Alios Lang, St.-Lukas-Strasse 15, Tel. 08822/4141 (L)
Wittelsbach, Dorfstrasse 21, Tel. 08822/4545 (M)
Alte Post, Dorfstrasse 19, Tel. 08822/6691 (E-M)

•**Garmisch-Partenkirchen**
Grand-Hotel Sonnenbichl, Burgstrasse 97, Tel. 08821/7020 (L)
Bernrieder Hof, Von-Müller-Strasse 12, Tel. 08821/71074 (L)
Bellevue, Riesserseestrasse 9, Tel. 08821/58008 (M)
Rheinischer Hof, Zugspitzstrasse 76, Tel. 08821/72024 (E-M)
Romantik Hotel Clausings Posthotel, Marienplatz 12, Tel. 08821/58071 (M-L)

•**Wallgau**
Parkhotel, Bermseestrasse 1, Tel. 08825/211 (L)

•**Kochel**
Schmied von Kochel, Schlehdorfer Strasse 6, Tel. 08851/216 (M)
Gasthof Herzogstand, Herzogstandweg 3, Tel. 08851/324 (E)

•**Benediktbeuren**
Alpengasthof Friedenseiche, Häusernstrasse 34, Tel. 08857/279 (E)

•**Kreuth**
Zur Post, Nördliche Hauptstrasse 5, Tel. 08029/1021 (M)

•**Rottach-Egern**
Bachmair am See, Seestrasse 47, Tel. 08022/6444 (L)
Gästehaus Haltmair am See, Seestrasse 47, Tel. 08022/26057 (M)
Lindl/Zum Rosser, Nördliche Hauptstrasse 25, Tel. 08022/24064 (E)

•**Tegernsee**
Haus Bayern, Neureuthstrasse 23, Tel. 08022/3951 (E-M)

•**Gmund**
Oberstöger, Tölzer Strasse 4, Tel. 08022/7019 (E)

•**Schliersee**
Schliersee-Hotel, Kirchbichlweg 18, Tel. 08026/4086 (M-L)
Reiter, Risseckstrasse 8, Tel. 08026/4057 (E-M)
Gästehaus Risseck, Risseckstrasse 4, Tel. 08026/6140 (E)
Bayerischzell Gästehaus Effland, Tannermühlstrasse 14, Tel. 08023/263 (E-M)
Romantik-Hotel Die Meindelei, Michael-Meindl-Strasse 13, Tel. 08023/318 (M)

•**Reit im Winkl**
Unterwirt, Kirchplatz 2, Tel. 08640/8811 (M)
Altenburger Hof, Frühlingstrasse 3, Tel. 08640/8994 (M)
Zum Löwen, Tiroler Strasse 1, Tel. 08640/8901 (E)

•**Inzell**
Dorint-Hotel, Lärchenstrasse 5, Tel. 08665/6051 (M)
Post, Reichenhaller Strasse 2, Tel. 08665/231 (E)

•**Bad Reichenhall**
Kurhotel Luisenbad, Ludwigstrasse 33, Tel. 08651/5011 (L)

Kurhotel Alpina, Adolf-Schmid-Strasse 5, Tel. 08651/2038 (L)
Panorama, Baderstrasse 3, Tel. 08651.61001 (M-L)
Kurfürst, Kurfürstenstrasse 11, Tel. 08651/2710 (E-M)
Haus Vroni, Paepkestrasse 3, Tel. 08651/5993 (E)

•Berchtesgaden
Alpenhotel Kronprinz, Am Brandholz, Tel. 08652/61061 (M-L)
Fischer, Königsseer Strasse 51, Tel. 08652/4044 (M-L)
Sporthotel Seimler, Maria am Berg 4, Tel. 08652/5031 (E-M)

MUNICH – THE SECRET CAPITAL

Vier Jahreszeiten, Maximilianstrasse 17, Tel. 089/230390 (LL)
Bayerischer Hof, Promenadenplatz 2, Tel. 089/21200 (LL)
Königshof, Karlsplatz 25, Tel. 089/558412 (LL)
Hilton, Am Tucherpark 7, Tel. 089/38450 (LL)
Excelsior, Schützenstrasse 11, Tel. 089/557906 (L)
Ambassador, Mozartstrasse 4, Tel. 089/530840 (L)
Admiral, Kohlstrasse 9, Tel. 089/226641 (L)
Apollo, Mittererstrasse 7, Tel. 089/539531 (L)
Bundesbahnhotel, Im Hauptbahnhof, Tel. 089/558571 (M)
Reinbold, Adolf-Kolping-Strasse 11, Tel. 089/222691 (M)
Mark, Senefelderstrasse 12, Tel. 089/592801 (M)
An der Oper, Falkenturmstrasse 10, Tel. 089/228711 (M)
City Hotel, Schillerstrasse 3a, Tel. 089/558091 (M-L)
Adria, Liebigstrasse 8a, Tel. 089/293081 (M)
Europäischer Hof, Bayerstrasse 31, Tel. 089/551510 (M)
Amba, Arnulfstrasse 20, Tel. 089/592921 (E-M)
Blauer Bock, Blumenstrasse 16, Tel. 089/2608043 (E-M)
Württemberger Hof, Marsstrasse 5, Tel. 089/598394 (E-M)

•Suburb of Schwabing
Holiday-Inn, Leopoldstrasse 194, Tel. 089/34097 (L)
Tourotel, Domagkstrasse 26, Tel. 089/360010 (M)
Leopold, Leopoldstrasse 119, Tel. 089/367061 (E-M)

•Suburd of Haidhausen
Preysing, Preysingstrasse 1, Tel. 089/4484011 (L)
Penta-Hotel, Hochstrasse 3, Tel. 089/4482424 (M)

•Suburb of Bogenhausen
Sheraton, Arabellastrasse 6, Tel. 089/924011 (L)
Crest Hotel, Effnerstrasse 99, Tel. 089/982541 (L)

•Herrsching
Alba-Seehotel, Seepromenade, Tel. 08152/2011 (M-L)
Piushof, Schönbichlstrasse 18, Tel. 08152/1007 (M)

•Diessen
Strandhotel, Jahnstrasse 10, Tel. 08807/5038 (M)
Gasthof Seefelder Hof, Alexander-Köster-Weg 6, Tel. 08807/1022 (E-M)

•Starnberg
Seehof, Bahnhofsplatz 4, Tel. 08151/6001 (M)
Tutzinger Hof, Tutzinger-Hof-Platz 7, Tel. 08151/3081 (E-M)

•Berg
Strandhotel Schloss Berg, Seestrasse 17, Tel. 08151/50021 (M-L)

•Seeshaupt
Hotel-Gasthof Zur Quelle, Tel. 08801/772 (E)

•Tutzing
Engelhof, Heinrich-Vogel-Strasse 9, Tel. 08158/6336 (M)

•Wolfratshausen
Gasthof Humplbräu, Obermarkt 2, Tel. 08171/7115 (E)

•Aying
Brauerei-Gasthof Aying, Zornedinger Strasse 2, Tel. 08095/705 (M)

•Rosenheim
Parkhotel Crombach, Kufsteiner Strasse 2, Tel. 08031/12086 (M)
Tirol, Kufsteiner Strasse 5, Tel. 08031/31001 (M)
Alpenhotel Wendelstein, Bahnhofstrasse 4, Tel. 08031/32108 (E-M)

•Prien am Chiemsee
Yachthotel Chiemsee, Harrasser Strasse 49, Tel. 08051/6960 (M)
Kur-und Sporthotel Charivari, Stauden 1, Tel. 08051/1063 (M-L)
Reinhart, Tel. 08051/1045 (M)
König-Ludwig-Stuben, Seestrasse 95 Tel. 08051/4802 (E)

•Gstadt am Chiemsee
Gästehaus Grünäugl, Seestrasse 1, Tel. 08054/235 (E)

EASTERN BAVARIA

•Freising
Isar-Hotel, Isarstrasse 4, Tel. 08161/81004 (M)
Bayerischer Hof, Untere Hauptstrasse 3, Tel. 08161/3037 (E)

•Deggendorf
Centralhotel, Östlicher Stadtgraben 30, Tel. 09916011 (M)
Zum Burgwirt, Im Stadtteil Nattenberg, Tel. 0991/3226 (E)

•Landshut
Kaiserhof, Papiererstrasse 2, Tel. 0871/6870 (M)
Goldenne Sonne, Neustadt 520, Tel. 0871/23087 (E-M)
Romantik-Hotel Fürstenhof, Stethaimer Strasse 3, Tel. 0871/82025 (M)

•Neustadt a.d. Donau
Löwenbräu/Gigl, Herzog-Ludwig-Strasse 6, Tel. 09445/351 (E)

•Kelheim
Ehrnthaller, Donaustrasse 22, Tel. 9441/3333 (E-M)
Aukoferbräu, Allestrasse 27 Tel. 09441/1460 (E)

•Regensburg
Parkhotel Maximilian, Maximilianstrasse 28, Tel. 0941/561011 (L)
Kaiserhof am Dom, Kramgasse 10, Tel. 0941/54028 (M)
Bischofshof, Krauterer Markt 3, Tel. 0941/59086 (E-M)
Karmeliten, Dachauplatz 1, Tel. 0941/54308 (E-M)
Müncher Hof, Tandler Gasse, Tel. 09421/51805 (E)

•Weiden
Stadtkrug, Wolframstrasse 5, Tel. 0961/32025 (M)
Europa, Frauenrichter Strasse (E) Tel. 0961/2 50 51 (E)
Hotel am Tor, Am Unteren Tor, Tel. 0961/5014 (E)

•Straubing
Heimer, Schlesische Strasse 131, Tel. 09421/6109 (L)
Seethaler, Theresienplatz 25, Tel. 09421/12022 (M)
Wenisch, Innere Passauer Strasse 59, Tel. 09421/22066 (E)

•Frauenau
Gartenhaus Poppen, Godehardstrasse 18, Tel. 09926/715 (E)

•Bodenmais
Atlas Hotel Sonnenhof, Rechensöldenweg 8, Tel. 09924/7710 (M-L)
Andrea, Tel. 09924/386 (M)

•Zwiesel
Kurhotel Sonnenburg, Augustinerstrasse 9, Tel. 09922/2031 (M)
Deutscher Rhein, Stadtplatz 42, Tel. 09922/1651 (E)
Pension Bergfeld, Hochstrasse 45, Tel. 09922/9554 (E)

•Grafenau
Steigenberger Hotel Sonnenhof, Sonnenstrasse 12, Tel. 08552/2033 (M-L)
Parkhotel, Kurpark 51, Tel. 08552/2444 (M)
Gasthof Nätscher, Grüber Strasse 1, Tel. 08552/2121 (E)

•Tittling

Gasthof Zur Post, Marktplatz 3, Tel. 08504/1737 (E)

•Passau

Wilder Mann, Rathausplatz, Tel. 0851/35071 (M-L)

Paussauer Wolf, Rindermarkt 6, Tel. 0851/34046 M-L)

Weisser Hase, Ludwigstrasse 23, Tel. 0851/34066 (E-M)

Dreiflüsse-Hof, Danziger Strasse 42, Tel.0851/51018 (E)

Schloss Ort, Am Dreiflußeck, Tel. 0851/34072 (E)

•Altötting

Zur Post, Kapellplatz 2, Tel. 08671/5040 (M)

Schex, Kapuzinerstrasse 11, Tel. 0867/4021 (E)

Gasthof Plankl, Schlotthamer Strasse 4, Tel. 08671/6522

CIRCLING AROUND LAKE CONSTANCE

•Pfronten

Bavaria, Kienbergstrasse 62, Tel. 08363.5004 (L)

Schönkahler, Kienbergstrasse 56, Tel. 08363/6001 (E-M)

•Nesselwang

Kurhotel Bergpanorama, Falkensteinstrasse 10, Tel. 08361/555 (E)

•Hindelang

Bad-Hotel Sonne, Marktstrasse 15, Tel. 08321/2026 (M)

•Sonthofen

Brauerei-Gasthof Hirsch, Grüntenstrasse 7, Tel. 08321/7016 (E)

Pension Johanna, Sonnenkopfstrasse 13, Tel. 08321/2641 (E)

•Immenstadt

Hirsch, Hirschstrasse 11, Tel. 08323/6218 (E)

Hotel-Pension Lamm, Kirchplatz 2, Tel. 08323/6192 (E)

•Oberstaufen

Allgäu Sonne, Am Stiessberg 1, Tel. 08386/7020 (L)

Aparthotel Interest, Auf der Höh 1, Tel. 08386/1633 (M)

•Lindenberg

Bode, Nadenberg 7, Tel. 08381/2828 (E)

•Lindau

Bayerischer Hof, Seepromenade, Tel. 08382/5055 (L)

Reutemann mit Seegarten, Seepromenade, Tel. 08382/5055 (M-L)

Insel-Hotel, Maximilianstrasse 42, Tel. 08382/5017 (M)

Am Holdereggenpark, Giebelbachstrasse 1, Tel. 08382/6066 (M)

Toscana, Aeschacher Ufer 12, Tel. 08382/3131 (E)

•Konstanz

Steigenberger Inselhotel, Auf der Insel, Tel. 07531/25011 (L)

Parkhotel am See, Seestrasse 25, Tel. 07531/51077 (L)

Seeblick, Neuhauser Strasse 14, Tel. 07531/54018 (M)

Mago-Hotel, Bahnhofsplatz 4, Tel. 07531/27001 (M)

Bucher-Hotel, Buchner Strasse 6, Tel. 07531/31025 (E-M)

•Radolfzell

Am Stadtgarten, Höllturmpassage Haus 2, Tel. 07732/4011 (M)

Gasthof Adler, Seestrasse 34, Tel. 07732/3473 (E-M)

Braun, Schäferhalde 16, Tel. 07732/3730 (E)

•Reichenau

Strandhotel Löchnerhaus, Schiffslände 12, Tel. 07534/411 (M-L)

Mohren, Pirminstrasse 141, Tel. 07534/401 (M)

Romantik Hotel Seeschau, An der Schiffslände 8, Tel. 07534/257 (M)

•Überlingen

Parkhotel St. Leonhard, Obere St.-Leonard-Strasse 83, Tel. 07551/8080 (M-L)

Kurhotel Seehof, Strandweg 6, Tel. 07551/63020 (M-L)

Romantik Hotel Hecht, Münsterstrasse 8, Tel. 07551/63333 (M)

•Meersburg

Terrassen-Hotel Weisshaar, Stefan Lochner-Strasse 24, Tel. 07532/9006 (L)

Strandhotel Wilder Mann, Bismarckplatz 2, Tel. 07532/9011 (M-L)

Seehotel Zur Münz, Seestrasse 7, Tel. 07532/9090 (E-M)

•Hagenau

Hansjakob, Hansjakobstrasse 17, Tel. 07532/6366 (M)

•Immenstaad

Strandcafé, Am Strandbad 10, Tel. 07545/768 (M)

•Friedrichshafen

Buchorner Hof, Friedrichstrasse 33, Tel. 07541/25041 (L)

Zeppelin, Eugenstrasse 41, Tel. 0754/25071 (M)

Goldenes Rad, Karlstrasse 43, Tel. 07541/21081 (E-M)

Sieben Schwaben, Hauptstrasse 37, Tel. 07541/55098 (E)

Zur Gerbe, Hirschlatter Strasse 14, Tel. 07541/51084 (E)

•Langenargen

Schiff, Marktplatz1, Tel. 07543/2407 (M)

Löwen Obere Seestrasse 4, Tel. 07543/3010 (E)

ADVENTURING IN THE BLACK FOREST

•Freiburg

Colombi-Hotel, Rotteckring 16, Tel. 0761/31415 (L)

Rheingold, Eisenbahnstrasse 47, Tel. 0761/36066 (L)

Central-Hotel, Wasserstrasse 6, Tel. 0761/31129 (M)

Atlanta, Rheinstrasse 29, Tel. 0761/272336 (E-M)

City-Hotel, Weberstrasse 3, Tel. 0761/31766 (E-M)

•Glottertal

Hirschen, Rathausweg 2, Tel 07684/810 (M-L)

Gasthof Kreuz, Landstrasse 14, Tel. 07684/206

•Hinterzarten

Park-Hotel Adler, Adlerplatz, Tel. 07652/711 (L)

Thomahof, Erlenbrucker Strasse 16, Tel. 07652/703 (M-L)

Schwarzwaldhof, Freiburger Strasse 2, Tel. 07652/310 (E-M)

•Titisee

Titisee-Hotel, Seestrasse 16, Tel. 07651/8152 (L)

Treschers Schwarzwald-Hotel am See, Seestrasse 12, Tel. 07651/8111 (M-L)

Seehotel Wiesler, Strandbadstrasse 5, Tel. 07651/8330 (M)

Bären, Neustädter Strasse 35, Tel. 07651/8223 (E-M)

Romantik Hotel Adler-Post, Hauptstrasse 16, Tel. 07651/5066 (M)

•Staufen im Breisgau

Zum Hirschen, Haupstrasse 19, Tel. 07633/5297 (E)

•Sulzburg

Gasthof Hirschen, Hauptstrasse 69, Tel. 07634/8208 (E)

•Badenweiler

Römerbad, Schlossplatz 1, Tel. 07632/700 (L)

Blauenwald, Blauenstrasse 11, Tel. 07632/5008 (M)

Romantik-Hotel Sonne, Moltkestrasse 4, Tel. 07632/5053 (M-L)

•Endingen

Pfauen, Hauptstrasse 78, Tel. 07642/8050 (E)

•Breisach

Am Münster, Münsterbergstrasse 23, Tel. 07667/7071 (M)

Kapuzinergarten, Kapuzinergasse 26, Tel. 07667/1055 (E)

•Riegel

Riegeler Hof, Hauptstrasse 69, Tel. 07642/1468 (E)

•Furtwangen

Kussenhof, Kussenhofstrasse 43, Tel. 07723/7760 (E)

•Schonach

Schwarzwaldgasthof Schwanen, Hauptstrasse 18, Tel. 07722/5296 (E-M)

•Schönwald

Zum Ochsen, Ludwig-Uhland-Strasse 18, Tel. 077224/424 (E-M)

•Triberg

Romantik Hotel Parkhotel Wehrle, Gartenstrasse 24, Tel. 07722/4081 (M-L)

•Alpirsbach

Gasthof Rössle, Aischbachstrasse 5, Tel. 07444/2281 (E)

•Freudenstadt

Steigenberger-Hotel, Karl-von-Hahn-Strasse, Tel. 07441/81071 (L)

Kurhaus Palmenwald, Tel. 0744/4001 (M)

Württemberger Hof, Lauterbadstrasse 10, Tel. 07441/6047 (M)

•Nagold

Romantik Hotel Post, Bahnhofstrasse 2, Tel. 07452/4048 (M)

•Calw

Rattsube, Marktplatz 12, Tel. 07051/1731 (E)

Gasthof zum Rössle, Hermann-Hesse-Platz 2, Tel. 07051/30052 (E)

•Tübingen

Krone, Uhlandstrasse 1, Tel. 07071/31036 (M-L)

Stadt Tübingen, Stuttgarter Strasse 97, Tel. 07071/31071 (M)

Barbarina, Wilhelmstrasse 94, Tel. 07071/26048 (E-M)

Am Bad, Europastrasse, Tel. 07071/73071 (E)

Adler-Hotel-Garni, Bebenhäuser Strasse 2, Tel. 070718/81806 (E)

•Stuttgart

Steigenberger Hotel Graf Zeppelin, Arnulf-Klett-Platz 7, Tel. 0711/ 299881 (L)

Am Schlossgarten, Schillerstrasse 23, Tel. 0711/299911 (L)

Royal, Sophienstrasse 35, Tel. 0711/625050 (L)

Intercity-Hotel, Arnulf-Klett-Platz 2, Tel. 0711/299801 (M)

Rieker, Friedrichstrasse 3, Tel. 0711/221311 (M)

Wartburg-Hospiz, Lange Strasse 49, Tel. 0711/294151 (M)

Ketterer, Marienstrasse 3, Tel. 0711/2945151 (M)

Wörtz, Hohenheimer Strasse 30, Tel. 0711/245396 (E-M)

Espenlaub, Charlottestrasse 27, Tel. 0711/240022 (E-M)

Alte Krone, Grossglocknerstrasse 4, Tel. 0711/330105 (E-M)

Seyboldt, Fenchelstrasse 11, Tel. 0711/445354 (E)

•Pforzheim

Goldene Pforte, Hohenstaufenstrasse 6, Tel. 07231/37920 (L)

Ruf, Bahnhofsplatz 5, Tel. 07231/16011 (M-L)

Mönch's Schlosshotel, Lindenstrasse 2, Tel. 07231/16051 (M)

Gute Hoffnung, Dillsteiner Strasse 9, Tel. 07231/22011

Gasthof Sonnenberg, Friedrichstrasse 41, Tel. 07231/71230 (E)

•Karlsruhe

Ramada Renaissance, Mendelssohnplatz, Tel. 0721/37170 (L)

Schlosshotel, Bahnhofsplatz 2, Tel. 0721/26615 (M)

Eden, Bahnhofstrasse 15, Tel. 0721/28718 (M)

Kübler, Bismarckstrasse 39, Tel. 0721/28718 (M)

Kübler, Bismarckstrasse 39, Tel. 0721/26849 (E-M)

Hasen, Gerwigstrasse 47, Tel. 0721/615076 (E-M)

•Baden-Baden

Brenners Parkhotel, Schillerstrasse, Tel. 07221/3530 (L)

Quisiana, Bismarckstrasse 21, Tel. 07221/3446 (L)

Holiday Inn Sporthotel, Falkenstrasse 2, Tel: 07221/33011 (L)

Allee-Hotel Bären, Lichtentaler Allee, Tel. 07221/71046 (M)

Greiner, Lichtentaler Allee 88, Tel. 07221/71135 (E)

ON THE TRAIL OF THE BROTHERS GRIMM

•Frankfurt

Steigenberger Hotel Frankfurter Hof, Kaiserplatz, Tel. 069/20251 (LL)

Inter-Continental, Wilhelm-Leuschner-Strasse 43, Tel. 069/230561 (LL)

Hessischer Hof, Friedrich-Ebert-Anlage 40, Tel. 069/75400 (LL)

Canadian Pacific Plaza, Hamburger Allee 2, Tel. 069/770721 (L)

Savoy, Weisenhüttenstrasse 42, Tel. 069/230511 (L)

Continental, Baseler Strasse 56, Tel. 069/68020 (L)

Jaguar, Theobald-Christ-Strasse 17, Tel: 069/439301 (M)

Merkur, Esslinger Strasse 8, Tel. 069/235054 (M)

Henninger Hof, Hanauer Landstrasse 127, Tel. 069/747007 (M)

Motel Frankfurt, Eschersheimer Landstrasse 204, Tel. 069/568011 (M)

Am Zoo, Alfred-Brehm-Platz 6, Tel. 069/490771 (M)

Meyn, Grüneburgweg 4, Tel. 069/590179 (M)

Pension Uebe, Grüneburgweg 3, Tel. 069/591209 (E-M)

Neue Kräme, Neue Kräme 23, Tel. 069/284046 (E)

Höchster Hof, Mainberg 3, Tel. 069/30040 (E-M)

Radilohof, Radilostrasse 39, Tel. 069/783287 (E-M)

Goldener Schlüssel, Eschersheimer Landstrasse 442, Tel. 069/520122 (E-M)

Waldhotel Hensels Felsenkeller, Buchrainstrasse 95, Tel. 069/652086 (E-M)

Maingau, Schifferstrasse 38, Tel. 069/617001 (E-M)

•At Frankfurt Airport

Sheraton Hotel, Hugo-Eckener-Ring 15, Tel. 069/69770 (L)

Steigenberger Airport-Hotel, Unterschweinsteige 16, Tel. 069/69851 (L)

•Bad Homburg

Maritim Kurhaus-Hotel, Ludwigstrasse, Tel. 06172/28051 (L)

Hardtwald-Hotel, Philosophenweg 31, Tel. 06172/25016 (M)

Villa Kisseleff, Kisseleffstrasse 19, Tel. 06172/21540

•Kronberg

Schlosshotel, Hainstrasse 25, Tel. 06173/7011 (L)

Viktoria, Viktoriastrasse 7, Tel. 06173/4074 (M)

Kronberger Hof, Bleichstrasse 12, Tel. 76071 (E)

•Königstein im Taunus

Sonnenhof, Falkensteiner Strasse 7, Tel. 06174/3051 (M-L)

Zum Hirsch, Burgweg 2, Tel. 06174/5034 (E-M)

Hotel-Pension Zacharias, Hugo-Amelung-Strasse 4, Tel. 06174/7305 (M)

•Oberursel

Parkhotel Waldlist, Hohenarkstrasse 168, Tel. 06171/2860 (M-L)

Mergner, Liebfrauenstrasse 20, Tel. 06171/3592 (E)

•Bad Nauheim

Parkhotel am Kurhaus, Nördlicher Park 16, Tel. 06032/3030 (L)

Am Hochwald, Carl-Oelemann-Weg 9, Tel. 06032/82074 (E)

•Hanau

Brüder-Grimm-Hotel, Kurt-Baum-Platz 6, Tel. 06181/3060 (M)

Royal, Salzstrasse 14, Tel. 06181/24157 (M)

Zur Linde, Steinheimer Vorstadt 31, Tel. 06181/61250 (M)

•Gelnhausen

Burg-Mühle, Burgstrasse 2, Tel. 06051/5005 (E-M)

Grimmelshausen-Hotel, Schmidtgasse 12, Tel. 06051/17031 (E)

•Bad Orb

Hohenzollern, Spessartstrasse 4, Tel. 06052/30455 (L)

Madstein, Am Orbgrund 1, Tel. 06052/2028 (M)

Stadt Hamburg, Sälzerstrasse 3, Tel. 06052/2063 (E)

•Bad Soden

Park-Hotel, Am Kurpark, Tel. 06196/2000 (L)

Rheinischer Hof, Königsteiner Strasse 76, Tel. 06196/26050 (M)

Türck, Bismarckstrasse 20, Tel. 061/26023 (E-M)

•Steinau an der Strasse

Brathähnchenfarm, Im Ohl, Tel. 06663/228 (E)

•Schlüchtern

Löwen, Obertorstrasse 2, Tel. 06661/2073 (E)

•Fulda

Maritim Am Schlossgarten, Paulus-promenade 2, Tel. 0661/2820 (L)

Zum Kurfürsten, Schlosstrasse 2, Tel. 0661/70001 (M)

Peterchens Mondfahrt, Rabanusstrasse 7, Tel. 0661/77094 (M)

Zum Ritter, Kanalstrasse 20, Tel. 0661 72083 (E-M)

Romantik Hotel Goldener Karpfen, Simpliziusplatz, Tel. 0661/70044 (L)

•Lauterbach

Schubert, Kanalstrasse 12, Tel. 0664/3075 (E-M)

•Alsfed

Krone, Schellenstrasse 2, Tel. 06631/4041 (E-M)

•Marburg

Waldecker Hof, Bahnhofstrasse 23, Tel. 06421/63011 (M)

Europäischer Hof, Elisabethstrasse 12, Tel. 0641/65400 (E-M)

Bahnhofshotel Rump, Bahnhofstrasse 29, Tel. 06421/26036 (E-M)

Gasthof zur Sonne, Markt 14, Tel. 06421/26036 (E-M)

Dammühle, Dammühlenstrasse 1, Tel. 06421/23036 (E)

•Schwalmstadt

Rosengarten, Muhlystrasse 3, Tel. 0669/3084 (E)

•Bad Hersfeld

Am Kurpark, Tel. 06221/1640 (M-L)

Parkhotel Rose, Am Kurpark 19, Tel. 06621/14454 (M)

Romantik Hotel Zum Stern, Lingplatz 11, Tel. 06621/72007 (M)

•Kassel

Dorint Hotel Reiss, Werner-Hilpert-Strasse 24, Tel. 0561/7880 (M)

Dimus, Erzbergerstrasse 1, Tel. 0561/102385 (M)

Park-Hotel Hessenland, Obere Königstrasse 2, Tel. 0561/14974 (M)

Westend, Friedrich-Ebert-Strasse 135, Tel. 0561/103821 (M)

Royal, Giesbergstrasse 53, Tel. 0561/85018 (E)

•Göttingen

Gebhards Hotel, Goetheallee 22, Tel. 0551/56133 (M-L)

Eden, Reinhäuser Landstrasse 22a, Tel. 0551/76007 (M)

Zur Sonne, Paulinerstrasse 10, Tel. 0551/56738 (M)

Central, Jüdenstrasse 12, Tel. 0551/57157 (E-M)

Gräfin von Holtzendorf, Eerst-Ruhstrat-Strasse 4, Tel. 0551/63987 (E)

FOLLOWING THE WESER VALLEY TO BREMEN

•Münden

Berghotel Eberburg, Tillyschanzenweg 14, Tel. 05541/4453 (E-M)

Jagdhaus Heede, Hermannshäger Strasse 81, Tel. 05541/5049 (E)

Schmucker Jäger, Wilhelmshäuser Strasse 45, Tel. 05541/5049 (E)

•Bad Karlshafen

Kurhotel Carolinum, Mündener Strasse 11, Tel. 05672/1011 (M)

•Beverungen

Stadt Bremen, Lange Strasse 13, Tel. 06273/1275 (E-M)

Pension Bevertal, Jahnweg la, Tel. 05273/5485 (E)

•Höxter

Niedersachsen, Möllinger Strasse 4, Tel. 06271/35333 (M)

Weserberghof, Godelheimer Strasse 1, Tel. 05271/7556 (E)

•Holzminden

Parkhotel Interopa, Altendorfer Strasse, Tel. 05531/2001 (E-M)

Schleifmühle, Schleifmühle 3, Tel. 05531/5098 (E)

•Bevern

Gasthaus Zum Goldenen Hirsch, Kaspul 2, Tel. 05531/8461 (E)

•Bodenwerder

Deutsches Haus, Münchhausenplatz 4, Tel. 05533/3925 (E-M)

Bad Pyrmont Kurhotel-Kurhaus, Heiligenangerstrasse 4, Tel. 05281/4001 (M-L)

Bergkurpark, Ockelstrasse 11, Tel. 05281/2554 (E)

•Hameln

Dorint Hotel, Weserbergland, Am 164er Ring 3, Tel. 05151/7920 (L)

Zur Börse, Osterstrasse 41, Tel. 05151/7080 (E-M)

Bellevue, Klüstrasse 34, Tel. 05151/61018 (E)

•Hannover

Inter-Continental, Friedrichswall 11, Tel. 0511/16911 (L)

Maritim, Hildesheimer Strasse 34, Tel. 0511/16531 (L)

Kastens Hotel Luisenhof, Luisenstrasse 1, Tel. 0511/16151 (L)

Königshof, Königshof 12, Tel. 0511/312071 (M)

Loccumer Hof, Kurt-Schmaucher-Strasse 16, Tel. 0511/326052 (M)

Köner, Könerstrasse 24, Tel. 0511/4666

Intercity Hotel, Ernst-August-Platz 1, Tel. 0511/327461 (M)

Thüringer Hof, Osterstrasse 37, Tel. 0511/326681 (M)

Hospiz am Bahnhof, Joachimstrasse 2, Tel. 0511/324297 (E)

•Braunschweig

Atrium, Berliner Platz 3, Tel. 0531/73001 (L)

Mövenpick Hotel, Welfenhof, Tel. 0531/48170 (L)

Deutsches Haus, Burgplatz 1, Tel. 0531/44422 (M)

Fürstenhof, Campestrasse 12, Tel. 0531/791061 (M)

Forsthaus, Hamburger Strasse 72, Tel. 0531/791061 (M)

An der Stadthalle, Leonhardstrasse 21, Tel. 0531/73068 (E)

•Wolfsburg

Holiday Inn, Rathausstrasse 1, Tel. 05361/12081 (L)

Goya, Poststrasse 34, Tel. 05361/23066 (M)

City Hotel, Kaufhofpassage 2, Tel. 05361/23333 (E-M)

•Hildesheim

Schweizerhof, Hindenburgplatz 6, Tel. 05121/39081 (M)

Bürgermeisterkapelle, Rathausstrasse 8, Tel. 05121/14021 (M)

Berghölzchen, Berghölzchen, Tel. 05121/42063 (E)

•Rinteln

Zum Brückentor, Weserstrasse 1, Tel. 05751/42095 (M)

•Bad Oeynhausen

Kur-und-Badehotel Wittekind, Am Kurpark 10, Tel. 05731/22910 (E-M)

Westfälischer Hof, Herforder Strasse 40, Tel. 05731/28061 (E)

•Minden

Bad Minden, Portstrasse 36, Tel. 0571/51049 (M-L)

Exquisit, In den Bärenkämpen 2a, Tel. 0571/43055 (M)

Victoria, Markt 13, Tel. 0571/22240 (E-M)

•Bückeburg

Forsthaus Heinemeyer, Harrl 2, Tel. 05722/4041 (M)

Haus Niedersachsen, Grüner Weg 13, Tel. 05722/5345 (E)

•Nienburg

Nienburger Hof, Hafenstrasse 3, Tel. 05021/13048 (M)

•Verden

Parkhotel Grüner Häger, Bremer Strasse 48, Tel. 04231/5091 (E-M)

Haag's Hotel Niedersachsenhof, Lindhooper Strasse 97, Tel. 04231/69033 (E)

•Bremen
Bremen Plaza CP Hotel, Hillmannplatz 20, Tel. 0421/17670 (L)
Park Hotel, Im Bürgerpark, Tel. 0421/34080 (L)
Zur Post, Bahnhofsplatz 11, Tel. 0421/30590 (L)
Überseehotel, Wachtstrasse 27, Tel. 0421/320197 (M)
Bremer Hospiz, Löningstrasse 16, Tel. 0421/321668 (M)
Westfalia, Langemarckstrasse 38, Tel. 0421/500440 (M)
Lichtsinn, Rembertistrasse 11, Tel. 0421/323235 (M)
Bölts Am Park, Slevogtstrasse 23, Tel. 0421/341348 (M)
Heldt, Friedhofstrasse 41, Tel. 0421/213051 (E)
Zum Klüverbaum, Mühlenstrasse 43, Tel. 0421/603312 (E)

•Bremerhaven
Nordsee-Hotel Naber, Theodor-Heuss-Platz, Tel. 0471/48770 (L)
Parkhotel, Im Bürgerpark, Tel. 0471/27041 (M)
Haverkamp/Seiffert, Prager Strasse 34, Tel. 0471/45031 (M)
Weser-Hotel, Weserstrasse 132, Tel. 0471/71156 (E)
Geestemünde, Am Klint 20, Tel. 0471/28800 (E-M)

LIVING WITH THE TIDE

•Leer
Ostfriesen Hof, Groniger Strasse 109, Tel. 0491/4505 (E)
Central-Hotel, Pferdemarktstrasse 47, Tel. 0491/2371 (E)

•Emden
Am Boltentor, Hinter den Rahmen 10, Tel. 04921/32346 (M)
Faldernpoort, Courbièrestrasse 6, Tel. 04921/21075 (M)
Schmidt, Friedrich-Ebert-Strasse 79, Tel. 04921/24057 (E-M)
Grosser Kurfürst, Neutorstrasse 41, Tel. 04921/20303 (E)

•Aurich
Piqueur Hof, Bahnhofstrasse 1, Tel. 0494/4118 (M-L)
Brems Garten, Kirchdorfer Strasse 7, Tel, 04941/5812 (M)

•Wiesmoor
Friesengiest, Am Rathaus 1, Tel. 04944/1044 (M)
Christophers, Marktstrasse 11, Tel. 04944/2005 (E)

•Norden
Deutsches Haus, Neuer Weg 26, Tel. 04931/2411 (E)
Reichshof, Neuer Weg 53, Tel. 04931/2411 (E)

•Borkum
Poseidon, Bismarckstrasse 40, Tel. 04922/811 (M-L)
Graf Waldersee, Bahnhofstrasse 6, Tel. 04922/1094 (M)

•Juist
Achterdiek, Wilhelmstrasse 36, Tel. 04935/1025 (L)
Buschhaus, Karl-Wagner-Strasse 7, Tel. 04935/1030 (M)

•Norderney
Kurhotel, Weststrandstrasse 8, Tel. 04932/771 (L)
Strandhotel Germania, Kaiserstrasse 1, Tel. 04932/648 (M-L)
Bruns-Hotel, Lange Strasse 7, Tel. 04932/531 (E-M)

•Baltrum
Stranhotel H. Wietjes, Haus-Nr. 58, Tel. 04939/237 (M-L)

•Langeroog
Flörke, Hauptstrasse 17, Tel. 04972/6097
Haus Westfalen, Abke-Hansen-Weg 6, Tel. 04972/265 (M)

•Spiekeroog
Upstalsboom, Pollerdiek, Tel. 04976/364 (M)
Hotel Pension Huus Süder Mens. Südermens 1, Tel. 04976/226 (M)

•Wangerooge
Strandhotel Gerken, Strandpromenade 21, Tel. 04469/611 (L)
Strandhotel Kaiserhof, Strandpromenade 27, Tel. 04469/202 (M)

•Jever

Friesen-Hotel, Harlinger Weg 1, Tel. 04461/2500 (E-M)

Hotel-Pension Stöber, Hohnholzstrasse 10, Tel. 04461/5580 (E)

•Wilhelmshaven

Kaiser's Hotel, Rheinstrasse 128, Tel. 04421/42071 (M)

Jacobi, Freiligrathstrasse 163, Tel. 04421/60051 (M)

Klatte, Marktstrasse 159, Tel. 04421/26238 (E)

Koppernhörner Mühle, Koppernhörner Strasse, Tel. 04421/31072 (E-M)

Maris, Wertstrasse 54, Tel. 04421/202096 (E)

•Oldenburg

City-Club-Hotel, Europaplatz 20, Tel. 0441/8080 (M)

Heide, Melkbrink 47, Tel. 0441/81001 (M)

Wieting, Damm 29, Tel. 0441/27214 (E-M)

Schützenhof, Hauptstrasse 38, Tel. 0441/502063 (E)

Beyer, Alexanderstrasse 105, Tel. 0441/82006 (E)

Bavaria, Bremer Heerstrasse 196, Tel. 0441/20745 (E)

•Brake

Wilkens Hotel/Haus Linne, Mitteldeichstrasse 51, Tel. 0440/5357 (M)

•Nordenham

Aits, Bahnhofstrasse 120, Tel. 04731/80044 (M)

Friedeburg, Oldenburger Strasse 2, Tel. 0473/4055 (E-M)

•Cuxhaven

Donners Hotel, Am Seedeich 2, Tel. 04721/37014 (M)

Seepavillon, Bei der Alten Liebe 5, Tel. 04721/38064 (M)

Deichgral/Nordsee-Hotel, Nordfeldstrasse 16, Tel. 04721/47091 (M-L)

Neue Liebe, Prinzessinnentrift 12, Tel. 04721/48270 (E-M)

Henning, Steinmarner Trift 8, Tel. 04721/48444 (E-M)

•Island of Heligoland

Kurhotel, Lung Wai 27, Tel. 04725/595 (M-L)

Villa Augusta, Am Südstrand 16, Tel. 04725/220 (M)

Haus Hanseat, Am Südstrand 21, Tel. 04725/663 (E-M)

•Otterndorf

Zum Weissen Ross, Marktstrasse 42, Tel. 04751/3308 (E)

•Wingst

Landgasthof, Forsthaus Dorock, Hasenbeckallee 39, Tel. 04778/290 (M)

•Stade

Vier Linden, Schölischer Strasse 63, Tel. 04141/44011 (M)

Stader Klubhaus, Grosse Schmiederstrasse 14, Tel. 04141/2479 (E-M)

Schwedenkrone, Richeyweg 15, Tel. 04141/81174 (E-M)

•Buxtehude

Zur Mühle, Ritterstrasse 16, Tel. 04161/3003 (M)

Pension Christel, Mühlenkempstrasse 19, Tel. 04163/6282 (E)

•Glückstadt

Tiessen/Holsteinischer Hof, Kleine Kremper Strasse 18, Tel. 04124/2116 (M)

Raumann, Am Markt 5, Tel. 04124/2170

•Brunsbüttel

Zur Traube, Markt 9, Tel. 04852/51011 (M)

•Meldorf

Stadt Hamburg, Nordermarkt 2, Tel. 04832/1461 (E)

•Heide

Berlin, Oester Strasse 18, Tel. 04832/3066 (E-M)

Heider Hof, Markt 74, Tel. 0481/2505 (E)

Kotthaus, Rüsdorfer Strasse 3, Tel. 0481/8011 (E)

•Büsum

Friesenhof, Nordseestrasse 66, Tel. 04834/2095 (M)

Strandhotel Hohenzollern, Strandstrasse 2, Tel. 04834/2293 (E-M)

•Friedrichstadt
Herzog Friedrich, Schmiedestrasse 11a, Tel. 04881/1771 (E-M)

•Husum
Thomas-Hotel, Zingel 9, Tel. 04841/6087 (E-M)
Hinrichsen, Süderstrasse 35, Tel. 04841/5051 (E-M)
Carstens am Wasserturm, Hinter der Neustadt 28, Tel. 04841/62062 (E-M)

•Nordstrand
Landgasthof Kelting, Tel. 04842/335

•Amrun-Nebel
Bahnhofshotel, Strunwai 1, Tel. 04682/2338 (E)

•Amrun-Norddorf
Graf Luckner, Tel. 04681/2367 (M)

Föhr-Nieblum
Haus Osterheide, Tel. 04681/2895 (E)

•Föhr-Süderende
Landhaus Altes Pastorat, Tel. 04681/226 (L)

•Föhr-Wyk
Kurhotel Am Wellenbad, Sandwall 29 Tel. 04681/2199 (M-L)
Duus, Hafenstrasse 40, Tel. 04681/708 (M)
Haus der Landwirte, Hafenstrasse 2, Tel. 04681/535 (E-M)

•Sylt-List
Silbermöve, Süderhörn 7, Tel. 04652/1214 (M)

•Sylt-Kampen
Rungholt, Kurhausstrasse, Tel. 04651/41041 (L)
Wuldenhof, Wuldeschlucht, Tel. 04651/41051 (L)

•Sylt-Westerland
Stadt Hamburg, Strandstrasse 2, Tel. 04651/8580 (L)
Sylt-Plaza, Elisabethstrasse 9, Tel. 04651/6006 (L)
Windhuk, Brandenburger Strasse 6, Tel. 04651/6033 (M-L)

•Sylt-Keitum
Wolfshof, Osterweg 8, Tel. 04652/3445
Romantik-Hotel Benen-Diken-Hof, Süderstrasse, Tel. 04652/31035 (L)

•Sylt-Wennigstedt
Strandhörn, Dünenstrasse 1, Tel. 04651/42990 (L)
Friesenhof, Hauptstrasse 16, Tel. 04651/41031 (E-M)

HAMBURG – GATEWAY TO THE SEVEN SEAS

Vier Jahreszeiten, Neuer Jungfernsteig 9, Tel. 040/34941 (LL)
Atlantic Hotel Kempinski, An der Alster 72, Tel. 040/248001 (LL)
Ramada Renaissance, Grosse Bleichen, Tel. 040/349180 (L)
Elysee, Rothenbaumchaussee 10, Tel. 040/414120 (L)
Canadian Pacific Plaza, Marseiller Strasse 2, Tel. 040/35020 (L)
Europäischer Hof, Kirchenallee 45, Tel. 040/248171 (L)
Aussen Alster, Schmilinskystrasse 11, Tel. 040/241557 (L)
Senator, Lange Reihe 18, Tel. 040/241203 (L)
Baseler Hospiz, Esplanade 11, Tel. 040/341921 (M)
St. Raphael, Adenauerallee 41, Tel. 040/241191 (M)
Alte Wache, Adenauerallee 25, Tel. 040/24129 (M)
Fürst Bismarck, Kirchenallee 49, Tel. 040/2801091 (M)
Graf Moltke, Steindamm 1, Tel. 040/2801154 (M)

•Suburb of Altona
Raphael Hotel Altona, Präsident-Krahn-Strasse 13, Tel. 040/3811239 (E-M)
Stadt Altona, Luise-Schroeder-Strasse 29, Tel. 040/381111 (E-M)

•Suburb of Blankenese
Strandhotel, Strandweg 13, Tel. 040/860993 (L)
Behrmann, Elbchaussee 528, Tel. 040/863673 (M)

•Lüneburg
Wellenkamp, Am Sande 9, Tel. 04131/43026 (E-M)
Bremer Hof, Lüner Strasse 13, Tel. 04131/36077 (E)

•Lauenburg
Möller, Elbstrasse 46, Tel. 04153/2011 (E-M)

ALONG THE COASTLINE OF THE BALTIC SEA

•Lübeck
Lysia-Mövenpick, Auf der Wallhalbinsel, Tel. 0451/15040 (L)
Kaiserhof, Kronsforder Allee 13, Tel. 0451/791011 M-L)
Jensen, An der Oberstrave 4, Tel. 045/71646 (M)
Altstadt-Hotel, Fischergrube 52, Tel. 0451/72083 (E-M)
Schwarzwaldstuben, Coberg 12, Tel. 0451/77715 (M)

•Suburb of Travemünde
Maritim-Strandhotel, Trelleborgallee 2, Tel. 04502/75001 (M-L)
Deutscher Kaiser, Vorderreihe 52, Tel. 04502/5028 (M-L)
Sonnenklause, Kaiserallee 21, Tel. 04502/73330 (M)

•Eutin
Voss-Haus, Vossplatz 6, Tel. 04521/1797 (M)
Wiesenhof, Leonhard-Bold-Strasse 25, Tel. 04521/2727 (E-M)
Freischütz, Braaker Strasse 1, Tel. 04521/2460 (E)

•Malente
Intermar, Hindenburgallee 2, Tel. 04523/4040 (L)
Dieksee, Diekseepromenade 13, Tel: 04523/3065 (M)
Hotel-Pension Godenberghorst, Godenbergredder 15, Tel 04523/3666 (E)

•Plön
Kurhotel, Ölmühlenallee, Tel. 04522/9535 (M-L)
Seeblick, Rodomstorstrasse 70, Tel. 04522/3993 (E)

•Basau
Strauers Hotel am See, Neuer Damm 2, Tel. 04527/207 (M)

•Preetz
Drillers Hotel, Bismarckplatz 2, Tel. 04342/81241 (E-M)

•Kiel
Maritim Bellevue, Bismarckallee 2, Tel. 0431/51150 (L)
Astor, Holstenplatz 1, Tel 0431/62050 (M)
Berliner Hof, Ringstrasse 6, Tel. 0431/62050 (M)
Rendsburger Hof, Rendsburger Landstrasse 363, Tel. 0431/69131 (E)

•Eckernförde
Sandkrug, Berliner Strasse 146, Tel. 04351/4193 (M)
Seegarten, Berliner Strasse 71, Tel. 04351/6028 (E-M)
Stadt Kiel, Kieler Strasse 74, Tel. 04351/2867 (E)

•Schleswig
Strandhalle, Am Yachthafen, Tel. 04621/22021 (M)
Waldhotel am Schloss Gottorf, An der Stampfmühle 1, Tel. 04621/23288 (E-M)
City-Hotel, Stadtweg 9, Tel. 04621/23013 (E)

•Kappeln
Motel-Café Tange, Flensburger Strasse 17, Tel. 0464/2180 (E)

•Flensburg
Flensburger Hof, Süderhofenden 38, Tel. 0461/17320 (M-L)
Am Rathaus, Rote Strasse 32, Tel. 0461/17333 (M)
Am Stadtpark, Nordergraben 70, Tel. 0461/23508 (E)

•Flensburg/Oeversee
Romantik Hotel Historischer Krug, Tel. 04630/334 (M)

SPECIAL BERLIN

Bristol Hotel, Kurfürstendamm 27, Tel. 030/881091 (LL)

Inter-Continental, Budapester Strasse 2, Tel. 030/26020 (LL)

Steigenberger Hotel, Los-Angeles-Platz 1, Tel. 030/21080 (LL)

Palace im Europa-Center, Budapester Strasse, Tel. 030/269111 (L)

Penta-Hotel, Nürnberger Strasse 65, Tel. 030/240011 (L)

Mondial, Kurfürstendamm 47, Tel. 030/884110 (L)

Schweizerhof, Budapester Strasse 21, Tel. 030/26960 (L)

Ambassador, Bayreuther Strasse 42, Tel. 030/219020 (L)

Berlin Excelsior, Hardenbergstrasse 14, Tel. 030/31991 (L)

Hamburg, Landgrafstrasse 4, Tel. 030/269161 (M-L)

Berlin, Kurfürstenstrasse 62, Tel. 030/269291 (M-L)

Berlin Plaza, Knesebeckstrasse 63, Tel. 030/884130 (M)

Meinecke, Meineckestrasse 10, Tel. 030/882811 (M)

Kronprinz, Kronprinzendamm 1, Tel. 030/896030 (M)

•Suburb of Charlottenburg

Seehof, Lietzensee-Ufer 11, Tel. 030/320020 (L)

Am Studio, Kaiserdamm 80, Tel. 030/302081 (M)

Kanthotel, Kantstrasse 111, Tel. 030/323026 (M)

Westerland, Knesebeckstrasse 10, Tel. 030/3121004 (M)

•Suburb of Wilmersdorf

Crest Hotel, Güntzelstrasse 14, Tel. 030/87024 (L)

Franke, Albrecht-Achilles-Strasse 57, Tel. 030/8921097 (M)

Lichtburg, Paderborner Strasse 10, Tel. 030/8918041 (M)

•Suburb of Friedenau

Hospiz Friedenau, Fregestrasse 68, Tel. 030/8519017 (E)

•Suburb of Grunewald

Belvedere, Seebergsteig 4, Tel. 030/8261077 (E-M)

ROMANTIK HOTELS

Should you have time during your journey through Germany, you might want to stop in one of the many Romantik Hotels. They are housed in historic buildings, offer first-class cuisine, and provide friendly service in a cordial atmosphere. Listed below (in alphabetical order of the towns) are the hotels which belong to this category. For more information contact: **Romantik Hotels and Restaurants,** Freigerichtstrasse 5 D-8757 Karlstein am Main Tel. 06188/5020. Prices and room rates vary, from inexpensive (E) to moderate (M) to expensive (L).

Romantik Hotel Lindner, 8202 Bad Aibling, Marienplatz 5, Tel 08061/4050 (M)

Romantik Hotel Der Kleine Prinz, 7570 Baden-Baden, Lichtentaler Strasse 36 Tel. 07221/3464 (M-L)

Romantik Hotel Weinhaus Messerschmitt, 8600 Bamberg, Lange Strasse 41, Tel. 0951/27866-7 (M)

Romantik Hotel Bierhütte, 8351 Bierhütte 10 (close to Passau), Tel. 08558/315-316 (M)

Romantik Hotel Höttche, 4047 Dormagen 1, Krefelder Strasse 14/18. (close to Cologne), Tel. 02106/4104 (M-L)

Romantik Hotel Lennhof, 4600 Dortmund-Varop, Menglinghauser Strasse 20, Tel. 0231/75726 (L)

Romantik Hotel Zum Alten Brauhaus, 5521 Dudedorf (close to Trier), Jerrengasse 2, Tel. 06565/2208 (M)

Romantik Hotel Residence, 4300 Essen-Kettwig, Auf der Forst 1, Tel. 02054/8911 (M)

Romantik Hotel Goldener Karpfen, 6400 Fulda, Simpliziusplatz 1, Tel. 0661/70044 (M-L)

Romantik Hotel Benen-Diken-Hof, 2280 Keitum (on the island of Sylt) Süderstrasse, Tel. 04651/31035-38 (L)

Romantik Hotel Hof zur Linde, 4400 Münster-Handorf, Handorfer Werseufer 1, Tel. 0251/325002 (M)

Romantik Hotel Spielweg, 7816 Münstertal (in the Black Forest), Hauptstrasse 61, Tel. 07636/618 + 1313 (M-L)

Romantik Hotel Alte Post, 7270 Nagold (in the Black Forest), Bahnhofstrasse 2-4, Tel. 07452/4048 + 4049 (M)

Romantik Hotel Schwan, 6227 Oestrich (close to Rüdesheim), Rheinallee 5/7, Tel. 06723/5041 (M)

Romantik Hotel Hahnenkamp, 4970 Bad Oeynhausen (close to Minden), Alte Reichsstrasse 4, Tel. 05731/5041 (M)

Romantik Hotel Jagdhaus Waldfrieden, 2085 Quickborn (close to Hamburg), Kieler Strasse B4, Tel. 04106/3771 (M-L)

Romantik Hotel Waldhorn, 7980 Ravensburg, Marienplatz 15, Tel. 0751/16021 (M-L)

Romantik Hotel zur Schwane, 8712 Volkach (between Würzburg and Bamberg), Hauptstrasse 12, Tel. 09381/515 (M)

Romantik Hotel Alte Post, 7988 Wangen (close to Lindau), Postplatz 2, Tel. 07522/4014 (M)

Romantik Hotel Jagdhaus Eiden, 2903 Bad Zwischenahn (next to Oldenburg), Tel. 04403/1022 (M)

USEFUL ADDRESSES

TOURIST INFORMATION

Tourist information is generally indicated with an "i" in bigger towns. In smaller towns and villages you will look in vain for the "i"; look for a *Fremdenverkehrsamt* instead. (Other terms are *Verkehrsverein, Verkehrsamt, Verkehrsbüro, Fremdenverkehrsverein*). One way or another, tourist information centres are found everywhere. They are usually housed in city halls, at train stations or in separate buildings in town centres. If necessary, you can find the full address in the local phone book under one of those terms mentioned.

These are the central tourist information offices throughout the Federal Republic:

Deutscher Fremdemverkehrsverband e.V.,
Niebuhrstrasse 16b, 5300 Bonn 1,
Tel. 02228/214071-73

Fremdenverkehrsverband Schleswig-Holstein e.V.,
Niemannsweg 31, 2300 Kiel 1,
Tel. 0431/56302/561061

Fremdenverkehrsverband Nordsee-Niedersachsen-Bremen-e.V.,
Gottorpstrasse 18, 2900 Oldenburg,
Tel. 0441/14535

Fremdenverkehrsverband Lüneburger Heide e.V.,
Glockenhaus, 2120 Lüneburg,
Tel. 0413/42006

Harzer Verkehrsverband e.V.,
Marktstrasse 45, 3380 Goslar 1,
Tel. 05321/20032

Fremdenverkehrsverband Weserbergland-Mittelweser e.V.,
Falkestrasse 2, 3250 Hameln 1,
Tel. 05151/24566

Landesverkehrsverband Westfalen e.V.,
Balkenstrasse 40, 4600 Dortmund 1,
Tel. 0231/571715

Landesverkehrsverband Rheinland e.V.,
Abraham-Lincoln-Strasse 38-43,
6200 Wiesbaden,
Tel. 06121/73725, 367226

Fremdenverkehrsverband Rheinland-Pfalz e.V.,
Löhrstrasse 103, 5400 Koblenz,
Tel. 0261/31079

Fremdenverkehrsverband Saarland e.V.,
Am Stiefel 2, 6600 Saarbrücken 3,
Tel. 0681/35376

Landesfremdenverkehrsverband Baden-Württemberg e.V.,
Bussenstrasse 23, 7000 Stuttgart 1,
Tel. 0711/481045

Fremdenverkehrsverband Neckarland-Schwaben e.V.,
Wolhausstrasse 14, 7100 Heilbronn,
Tel. 07131/629021, 629062

Fremdenverkehrsverband Schwarzwald e.V.,
Bertoldstrasse 45, 7800 Freiburg i. Br.,
Tel. 0761/31317

Fremdenverkehrsverband Bodensee Oberschwaben e.V.,
Schützenstrasse 8, 7750 Konstanz,
Tel. 07531/22232

Fremdenverkehrsverband Franken e.V.,
Am Plärrer 14, 8500 Nürnberg 81,
Tel. 0911/264202, 264204

Fremdenverkehrsverband München-Oberbayern e.V.,
Sonnenstrasse 10, 8000 München 2,
Tel. 089/597347

Verkehrsverein der Freien Hansestadt Bremen,
Bahnhodsplatz 29, 2800 Bremen 1,
Tel. 0421/3636-1

Fremdenverkehrsverband Allgäu/Bayerisch-Schwaben,
Landshuter Strasse 13, 8000 Augsburg 1,
Tel. 0821/33335

Fremdenverkehrsverband Ostbayern e.V.,
8400 Regensburg,
Tel. 0941/560260, 520262

Verkehrsamt Berlin
Europa-Center, 1000 Berlin 30,
Tel. 030/21234

Hamburg-Information GmbH,
Neuer Jungfernstieg 5, 2000 Hamburg 36,
Tel. 040/351301

EMBASSIES & CONSULATES

Algeria
5300 Bonn 2, Rheinallee 32,
Tel. 0228/356054

Argentina
5300 Bonn 1, Adenauerallee 55,
Tel. 0228/223973

Australia
5300 Bonn 2,
Godesberger Allee 107,
Tel. 0228/81003-0

Austria
5300 Bonn, Johanniterstrasse 2,
Tel. 0228/230051

Belgium
5300 Bonn,
Kaiser-Friedrich-Strasse 7,
Tel. 0228/212001

Bolivia
5300 Bonn 2, Konstantinstrasse 16,
Tel. 0228/362038

Brazil
5300 Bonn 2, Kennedyallee 74,
Tel. 0228/376976

Bulgaria
5300 Bonn 2, Auf der Hostert 6,
Tel. 0228/363061

Burma
5300 Bonn 1, Schumannstrasse 112,
Tel. 0228/211091

Canada
5300 Bonn 1,
Friedrich-Wilhelm-Strasse 18,
Tel. 0228/231061

Chile
5300 Bonn 2,
Kronprinzenstrasse 20,
Tel. 0228/363089

China, The People's Republic of
5300 Bonn 2, Kurfürstenallee 12,
Tel. 0228/361095

Colombia
5300 Bonn 1,
Friedrich-Wilhelm-Strasse 35,
Tel. 0228/234565

Costa Rica
5300 Bonn 1, Borsigallee 22,
Tel. 0228/254940

Cuba
5300 Bonn 2, Kennedyallee 22,
Tel. 0228/309-0

Cyprus
5300 Bonn 2, Kronprinzenstrasse 58,
Tel. 0228/363330

Czechoslovakia
5300 Bonn 3, Im Rheingarten 7,
Tel. 0228/471277

Denmark
5300 Bonn 1, Pfälzer Strasse 14,
Tel. 0228/72991-0

Dominican Republic
5300 Bonn 2, Burgstrasse 87,
Tel. 0228/364956

Ecuador
5300 Bonn 2,
Koblenzer Strasse 37,
Tel. 0228/352544

Egypt
5300 Bonn 2, Uhlandstrasse 32,
Tel. 0228/352901

Ethiopia
5300 Bonn 1, Brentanostrasse 1,
Tel. 0228/233041

Finland
5300 Bonn 2, Friesdorfer Strasse 1,
Tel. 0228/311033

France
5300 Bonn 2, Kapellenstrasse 1a,
Tel. 0228/362031

Great Britain
5300 Bonn 1, Friedrich-Ebert-Allee 77,
Tel. 0228/344061

Greece
5300 Bonn 1, Weberstrasse 83,
Tel. 0228/215654

Guatemala
5300 Bonn 2, Zietenstrasse 1b,
Tel. 0228/351579

Haiti
5300 Bonn 2, Schlossallee 10,
Tel. 0228/340351

Honduras
5300 Bonn 2, Ubierstrasse 1,
Tel. 0228/356394

Hungary
5300 Bonn 2, Turmstrasse 30,
Tel. 0228/376794

Iceland
5300 Bonn 2, Kronprinzenstrasse 6,
Tel. 0228/375937

India
5300 Bonn 1, Adenauerallee 264,
Tel. 0228/5405-1

Indonesia
5300 Bonn 2, Godesberger Allee 133,
Tel. 0228/81005-0

Iraq
5300 Bonn 2, Dürenstrasse 33,
Tel. 0228/8203-1

Ireland, The Republic of
5300 Bonn 2,
Godesberger Allee 119,
Tel. 0228/376937

Israel
5300 Bonn 2, Simrockallee 2,
Tel. 0228/823-1

Italy
5300 Bonn 2,
Karl-Finkenburg-Strasse 49,
Tel. 0228/82006-0

Japan
5300 Bonn 2, Bonn-Center,
Tel. 0228/500-1

Kenya
5300 Bonn 2, Villichgasse 23,
Tel. 0228/353066

Korea, The Republic of
5300 Bonn 2,
Adenauerallee 124,
Tel. 0228/214358

Kuwait
5300 Bonn 2,
Godesberger Allee 77,
Tel. 0228/378081

Lebanon
5300 Bonn 2, Rheinallee 27,
Tel. 0228/352075

Liberia
5300 Bonn 2, Hohenzollernstrasse 73,
Tel. 0228/351810

Luxembourg
5300 Bonn, Adenauerallee 110,
Tel. 0228/214008

Malaysia
5300 Bonn 2, Mittelstrasse 23,
Tel. 0228/351056

Malta
5300 Bonn 2, Victoriastrasse 1,
Tel. 0228/363017

Mexico
5300 Bonn 1, Oxfordstrasse 12,
Tel. 0228/631226

Monaco
5300 Bonn 1, Zitelmannstrasse 16,
Tel. 0228/232007

Morocco
5300 Bonn 2, Gotenstrasse 7,
Tel. 0228/355040

Nepal
5300 Bonn 2, Im Hag 15,
Tel. 0228/343097

Netherlands
5300 Bonn, Straschenweg 10,
Tel. 0228/238091

New Zealand
5300 Bonn, Bonn-Center HI 902,
Tel. 0228/214021

Nicaragua
5300 Bonn 2, Konstantinstrasse 41,
Tel. 0228/355938

Nigeria
5300 Bonn 2, Goldbayweg 13,
Tel. 0228/322071

Norway
5300 Bonn 2, Gotenstrasse 163
Tel. 0228/374055

Oman
5300 Bonn 2, Lindenallee 11,
Tel. 0228/357031

Pakistan
5300 Bonn 2, Rheinallee 24,
Tel. 0228/351036

Panama
5300 Bonn 2, Lützowstrasse 1,
Tel. 0228/351036

Paraguay
5300 Bonn 2, Plittersdorfer Strasse 121,
Tel. 0228/356727

Peru
5300 Bonn, Mozartstrasse 34,
Tel. 0228/638012

The Philippines
5300 Bonn 1, Argelanderstrasse 1,
Tel. 0228/213071

Poland
5300 Köln 51, Lindenallee 7,
Tel. 0221/380261

Portugal
5300 Bonn 2, Ubierstrasse 78,
Tel: 0228/363011

Rumania
5300 Bonn 1, Legionsweg 14,
Tel. 0228/670001

Saudi Arabia
5300 Bonn 1, Godesberger Allee 42,
Tel. 0228/379007

Singapore
5300 Bonn 2, Südstrasse 133,
Tel 0228/312007

Somalia
5300 Bonn 2, Hohenzollernstrasse 12,
Tel. 355084

South Africa
5300 Bonn 2, Auf der Hostert 3,
Tel. 0228/8201-0

Spain
5300 Bonn, Schlosstrasse 4,
Tel. 0228/217511

Sri Lanka
5300 Bonn 2, Rolandstrasse 52,
Tel. 0228/332055

Sweden
5300 Bonn 1, Heussallee,
Tel. 0228/26002-0

Switzerland
5300 Bonn 2, Gotenstrasse 156,
Tel. 0228/376655

Tanzania
5300 Bonn 2, Theaterplatz 26,
Tel. 0228/355065

Thailand
5300 Bonn 2, Ubierstrasse 65,
Tel. 0228/355065

Tunisia
5300 Bonn 2, Godesberger Allee 103,
Tel. 0228/344081

Turkey
5300 Bonn 2, Utestrasse 47,
Tel. 0228/344081

Uruguay
5300 Bonn 2, Gotenstrasse 1,
Tel. 0228/356570

U.S.A.
5300 Bonn 2, Deichmanns Aue,
Tel. 0228/339-1

U.S.S.R.
5300 Bonn 2, Waldstrasse 42,
Tel. 0228/312086

Venezuela
5300 Bonn 2, Godesberger Allee 119,
Tel. 0228/376631

Yemen, The Republic of
5300 Bonn 2, Godesberger Allee 125,
Tel. 376851

Yugoslavia
5300 Bonn 2, Schlossallee 5,
Tel. 0228/344051

Zaire
5300 Bonn 2, An der Nesselburg 38,
Tel. 0228/349193

Zimbabwe
5300 Bonn 2, Viktoriastrasse 28,
Tel. 0228/356071

ART/PHOTO CREDITS

Aga, Heimo	18, 201, 206, 210
Archiv für Kunst und Geschichte	20, 23L& R, 25L& R, 27, 29-36, 39-46, 48/49, 50/51, 52-58, 59L& R, 61, 63, 65, 66, 68, 69
Baumeister, Ossi	232, 233
Bucher, Siegfried	19, 37, 125, 126, 128, 130, 132, 133, 134/135, 138L& R, 139, 141R, 143, 149, 168, 188/189, 190, 191L& R, 193L& R, 194, 196, 198, 300
Deutsche Presse Agentur	67, 70, 72, 73
D. & J. Heaton/APA Photo Agency	118/119, 124, 180
Feurer, Jonny	185, 304
Fotostudio Furtner	120/121, 176, 178/179, 181, 182, 184
Fremdenverkehrsamt Augsburg	170, 171, 209
Fremdenverkehrsamt Dinkelsbühl	174L
Fremdenverkehrsamt Landau	294
Fremdenverkehrsamt Landshut	205
Fremdenverkehrsamt Nürnberg	151, 152, 158, 160, 161L& R, 164
Fremdenverkehrsamt Oberbayern	203
Fremdenverkehrsamt Rheinland Pfalz	303
Fremdenverkehrsamt Würzburg	141L
Gaertner, Rainer	106/107
Gundle, Barbara	16
Halliday, Tony	197
Höfer, Hans	38, 113, 200
Hoff, May	186, 219
Landesbildstelle München	299
Landesbildstelle Südbayern	22, 24R, 26, 28, 175
MAGO-Luftbild	156/157, 211, 242
Nakayama, Ben/APA Photo Agency	129
Pansegrau, Erhard	Cover, 3, 8/9, 14, 24L, 74, 80/81, 82/83, 86/87, 88, 90, 91L& R, 92, 93, 94L& R, 95, 97, 98/99, 100, 101L& R, 102-105, 108-117, 140, 142, 144, 145, 147, 148, 150, 153, 212, 215, 216-218, 234/235, 236/237, 240, 241, 243-245, 246L& R, 247-250, 253, 254L& R, 255-258, 260/261, 262, 264-267, 270, 276-281, 282/283, 284-289, 295, 297
Reichelt, G.P.	15, 75, 76, 78, 79, 199, 259, 269, 272, 273L, 274, 275
Schaffer, Manfred/Dennis Lane	154
Schneider, Günter	282/283
Schumann, Jens	12/13
Specht, Maja	163, 167, 173L
Spielcasino Baden-Baden	231
Stadtarchiv Ulm	296
Süddeutsche Zeitung	64, 71
Tony Stone Worldwide	187, 291
Tetzner, Marina	252
Unger, Klemens	204, 301
Vogel, Dieter	207
Wagner, Horst	268
Wittelsbacher Augsleichsfond	177
Zange, Christoph	6/7, 17, 172, 222-225, 226L& R, 228, 230, 292/293

INDEX

A

B

C

D

E

G

H

I – J

K

L

M

N

O

P

Q – R

S

Z

A
B
C
D
E
F
G
H
I
J
a
b
c
d
e
f
g
h
i
j
k
l

NOTES

NOTES

NOTES

NOTES

NOTES

APA

INSIGHT

Letter from the Publisher

Apa Khabar!

Old friends in many parts of Asia greet each other with the salutation 'Apa Khabar' (ah-pah car-bar). They are saying 'How are you?' and 'What's news?'. In the Malay-Indonesian tongue, 'Apa' is a word that denotes a question. That is why we are called APA Publications. Our books are designed for a traveller with an enquiring mind, who wants to get beneath the skin of a place and find out what goes on beneath the surface.

The first Insight guide – Insight Bali – was published in 1970. The team of young writers, designers and photographers who contributed to that guide had never produced a book before. Their ambition was to capture the essence of that fascinating island, its people and its vital culture. The result was hailed as a totally new type of guide, praised for its evocative photography and perceptive writing and above all for presenting an honest and penetrating portrait of the real Bali.

Twenty years on, we are still winning awards and critical acclaim for our guides. We have grown from a small, Asia-oriented firm into an internationally renowned company which operates worldwide. We have over 100 titles in print in a variety of languages, distributed by our co-publishers and distributers in more than 40 countries. Many more titles are in preparation.

Yet our essential philosophy has not changed; each guide is produced by a team of creative photographers and journalists – some are seasoned professionals, others are talented young people at the start of their career. All have an intimate knowledge of their subject and are motivated by the challenge of capturing the spirit of a place: not only to produce a thoroughly practical guide but also to convey a sense of what it is like to be one of the people who live there.

That is why, when you turn the pages of an Insight guide, you will find pictures full of people – not posing for the camera but going about their everyday life and work. That is why you will read articles on subjects as diverse as pub culture in Dublin, the art of political compromise in Brazil or the movie industry in India – each one providing a real insight into what makes each place and its people unique.

You will not find such material in other guide books and – with sales of over a million and a half Insight guides a year – it is clear that many readers share our philosophy. We view our readers as true explorers, people who travel in order to learn. They know that the experience of travel is much more rewarding when based on a broad understanding of all the vital aspects of a place and its people.

As a logical extension of that philosophy, we also want to build a closer relationship with our readers. We want your feedback – tell us how you use the guides – before, during or after a journey, what you like and dislike about them; tell us about any error or omission that you find, either using the enclosed reply card, or by letter. Let's keep the communication lines open!

Selamat jalan; Happy travelling

Hans Höfer
APA Publications

A P

Facts

The era of Glasnost

As the political hostilities of the Cold War give way to a new era of openness and peace, the Soviet Union is set to become the travel destination of the 1990s.

Intourist, the USSR travel authority, has signed joint venture agreements with overseas companies to build new hotels and highways, to make travel more comfortable and to open up areas that have been inaccessible or closed to visitors.

APA is responding to the need for information on this vast country – bigger than China and the USA combined – with three new guides: Insight USSR and Cityguides Moscow and Leningrad. Contributors include prominent Soviet writers and former dissidents, including the world-renowned poet, Yevgeni Yevtushenko.

The Great Trains of India

Listeners to the BBC's World Service will be familiar with the voice of Mark Tully, the BBC's India correspondent for 25 years. Travelling the length and breadth of the huge subcontinent to cover the great events of recent Indian history, Mark often takes the train for preference – he says that every train journey is an event, and always leads to memorable encounters.

Now Mark Tully and a team of experts are preparing a new title in our growing 'Special Interest' series – *The Great Trains of India*. The book will appeal to anyone nostalgic for the great days of steam-engine travel, and will trace the routes that criss cross the country, linking the lake-filled mountains of Srinagar to the golden sands and colourful temples of the south.

Into Vietnam

Vietnam – so often in the news over the last two decades – has been virtually closed to visitors since the end of the war. Now the country is looking to tourism as part of its plans for economic reconstruction. The government has invited APA Publications to send an editorial delegation, led by founder-publisher Hans Höfer, to explore the country and produce the first-ever modern guide. Contributions will also come from the professors and staff of Hanoi University's Institute of Anthropology.

Top titles

Where do Insight Guide readers go for their holidays? This list of our top ten bestsellers shows that Thailand is the favourite destination, and that the age of the Grand Tour is not yet over – long journeys across Australia and the USA are clearly popular with today's adventurous young explorers.

1 Thailand
2 Florida
3 Australia
4 Hawaii
5 Kenya
6 Hongkong
7 India
8 Crossing USA
9 Germany
10 Continental Europe

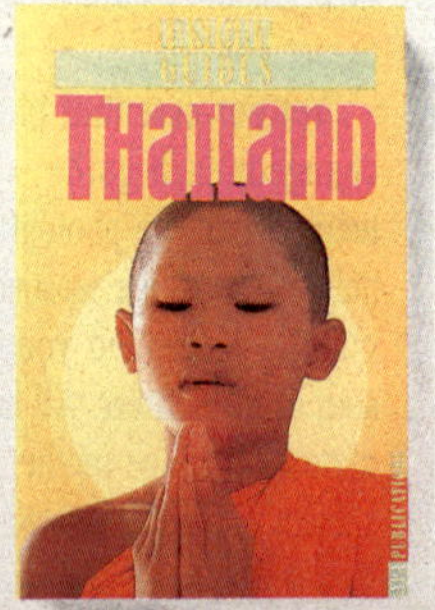

News

Europe

Bestsellers in the English language are Florida, India and Hawaii; in German they are Continental Europe, California and Florida; in French, Greece is number one, followed by Mexico and Egypt; in Spanish, Great Britain, Italy and London; in Chinese, Nepal, Continental Europe and Crossing USA.

Short Stay Guides

Comprehensive, authoritative": that is how the Times of London assessed the APA guides. But what if you are making a brief visit to a place and do not have the time to see and do everything? APA is responding to the needs of the growing number of busy people who take short break holidays. Our Short Stay Guides will tell you what to do if you only have three days in, say, London, Manhattan or Bangkok. Written by destination specialists, Short Stay Guides will cut out the frustration of wasted time and ensure that every moment of your visit is packed with interest.

Expansion

APA now has its own printworks in Singapore which enables us to produce a book from conception to bookshop delivery in barely six months. Our editorial offices in Singapore, London, Munich and Hong Kong prepare the books using desktop publishing systems, linked by electronic mail. With these facilities we plan to have 200 titles in print within the next three years – and we are updating and upgrading all the existing guides continuously.

New Insight Guide identity

As part of our commitment to updating, all new guides are appearing in a fresh new style. Art Director Professor V Barl has combined bright colours and modern graphics and eye-catching, specially designed typefaces to produce a new generation of visually up-to-date Insight Guides.

APA Photo Agency

The APA Photo Agency, located in a beautiful old Chinese Baba-style house in downtown Singapore, covers destinations around the world – including the world's largest collection of Asian travel photographs.

We are constantly looking for pictures to extend the collection. If you have quality material, send us a letter and description – but please do not send the photographs themselves.

Ideas, please

Ideas and proposals for our new titles are also highly welcome. APA is always open to suggestions from would-be contributors, editors and travel experts. Write to Höfer Media, 38 Joo Koon Road, Singapore 2262 and we will forward your ideas to our regional editors.

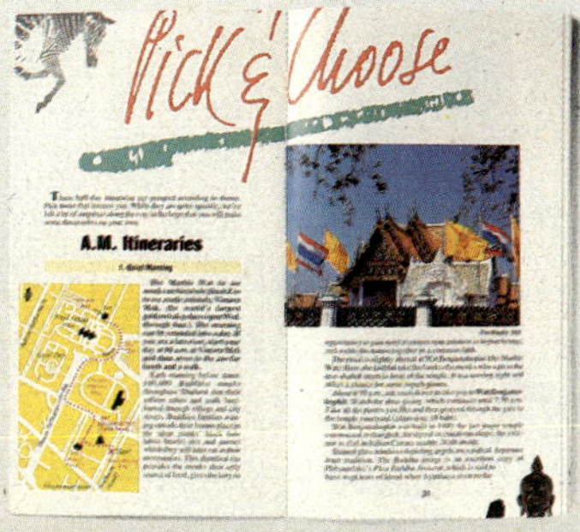

HT
ES

events that have shaped the nation and its culture, glimpses of the life, work, pleasures and pastimes, politics, passions, appetites, festivities and fascinating anomalies of a people.

Section two – Places – the most substantial part of each book – presents a comprehensive guide to all locations of interest. In the last section-Travel Tips – we provide a compendium of vital and up-to-date information for planning your trip and making the most of your stay.

Insight Guides now cover scores of destinations, from Alaska to Rajasthan, and our Special Interest Guides – such as Waterways of Europe, Indian Wildlife and East African Wildlife – are already proving to be bestsellers.*

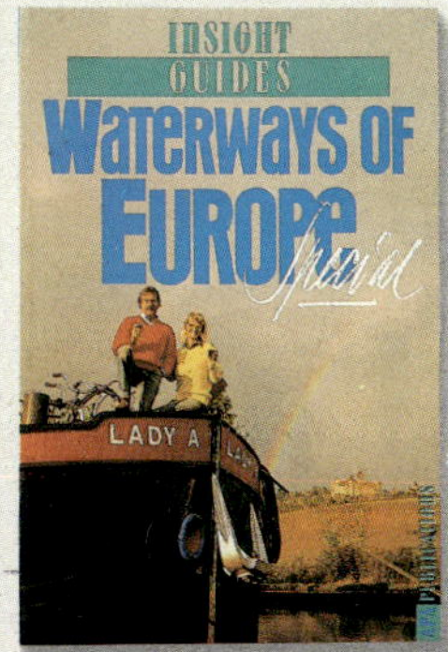

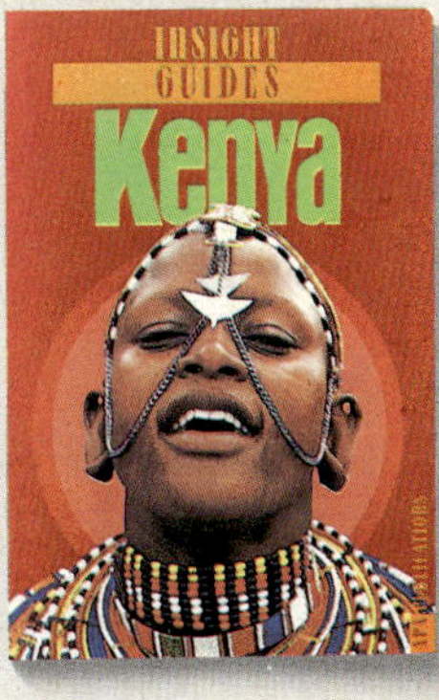

* Don't just take our word for it!

Check us out at any major bookshop or Hotel drug store.

INS
CITY

The Cityguides series, launched in 1988, follows the same format as the Insight Guides, combining comprehensive sightseeing information with revealing features on those aspects that make each city unique: carnival in Venice, the wit of a London taxi driver, enchanting flower-filled courtyards in Lisbon or the markets and bazaars of Istanbul.

Cityguide Bangkok has already won the prestigious Top Honours Gold Award given by the 35-nation Pacific-Asian Travel Association for the best travel guide in 1989.

Twenty-five titles are already available. They are soon to be joined by new guides to Glasgow –

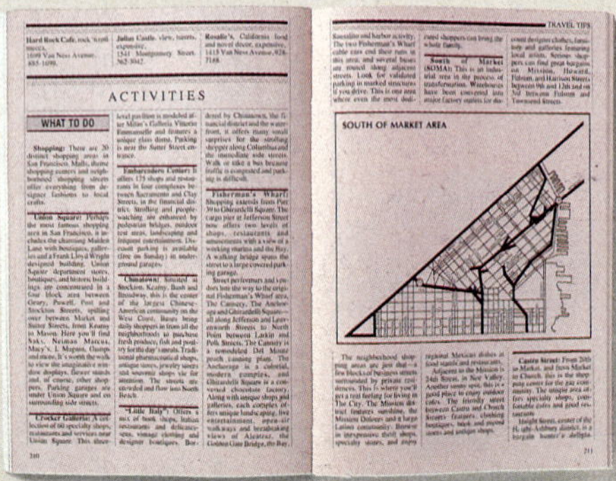

HT
IDES

European City of Culture for 1990 – and Barcelona – host to the 1992 Olympics, and many more.

So, if you want to visit Eastern Europe and see how events are unfolding, don't forget to pack our Cityguide Prague or Budapest. Or let us guide you through the romantic boulevards of Paris or Vienna, the historic streets of London and Florence, the winding canals of Venice or the dazzling sights of Sydney, San Francisco or Singapore.

If your local bookshop does not stock our complete range of titles, the bookshop assistant can order the titles you need. Our local global network of distributors can speed books to your local book dealer!

"I was first drawn to the Insight Guides by the excellent "Nepal" volume. I can think of no book which so effectively captures the essence of a country. Out of these pages leaped the Nepal I know — the captivating charm of a people and their culture. I've since discovered and enjoyed the entire Insight Guide Series. Each volume deals with a country or city in the same sensitive depth, which is nowhere more evident than in the superb photography."

Sir Edmund Hillary